Information, Cyber and Space Domain and its Application in Future Land Warfare

Information, Cyber and Space Domain and its Application in Future Land Warfare

PK Mallick

KW Publishers Pvt Ltd
New Delhi

Centre for Land Warfare Studies
Delhi Cantt
New Delhi

Reprint 2024

The Centre for Land Warfare Studies (CLAWS), New Delhi, is an independent Think Tank dealing with contemporary issues of national security and conceptual aspects of land warfare, including conventional & sub-conventional conflicts and terrorism. CLAWS conducts research that is futuristic in outlook and policy-oriented in approach.

CLAWS Vision: To establish CLAWS as a leading Think Tank in policy formulation on Land Warfare, National Security and Strategic Issues.

Centre for Land Warfare Studies
RPSO Complex, Parade Road, Delhi Cantt, New Delhi 110010
Tel: +91-11-25691308 **Fax:** +91-11-25692347
Email: landwarfare@gmail.com; **Website:** www.claws.in
CLAWS Army No. 33098

ISBN 978-93-91490-56-0 Hardback
ISBN 978-93-91490-64-5 ebook

KW Publishers Pvt Ltd
4676/21, First Floor, Ansari Road
Daryaganj, New Delhi 110002
Phone: +91 11 43528107
Marketing: kw@kwpub.in
Editorial: production@kwpub.in
Website: www.kwpub.in

Printed and bound in India

This book is dedicated
To
Three women in my life
My wife Ratna
and
Daughters Piyali and Pritha

Contents

Foreword ix

Acknowledgements xiii

Abbreviations xv

1 Abstract 1

2 Introduction 14

3 Information Domain 30

4 Cyber Domain 121

5 Space Domain 246

6 Summary of Recommendations 389

7 Conclusion 414

Foreword

Rapid technical advancements are taking place in the information, cyber and space domains especially in the Civil Sector. The domains of information, cyberspace and space have joined conventional warfighting domains of land, sea and air. Space and cyber forces offer flexible, low-signature or small-footprint capabilities that are rapidly deployable, capable of operating freely from logistically intensive forces, have the operational reach and can be persistent.

The information, cyber and space domain are omnipresent and permeates all other domains of land, sea and air, however, these are the least understood domains. Although the doctrine for land operations is relatively mature, the doctrines for information, cyberspace and space are still growing, often in an unstructured manner.

The current domains of information, cyber and space operates seamlessly across all domains, including land, water & air, and can span over different geographical locations. The commanders may employ some of these capabilities to enhance operational effectiveness in conjunction with Electronic Warfare (EW) and Electro Magnetic Spectrum (EMS) management.

Information, cyber and space will become both a precursor to and an integral part of armed combat in land, maritime and air domains. Advanced armed forces are trying to take maximum advantage of these domains.

Capabilities in these domains provide commanders, at all levels, the ability to share information and influence adversary opinions, communicate, integrate and synchronise operations across all warfighting functions and echelons. These capabilities and physical actions would create desired efforts on the adversary. Similarly, there is a challenge of defence against the use of these domains by a skilful adversary.

Integrating all domains of information, cyber, space, land, maritime and air will change how we operate, fight and develop capability. It adds up to far more than the sum of parts. Integration is now required at the tactical level of war, not just at the operational level where the term 'Joint' applies.

In the emerging Multi-Domain Operations (MDO) concept, the ability to integrate information, cyberspace, intelligence and space will be crucial to operational success. Modern armed forces cannot carry out high-tempo, effective operations without reliable information and communication networks and assured access to information, cyberspace and space.

Commanders, at all echelons, must understand the fundamental principles and advantages information, cyber and space operations bring to all Army operations, the disadvantages associated with not understanding their capabilities and the impact on military operations when friendly forces are denied the use of these capabilities.

Modern armed forces, worldwide, are developing new technologies to operate in these domains. U.S. Army has incorporated teams with specialists from Cyber, Military Intelligence, EW, SIGINT and Space to their Brigade Combat Team (BCT) to deliver effects at the cutting edge of the battlefield. PLA of China has established Strategic Support Force (SSF) to fight and win, incorporating information, cyber and space domains under one roof.

How the Indian Armed Forces' military operations, especially the land forces, are being integrated with these new domains, will be critical for the success in operations. Commanders, at all levels, should consider how information, space, cyberspace and electromagnetic spectrum (EMS) capabilities enhance the effectiveness and execution of joint land operations. As a modern Army, we must adopt latest technological advancements in these domains to remain relevant and contemporary.

The commanders will not have control of all the domains at all times. For instance, offensive cyber is not under the exclusive control of armed forces. Activities in space will have immediate consequences for other departments, and this adds layers to military judgement and mission command.

We must remember that information, cyber or space can enable a military operation. They cannot win the war on their own. As the author concludes: "In our effort to capture the leading edge of the info age, it is important to remember that at night, in the rain, attacking uphill in the mud, it is the quality of the leadership, not the speed of the processor, that will carry the battle."

Maj Gen PK Mallick, VSM (Retd), is from the Corps of Signals of the Indian Army. He has vast experience in Communications, EW and Signal Intelligence (SIGINT). He has been a keen observer of the developments in information, cyber and space domains. He has written extensively and delivered talks at different for a on these issues. He has written this book as part of the COAS Chair of Excellence project at CLAWS.

He has covered the subject in detail. Thoughtfully, he has explicitly included the Chinese activities in these very domains. I am sure this book will throw some new light on the subject.

I am confident that this timely book will enrich the ongoing discourse on information, cyber and space warfare.

November 2022

Lt Gen (Dr.) **Ranbir Singh**
PVSM, AVSM**, YSM, SM (Retd)
Director General, CLAWS
Former Army Commander, Northern Command and
Director General Military Operations

Acknowledgements

I have been studying the Information, Cyber and Space domain and their implications on warfare for a long time. I have written extensively and delivered talks at different fora on the subject. This book is the culmination of all these efforts.

Many subject matter experts, both serving and retired, from the armed forces, industry and academia, have helped me immensely to research and clarify various issues. Without naming them individually, I owe a debt of gratitude to all of them.

At the outset, I want to thank the Centre of Land Warfare Studies (CLAWS) for conferring the COAS Chair of Excellence to me for the year 2020, tenanted as a Distinguished Fellow. This book is part of the project.

I want to place on record my gratitude to Lt Gen (Dr) Vijay Kumar Ahluwalia, PVSM, AVSM**, YSM, VSM (Retd), former Director CLAWS, during whose time the book was written. Without his kindness, motivation, encouragement and advice, this book would not have seen the light of the day. Special thanks to the present Director, Lt Gen (Dr) Ranbir Singh, PVSM, AVSM**, YSM, SM (Retd), for helping me finalise the book.

I am indeed grateful to Maj Gen Vivek Sehgal, VSM (Retd), with whom I shared the same room during the research and, with endless cups of tea and coffee, discussed various aspects of the book, especially the Chinese angle.

My special thanks to Col (now Brig) Hardeep Singh Burn, Col PS Ranawat and Col SK Singh as Deputy Directors for providing all the support for writing the book.

No appreciation is enough for Ms Shreya Das Barman, the Publication Manager of CLAWS, for keeping me on my toes for meeting the timeline and helping me in various aspects of checking the manuscript, copy editing, etc.

I am grateful to Capt AK Das, the Librarian Nitesh Khandelwal for all the library support often going beyond his means, Darmender Bansiwal, our man Friday for all issues regarding IT and Internet, Naik Anuj JV and all the administration and support staff of CLAWS for keeping me going during the project of writing.

I am thankful to my brother in arms from the Corps of Signals of Indian Army who have been standing behind me like a rock in all my endeavours. My grateful thanks to Subedar S Nayak, Naib Subedar Santanu Nandi, Havildar Kamal Mahata, Havildar Sundar Singh and Havildar Dhirendra Kumar. I shall be failing in my duties if I do not specially mention Havildar Kamal Mahata, who has helped me immensely in word processing, making charts and illustrations of the book.

I would like to convey my gratitude to Ms Kalpana Shukla, Managing Director of KW Publishers and her editorial team for their untiring work in finalising the book.

What can I say about three women in my life? My ever-supporting wife Ratna and two of my fiercest critics, my daughters Piyali and Pritha who also are immensely proud of me. They have always suffered all my idiosyncrasies with good humour and always kept the home front happy.

In the end, as always, all errors and omissions are mine.

PK Mallick

Abbreviations

A2/AD	Anti-Access/Area Denial
ADGPI	Additional Directorate General of Public Information
AEHF	Advanced Extremely High Frequency
AFRL	Air Force Research Laboratory
AI	Artificial Intelligence
AJ	Anti-Jam
AOR	Area of Responsibility
AQI	al Qaeda in Iraq
ASAT	Anti-Satellite Weapons
BBG	Broadcasting Board of Governors
BIS	Bureau of Indian Standards
BLOS	Beyond-Line-Of-Site
BMD	Ballistic Missile Defense
BRI	Belt and Road Initiative
C2W	Command and Control Warfare
C4ISTAR	Command, Control, Communications, Computers, Intelligence, Surveillance, Target Acquisition and Reconnaissance
CA	Civil Affairs
CAD	Computer Aided Design
CAIR	Centre for Artificial Intelligence and Robotics
CASC	China Aerospace Science and Technology Corporation
CBDT	Central Board of Direct Taxes

CBEC	Central Board of Excise and Customs
CBI	Central Bureau of Investigation
CCD COE	Cooperative Cyber Defence Centre of Excellence
CCMP	Cyber Crisis Management Plan
CCPWC	Cyber Crime Prevention for Women and Children
CCS	Cabinet Committee on Security
C-DOT	Centre for Development of Telematics
CERT	Computer Emergency Response Team
CGI	Computer-Generated Imagery
CGTN	China Global Television Network
CI/ CT Ops	Counter Insurgency/Counter Terrorism Operations
CIA	Central Intelligence Agency
CII	Critical Information Infrastructure
CIO	Cyber-Enabled Information Operations
CIS	Cyber and Information Security
CISOs	Chief Information Security Officers
CMA	China Meteorological Administration
CMC	Central Military Commission
CMS	Centralised Monitoring System
CNA	Computer Network Attack
CND	Computer Network Defence
CNE	Computer Network Exploitation
CNO	Computer Network Operations
CNSA	China National Space Administration
CO	Cyberspace operations
CoE	Centre of Excellence
CPC	Communist Party of China
CSC	Cyberspace Solarium Commission
CSD	Countering State-Sponsored Disinformation
CVE	Countering Violent Extremism
CW	Cyber Warfare
DCA	Defence Cyber Agency
DDoS	Distributed Denial of Service

DGCEI	Directorate General of Central Excise and Intelligence
DHS	Department of Homeland Security
DIARA	Defence Information Assurance Research Agency
DIMEFIL	Diplomatic, Information, Military, Economic, Financial, Intelligence and Legal
DIPAC	Defense Imagery Processing and Analysis Center
DISA	Defense Information Systems Agency
DoD	Department of Defense
DoS	Department of Space
DPSU	Defence Public Sector Undertaking
DRDO	Defence Research and Development Organisation
DRI	Directorate of Revenue Intelligence
DSA	Defence Space Agency
DSB	Defense Science Board
DSC	Defensive Space Control
DSCI	Data Security Council of India
DSN	Deep Space Network
DSPD	Defence Support To Public Diplomacy
DSRO	Defence Space Research Organisation
DSSC	Defense Satellite Control Center
DTH	Direct to Home
ECM	Electronic Countermeasures
ED	Enforcement Directorate
EDD	Equipment Development Department
ELaNa	Educational Launch of Nanosatellites
EMI	Electromagnetic Interference
EMP	Electromagnetic Pulse
EMS	Electromagnetic Spectrum
EO	Electro-Optical
EO/IR	Electro-Optical and Infrared
EW	Electronic Warfare
FIU	Financial Intelligence Unit

FNC3	Fully Networked C3
GAN	Generative Adversarial Network
GBS	Global Broadcast Service
GCI	Global Cyber security Index
GEC	Global Engagement Centre
GEO	Geosynchronous Earth Orbit
GNSS	Global Navigation Satellite System
GPS	Global Positioning System
GSAT	Geostationary Satellites
GTO	Geosynchronous Transfer Orbit
HEO	Highly Elliptical Orbit
HPM	High-Power Microwave
HPRF	High Power Radio Frequency
HUMINT	Human Intelligence
I4C	Indian Cyber Crime Coordination Centre
IAI	Israeli Aerospace Industries
IB	Intelligence Bureau
ICS/OT	Industrial Control System and Operational Technology
ICT	Information-Communications Technologies
IDF	Israeli Defense Forces
IDS	Intrusion Detection Systems
IE	Information Environment
IIO	Information and Influence Operations
IISS	International Institute for Strategic Studies
IN-SPACe	Indian National Space Promotion and Authorisation Centre
INSS	Institute for National Security Studies
IO	Information Operations
IoT	Internet of Things
IP	Internet-Protocol
IPS	Intrusion Protection Systems
IRA	Internet Research Agency

IRC	Information-Related Capabilities
IRNSS	Indian Regional Navigation Satellite System
ISAC	Information Sharing and Analysis Centre
ISAO	Information Sharing and Analysis Organisation
ISEA	Information Security Education and Awareness
ISI	Indian Standards Institute
ISIS	Islamic State of Iraq and Syria
ISP	Internet Service Providers
ISpA	Indian Space Association
ISR	Intelligence, Surveillance and Reconnaissance
ISRO	Indian Space Research Organisation
ISS	International Space Station
ITO	Information Technical Operations
ITU	International Telecommunication Union
IW	Information Warfare
JPL	Joint Propulsion Laboratory
JSpOC	Joint Space Operations Centre
KKV	Kinetic Kill Vehicle
KNPP	Kudankulam Nuclear Power Plant
LEAs	Law Enforcement Agencies
LEO	Low Earth orbit
LOAC	Laws of Armed Conflict
LOS	Line of Sight
LPD	Low Probability of Detection
LTE	Long Term and Evolution
MASINT	Measurement and Signature Intelligence
MBN	Middle East Broadcasting Networks
MCIT	Ministry of Communication and Information Technology
MDO	Multi Domain Operations
MDU	Mission Data Unit
MeitY	Ministry of Electronics and Information Technology
MEO	Medium Earth Orbit

MHA	Ministry for Home Affairs
MHRD	Ministry of Human Resource Development
MILDEC	Military Deception
MISO	Military Information Support Operations
ML	Machine Learning
MLAT	Mutual Legal Assistance Treaties
MNC	Multi-National Corporations
MoU	Memorandum of Understanding
MS	Military Secretary
NASA	National Aeronautics and Space Administration
NATGRID	National Intelligence Grid
NATO	North Atlantic Treaty Organisation
NAVWAR	Navigation Warfare
NCB	Narcotics Control Bureau
NCCC	National Cyber Coordination Centre
NCCIC	National Cyber security and Communications Integration Centre
NCIIPC	National Critical Information Infrastructure Protection Centre
NCPI	National Cyber Power Index
NDMA	National Disaster Management Authority
NDRC	National Development and Reform Commission
NDU	National Defence University
NETRA	Network Traffic Analysis
NGO	Nongovernmental Organisations
NGPEs	Non-Government Private Entities
NIC	National Information Centre
NIOR	Non- Indian Orbital Resources
NIST	National Institute of Standards and Technology
NOAA	National Oceanic and Atmospheric Administration
NRSC	National Remote Sensing Centre
NSA	National Security Agency
NSCS	National Security Council Secretariat

NSD	Network Systems Department
NSIL	New Space India Ltd
NTRO	National Technical Research Organisation
OCO	Offensive Cyber Operations
ODNI	Office of the Director for National Intelligence
OFB	Ordnance Factory Board
OIE	Operational Information Environment
OPIR	Overhead Persistent Infrared
OPSEC	Operations Security
OSC	Offensive Space Control
OST	Outer Space Treaty
OTH	Over the Horizon
PA	Public Affairs
PAROS	Prevention of an Arms Race in Outer Space
PD	Public Diplomacy
PI	Public Information
PLA	People's Liberation Army
PLAAF	People's Liberation Army Air Force
PLASSF	People's Liberation Army Strategic Support Force
PNT	Positioning, Navigation and Timing
POG	Psychological Operations Group
PPP	Public-Private Partnership
PSLV	Polar Satellite Launch Vehicle
PsyW	Psychological Warfare
PTW	Protected Tactical Waveform
R&AW	Research & Analysis Wing
R&D	Research and Development
RBI	Reserve Bank of India
RC	Reserve Component
RDT&E	Research, Development, Test & Evaluation
RFA	Radio Free Asia
RoE	Rules of Engagement
RPO	Rendezvous and proximity operations

RSSC	Regional Satellite Communications Support Centre
SAR	Synthetic Aperture Radar
SAST	Shanghai Academy of Space Technology
SASTIND	State Administration for Science and Technology and Industry for National Defence
SATCOM	Satellite Communications
SBIRS	Space-Base-Infra-Red System
SCADA	Supervisory Control and Data Acquisition
SIGINT	Signals Intelligence
SLE	Soldier and Leader Engagement
SLOC	Sea Lines of Communication
SLV	Space Launch Vehicle
SMPs	Social Media Platforms
SNAS	Secure Network Access System
SOE	State-Owned Enterprise
SR	Space Radar
SRoE	Standing Rules of Engagement
SRUF	Standing Rules for the Use of Force
SSA	Space Situational Awareness
SSD	Strategic Studies Detachment
SSF	Strategic Support Force
SSN	Space Surveillance Network
SSO	Sun-Synchronous Orbit
STM	Space Traffic Management
STO	Special Technical Operations
STQC	Standardisation Testing and Quality Certification
Strat Comn	Strategic Communication
SUPARCO	Space and Upper Atmosphere Research Commission
TAO	Tailored Access Operations
TCS	Tata Consultancy Services
TDRSS	Tracking Data Relay Satellite System
TOR	The Onion Router
ToT	Transfer of Technology

TRANSEC	Transmission Security
TRB	Technical Reconnaissance Bureau
TSP	Telecom Service Provider
TT&C	Telemetry, Tracking and Commanding
TTP	Tactics Techniques and Procedure
UAV	Unmanned Aerial Vehicle
UFWD	United Front Work Department
USAID	United States Agency for International Development
USASOC	US Army Special Operations Command
USCYBERCOM	United States Cyber Command
USSF	United State Space Forces
USSPACECOM	United States Space Command
VCOAS	Vice Chief of Army Staff
VOA	Voice of America
WHAM	Winning Hearts of Minds
WMD	Weapons of Mass Destruction

1 Abstract

Introduction

The ubiquity of information and the pace of technological change is transforming the character of warfare. Old distinctions between peace and war, public and private, foreign and domestic and state and non-state are increasingly getting out of date. As observed in recent conflicts, commercial technologies have disrupted the economics and character of warfare. They are cheaper, faster, lighter, smaller and stealthier.

The domains of air, space, information and cyberspace have joined the conventional warfighting domains of land and sea. Space and cyberspace forces offer flexible, low-signature or small-footprint capabilities that are rapidly deployable, mainly able to operate freely from logistically intensive forces, have the operational reach and can be persistent. Although the doctrine for land operations is relatively mature, the doctrine for information, cyberspace and space continue to grow, often in an unstructured manner.

Information, cyber and space will become both a precursor to and integral part of armed combat in the land, maritime and air domains. How the Indian armed forces' military operations, especially the land army is being integrated with these new domains will be critical to its success in operations. Commanders at all levels should consider how information, space, cyberspace and electromagnetic spectrum (EMS) capabilities enhance the effectiveness and execution of joint land operations.

All the recent domains of information, space and cyber operate seamlessly across all domains, including land, water and air and can span different geographical locations. The commanders may employ some of these capabilities to enhance operational effectiveness in conjunction with Electronic Warfare (EW) and Electro Magnetic Spectrum (EMS) management. The five operational domains are not equivalent or equal. The cyber and information domain is omnipresent and permeates all other domains. The information, cyber and space domains are the least understood domains.

Home is no longer a secure place. The 'front' is within the country. Fake news appears to originate at home gaining credibility and reach. It fuels confusion, disagreement, division and doubt in our societies. Soldiers have to perform their duties with greater skill and understanding of information and cyberspace. Commanders have to seek information advantage, think beyond the enemy and examine the additional effects that are to be applied before coordinating the appropriate mix of physical, virtual and cognitive actions. Providing information advantage for commanders and decision dominance will require a range of capabilities to include cyber, information, intelligence, public affairs and space.

In the emerging Multi Domain Operations (MDO) concept, the ability to integrate information, cyberspace, intelligence and space will be crucial to operational success. Modern armed forces cannot carry out high-tempo, effective operations without reliable information and communication networks and assured access to cyberspace and space.

Emerging technologies like artificial intelligence, machine learning, hypersonics, robotics, 3D printing, quantum computing, 5G and nanotechnology are driving a fundamental change in the character of war. As these technologies mature and their military applications become clear, the impacts can revolutionise battlefields.

Integrating all Domains of Information, Cyber, Space, Land, Maritime and Air will change the way we operate, fight and develop capability. It adds up to far more than the sum of the parts. Integration is now required at the tactical level of war, not just at the operational level where the term 'Joint' applies.

The level of jointness and integration of all these domains in the Indian Armed forces and what can be done to improve is the most critical question that stares at the Indian Armed Forces.

Information Domain

Information is a well-developed element of national power and a strategic, operational and tactical weapon. Information Warfare (IW) takes place below the level of armed conflict. Most of the information warfare today occurs on the internet. IW is a means through which nation states achieve strategic objectives and advance foreign policy goals.

The Information Environment (IE) is part of the operational environment. Activities occurring in and through the IE substantially affect military operations and outcomes. Commanders and staffs at all levels must know the IE in all its complexity and the likely impacts it will have on current and planned military operations.

Cyberspace is a global domain within the IE comprising the interdependent network of information technology infrastructures and resident data, including the Internet, telecommunications networks, computer systems and embedded processors and controllers.

Cyber Enabled Information Operations (CIO). Cyber-enabled information operations (CIO) is defined as the conduct of information warfare that makes substantial use of modern information technologies, such as social media, search engines, artificial intelligence and the Internet as well as traditional communications media technologies.

Confusion of Terminologies. Various terms are used in the doctrines of information warfare and later information operations. The terms used in these doctrines somehow are confusing and lack clarity. The strategic community and the Department of Defense of U.S. use the terms information warfare, information operations, psychological operations, military information support operations (MISO), strategic communication, influence operations and possibly cyberspace operations interchangeably, though they are not synonymous.

There is a difference between cyber-enabled psychological operations and offensive cyber operations. The competence required to conduct psychological operations goes beyond the skill set of cyber operators. The expertise of cyber forces generally focuses on the information delivery side of cyber-enabled psychological operations. Contesting information warfare requires content. The issue of content, themes, etc., are the most critical part. The government has to take a whole of government approach to bring all of the relevant expertise from all parts of government and the nation to address the problem.

Considerable resources are put on cyber security globally. These activities are centred around technical expertise in computer science, communications, mathematics, etc. Much less activity and funds are dedicated to understanding the science and practice of psychological operations.

Intelligence. There is a general lack of coordination and understanding between the practitioners of information operations (IO) and intelligence communities, which adversely affect operational planning. A clear understanding of the information environment is the responsibility of intelligence practitioners. The ability to conduct operations in and through the IE is the responsibility of IO practitioners.

Generally, there is a lack of understanding, shared processes and a shared lexicon about what the other community does. Gaps in knowledge hinder close coordination between the two communities and lead to reduced operational effectiveness. Both intelligence and IO professionals need training to support and conduct Operational Information Environment (OIE) effectively. Training and education must grow as needs change.

Use of Social Media. Social Media Platforms (SMPs) like Facebook, Twitter, YouTube, Instagram are websites, tools, applications and gizmos that provide social media services. SMP industry has created an addiction. It has a damaging side-effect on democracy.

Social media is not just a communication space but a new kind of battlespace. The boundaries between foreign and domestic sources of information chaos and dysfunction are blurring. Nation-states and non-state actors alike are leveraging social media to manipulate like-minded populations' cognitive biases to influence conflict dynamics.

The use of propaganda, disinformation, deception and information warfare is not new. What is new is the ease, efficiency, low cost of such efforts, global reach, propagation speed and our political sensitivity to national and international opinion. We cannot control who accesses this capability. The agile player who can shape perceptions will more likely achieve their objectives.

Private sector now owns Facebook, Twitter, YouTube, Instagram and the other popular platforms. They shape and influence what we think. Responding to these challenges will not be easy. It will involve making complex and controversial decisions about the private sector's responsibility, restrictions on speech and national security issues.

The dichotomy between Freedom of Speech in Social Media and National Security Concerns

Social Media. Social media platforms like Facebook, Google, Twitter and Microsoft are global private players. They have no public accountability. There is no regulatory oversight. They are not law enforcers. They do not have mandate to address issues of national security. They do not police their platforms. They do it as per their internal policies. Social media platforms make decisions about content take-downs according to criteria that include corporate risk factors.

Big Brother is no longer the state. The tech giants have taken that position, who misuse privacy protections based on their own politically driven algorithms rather than submitting themselves to the government's due process. Social media companies are reluctant to let intelligence and law enforcement agencies look behind the privacy walls of active accounts. This would cause a public outcry as user privacy is at stake. However, making those walls impenetrable prevents those agencies responsible for keeping us safe from doing their job. A balance has to be struck as our safety depends on it.

National Security Concerns. Due to the very structure of the Internet, there is no solution to stop or deter malicious foreign cyber activity. It's near impossible to know quickly and with certainty if a foreign government is behind a disinformation campaign, ransomware implant or data theft. With uncertain attribution, the government's hands are tied.

PLA in Information Domain. Along with the technical aspects of information operations, the PLA combines psychological warfare in manipulating public opinion, media warfare and legal warfare to strengthen China's diplomatic and security position. China calls this Three Warfare. China effectively integrates this Three Warfare in a comprehensive information operations doctrine.

Information Operations and India. In Indian Army's Land Warfare Doctrine published in 2018[1] it is stated that Indian Army will develop capabilities to prosecute Information Warfare Operations over the entire spectrum of conflict as well as in 'No War No Peace' scenario, with the aim to achieve full spectrum information dominance over the adversary. It will have the following components: Cyber Warfare (CW), Electronic Warfare (EW) and Psychological Warfare (PsyW).

Information warfare capabilities, both offensive and defensive, must be integrated with traditional warfare for success on the modern battlefield. Information warfare's ability to drive offensive operations while denying or manipulating enemy perceptions of the battlefield will not get us victories in isolation. Information warfare capabilities defined as combat capabilities will only be effective in the context of consequences. Ultimately war is won in the land, which involves violence, killing people and destroying things.

Cyber Domain

The internet and Information technology have advanced to such a level that they have become a major element of national power. Nation-states are preparing themselves for the cyber battlespace. Many states are creating offensive cyberwar capabilities, developing national strategies and engaging in cyber attacks regularly. Cyber is a man-made domain. Unlike the other domains, cyberspace is not geographically constrained. Cyberspace simultaneously occupies the space of the other strategic domains.

Cyber Power. Cyberspace is transforming how information is created and the connectivity used to transmit and exchange that content. The crucial elements of cyber power are the use of the electromagnetic spectrum, electronics technology and integrated man-made infrastructure.

The vital aspect of cyber power is its capability to manipulate a target's cyber infrastructure via exploitation and attack.

Cyber Deterrence. Cyber deterrence is a result of states' desire to avoid being attacked in or via cyberspace. The efficacy of cyber deterrence relies on the ability to impose or raise costs and deny or lower benefits related to a cyber attack in a state's decision making calculus. Deterrence in cyberspace is more challenging to achieve than deterrence in conventional domains.

Military Domain

Integration of Cyber Warfare in a Conventional Military Operations. Armed conflict takes place at the strategic, operational and tactical level. In conventional warfare, the battlefield is clearly defined within the various domains. With the emergence of cyberspace, tactical and operational questions have taken precedence over strategic ones. Cyber operations and tactics are different from conventional ones due to the battlefield's unique nature and scope.

Cyber Weapons. Intelligence Community and militaries worldwide have developed new tools for exploiting, subverting, degrading and destroying adversaries' informational assets. Cyber weapons are written in computer code. They can infiltrate whole networks or infect individual computers. Cyber weapons can be installed in hardware also. If the payload causes data exfiltration, we call this cyber exploitation. If the payload causes damage, destruction, degradation, or denial, the use is called a cyber attack.

Use of Cyber Weapons. There is a growing tendency of using cyber weapons on the battlefield or in peacetime. U.S. has publicly acknowledged using cyber weapons in its fight against the Islamic State of Iraq and Syria (ISIS). There has been no reported loss of life directly linked to cyber attacks till date.[2] There is no international agreement on how cyber weapons should be regulated.

Cyber Weapon Market. Cyber weapons are cheap and widely available in the market at a price for nation-states, criminals and harmful actors. There is a rising demand for offensive cyber tools and systems.

In cyber operations, rules of engagement are not clear. The policies and laws governing the use of cyber weapons are still under development. Cyber warfare has blurred the line between nation-states and non-state actors and even between traditional notions of sovereignty and loyalty.

China and Cyber War

Concept of Warfare. The PLA differs substantially from its Western counterparts in its approach to cyber operations. PLA does not consider cyber power as a distinct capability like land, sea, air and space. PLA's experts view cyber operations as occurring in an information domain. This domain includes network, electronic warfare, psychological and media operations.

Strategic Support Force (SSF). The Strategic Support Force is responsible for collecting and managing technical intelligence, from cyber and space assets; supporting joint operations and carrying out attacks against an adversary's command network. The PLA wants to use offensive cyber operations to disrupt, degrade, or damage opponent systems, including critical infrastructure, preceding and during various stages of a conflict and in a range of conflict scenarios.

Indian Cyber Space

Indian has put policies and organisation in place for cyber security. India has taken several steps to strengthen its cyber defence capabilities. Things are moving in the right directions. But in the cyber domain, things move very fast. Most government organisations, because of the bureaucracy, are always in the catch-up mode.

Public-Private Partnership (PPP). Except for few exceptions, there has hardly been any progress on the PPP model. Indian IT industry is worth $150 billion. They have some well-established cyber security procedures. Indian IT industry, showing huge profits in their balance sheets must be goaded into participating in national cyber security efforts.

There is a serious mismatch of understanding between the civil sector and the government agencies dealing with cyber security. Surely, there has to be a middle ground where the sharply divergent views can be met.

We need to place particular emphasis on building adequate technical capabilities in the areas of cryptology, digital signatures, testing for malware in embedded systems, operating systems, fabrication of specialised chips for defence and intelligence functions, Search engines, Artificial intelligence, Routers, Supervisory Control and Data Acquisition (SCADA) systems, etc.

Space Domain

Space is more diverse, disruptive, disordered and dangerous than in the past. A new set of non-state space actors have become foundational and catalytic elements of space activity. Approximately 90 per cent of satellites launched in 2020 were commercial rather than the government owned.

Space is an integral part of modern warfare. There are a variety of military space capabilities and activities, including space situational awareness, space lift, space control, positioning, navigation, and timing; satellite communications, environmental monitoring, missile warning, space-based Intelligence, Surveillance and Reconnaissance (ISR) and nuclear detonation detection. Space capabilities have proven to be significant force multipliers when integrated into military operations.

Threats in space can be broadly categorised into four distinct segments: lethal physical weapons, non-lethal physical weapons, directed energy attacks and cyberspace attack.

Space Weapons. A space weapon is used to apply force directly against an adversary or to directly interfere with an adversary's ability to conduct military operations in, through or enabled by space. Space-to-Earth weapons can attack targets deep inside enemy territory without the risk of aircraft and cruise missiles getting shot down. However, Space-based weapons are vulnerable to non-kinetic attacks like jamming or laser attacks. The use of destructive, non-reversible kinetic Earth-to-Space or Space-to-Space weapons would leave a cloud of debris and produce a long-term hazard to all satellites.

Armed Forces in Space Domain. There are several distinct advantages of using space for operational purposes. Now developing states and non-state actors can increase their influence by purchasing or leasing chosen space capabilities, products and applications easily.

Space assets provide commanders with coverage beyond the geographical areas and access to otherwise denied areas. This characteristic makes space-based ISR, remote sensing, SATCOM and PNT more responsive than terrestrial alternatives. The armed forces are getting more and more dependent on the use of commercial space systems. There are additional risks connected with using commercial services. These have to be balanced against the potential benefits.

Space Situational Awareness (SSA). SSA is "the requisite current and predictive knowledge of space events, threats, activities, conditions and space system (space, ground, link) status capabilities, constraints and employment—to current and future, friendly and hostile—to enable commanders, decision makers, planners and operators to gain and maintain space superiority across the spectrum of conflict." SSA depends on integrating space surveillance, collection and processing, environmental monitoring, status of own satellite systems and analysis of the space domain. SSA should include understanding of the space capabilities and intent of adversaries.

Intelligence, Surveillance and Reconnaissance (ISR). Space-based intelligence collection complements air and ground based information collection. Surveillance from the space domain enables the forces to overcome terrestrial line of sight restrictions and affords coverage of large area of interest.

Satellite Communications (SATCOM). SATCOM systems facilitate beyond Line of Sight connectivity. SATCOM provides crucial connectivity for tactical maneuver forces.

Space Treaties. There is no legally binding Treaties or Norms on the use of space, especially for weapons. Several attempts have been made but proved elusive. It is debatable that the U.S. or Russia and China would agree to ban capabilities that are essential to protect their military operations.

Role of Private Players. Several private companies have emerged to make space more accessible and reduce the overall cost of space operations.

Termed as New Space companies, they have brought about innovations in the space industry. Services such as high-resolution imaging, geo-location and remote sensing are now available through cube and microsatellites. These can be purchased on the commercial market. Many private companies have come up in China and India, which can offer affordable and reliable launch services for small, micro and nano-satellites.

China

China's space program is serving its political, economic and military interests. Today, China has more than 300 satellites, the second largest number of satellites in orbit. The reliability of its space launch vehicles is of international standards. China is fast narrowing the gap in quantity and quality of space technologies with global space powers.

To further integrate space into military operations, the PLA created the Strategic Support Force (SSF), an organisation that is, in part, responsible for elements of the PLA's space program. The Space Systems Department (SSD) under SSF is responsible for space operations, including space launch and support, space surveillance, space information support, space telemetry, tracking and control and space warfare. The SSD integrates space-related Research, Development and Acquisition, operations and training under a single authority.

India in Space Domain

India is now a major spacefaring nation. India has had its fair share of achievements in the space domain. India has achieved self-reliance in launch vehicles and satellite technology. India is moving towards integrated application of different space technologies. These technologies are being used for social welfare purposes. Schemes like village resource centers and e-governance are significant for large populations in the most remote places.

Indian Space Research Organisation (ISRO). ISRO is now one of the largest space agencies in the world. It maintains a large fleet of communication, (INSAT)/Geostationary Satellites (GSAT) remote sensing, navigation and scientific satellites. It provides multiple application-specific products and tools for broadcasting, communication, disaster management, weather forecasting, GIS, cartography, navigation, telemedicine, among many other functions.

ISRO, by itself, does not have the capacity in terms of capital, skilled labour, equipment to develop and exploit all benefit single-handedly. This makes a strong case for unlocking the potential of private capital and skills. In a major policy change, the present government has permitted the reforms in the space sector by allowing private players' participation.

Indian Space Association (ISpA). Prime Minister Narendra Modi, on October 11, 2021, launched the Indian Space Association (ISpA). It is an industry body of various stakeholders of the Indian space domain. The members of ISpA include government organisation (ISRO) and private telecom companies.

ISRO will continue to function as the core space organisation in India with decision-making authority related to activities, missions and projects. It will focus more on Research and Development (R&D), exploring new technologies, and planning new space missions.

Armed Forces

Indian armed forces had been aware of the importance of space in today's warfare. In 2019, the Union Government announced the creation of a new agency called the Defence Space Agency (DSA), comprising members from the Army, Navy and Air Force and supported by a new research organisation, the Defence Space Research Organisation (DSRO). DSA may be a precursor to something like that of a space command in the U.S., integrating space assets from the Army, Navy and Air Force.

Commanders at all echelons must understand the fundamental principles and advantages space operations bring to all operations, the disadvantages associated with not understanding space capabilities and the impact to mission operations when friendly forces are denied the use of space capabilities.

Notes

1. Indian Army, 'Land Warfare Doctrine 2018', at https://www.ssri-j.com/MediaReport/Document/IndianArmyLandWarfareDoctrine2018.pdf
2. Clay Wilson, 'Cyber Weapons: 4 Defining Characteristics', GCN, June 4, 2015, at https://gcn.com/articles/2015/06/04/cyber-weapon.aspx

2 Introduction

The domains of air, space, information and cyberspace have joined the conventional warfighting domains of land and sea. Although the doctrine for land operations is relatively mature, the doctrine for information, cyberspace and space continue to grow, often in an unstructured manner.[1]

Expensive, manned platforms cannot be replaced easily. These will be more and more vulnerable to swarms of self-coordinating smart munitions, arriving with hypersonic or ballistic weapons from space, designed to swamp defences already weakened by pre-emptive cyber-attack. The business of warfare is changing the balance between platforms and weapons and between manned and unmanned systems. We are facing an inflexion point between the Industrial Age and the Information Age. We have to respond to these challenges if we want to retain a competitive edge.

The ubiquity of information and the pace of technological change are transforming the character of warfare. Old distinctions between peace and war, between public and private, between foreign and domestic and between state and non-state are increasingly getting out of date. As observed in Syria and Iraq, commercial technologies have disrupted the economics and character of warfare. They are cheaper, faster, lighter, smaller and stealthier. They are available readily in large numbers and at low cost. They are persistent and omnipresent in the battlespace.[2]

Information, cyber and space will become both a precursor to and integral part of armed combat in the land, maritime and air domains. How the Indian armed forces' military operations, especially the land army is being integrated with these new domains will be critical to its success in operations. U.S. Joint Doctrine JP 3-31 states up front, "commanders at all levels should consider how space, cyberspace and electromagnetic spectrum (EMS) capabilities enhance the effectiveness and execution of joint land operations."

Space and cyberspace forces offer "flexible, low-signature or small-footprint capabilities" that are rapidly deployable, mainly able to operate freely from logistically intensive forces, have the operational reach, and can be persistent. Most importantly, their use does not always constitute an irreversible policy commitment. The integrated operations include the key element of cross-domain synergy that will allow an integrated joint force "to exploit even small advantages in one domain to create or increase advantages in others, compounding those mutually reinforcing advantages until they overwhelm an enemy."[3]

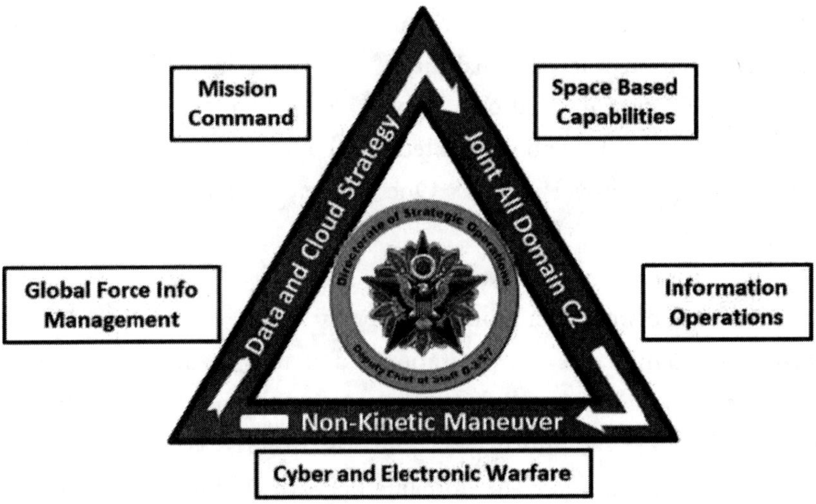

The growing importance given to cyber and space can be seen from the following:

In 2018, the U.S. elevated United States Cyber Command to a full and independent unified combatant command, recognising that cyber warfare constitutes a unique theatre of combat.

In 2019, President Donald Trump launched U.S. Space Command, acknowledging the importance and the centrality of space communications and infrastructure to America's security and defence.

Domain Overlap. All the recent domains of information, space and cyber operate seamlessly across all domains, including land, water, air and can span different geographical locations. The commanders may employ some of these capabilities to enhance operational effectiveness in conjunction with Electronic Warfare (EW) and Electro Magnetic Spectrum (EMS) management. Advancements in technology have made an increasingly complex Operational Environment (OE). Cyber, Information and space operations can be conducted against targets using part of the EMS. These can be integrated with other information related capabilities as part of Information Operations (IO). IO, cyber, space and EW operations are often conducted under specific authorities. Similarly, some information-related capabilities supported by cyber operations, such as military information support operations (MISO), military deception (MILDEC) and special technical operations (STO), have their own execution approval process. One can say that these are stovepipe organisations.

Relationship between the Domains

Unequal Domains. The five operational domains are not equivalent or equal. There is a significant difference when considering the relationship of space and the cyber and information domains. Space is a constant in relation to the land, maritime and air domains beneath it, and being a domain in which discrete activity is also possible. We rely on space for critical services such as Position, Navigation and Timing (PNT) and satellite communications. The cyber and information domain is omnipresent and permeates all other domains. The information, cyber and space domains are the least understood domains.

Illustration of Domains as Described in UK Doctrine

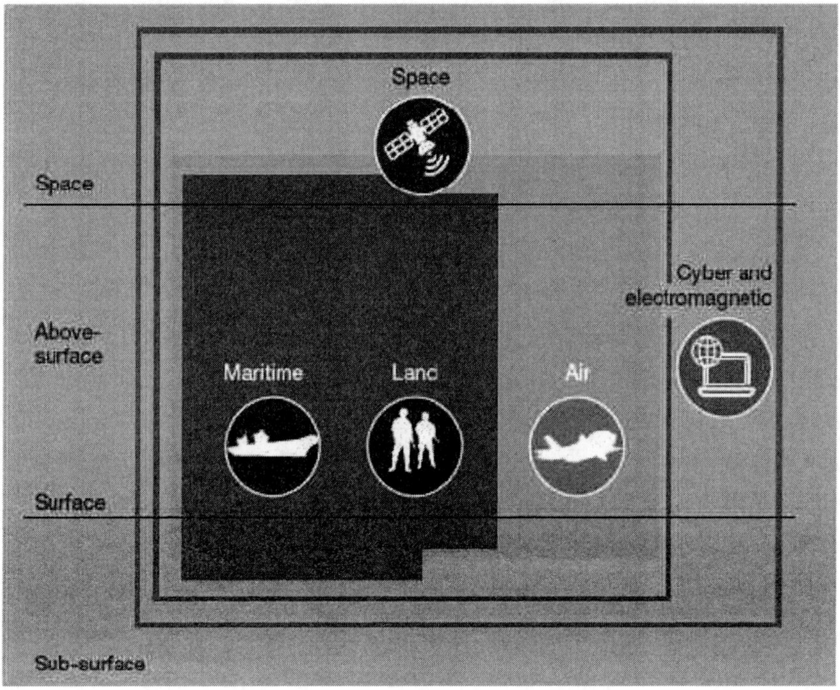

Source: Multi-Domain Integration, Joint Concept Note 1/20, UK Ministry of Defence (MOD), P 18, available at: https://assets.publishing.service.gov.uk/government/uploads/system/uploads/attachment_data/file/950789/20201112-JCN_1_20_MDI.PDF

Space and Cyber. Space systems comprise many governments and commercial components where cyber security and space operations are intimately linked. The vulnerability of satellites and other space assets to a cyberattack is often overlooked in discussions of cyber threats to critical national infrastructure. A space system should have cyber security protections applied to all four segments: space, ground, link and user. Neither space policy nor cyber security caters to the challenges created by the meshing of space and cyberspace, especially for spacecraft. To meet the space cyber challenges, government, industry and international action is needed.

Many capabilities reserved earlier to superpowers are now available to other states on a commercial basis. These capabilities are earth observation, optical sensing, space-based internet and communications services. An array of Anti-Satellite weapons (ASAT) able to disrupt or destroy the space, electromagnetic and ground segments of these constellations will become more common.

Cyber and Information Operations. The success of the narrative increasingly determines defeat or victory. This is why information operations are important. They can be used in support of conventional military operations and those utilising proxies and deniable paramilitary forces, military coercion, offensive cyber operations and lawfare. Traditional techniques, such as assassination, deception, economic coercion, espionage, theft of intellectual property and subversion, gain potency through the clever use of cyber, digitised information and social media.

The emergence of state-sponsored actors and associated organisations with more advanced cyber warfare capabilities is a reality. State-based cyber advocates will develop strategies that will attempt to "leap over" traditional military power and directly influence political and military leadership decisions. Several states will have offensive cyber warfare capabilities to disrupt adversary's cyber-connected systems. They will use this capability to cause social unrest. Attacks will undermine the trust and data integrity central to advanced societies, mainly financial, legal and technical infrastructure. This competition may feature strategic surveillance as well as industrial and scientific espionage.

When 'fake news' appears to originate at home, it gains credibility and reach. It fuels confusion, disagreement, division and doubt in our societies. Home is no longer a secure place from where we may launch interventions. The 'front' is no longer in some distant theatre of operations but is within the country. It sits across the electromagnetic spectrum, space and inside our networks. Sub-conventional operations are carried out continuously by our adversaries who want to weaken our military readiness, critical national infrastructure, economy and way of life.

Urbanisation and extensive access to social media will increase operational complexity. Soldiers and commanders may be deluged with information and face multiple dilemmas, in shorter periods, across multiple operational domains. The increase in overall operational complexity will need army personnel to perform their duties with greater skill and understanding of information and cyberspace.[4]

Commanders have to seek information advantage because it is central to how we operate and fight. Commanders have to think beyond the enemy and examine the additional effects that are to be applied to the many other actors, especially local populations relevant to the achievement of the objective, before coordinating the appropriate mix of physical, virtual and cognitive actions. Information advantage facilitates improved understanding, assessment, decision-making and execution.[5]

New Thinking. U.S. Army Cyber Command has spent two years integrating cyber, electronic warfare and information operations with new units under the banner of information warfare to offset adversary capabilities. Army Cyber Command is shifting from "information warfare" as a concept, opting instead for "information advantage." Lt. Gen. Stephen Fogarty, Commander of U.S. Cyber command, has been pushing for renaming ARCYBER as Army Information Warfare Command.[6]

Gen Fogarty, during the virtual CEMAlite Conference on September 29, 2020, hosted by the Association of Old Crows, said, "This is not only the cyber domain, it's not only in the [radio frequency] spectrum, but it's in the larger or, the greater information environment.... The stunning social media-powered rise of ISIS [the Islamic State group] in 2015, Russia's interference in the 2016 U.S. Presidential election, Iran's increasing digital belligerence, and China's disinformation surrounding the COVID-19 pandemic are upending that perception and igniting a conversation across the defense establishment regarding appropriate roles for the uniformed armed services in this environment of unprecedented information warfare."

Providing information advantage for commanders and decision dominance will require a range of capabilities to include cyber, information, intelligence, public affairs and space.[7]

Operating Effectively in Cyberspace, Space and Information domains

In the context of the emerging multi-domain operations (MDO) concept or its next avatar, all domain operations, the ability to integrate information, cyberspace, intelligence and space will be crucial to operational success. The integration, especially at the tactical level, will ensure commanders' access to cross-domain combined arms capabilities for mounted and dismounted operations. Modern armed forces cannot carry out high-tempo, effective operations without reliable information and communication networks and assured access to cyberspace and space.

As the MDO concept grows, non-lethal fires such as space control, cyber warfare and information warfare will provide capabilities and effects that will be integral to the evolution of warfare. The inclusion of Information Operations (IO) as an integrator of joint fires, both lethal and non-lethal, to affect adversary behaviour is indispensable.

For example, information operations, cyber and space operations may be used for an operation directed at an enemy weapons system comprising of the targeted platform and its operators. The space capability may help in identifying and targeting the target. Cyber capability could create degrading effects on the platform while an information-related capability influences, disrupts, corrupts or preempts the operator's decision-making.

Operations in space, cyber and information domains will be continuous. These operations are likely to commence long before lethal combat begins and even before combat forces begin to deploy. These could be part of efforts to shape the operational area.

In this era of persistent competition, we should be able to operate and fight in a manner that generates advantage through being better integrated across three levels of warfare and all five operational domains: maritime, land, air, space, cyber and information. This multi-domain integration will change the way we operate and fight and develop capability. This is moving beyond 'joint' to an era when effects from all domains will enable modern manoeuvre in any domain.

Sophisticated operations that target systems can be combined with more conventional military operations such as proxies, coercion, offensive cyber and lawfare. This may result in achieving without escalating above the threshold of armed conflict. They could turn 'shaping' operations into 'decisive' ones.

Technology and People

Humans in Command. The requirement of command, control, communications, computers, intelligence, surveillance, target acquisition and reconnaissance (C4ISTAR) system is well understood. The machine will bring advantages of automation and augmentation by artificial intelligence for bounded less-complex data-centric tasks. They will allow analysis that covers descriptive, diagnostic, predictive and ultimately prescriptive capabilities. However, as well as conveying data, the system will need to connect the right people at the right time for decision-making, the delegation of authorities, and legal/ethical assurance. These interventions and inputs of guile, judgment, emotional intelligence and understanding of subtle complexities will remain the basis for military success. Human inputs will endure at least till the near foreseeable future.

Commanding with Machines. Commanders will have to be comfortable with the options generated by machines and understand why they offer the solutions they do or make the 'mistakes' they make. Robotics, intelligent and autonomous systems will need to be complemented with carefully calibrated levels of appropriate human control according to the complexity of the task. To command effectively within a multi-domain system, the human operator must be involved.[8]

Emerging technologies like artificial intelligence, machine learning, hypersonics, robotics and nanotechnology are driving a fundamental change in the character of war. Just as these technologies mature and their military applications become clear, the impacts can revolutionise battlefields, unlike anything.[9]

This increased complexity is designed to offer options for military commanders and complicate adversary decision making. The challenge is that even the advanced military like the U.S. is not organised to make these decisions. The complexity and speed of the technology being used can exceed the ability of human cognition.

Coordinating operations between two domains is an age-old phenomenon. For example, close air support, which uses aircraft to support ground fires and manoeuvre against adversary ground forces, has been used since Second World War. Today joint forces are grappling with integrating information, cyber and space which are emerging as essential warfighting domains.

It is no longer possible to maintain total dominance in all domains all the time. Operations in one domain may be used to create a window of opportunity in another. For instance, a cyberattack on adversary integrated air defence systems may open up a window of air superiority in a limited geographic area, allowing friendly aircraft to safely transit the area to strike a target Command-and-Control set up.

Culture Issues. The Army wants to focus on using space, cyberspace, EW and IO to support the ground fight. Air Force intends to concentrate on integrating air, space and cyberspace capabilities to create windows of superiority. Information operations is absent here. The Army wants to empower forward forces to conduct operations within the commander's intent, a principle known as the directive style of command, to seize opportunities during fast-moving operations and sustain operations even when communications are disrupted. Air Force has historically sought to centralise air power to remain flexible and shift priorities rapidly in response to changes in the battlefield.

A single domain or service-centric mindset is there. Service components may have cultural biases or organisational structures that prioritise missions in some domains over others. These biases could guide planners to overlook or avoid solutions in other domains or to sidestep prioritising support to missions that take place primarily in different domains.

Command and Control Characteristics

Planners have insufficient expertise in or access to information about relevant domains. Decision-makers need to understand both the capabilities and limitations of operations in all domains. They need information about availability of forces and what activities are taking place in the operating environment. Significant expertise is required to identify planning considerations for a particular domain and to interpret information about the operating environment to generate situational awareness.

This does not mean that the decision-makers need access to the highly detailed information that domain experts need to conduct planning or execute operations in their domain. It means that decision-makers at the operational level need access to sufficient expertise and information to know what appropriate options are available in a given situation.

Combined Joint All Domain Command and Control

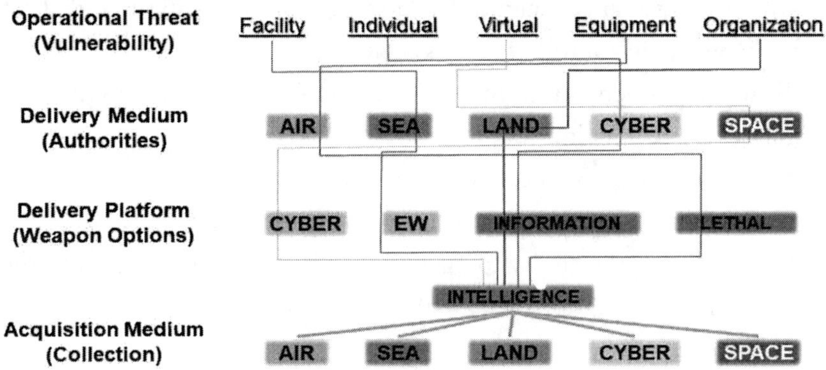

Source: https://disa.mil/-/media/Files/DISA/News/Events/2020-Virtual-Experience/AFCEA_Agile_EMSO_Rosner_Coyle_Pugh_11-3-20_Final_PAO_Approved.ashx

Communications. In January 2012, President Barack Obama and Secretary of Defense Leon Panetta endorsed new strategic guidance for 21st-century defence priorities of the U.S. The guidance asserted: "Modern armed forces cannot conduct high-tempo, effective operations without reliable information and communication networks and assured access to cyberspace and space.[10]"

In such operations, dependence on communications increases. Attack on a smaller number of high-payoff targets such as undersea cables and infrastructure for satellite communications could disrupt or degrade the communications. Command and control nodes, such as large operations centres and headquarters, are likely to be targeted for kinetic and non-kinetic attacks. The proliferation of electronic jammers requires resilience or anti-jam properties to maintain communications while being actively jammed.

Satellite communication systems face latency (time delay) issues. It is not designed to operate effectively in the presence of electronic warfare. New applications, like Artificial Intelligence (AI), will require additional data rates that current communications networks will not be able to support. Data links, which share data with all available users, do not necessarily require high data rates. However, data links do need low latency for fast-moving systems like cruise missiles and aircraft. The introduction of autonomous systems would demand secure communications and short latency to maintain control of these systems.

To develop a network to meet the future requirements, the following capabilities are required:

- Data throughput, i.e., the rate at which data can be transported.
- Latency, i.e., the time delay in receiving a message/data.
- Resiliency, the ability to maintain a communications signal in the event of disruption by natural or intentional sources.

The figure below illustrates how these three competing requirements must be balanced to develop a new waveform. Radio signals can offer each capability. However, prioritising one requirement means that the other two requirements may suffer. It creates a dilemma for policymakers in terms of which capabilities to prioritise in acquisition.

Balancing Communications Requirements

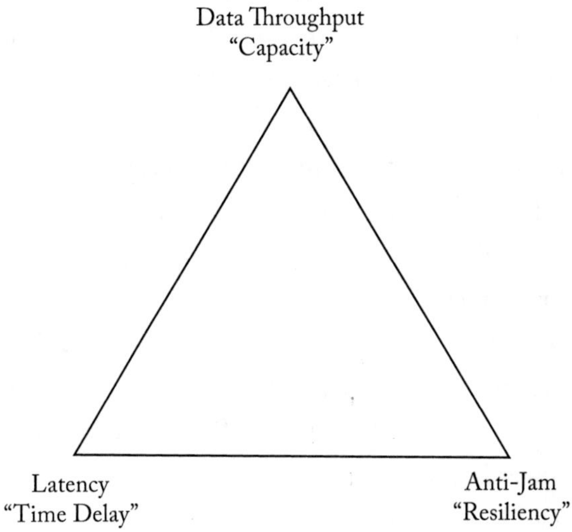

Source: Congressional Research Service.

Automation and Artificial Intelligence

In a January 2021 article, Lt Gen Michael Groen, director of the Pentagon's Joint Artificial Intelligence Center, stated that the role of artificial intelligence (AI), and by extension the role of data and data structures, is to enable these algorithms to inform commanders. Lt Gen Dennis Crall, Director of the Joint Staff's command, control, communications, and computers/cyber chief information officer, wrote: "It is about taking advantage of that sensor-rich environment—looking at things like data standards; making sure that we can move this information into an area that, again, we can process it properly; bringing on cloud; bringing on artificial intelligence, predictive analytics; and then undergirding this with a network that can handle this, all domains and partners."

Mosaic Warfare. It represents a series of DARPA-sponsored projects designed to use AI to combine systems and networks not traditionally designed to interoperate. Conceptually, these projects would take raw intelligence collected from a satellite and turn that data into targetable information passed to a "shooter" like a cyber-weapon, electronic jammer, missile, aircraft or any other weapon might be able to affect the desired target. Rather than relying on many specialised personnel to manually identify the location and status of air assets, DARPA software automatically tracks this information and relays it to commanders. It balances Communications Capabilities in a Degraded Environment.[11]

Operational Challenges

Dealing with Disruption. The commanders should be able to deal with disrupted and degraded space and cyberspace capabilities that may be attacked using advanced weapons like EMP (Electromagnetic Pulse) and HPRF (High Power Radio Frequency).

Cross-domain Deterrence. It is an action of deterring in one domain with a threat in another domain. The domains are defined as land, sea, air, space, information and cyber and may use economic sanctions and other diplomatic and political tools. Cross-domain synergy can clarify the intentions of deterrence measures as well as enhance their effectiveness.

The Leadership Dimension. With space and cyberspace capabilities available to the commanders, commanders tend to micromanage their troops rather than follow mission command.

Electromagnetic Spectrum. EMS is normally viewed as a critical enabler to operations in all domains. Many scholars and practitioners argue that EMS is worthy of being named as the sixth warfighting domain. This remains an open dialogue.

Space and Cyberspace in the Lead. Currently, cyber and space operations are considered as the supported activities. In future, these may become the primary efforts. The traditional domains may have to support main efforts in space or cyberspace domains.

Priorities for Cyberspace Resources. There are high expectations from future cyber and space operations, which may be unrealistic. A realistic evaluation should be carried out.

Military Theory for Space and Cyberspace. Military activities in space and cyberspace are the least intuitive to comprehend and the least understood by military planners and operators. A military theory should be developed and promulgated throughout the spectrum of professional military education.

China. The PLA uses the term "informatised or informationised warfare" to describe the process of acquiring, transmitting, processing and using the information to conduct joint military operations across the domains of land, sea, air, space, cyberspace and the electromagnetic spectrum during a conflict. Informationised warfare obscures the lines between peacetime and wartime. Informationised warfare is a superset of cyber warfare; cyber warfare is just one piece of the larger whole.

Informationised warfare goes beyond the addition of information technology into individual weapons or broader systems. It creates systems-of-systems, including the inclusion of information technology into every facet of military activities, e.g., logistics, intelligence collection and exploitation, transportation, etc. One of the characteristics of informationised warfare is that conflicts are not platform-vs-platform or system-versus-system. Battles are now between rival arrays of systems-of-systems.

Conclusion

The use of advanced technologies in global communications, networked operations, space, cyberspace, robotics, platforms, etc., cost money. Such technologies, in a time of restricted budgetary constraints, may prove unaffordable.

The commanders will not have control of all the domains. For instance, offensive cyber is not under the exclusive control of armed forces. Activities in space will have immediate consequences for other departments. This adds layers to military judgement and mission command.

As we look to the future, the technologies such as the universal data availability via cloud connectivity, artificial intelligence, machine learning and quantum computing will create not only a new generation of weapons systems but a totally new way of warfare. A mix of manned, unmanned and autonomous systems will improve lethality and utility. The ubiquitous nature of data, private, commercial, governmental and military combined, gathered from constellations of sensors and analysed at high speed by artificial intelligence, will make it extremely hard to hide today's military signature anywhere on the globe.

Integrating all five Operational Domains: Space, Cyber, Maritime, Air and Land will change the way we operate, fight and develop capability. It adds up to far more than the sum of the parts. Integration is now required at the tactical level of war, not just at the operational level where the term 'Joint' applies.

The level of jointness and integration in the Indian Armed Forces and what can be done to improve are the most critical question that stares at the Indian Armed Forces.

This book will be covered in six main chapters: Introduction, Information, Cyber and Space domains, Summary of Recommendations and Conclusion.

Notes

1. Jeffrey L. Caton, 'The Land, Space, and Cyberspace Nexus: Evolution of the Oldest Military Operations in the Newest Military Domains', U.S. Army War College Press, 2018, at https://press.armywarcollege.edu/cgi/viewcontent.cgi?article=1399&context=monographs
2. 'The Integrated Operating Concept 2025', UK Ministry of Defence, September 30, 2020, at https://www.gov.uk/government/publications/the-integrated-operating-concept-2025/the-integrated-operating-concept-2025-accessible-version
3. Jeffrey L. Caton, n. 1.
4. 'The U.S. Army Concept for Cyberspace and Electronic Warfare Operations', TRADOC Pamphlet 525-8-6, January 2018, at https://adminpubs.tradoc.army.mil/pamphlets/TP525-8-6.pdf
5. 'The Integrated Operating Concept 2025', n. 2.
6. Mark Pomerleau, 'Out: "information warfare". In: "information advantage",' C4ISRNET, September 29, 2020, at https://www.c4isrnet.com/information-warfare/2020/09/29/out-information-warfare-in-information-advantage/

7. Ibid.
8. Joint Concept Note 1/20, Multi-Domain Integration, Joint Concept Note (JCN) 1/20, November 2020.
9. 'The U.S. Army in multi-domain Operations 2028', n. 4.
10. 'Sustaining U.S. Global Leadership: Priorities for 21st Century Defense', U.S. Department of Defense, January 2012, p. 5, at http://archive.defense.gov/news/Defense_Strategic_Guidance.pdf
11. Joint All-Domain Command and Control: Background and Issues for Congress, Congressional Research Service, R46725, March 18, 2021.

3 Information Domain

> "I began to understand that I was caught up in two wars: one fought on the ground with tanks and artillery, and an information war fought largely, though not exclusively, through social media. And, perhaps counter-intuitively, it mattered who won the war of words and narratives (rather) than who had the most potent weaponry."
>
> —David Patrikarakos, *War in 140 Characters*, 2017

Introduction

From the beginning, the battle over information has been a part of warfare. The use of information as a tool in warfare and its emphasis on accurate intelligence for decision superiority over a mightier foe has been enunciated in Chinese military strategist Sun Tzu's book, The Art of War, in fifth-century BC. In 480 BC, in the Battle of Thermopylae, Persian ruler Xerxes used intimidation tactics to break the will of Greek city-states. In 1870, Alexander the Great used cultural assimilation to subdue dissent and maintain conquered lands. Otto von Bismarck was able to incite the French into a very unfavourable declaration of war against Prussia by manipulating the reported text of one telegram. These earliest strategists laid the foundation for information warfare strategy in modern times.

We live in the data-rich Information Age. The exponential growth in computer capability, data and connectivity is shaping the way people live and work. The ability to share information in near real-time, securely and anonymously, is a capability that is an asset as well as a potential vulnerability to our adversaries and us. The intelligent use of information through the mass customisation of messaging, narrative and persuasion, can immensely extend reach and deliver uneven influence on targeted audiences. Information is no longer just an enabler. It is a well-developed element of national power and a strategic, operational and tactical weapon. If used in a timely and logical manner, it can generate an advantage over an opponent and deliver mass effect and precision 'fire', to disrupt, confuse, agitate and radicalise.

In a foreword to Rand Corporation Report on Changing Role of Information in Warfare, Andrew W Marshall 23 years back in 1998 stated prophetically.[1]

- Information advances will affect more than just how we fight wars. The nature and purpose of war itself may change. How wars start, how they end, their length, and the nature of the participants may change as shifts in the relative power of states and non-state entities occur.
- New technologies cut both ways in terms of their effects on national security. Together, advances create new vulnerabilities; new threats create new opportunities. We should resist the temptation to see the changes documented here either as wholly bad or wholly good. Rather, we need to understand that profound technological changes are inevitably two sided.
- The Department of Defense (DoD) has little control over the pace and direction of the information revolution. Although in the past DoD played an important role in developing, refining and implementing new information technologies, today the technological envelope is being pushed largely by the commercial sector. DoD needs to manage a difficult transition from being a pioneer to being a leading user. This transition will require not only keeping abreast of new technological developments but also accepting that technology will no longer be developed exactly to military specifications.

The increasing capacity to produce, communicate and use information will have an important effect on every area of national security. Information is everywhere. As a result, we will not be able to understand how these new technologies will change our own jobs unless we understand how they will change the jobs of others. The advent of the information age will require, as never before, that we take a wider perspective and avoid stovepipes that blind us to changes taking place outside our own spheres of direct responsibility.

The information dimension is becoming central to the outcome of battles. Defending own information systems and being able to degrade, destroy or disrupt the functioning of the opponent's information systems will be the central focus of the operational art. Obtaining early superiority in the information domain will become central to success in future warfare.

Information Warfare (IW) takes place below the level of armed conflict. As cyberspace presents a cost-effective and easy method to communicate a message to a large population, most of the information warfare today occurs on the internet. This leads to some confusion between cyber warfare and information warfare. IW is a strategy for using the information to pursue a competitive advantage, including defensive and offensive efforts. It is a form of political warfare. IW is a means through which nation states achieve strategic objectives and advance foreign policy goals.

There is a subtle difference between cyber warfare and information warfare. Both deals with information. Cyber warfare does it exclusively in its digitised and operationalised form. Information warfare does so in a much broader sense. With IW, information itself is the weapon. In cyber conflict, information systems are leveraged as the terrain over which diverse effects might be realised. The national cyber mission force of the U.S. Cyber Command carry out operations to target and dismantle violent extremist websites that cause an operational threat to troops on the ground. But, this cyber force is structurally and conceptually separated from the troops responsible for conducting information operations. The two forces operate under the separate doctrine.

There are debates in the U.S. about where the IW centre of gravity should be. During the Cold War, it was the Department of State and the U.S. Information Agency. Since 9/11, much of the current doctrine and capability exists in the military. Some experts worry that the army should not be involved in the production of propaganda.[2]

Information Operations are an evolving construct. The late 1970s saw the emergence of Information Warfare (IW) and Command and Control Warfare (C2W) as war-fighting concepts integrating several diverse capabilities. These further evolved into Information Operations, recognising the role of information as an element of power through the spectrum of peace, conflict and war.

Defining Information Warfare (IW)

Currently, there is no official definition of IW specially from U.S. government. It is theorised as using and managing information to pursue a competitive advantage, including offensive and defensive efforts. According to Cold War diplomat George Kennan's definition:

> Political warfare is the employment of all the means at a nation's command, short of war, to achieve its national objectives. Such operations are both overt and covert. They range from such overt actions as political alliances, economic measures, and "white" propaganda to such covert operations as clandestine support of 'friendly' foreign elements, "black" psychological warfare and even encouragement of underground resistance in hostile states.[3]

In this sense, IW is a form of political warfare, where targets are a nation state's government, military, private sector and the general population.

As a term, information warfare, or IW, remains in use worldwide. Rand Corporation defined IW as: "Information warfare is conflict or struggle between two or more groups in the information environment". Dan Kuehl of the National Defence University defines IW as "military offensive and defensive actions to control/exploit the environment."

IW is the assortment of military and government operations to protect and exploit the information environment. It takes place below the level of armed conflict. It comprises both offensive and defensive operations. It is conducted in crisis, conflict, warfare as well as in peacetime also. Whether attacking government organisations, political leadership or news media to influence public opinion or compel decision-makers to take specific actions, ultimately, the target of information warfare activities is human cognition. That is why IW is sometimes referred to as influence operations or psychological operations.

Information warfare may be a preamble to an armed conflict. Information operations set the conditions to gain the support of locals, "winning the hearts and minds." Alternatively, IW may be an end in itself, achieving the goal without the use of force.

Information Warfare vs Information Operations

Information warfare occurs at the strategic level, while information operations (IO) involve using various information-related capabilities to implement the strategy. The operational level is when campaigns and major operations are planned, conducted and sustained to achieve strategic objectives within theatres or other operational areas. Operations link these strategic objectives with particular tactics, techniques and procedures to achieve them. IO takes places at the operational level, linking information-related capabilities and tactics to a broader strategy.[4] However, in this book IW and IO have been used interchangeably meaning the same.

Information Operation Domain

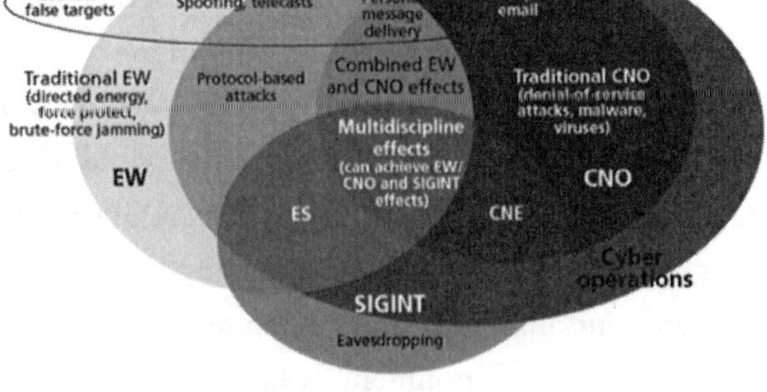

Source: CERDEC I2WD. RAND MG1113-5.2

Information Environment

The Information Environment (IE) is part of the operational environment. Therefore, any activity that occurs in the information environment simultaneously takes place in and affects one or more of the operational environment domains.

The information environment is becoming more and more complex. Because of the extensive availability of internet, mobile communications and information, the information environment is an essential consideration to military planning and operations. The armed forces also rely on these technologies. As a result, activities occurring in and through the IE substantially affect military operations and outcomes. Commanders and staffs at all levels must know the IE in all its complexity and the likely impacts it will have on current and planned military operations.

Information environment is defined as "The aggregate of individuals, organizations, and systems that collect, process, disseminate, or act on information.[5]"

The recent model of the IE focuses on the transmission, processing and storage of information within three interrelated but distinct dimensions: physical, informational and cognitive domains.

The Information Environment

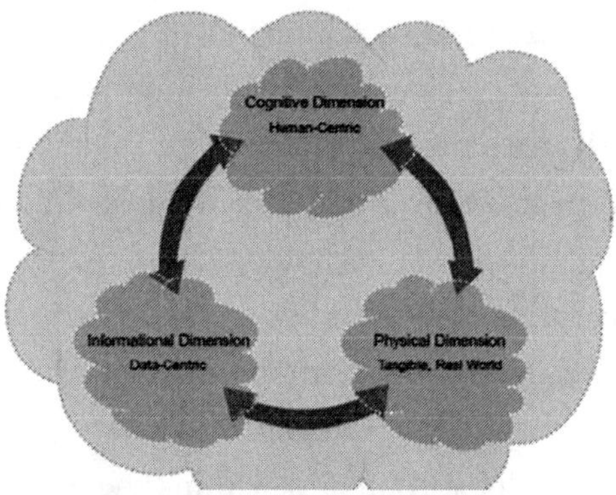

Source: Joint Concept for Operating in the Information Environment (JCOIE), available at: https://www.jcs.mil/Portals/36/Documents/Doctrine/concepts/joint_concepts_jcoie.pdf?ver=2018-08-01-142119-830

Information Environment Dimensions

Types	Affects	Examples
Physical	Content	• The physical world and its content, particularly that which enables and supports exchanging ideas, information, and messages. • Information systems and physical networks. • Communications systems and networks. • People and human networks. • Personal devices, handheld devices, and social media graphical user interface. • Mobile phones, personal digital assistants, and social media graphical user interfaces.
Informational	Code	• Collected, coded, processed, stored, disseminated, displayed, and protected information. • Information metadata, flow, and quality. • Social media application software, information exchange, and search engine optimization. • The code itself. • Any automated decision making.
Cognitive	Context	• The impact of information on the human will. • The contextualized information and human decision making. • Intangibles, such as morale, values, worldviews, situational awareness, perceptions, and public opinions. • Mental calculations in response to stimuli, such as liking something on a social media application.

Source: The Conduct of Information Operations, ATP 3-13.1, October 2018, available at: https://irp.fas.org/doddir/army/atp3-13-1.pdf

In 2017, U.S. DOD updated its Doctrine for the Armed Forces. It created information as the seventh joint function of the military in addition to the joint functions of command and control, intelligence, fires, movement and manoeuvre, protection and sustainment.

Information technology has considerably improved human interaction around the globe and raised the importance of information as an instrument of power employed by individuals and societies in politics, economics and warfare. Advances in information technology have changed the generation, transmission and reception of information and reaction to them. Particularly social media empowers swift mobilisation of people and resources around ideas and causes, even before they are fully understood.

Cyberspace is a global domain within the IE comprising the interdependent network of information technology infrastructures and resident data, including the internet, telecommunications networks, computer systems and embedded processors and controllers.

The Information Environment is Increasingly Digital and Wireless

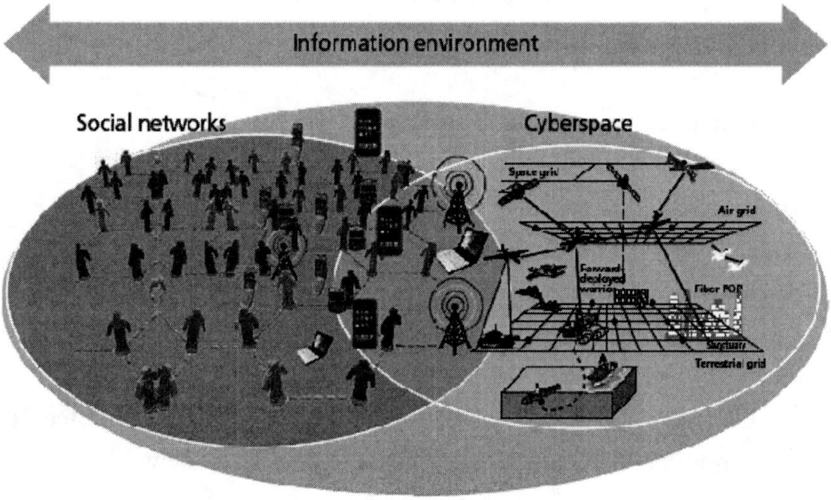

Source: Isaac R. Porche III et al., Redefining Information Warfare Boundaries for an Army in a Wireless World, RAND Corporation, 2013, available at: https://www.rand.org/pubs/monographs/MG1113.html

The recent developments in the entertainment industry and social media have made some fundamental changes in the IE. The entertainers, advertisers, politicians and others always try to build audiences with attention-grabbing techniques. The attention economy, which translates online views of content into money, has made it almost impossible for humans to turn away. The same techniques can expose individuals to information that is specifically designed to feed their biases and prevent objective analysis of facts.

An example of cyber-based exploitation is YouTube. Algorithms produce video after video to viewers based on previously viewed content. This is more concerning when combined with big data. The manipulation and targeted use of information are creating threats to democracy that are as real as military threats.

The information-capable adversaries can promote narratives that exploit social division, strategically target information and selectively manipulate the truth. Cyber-enabled information operations are a threat to democracies. Democratic nations will have to come to grips with the modern information environment.[6]

Components of Information Operations (IO)

Information Operations

The U.S. government has theorised information operations as a purely military activity involving a set of tactics or capabilities. In the 2003 version of U.S. DoD's Joint Publication 3-13 and the Information Operations Roadmap, IO consists of five pillars:

- Computer network operations (CNO), which consisted of computer network attack (CNA), computer network defence (CND) and computer network exploitation (CNE).
- Psychological operations (PSYOP).
- Electronic warfare.
- Operations security (OPSEC).
- Military deception (MILDEC).

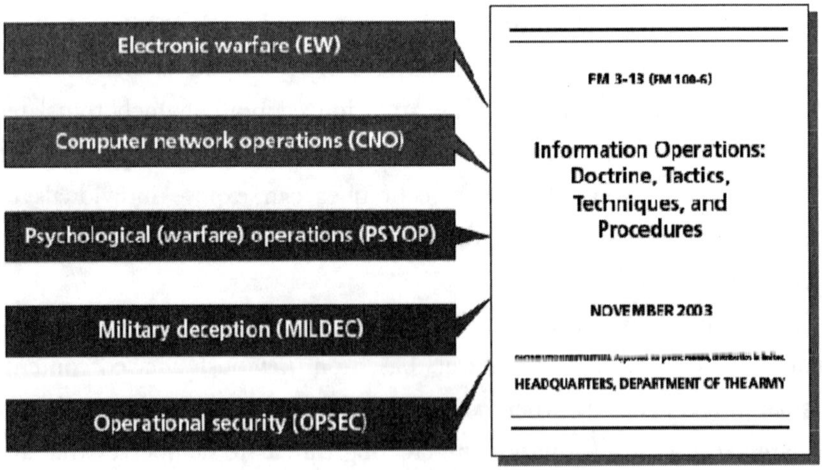

Source: Isaac R. Porche III et al., Redefining Information Warfare Boundaries for an Army in a Wireless World, RAND Corporation, 2013, available at: https://www.rand.org/pubs/monographs/MG1113.html

Later CNO became cyberspace operations, offensive and defensive, with its separate doctrine in Joint Publication 3-12.

Psychological Operations (PSYOPS) involve the prepared use of information to influence the emotions, objective reasoning motives and ultimately the behaviour of foreign governments, organisations, groups and individuals. At the strategic level, PSYOPs are the handing over of information to influence foreign target audiences in support of nation's goals and objectives. PSYOPs at the operational level are conducted to support the combatant commander's mission accomplishment, either independently or as an integral part of other operations. In the later doctrine, PSYOP term was changed to military information support operations (MISO).

Electronic Warfare is defined as military action involving electromagnetic and directed energy to control the electromagnetic spectrum or attack the enemy. Examples are jamming command and control systems, satellites used for global positioning systems and radio communications.

Operations Security is the system of identifying critical information and analysing friendly actions attendant to military operations and other activities.

Military Deception is actions to knowingly mislead adversary military, paramilitary or violent extremist organisation decision-makers, thereby causing the adversary to undertake specific actions or inactions that will contribute to accomplishing the friendly mission. A pillar closely related to PSYOP, MILDEC focuses on false information or disinformation.

In JP 3-13 of November 20, 2014, IO has been defined as "the integrated employment, during military operations, of information-related capabilities in concert with other lines of operation to influence, disrupt, corrupt, or usurp the decision making of adversaries and potential adversaries while protecting our own." This definition transfers the focus from a set of tactics or pillars toward the desired effects and how to achieve them. It defines information-related capability as a tool, technique or activity used within a dimension of the information environment that can be employed to create effects and operationally desirable conditions. Strategic communication, public diplomacy, public and civil affairs, and cyberspace operations may be considered supporting capabilities. They may occur outside of cyberspace, such as dropping pamphlets, cultural exchanges, civil affairs and foreign aid programs to gain favour with a target population.

Facebook has published an interesting White Paper on Information Operations. Its definition of IO would have been read by many more people than U.S. DoD Publication. It defines IO as:

Information operations, as actions taken by organised actors (governments or non-state actors) to distort domestic or foreign political sentiment, most frequently to achieve a strategic and/or geopolitical outcome. These operations can use a combination of methods, such as false news, disinformation, or networks of fake accounts aimed at manipulating public opinion.[7]

A main component of IO is now MISO (formerly PSYOP), which are planned operations to convey selected information and indicators to foreign audiences to influence the emotions, objective reasoning, motives and ultimately foreign governments behaviour, groups, and individuals. It focuses on the cognitive element of the information environment where its target audience includes potential and actual adversaries and friendly and neutral populations.

Types of Information

Different categories of information may be used in IO, including the following:

Propaganda. It is the propagation of an idea or narrative intended to influence, similar to psychological or influence operations. This can be misleading but true and can include stolen information. A government communicating its resolve, policies and values through press releases, speeches and other public affairs can be treated as propaganda as well as public diplomacy. These communications have strategic value. Over time they can generate perceptions that steer decision-makers towards a particular course of action.

Misinformation. It is the spreading of inadvertent false information. Examples include internet trolls which spread unfounded conspiracy theories or web hoaxes through social media, believing them to be true. Misinformation can sow divisiveness and chaos in a target society, as the truth becomes harder to discern.

Disinformation. Disinformation is deliberately false. Examples include planting intentional false news stories in the media, doctoring pictures, manufacturing protests and tampering with private or classified communications before their widespread release.

These activities occur within the information environment, which is the aggregate of individuals, organisations and systems that collect, disseminate or act on information. This includes:

- **The physical layer.** Command and control systems and associated infrastructure.
- **The informational layer.** Networks and systems where information is stored.
- **The cognitive layer.** The minds of people who transmit and respond to information.

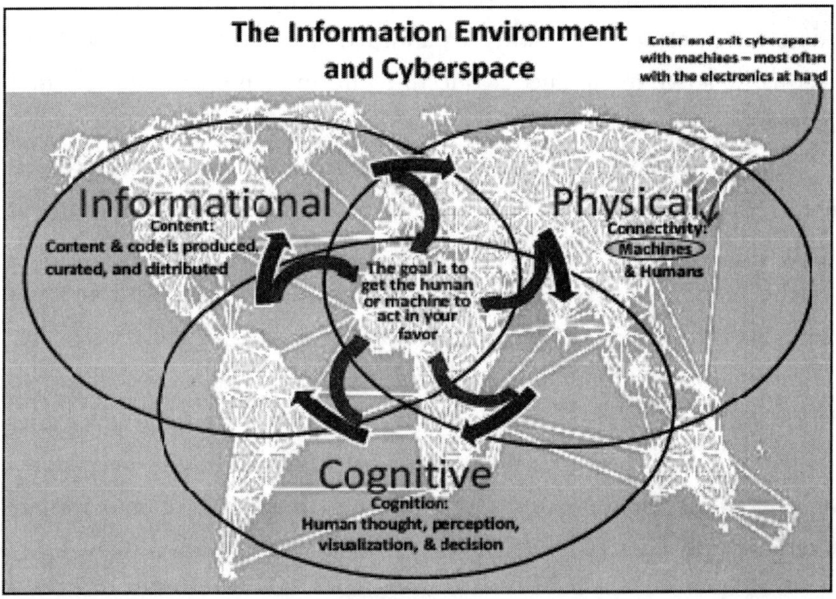

All instruments of national power, diplomatic, informational, military and economic (DIME), can be projected and employed in the information environment.[8]

Information Operations in Cyberspace

In JP 3-12, cyberspace is defined as "the global domain within the information environment consisting of the interdependent network of information technology infrastructures and resident data, including the Internet, telecommunications networks, computer systems, and embedded processors and controllers." Some have criticised this as lacking the cognitive, human element that the internet represents, which could adversely affect how the military organises, trains and equips for IO.[9]

Cyberspace is a force multiplier for IW activities. Social media and botnets can magnify a message or narrative, using all three information elements to generate discord and confusion in a target audience. Cyberspace operations can be used to attain strategic information warfare goals. For example, an offensive cyberattack may be used to create psychological effects in a target population.

IO may be covert or overt. In covert operations, government sponsorship is denied if disclosed. The anonymity afforded by cyberspace can produce an ideal battle space to conduct clandestine information operations. IO may also take place outside of cyberspace.

Intelligence Agencies. Earlier intelligence agencies like the Central Intelligence Agency (CIA) used to carry out information warfare or psychological operations. Intelligence agencies still have a role to play.

The Nation States and Terrorist Organisations. Both nation-states and terrorist organisations conduct information warfare to achieve strategic objectives. The latest U.S. National Defense Strategy refers specifically to information warfare as a means through which "competitors and adversaries seek to optimise their targeting of our battle networks and operational concepts, while also using other areas of competition short of open warfare to achieve their ends.[10]"

The information content is the key to the psychological part. The means to deliver content or prevent delivery is critical for the technical function. Ultimately, it has been suggested that most of what falls into the psychological realm be redefined as inform and influence operations (IIO). Most of what falls into the technical domain be considered information technical operations (ITO). The Dividing Line is the Technical Operations Versus Inform and Influence Operations. This has been illustrated in the following diagram.[11]

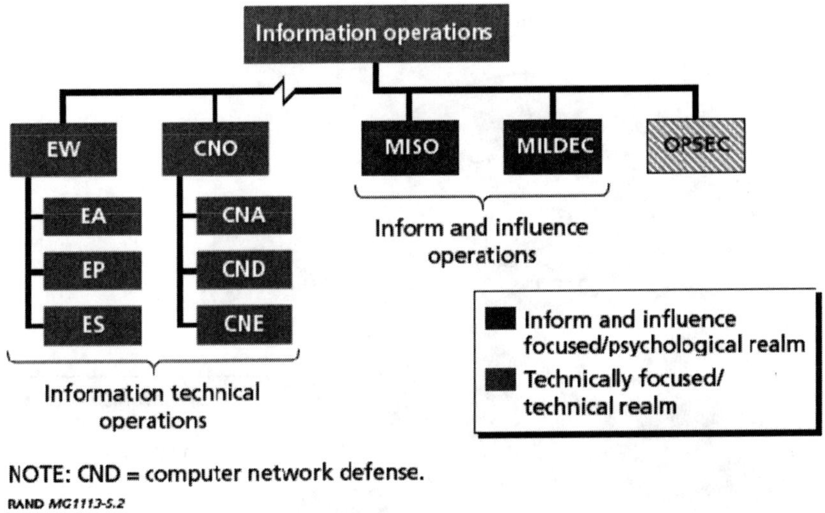

Source: Isaac R. Porche III et al., 'Redefining Information Warfare Boundaries for an Army in a Wireless World', RAND Corporation, 2013, available at: https://www.rand.org/pubs/monographs/MG1113.html

Influence Operations

As per Rand Corporation, Influence operations are the coordinated, integrated and synchronised application of national diplomatic, informational, military, economic and other capabilities in peacetime, crisis, conflict and post-conflict to foster attitudes, behaviours or decisions by foreign target audiences that further U.S. interests and objectives. This definition has a striking resemblance to the definition of strategic communications. U.S. DoD defines strategic communication as, Focused U.S. government efforts to understand and involve key audiences to create, strengthen or keep conditions favourable for the advancement of U.S. government interests, policies and goals through the use of coordinated programs, themes, plans, messages and products synchronised with the actions of all instruments of national power.[12]

Thus, influence operations can be considered synonymous with strategic communications.

Elements of Influence Operations

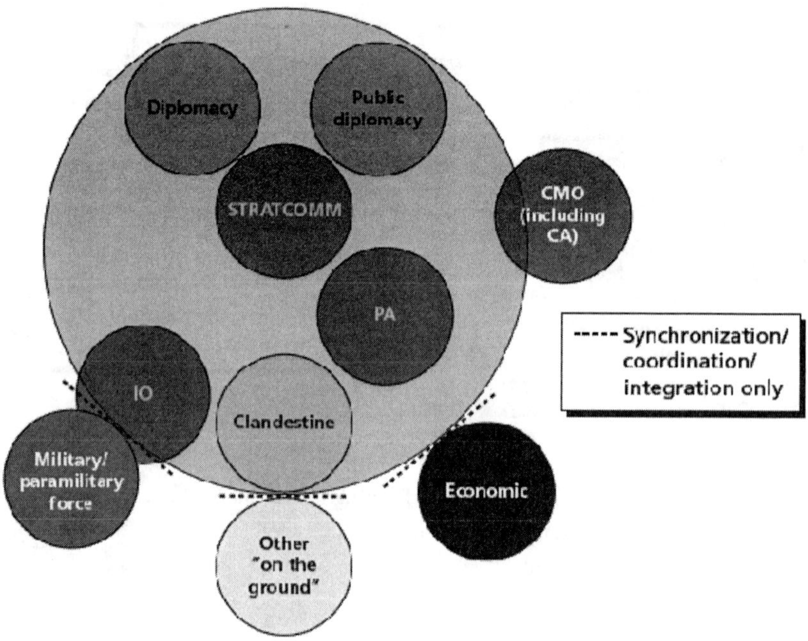

Source: Eric V. Larson et al., 'Foundations of Effective Influence Operations', RAND Corporation, 2009.

Psychological Dimension

Similar logic can be applied to the psychological realm, where there is an opportunity for consolidation. Specifically, Public Affairs (PA) and MISO, formerly PSYOP have enough reason to be better integrated.

Presently, there is a clear dividing line between PA and MISO. The main reason for separation is the commitment to use or not use truthful information. You cannot lie to your own population. You do not carry out psychological operations against your own countrymen. Truth can become a casualty here like what Yudhistir said in the great battle of Mahabharata, "Ashwatthama Hata:ha Iti, Narova Kunjarova" (Aswathhama is dead, and then he murmured, I don't know if its a man or an Elephant).

The Concept for Information Advantage

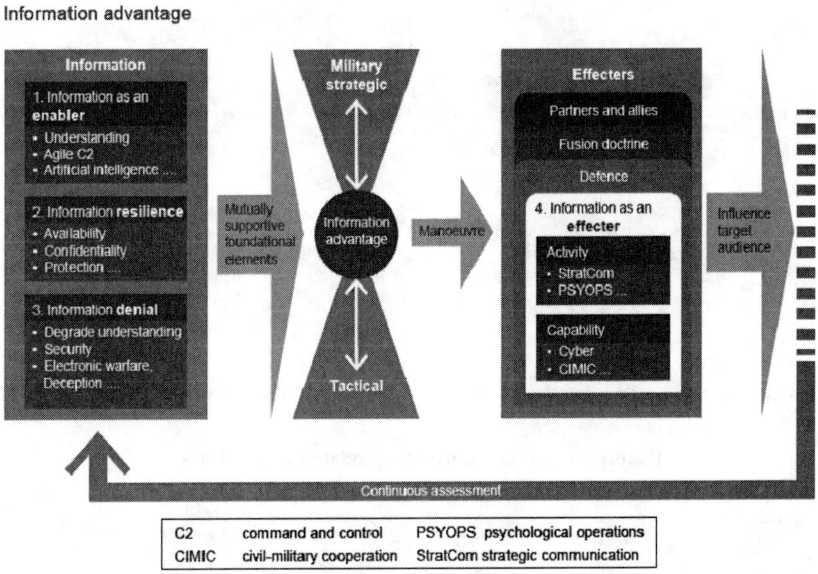

Source: Information Advantage, Joint Concept Note 2/18, UK Ministry of Defence (MOD), available at: https://assets.publishing.service.gov.uk/government/uploads/system/uploads/attachment_data/file/919262/20200909-JCN_2_18_Information_Advantage_accessible.pdf

Cyber Enabled Information Operations (CIO)

Cyber-enabled information operations (CIO) is defined as the conduct of information warfare that makes substantial use of modern information technologies, such as social media, search engines, artificial intelligence and the internet as well as traditional communications media technologies.[13]

The information environment broadly includes military information support operations, military deception, cyber operations, electromagnetic warfare, operations security and information operations.

Information Operations and Selected Information-related Capabilities

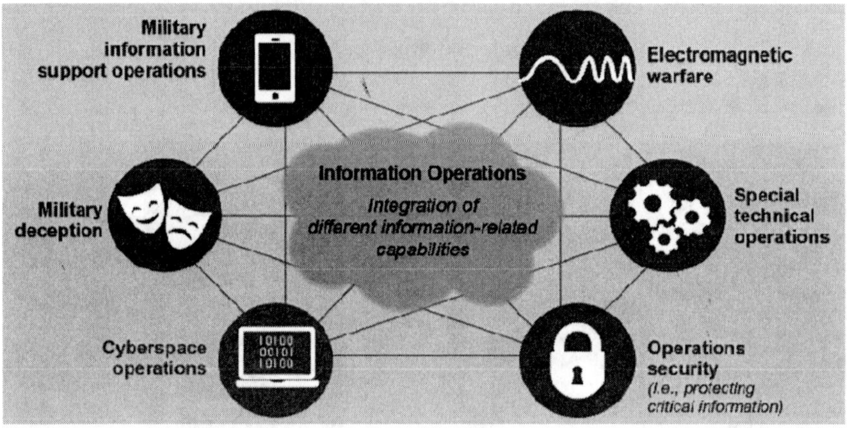

Source: GAO analysis of Department of Defense (DOD) information. GAO 21-525T

Example of DoD Information-related Capabilities

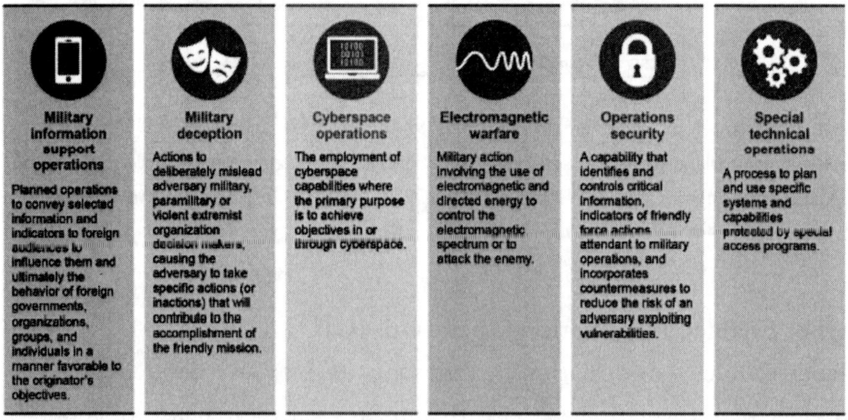

Source: GAO analysis of Department of Defense (DOD) information. GAO 21-525T

Information Operation-Related Terms Defined by DOD and Others		
DOD-defined terms	Information environment	The aggregate of individual, organisation and systems that collect, process, disseminate or act on information. This environment consists of three interrelated dimensions, which continuously interact with individuals, organisations and systems. These dimensions are known as the physical, information and cognitive (or human) dimensions.
	Information operations	The integrated employment during military operations of information-related capabilities in concert with other lines of operations to influence, disrupt, corrupt or usurp the decision-making of adversaries and potential adversaries while protecting our own.
	Information-related capability	A tool, technique or activity employed within an dimension of the information environment that can be used to achieve a specific end. DOD does not have a definitive list of information-related capabilities because any capability could be used in a way that meets the definition, according to DOD officials. A DOD official recently told us that the term information-related capability will be retired from the common vocabulary, but for the purpose of this testimony the term will continue to be used.
Non-DOD-defined terms	Influence activities/operations	DOD's current dictionary does not refer to the term "influence activities" or "influence operations." However, DOD's IO policy document refers to "influence activities" as an information-related capability, although the policy document does not define or describe these activities." In 2009, RAND issued a study on behalf of the U.S. Army. In that study, RAND defines influence operations as "the coordinated, integrated, and synchronised application of national diplomatic, informational, military, economic and other capabilities in peacetime, crisis, conflict and post-conflict to foster attitudes, behaviors, or decisions by foreign target audiences that further U.S. interests and objectives. A key difference between this definition of influence operations and DOD's definition of "information operations" is that RAND's definition includes all instruments of national power (i.e. diplomacy, information, military and economics) whereas DOD's joint doctrine focuses on activities and operations conducted by the military.
	Information warfare	Neither the U.S. government (as a whole) nor DOD (as a department) have a definition for "information warfare." However, the Congressional Research Service notes that information warfare is a form of political warfare where targets include a nation state's government, military, private sector and general population. Taking place below the level of armed conflict, information warfare is the range of military and government operations to protect and exploit the information environment. It consists of both offensive and defensive operations: the protection and assurance of one's own information (information security), and information operations to advance interests. As noted in our 2019 report about DOD information operations, while DOD does not have a department-wide definition for information warfare, we found that several of the services were using the term. "For example, the U.S Navy defines information warfare as the integrated application of capabilities to degrade, deny, deceive or destroy an enemy's information environment or to enhance the effectiveness of friendly operations. Our report also noted that the U.S. Army has begun to use the term information warfare as well, but this change has not been made in doctrine or guidance.

Source: GAO analysis of Congressional Research Service, Department of Defense (DOD), GAO-21-525T

Conflict occurs in cyberspace's information environment and involves the cognitive and emotional parts of the brain. Victory in influence operations is when the adversary willingly accepts and adopts the victor's political goals not because the adversary no longer has the means to resist but because the adversary no longer views the victor as the enemy. Knowledge, truth and confidence are all damaged due to infection of the adversary's decision process with fear, anger and uncertainty. There are no noncombatants in influence operations. Everyone, including governments, universities and news media is a potential target. Influence operations take advantage of the features of information technology, whereas cyber war takes advantage of the virtues of information technology.

It isn't easy to use influence operations against authoritarian regimes. Such regimes normally have strict information control systems that limit the types of communication citizens can access.

'Big data' enables unprecedented speed at which information is collected by connected devices, accumulating massive data that can be used for actionable insight, improved decision-making and competitive advantage. Information gathered through shopping loyalty programmes, credit cards, online shopping and social networking has increased available data exponentially. Analysis of these big data can predict political attitudes, affiliations, household income and many other personal details. This type of analysis can be used to narrow down the information to receptive audiences.

The widespread loss of information gatekeepers is unprecedented and has contributed to the scope and effectiveness of modern influence campaigns. Even the reputed media houses like BBC's reputation have suffered. A recent poll showed a fifth of Britons had no trust in the BBC to tell the truth.

There has been a general loss of faith in government, mainstream media and other traditional institutions. People are assisted by algorithms, pushing information that data indicates will be of interest to them. This fragmented information environment makes building a shared national narrative to protect society against hostile influences tough. Cyber-enabled information operations are a threat to the well-being of democratic states. For democracies will have to come to grips with the modern information environment.[14]

Today, cyberspace looks to be ideal for conducting Influence Operations. As Tim Stevens puts it, 'cyber warfare of the future may be less about hacking electrical power grids and more about hacking minds by shaping the environment in which political debate takes place.[15]'

Cyber-enabled disinformation corroding democracy and governmental institutions and threatening public safety is a national security problem. It presents unique challenges to the armed forces. Those challenges are likely to get worse, with the ongoing march of technology and increasing willingness of our adversaries to use the tool of disinformation to advance their interests. Responding to these challenges will not be easy. It will require making difficult and controversial decisions about the responsibility of the private sector or foreign social media companies for our national well-being and about restrictions on speech.[16]

The information function encompasses the management and application of information and its deliberate integration with other joint functions to influence relevant actor perceptions, behaviour, action or inaction and human and automated decision making. The information function helps commanders and staffs understand and leverage the pervasive nature of information, its military uses and its application during all military operations. This function provides commanders the ability to integrate the generation and preservation of friendly information while leveraging the inherent informational aspects of all military activities to achieve the commander's objectives and attain the end state.

Confusion of Terminologies

Post Gulf War, U.S. DoD has pioneered all the thinking and doctrines of information warfare and later information operations. However, various terms used in their doctrines somehow are confusing and lack clarity. It is not surprising that the strategic community and the Department of Defense itself, uses the terms information warfare, information operations, psychological operations, military information support operations (MISO), strategic communication, influence operations and possibly cyberspace operations interchangeably, though they are not synonymous. Currently, U.S. Cyber Command wants to expand its ambit to include information operations and information warfare.

These inconsistencies eventually can create conceptual confusion. This results in misallocation and misalignment of resources and capabilities. For instance, such confusion will make it difficult to recruit, hire and train the right people for cyber and psychological operations/MISO positions due to a lack of understanding of what skill sets different missions require.

Psychological Operations

Psychological operations often have been singled out for some negative comparisons among the non-kinetic combat capabilities. In 2011, the then Secretary of Defence Robert Gates directed that the term "psychological operations" (PSYOP) be replaced by "military information support operations."The explanation for the name change was that "although psyop activities rely on truthful information, credibly conveyed, the term PSYOP tends to connote propaganda, brainwashing, manipulation and deceit.[17]"

The conduct of psychological operations requires sanction from higher authorities than for kinetic operations. During Operation INHERENT RESOLVE, the authority to attack ISIS kinetically required a Brigadier or even below. Whereas for an information operation, approval of at least a Major General or above was required. Any operation conducted via the Internet or social media required Pentagon level approval. These constraints led to an often-expressed sentiment that "it is easier to get permission to kill terrorists than it is to lie to them".[18]

Armed forces worldwide generally consider kinetic military specialisations like armour, infantry, artillery as worthy of a higher degree of respect than non-kinetic specialisations. Everyone is busy. Incentives to familiarise oneself with matters deemed of lesser importance are likely to be scarce. Military specialities in information operations rank lower in the military pecking order and are accorded less respect than those specialising in traditional combat arts.

Despite the rhetoric and doctrinal statements, the military culture is oriented towards the operational environment where battles are won. Mass, firepower and technology have been regarded as the tools with which to win battles.

The evolution of the concept of Information Operations and its components have been covered in the chapter on components of information operations. The dichotomies between various terms and specific relevant terms like Public Field Diplomacy and strategic communication are discussed here.

Cyber Operations and Information Operations. The main restriction of carrying out any offensive psychological operation is being truthful and not misleading. This was valid in the Cold War era. The introduction of the internet, social media, search engines and other information technologies have changed the information environment by many orders of magnitude. The successes of information warfare carried out by autocratic countries against democracies in recent times have exhibited that truth does not always prevail, in part because lies spread faster than truth. Authoritarian governments exercise maximum control and influence over the information that flows through their borders or into their spheres of influence. How to do information operations against adversaries like these countries or non-state actors need careful examination.[19]

In late December 2019, Army Times reported that U.S. Army Cyber Command was coming up with a proposal to change its name to Army Information Warfare Command. The Washington Post reported that U.S. Cyber Command is "developing information warfare tactics that could be deployed against senior Russian officials and oligarchs if Moscow tries to interfere in the 2020 U.S. elections through hacking election systems or sowing widespread discord." Various service cyber command components across the globe, including U.S. Cyber Command have concentrated on getting the technical expertise that cyberspace operations require. However, the expertise needed to conduct psychological operations goes beyond the skill set of cyber operators. Cyber operations is the core competence of U.S. Cyber Command's operational activities, not the psychological operations.[20]

Cyber Command is responding to Russian election interference as Russian activities have mainly conducted through cyber means. Nevertheless, much of election interference is not a cyber problem. It is a problem of malign influence operations.

As long as these operations want to influence senior Russian or ISIL leadership behaviour, they are unmistakably influence operations. The use of information makes them information operations. The influence is psychological; hence they could be psychological operations. They are enabled by cyber operations that use computer hacking techniques to locate, identify and manipulate the sensitive data of the targeted individuals. They may be considered as information warfare activities since they respond to an information warfare campaign waged by Russia against the United States and its democratic institutions.[21]

In September 2019, NPR reported some Cyber Command activities to cause psychological effects on adversaries. Specifically, Operation Glowing Symphony was planned to degrade and disrupt online Islamic State efforts for propaganda, communications, fundraising and recruitment. Most of this effort concentrated on creating an unending series of technology annoyances and time-wasting interruptions that degraded and disrupted the workflow of Islamic State network operators significantly.

Glowing Symphony activities conveyed selected information to Islamic State network and cyber operatives to influence their emotions, motives, objective reasoning and ultimately the behaviour of the Islamic State in a manner favourable to the anti-Islamic State objectives of the United States. It is not clear about the nature of integrating military forces specialising in psychological operations into cyber operations. Usually this type of joint activity between cyber and psychological operations experts is rare.[22]

Can these cyber operations be considered psychological operations? Cyber operations are essential instruments through which psychological effects can be generated.

The expertise of U.S. Army Cyber Command is on the information delivery side of psychological operations. U.S. Special Operations Command has developed extensive psychological and cultural knowledge on the information content side of psychological operations because of long experience in executing influence operations. Bringing together the respective expertise of each command should enhance the synergies possible between cyber-enabled psychological operations and offensive cyber operations. The competence required to conduct psychological operations goes beyond the skill set of cyber operators. The cyber commands are not particularly interested in acquiring such expertise.

The technical dimensions of combating adversarial influence operations are important. The expertise of cyber forces generally focuses on the information delivery side of cyber-enabled psychological operations. Contesting information warfare requires content. The issue of content, narrative themes etc., are the most critical part. The government has to take a whole of government approach to bring all of the relevant expertise from all parts of government and the nation to address the problem.

Considerable efforts are in progress on cyber security in the world. These activities and the funds that support them are centred around technical expertise in computer science, communications, mathematics, etc. Much less activity and funds are dedicated to understanding the science and practice of psychological operations. Practitioners of psychological operations have to know about social cognition and behavioural economics as the fundamental psychological science behind influence operations.

For defence against adversary psychological operations, the practitioners need critical thinking skills to resist propaganda. They need to learn techniques for inoculating against misinformation. For offensive operations against the Islamic State, persuasion techniques are required. Experts on marketing and advertising are a must to carry out these operations.

Countering Violent Extremism (CVE)

> "We typically design physical operations first, then craft supporting information operations to explain our actions. This is the reverse of al-Qaida's approach. For all our professionalism, compared to the enemy's, our public information is an afterthought. In military terms, for al-Qaida the 'main effort' is information; for us, information is a 'supporting effort'."
>
> —David Kilcullen, Countering the Terrorist Mentality, New Paradigms for 21st Century Conflict

ISIL's Online Output. It is interesting to look at ISIL's organisation for psychological operations.

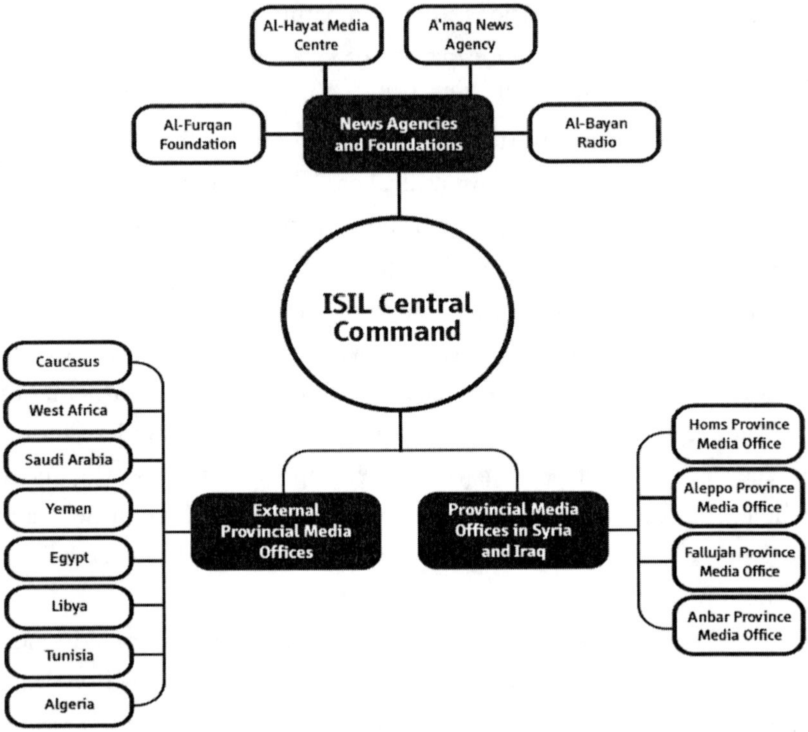

Organisation for Psychological Operations in U.S. Army

Psychological Operations Group.[23] The U.S. Army has the Psychological Operations Group (POG) for carrying out PsyOps. It is part of U.S. Army Special Operations Command (U.S.ASOC). The 4th POG(A) is divided into four regional PSYOP battalions, a tactical PSYOP battalion, a dissemination battalion and the Strategic Studies Detachment (SSD). The majority of PSYOP units are in the Reserve Component (RC). Two additional PSYOP groups, the 2nd and 7th Psychological Operations groups (POGs), provide tactical and dissemination battalions to support worldwide contingencies and exercises. The 2nd and 7th POGs are each comprised of three tactical PSYOP battalions and a dissemination battalion. The strategic studies detachment (SSD) of 4th Psychological

Operations Group (Airborne) augments this capability with civilian regional experts.

- The active Component PSYOP Group has approximately 1300 personnel with elements deployed globally. There are two Reserve Component PSYOP Groups with around 2600 Personnel with elements deployed in Iraq, Afghanistan and Balkans. In addition, they have one Special Operations Wing with six aircraft. It has the capability to broadcast deeply into denied areas rapidly.
- **Strategic Studies Detachment (SSD).** It has about 40 total analysts; most have PhDs. The majority are historians. There are some anthropologists, political scientists; all have extensive experience in the regions they cover.

The current challenge is to balance between operational support to analytic production.

Professional Skill Sets that have Direct Relevance to Psychological Operations

The skill sets needed to perform psychological operations are:

- Communications technologists provide insight toward methodologies that maximise the utility of existing communication modalities and identify emerging technical capabilities.
- Behavioural scientists and cultural anthropologists provide a deep understanding of human cultures, identities, attitudes and behaviours.
- Educators with knowledge of culturally relevant pedagogies offer valuable perspectives.
- Historians are versed in cultural perspectives and can act as interpreters of current and future events.
- Economists provide data models to understand and forecast financial events.
- Religious scholars and leaders offer insight into important dimensions of cultural life.

- Linguists and translators develop cultural sensitivities that are of great value in selecting keywords, messages, and communication formats that resonate with intended audiences.
- Political scientists provide insights into power and influence in modern societies.
- Librarians and researchers provide expert information access and data management skills and have a country and culture-specific knowledge, contacts, and capabilities.
- Corporate business managers and entrepreneurs have country and regional cultural experience and ongoing relationships with international audiences, government leaders, and non-governmental voluntary organisations.
- Marketing managers of products and services are accustomed to leading the complex and interdisciplinary management process associated with building and maintaining brand equity.
- Market researchers who advise global brand management teams have developed a wide range of measurement techniques to research and monitor international consumer interests, attitudes and preferences.
- Advertising copywriters, art directors and media planners have proven abilities to transform copy and media strategies into compelling messages, events and programs and identify media vehicles that attract target audiences.
- Producers and directors of films, television programming, radio, video games and advertising commercials are expert in crafting compelling and persuasive storylines and images.
- Artists, authors and musicians live lives of demonstrated creativity that transcends national boundaries and their personal stories and bodies of work offer windows into the host population.
- Retired government officials can provide historical perspective as well as program continuity.[24]

Ethnography. For doing psychological operations, professional ethnographers are needed. A typical ethnographer does the following:

- Learns the local language.
- Works to build rapport with key members of the local community and gains "entry" into that community.
- Spends multiple hours per day for months or even years observing how people go about their everyday business and recording these observations.
- Transcribes and codes these observations into field journals to be used as primary source materials.
- Analyses this data to assess patterns of behaviour.
- Conducts formal and informal interviews with key informants, focus groups or target populations to cross-reference different interpretations and learn the underlying meaning.

These practices enable the ethnographer to develop an understanding of underlying meanings, shared world view and ultimately a tacit understanding of "what makes that group of people tick.[25]"

Public Diplomacy

The concept of "public diplomacy" was coined in the United States in the 1960s. In 2016, the U.S. government made a concentrated effort to adjust its resources to counter the growing threat of disinformation. Initially, the response was uncoordinated, with many actors responding independently based on their policy focus. With the creation of the Global Engagement Center (GEC), a coordinated effort to counter disinformation effects started taking shape.[26]

Public Diplomacy is defined as: The efforts by a country's government to communicate and interact openly and directly with foreign audiences, including academics, NGOs, business, institutions and even the general public, to deepen mutual understanding and promote/protect its national interests.

The aim of a country's Public Diplomacy activities is to:

- Influence how foreign citizens perceive that country, correcting misperceptions about its policies and values, battling stereotypes etc.
- Promote general mutual understanding of people.
- Impact official relations with the foreign government in a way that serves the country's national interests.

Initially, in the U.S. the initiative for psychological opearations or strategic communications was with DoD for the simple reason of availability of funds. Department of State could not garner adequate finances. That has changed now. In February 2018, the Department of State announced that it had reached an agreement with the Department of Defense (DoD) to transfer a maximum of $40 million to the GEC to fund "counter propaganda and disinformation from foreign nations." In FY 2018, GEC's Countering State-sponsored Disinformation (CSD) funding totalled $41.1 million, meaning that 49 per cent of its CSD operations were dependent on DoD, but they were wholly GEC-led and added a significant new element to the Department of State programming mix.[27]

Strategic communication

White House 2010 National Framework for Strategic Communication defined strategic communication as:

"Strategic communication(s) refers to (a) the synchronization of words and deeds and how they will be perceived by selected audiences, as well as (b) programs and activities deliberately aimed at communicating and engaging with intended audiences, including those implemented by public affairs, public diplomacy, and information operations professionals".

Strategic communications refers to

- The synchronisation of words and deeds and how they will be perceived by selected audiences.

Programs and activities deliberately aimed at communicating and engaging with intended audiences, including those implemented by public affairs, public diplomacy and information operations professionals.[28]

Strategic Communication Relationships

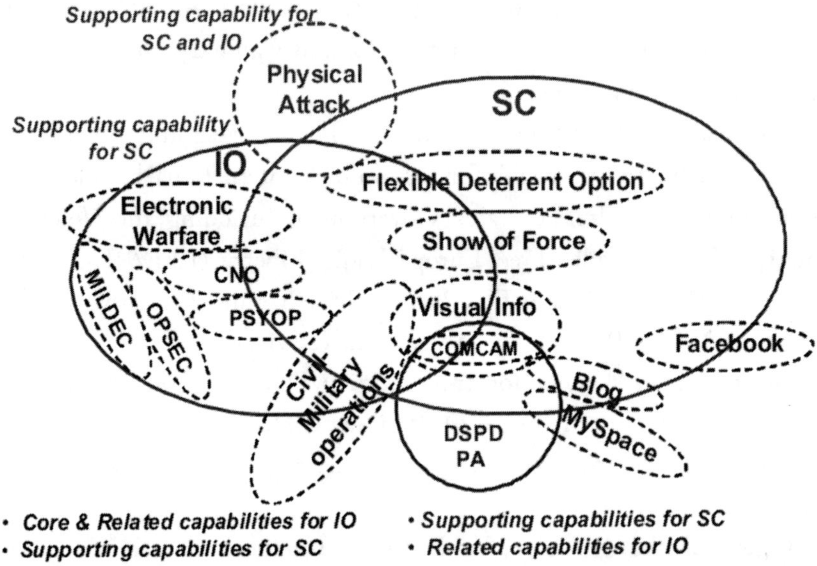

Source: Lysychkina, Iryna. (2017). 'The Image of Security Sector Agencies as a Strategic Communication Tool.' *Connections: The Quarterly Journal.* 16. 5-22. 10.11610/Connections.16.3.01.

Relationship between Strategic Communication (SC), Information Operation (IO), Public Diplomacy (PD) and Public Affairs (PA)

Roles and Responsibilities, U.S. Example

The Department of State carries out Public Diplomacy as an essential part of foreign policy.

The Department of State distinguishes between Public Affairs, which includes outreach to domestic publics, and Public Diplomacy (PD) which seeks to promote the national interest through understandingly engaging, informingly and influencing foreign publics/and by promoting mutual understanding between the people of the United States and people from other nations around the world.

The Department of Defense (DOD) is a crucial contributor to communication and engagement efforts. The critical elements of DOD involved include, but are not limited to information operations (IO), defence support to public diplomacy (DSPD), public affairs (PA) and civil affairs (CA), all working together to accomplish military objectives that support national objectives.

Broadcasting Board of Governors. The Broadcasting Board of Governors (BBG) is responsible for non-military, international broadcasting sponsored by the United States Government, including the Voice of America (VOA). Radio Free Europe/Radio Liberty (RFE/RL), Radio Free Asia (RFA), Radio and TV Marti, and the Middle East Broadcasting Networks (MBN)-Radio Sawa and Alhurra Television.

United States Agency for International Development. The United States Agency for International Development (USAID) works to inform recipients and partners of U.S. humanitarian and development aid initiatives.

Office of the Director for National Intelligence (ODNI). It is responsible for coordinating the efforts of intelligence agencies to conduct research and analysis on foreign public opinion, communication modes and mechanisms and violent extremist communication.

National Counterterrorism Centre. It coordinates, integrates, and synchronises United States Government efforts to counter violent extremism and deny terrorists the next generation of recruits.

Other departments and agencies with specific subject matter expertise and related communication and engagement capabilities may be asked to participate in communication and engagement strategy development and implementation as needed.[29]

Since there were lot of overlapping responsibilities and additional layers were being formed the U.S. DoD decided not to use the term Strategic Communication.

OFFICE OF THE ASSISTANT SECRETARY OF DEFENSE
1400 DEFENSE PENTAGON
WASHINGTON, DC 20301-1400

PUBLIC AFFAIRS

November 28, 2012

MEMORANDUM FOR COMMANDERS OF THE COMBATANT COMMANDS

SUBJECT: Communications Synchronization – A Local Coordination Process

This memorandum is in response to questions from the field about the status of Public Affairs and Strategic Communication (SC) in Office of the Secretary of Defense (OSD). The responsibility for SC in OSD was shared by the Office of the Assistant Secretary of Defense for Public Affairs (OASD-PA) (Communications Planning and Integration) and USD(P) (Global Engagement). COCOMs typically sent SC plans to these organizations for coordination and approval. SC was viewed as a means to synchronize communication efforts across the department, however, over the last six years we learned that it actually added a layer of staffing and planning that blurred the roles and functions of traditional staff elements and resulted in confusion and inefficiencies. As a result, this year we stood down these staff elements. We also realized that these SC plans mostly contained public affairs planning that we once again expect to come through public affairs channels.

We avoid using the term SC to avoid causing confusion. The more accurate terminology, which will be used in future Joint Publications, is communication synchronization. We are continuing our leadership role in communication and reminding those in the communication business that most things previously termed "SC" are in fact Public Affairs responsibilities.

IO During Military Operations

As explained earlier, Information Operations (IO) is "the integrated employment, during military operations, of information-related capabilities in concert with other lines of operation to influence, disrupt, corrupt, or usurp the decision-making of adversaries and potential adversaries while protecting our own" (JP 3-13). Army conducts operations across the conflict continuum and range of military operations. IO is essential during all phases of a military operation.

Employment of Information-Related Capabilities (IRC). Generally, the term IRC refers to those tools, techniques or activities that are inherently information-based. These include:[30]

- Military deception.
- Military information support operations (MISO).
- Soldier and leader engagement (SLE), to include police engagement.

- Civil affairs operations.
- Combat camera.
- Operations security (OPSEC).
- Public affairs.
- Cyberspace electromagnetic activities.
- Electronic warfare.
- Cyberspace operations.
- Space operations.
- Special technical operations.

A wide variety of unit functions and activities can be adapted for the purposes of conducting information operations or serve as enablers to its planning, execution and assessment. Some of these include, but are not limited to:

- Commander's communications strategy.
- Presence, profile and posture.
- Physical security.
- Foreign disclosure.
- Physical manoeuvre.
- Civil-military operations.
- Special access programs.
- Intelligence.
- Destruction and lethal actions.

Purpose of Information Operations. The purpose of IO is to create effects that provide commanders decisive advantage over adversaries. IO employs and synchronises Information Related Capabilities (IRCs) to affect the will, awareness, understanding and capability of these audiences while protecting their own. Commanders achieve an advantage when they preserve their freedom of action in the information environment while degrading enemy or adversary freedom of action.

Information Operations and Decisive Action

Defend. In defensive IO, it seeks to create effects in the information environment that accomplish any one or combination of the following (not all-inclusive):

Physical Dimension

- Locking or otherwise physically securing documents, equipment and infrastructure that facilitate decision making.
- Protecting documents, equipment and structures from destruction or degradation.

Using Obscurants to Mask Movements. Protecting key personnel from attack or exploitation.

Informational Dimension

- Preserving the free-flow of information and access to data and information sources.
- Encrypting communications.
- Using forensics to determine sources of attack.
- Employing knowledge management principles.
- Proactively identifying instances of social engineering or malware and keeping virus and other protections current.
- For countering adversary information efforts.

Cognitive Dimension

- Making decentralised decisions.
- Using precedents or best practices.
- Checking facts and assumptions.
- Using red teaming.

IRCs that are synchronised to attain defence orientation include, but are not limited to:

- Cyberspace operations.

- Electronic warfare.
- Operations security (OPSEC).
- Military deception.
- MISO.
- Physical security.
- Destruction and lethal actions.
- Special technical operations.

Attack

When the IO effort necessitates an attack orientation, it seeks to create effects in the information environment that accomplish any one or combination of the following (not all inclusive):

Physical Dimension

- Destroying or degrading threat command and control (C2) systems.
- Destroying or impairing threat networks and critical nodes (human or infrastructure).
- Degrading or destroying threat leadership.
- Using feints, ruses, demonstrations and displays.
- Corrupting data and information.

Informational Dimension

- Jamming communication and signals.
- Employing denial of service attacks.
- Attacking the enemy's or adversary's narrative(s).
- Intercepting or misdirecting data or content.
- Manipulating information provided to adversary leaders.
- Using social engineering or spoofing.

Cognitive Dimension

- Creating ambiguity or confusion.
- Creating hesitancy or procrastination.
- Causing an incorrect understanding of friendly intent.

- Enabling overconfidence in false signals and signs; under confidence or uncertainty in the true ones.
- Degrading legitimacy of threat narrative(s).
- Degrading support for the threat.

IRCs that are synchronised to achieve an attack orientation in the information environment include, but are not limited to:

- Cyberspace operations.
- Electronic warfare.
- Military deception.
- MISO.
- Destruction and lethal actions.
- Special technical operations.
- Space operations.
- Soldier and leader engagement (SLE).

The Commander

Commanders, at all levels, are responsible for knowing what threats their units face and how to exploit or defeat them. To affect the information environment to their advantage, commanders should be aware of the following[31]:

- Every operation has, to some degree, an effect on the information environment.
- IO planning is integral to operations from the start.
- Effects in and through the information environment, if essential to success, are part of the commander's intent.
- Combat power cannot be optimised without IO.
- The warfighting functions (particularly movement and manoeuvre and fires) produce effects in the information environment, whether intentional or not.
- IO is essential to operational success at all levels.
- All communication can quickly become global and have strategic consequences.

- IRCs can have long lead times to coordinate and employ and lengthy lag times before their effects are realised.
- The alignment of words, deeds, and images is essential to building trust and confidence with relevant audiences in operations.
- IO requires prioritised intelligence support.
- Effects in the information environment are not always caused as expected; assessment is difficult and benefits from commanders' interest, prioritisation and support.
- IO can be constrained by policy and law, while the threat is often unconstrained in its use of information.

Three obstacles prevent achievement of the desired IW state:

- Communication gap exists between information warfare subject matter experts and the formation commanders.
- IW capabilities are mostly highly classified. This makes planning difficult as decision-makers across domains involved in the planning process may not be aware of a particular program or capacity.
- More must be done to allow lower-level decision-makers to take the initiative.

Public Affairs

As per JP 3-61, Public Affairs (PA) provides information to domestic and international audiences and contributes to global influence and deterrence of attacks. This guidance does not differentiate between adversaries and own audiences. It includes both. The target audiences may differ, but the consistency of messages is essential to credibility. PA focuses on truth and credibility and must be fact-based.[32]

To successfully tell the Army's story, a range of digital communication tools are used to tell the Army's story instantaneously. Some of the tools required for the current and emerging demands of the communication environment are:

- Digital Media Management and Media Relations sections.
- Conduct Assessments and Counter Misinformation/ Disinformation core tasks.

- Public Affairs Code of Ethics and Commander's Communication Synchronisation concepts.
- Clear guidance on crucial responsibilities:
  - o Crisis Communication.
  - o Community Engagements.
  - o Drone Usage.
  - o Social Media Management.

The following efforts focuses on the future directionality of timely and accurate information release on most platforms:

- **Dissemination.** Impartial and objective dissemination of information about own action.
- **Social media.** Army social media platforms are official representations of the Army. Social media managers on official Army social media accounts must be granted release authority by the commanding officer. Getting ratified by higher headquarters means loss of precious time.
- **Countering misinformation/disinformation.** A commander cannot counter false information without being credible. PA can mitigate and counter adversary disinformation and misinformation with accurate and timely public information and imagery.

Use of low-cost, daily use equipment for deception. Recently mobiles have been used for effective military deception operations. Device exploitation, excessive sharing of sensitive data and the challenge in determining information credibility will increase as connected devices continue to proliferate. Examples are:

- A smartwatch or cell phone with a fitness tracking app used by troops can give away their location and activities. Adversaries have already employed tactics to exploit vulnerabilities arising from Soldier cellphone use.
- In Ukraine during 2014/15, a Russian tactic was to send spoofed text messages to Ukrainian soldiers telling them that their support unit has retreated, their bank account has been exhausted and they

are surrounded and abandoned. They have sent false messages to the families of soldiers, informing them that their loved one was killed in action. This sets off a chain reaction where the family member will call or text the soldier immediately, followed by another spoofed message to the original phone. With many messages to enough targets, an artillery strike is ordered on the area where an excess of cellphone usage has been detected. Hacking of apps used by artillery units in Ukraine causing the decimation of their artillery guns also have been reported.[33]

- A NATO red team was able to infiltrate their own forces easily through information gathered on social media sites by collecting locations, dates and other data to influence their Soldiers' behaviour. Facebook and Instagram permitted them to track Soldiers, determine exact locations of exercises and identify all members of a particular unit.
- Hamas employed a similar tactic against soldiers of Israeli Defense Forces, using fake accounts to pose as attractive women in honey trap operations to access sensitive operational information.

Intelligence

Defence intelligence organisations provide detailed enemy orders of battle and other related and valuable products. Information warfare professionals also gather such intelligence, which sometimes is overlapping. There is a general lack of coordination and understanding between the information operations (IO) and intelligence communities, which adversely affect operational planning.

From the very beginning, intelligence organisations are there for every level of organisation in the armed forces. Over such long periods, they have fine-tuned their organisation, doctrine, leadership, methods of gathering intelligence and analysis capabilities, human resource policies, etc. What distinguishes them from practitioners of information warfare is how each community compiles, sorts, analyses and uses information. A clear understanding of the information environment is the responsibility of intelligence practitioners. The ability to conduct operations in and through the IE is the responsibility of IO practitioners.

There is friction between the intelligence and IO communities about collecting the information and conducting the analyses necessary to support operation in the information environment (OIE). Generally, there is a lack of understanding, shared processes and a shared lexicon about what the other community does. Gaps in knowledge hinder close coordination between the two communities and lead to reduced operational effectiveness.

Both intelligence and IO professionals need training to support and conduct OIE effectively. Training and education must grow as needs change.[34]

Command and Control

Information warfare has two aspects: the psychological and the technical. The information content is vital for the psychological part. The means to deliver content or counter its delivery are crucial to the technical function. There is a logic for most of what falls into the psychological realm to be redefined as IO. Most of what falls into the technical realm should be considered cyber electronic. The exception must be for operating and maintaining the networks, which itself is a vital and mammoth task.

Virtually all core, supporting and related capabilities of IO tend to operate inside their own stovepipes. On the technical side, cyber operations, EW, EMSO, and so on are all separate organisations. Correspondingly, PA and MISO have many overlapping objectives, capabilities, and processes on the content side but are separate and sometimes competing organisations. Suppose the vision of IO includes certain capabilities working together in seamless harmony. In that case, those capabilities need to be combined or placed under the tight control of a single integrating authority.

Currently, authorities for Cyber and EW are not the same. The use of EW capabilities at all echelons has well-established tactics and procedures. Many policy changes are needed for cyber to enjoy the same level of permission, understanding and use. Training will have to be commensurate.

Use of Social Media

In a remarkable book on social media, P. W. Singer and Emerson T. Brooking brought out the essence of weaponisation of social media.[35] The following quotes from the book will be apt.

"Social media had changed not just the message, but the dynamics of conflict. How information was being accessed, manipulated, and spread had taken on new power. Who was involved in the fight, where they were located, and even how they achieved victory had been twisted and transformed. Indeed, if what was online could swing the course of a battle—or eliminate the need for battle entirely—what, exactly, could be considered 'war' at all?"

"The modern internet is not just a network, but an ecosystem of 4 billion souls.... Those who can manipulate this swirling tide, steer its direction and flow, can ... accomplish astonishing evil. They can foment violence, stoke hate, sow falsehoods, incite wars, and even erode the pillars of democracy itself."

"Attacking an adversary's most important center of gravity—the spirit of its people—no longer requires massive bombing runs or reams of propaganda. All it takes is a smartphone and a few idle seconds. And anyone can do it."

"Whether the cause is dangerous (support for a terrorist group), mundane (support for a political party), or inane (belief that the earth is flat), social media guarantees that you can find others who share your views and even be steered to them by the platforms' own algorithms.... As groups of like-minded people clump together, they grow to resemble fanatical tribes, trapped in echo chambers of their own design."

Social Media Platforms (SMPs) are websites, tools, applications and gizmos that provide social media services. Any social media service like Facebook, Twitter, YouTube, Instagram is a social media platform. SMP industry connected the world to push information to millions with a single click. It has created an addiction. At the same time, it has had a damaging side-effect on democracy. Critical thinking has taken a back seat. The average human attention fell to eight seconds, hurting critical thinking skills. As mobile device and SMP use increases, users' attentions span and critical thinking decrease. This cognitive environment is ripe for social manipulation and gave birth to 21st century IW.

Social media is not just a communication space but a new kind of battlespace. The boundaries between foreign and domestic sources of information chaos and dysfunction are blurring. Nation-states and non-state actors alike are leveraging social media to manipulate like-minded populations' cognitive biases to influence conflict dynamics.

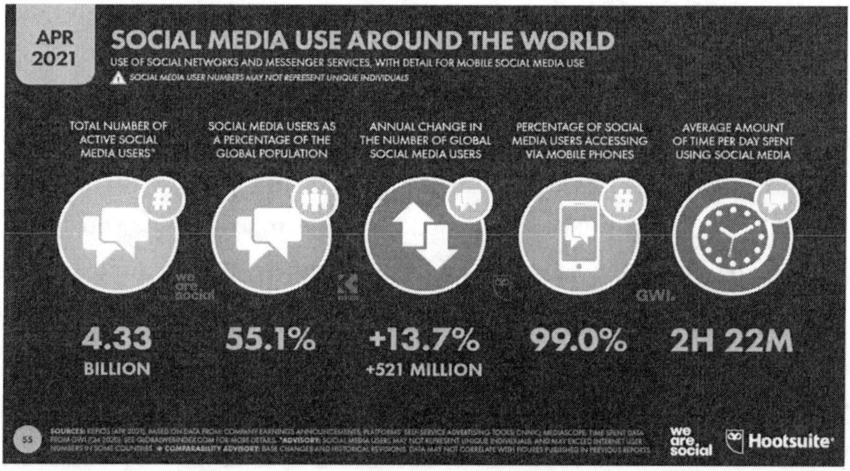

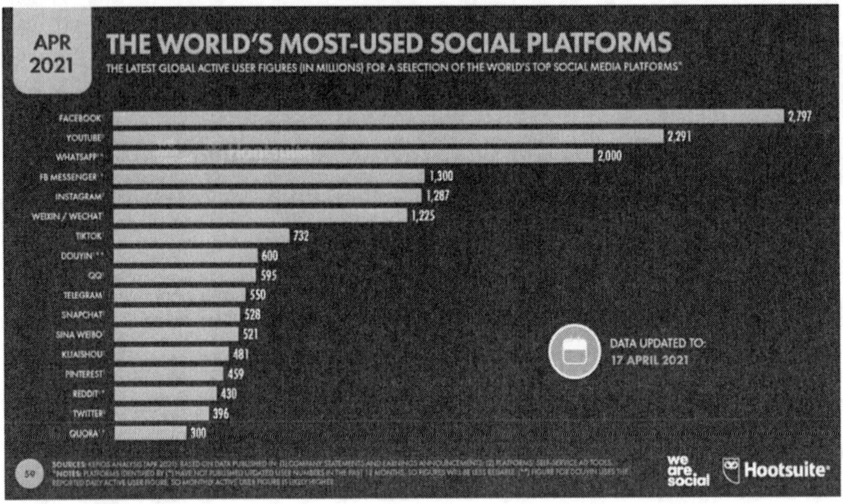

The use of propaganda, disinformation, deception and information warfare is not new. What is new is the ease, efficiency, low cost of such efforts, global reach, propagation speed, and our political sensitivity to national and international opinion. It is driven by commercial, societal and geopolitical forces determining how the technology unfolds and is used. We cannot control who accesses this capability. The agile player who can shape perceptions will more likely achieve their objectives.

A study in Science examining the spread of information on Twitter found that false information framed as news spread more widely and rapidly than actual information. The motivation of companies for providing such content is profit-driven. Private sector, now owns Facebook, Twitter, YouTube, Instagram and the other popular platforms. They shape and influence what we think.

A recent Gallup poll revealed that, due to erroneous fears spread on social media about the safety of COVID vaccines, about a third of the U.S. nationals had doubts about getting the vaccination. As a result, many refused to follow the advice of doctors and scientists and wear face masks. Instead, they chose to believe false online claims that masks are useless. Thus, even a public health issue can be politicised and damaged by cyber-disinformation.

Responding to these challenges will not be easy. It will involve making complex and controversial decisions about the private sector's responsibility, restrictions on speech and national security issues.

Weaponisation of Information

The advent of Social Media about 20 years ago has changed how we wage war. Both Nation states and non-state actors are leveraging social media to manipulate like-minded populations' cognitive biases to influence conflict dynamics. The social media battlefield has developed into an inevitable appendage to every international conflict. The Azerbaijan-Armenia conflict was a prime example late last year, with unverified or outdated videos spreading rapidly online.[36]

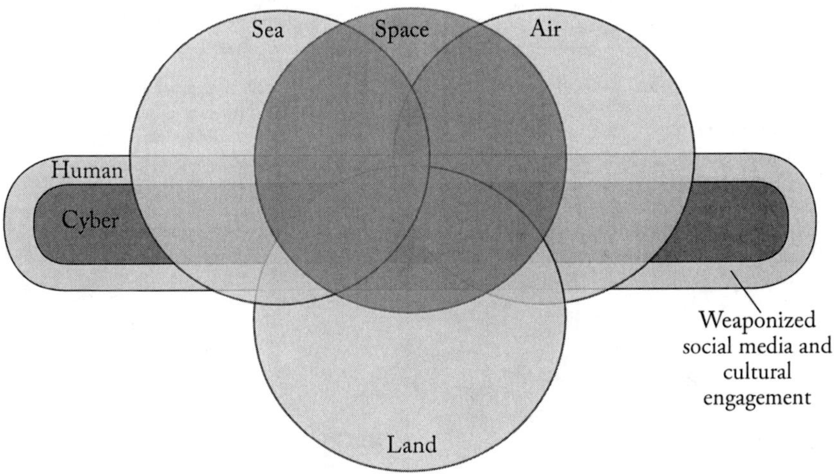

Source: The Information Environment Competition and Conflict, A Mad Scientist Laboratory Anthology, available at: https://community.apan.org/wg/tradoc-g2/ mad-scientist/m/articles-of-interest

Earlier awkward efforts to photo-shop images and fabricate grainy videos and poorly executed computer-generated imagery (CGI) have given way to refined Deepfakes, using AI algorithms to create nearly undetectable fake photos, videos and audio tracks. These quickly go viral online to dupe, deceive and manipulate. Now FakeApp has been launched as free software. It enables anyone with an artificial neural network and a graphics processor to create and share bogus videos via Social Media. The introduction of the internet brought with it the global spread of numerous hoaxes, urban myths and the fake news.[37]

The SMP's efforts to make the world open and connected are enormously successful financially. They also present an opportunity to manipulate national instruments of power. The problem is becoming more complex as SMP use around the world becomes omnipresent.

The Boundaries of Social Manipulation

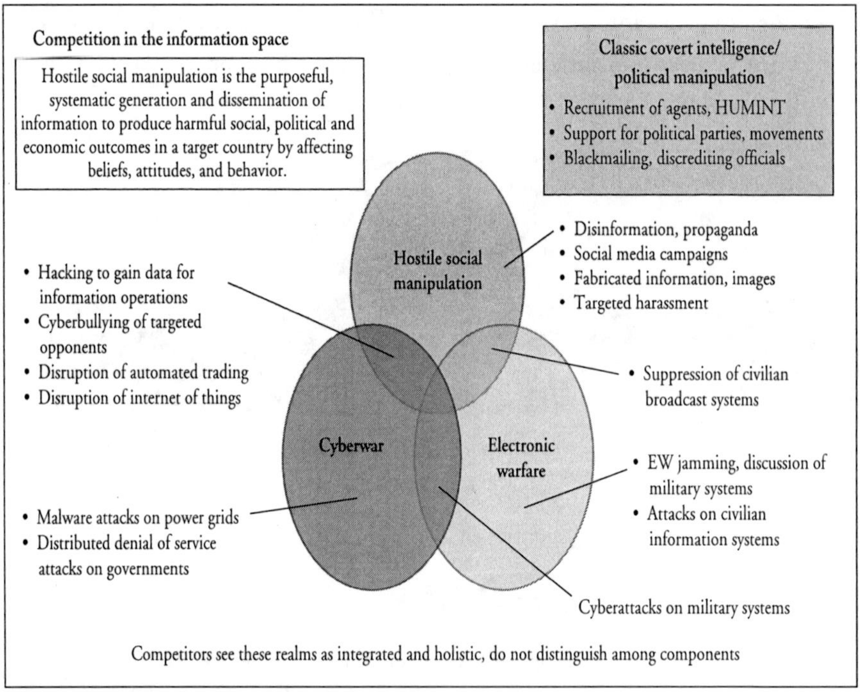

Note: HUMINT - human intelligence
Source: Michael J. Mazarr et al., 'Hostile Social Manipulation Present Realities and Emerging Trends', RAND Corporation, 2019, at https://www.rand.org/content/dam/rand/pubs/research_reports/RR2700/RR2713/RAND_RR2713.pdf

Post-2000, the rise of SMPs amplified cognitive bias, drastically reshaped the information consumption of the people. As a result, there is Truth Decay because of blurred lines and enlarged volume of opinions over fact, disagreement over those and interpretation and declining trust in traditional media.[38]

How social media is being manipulated today is explained in the following diagram.

Overview of Hostile Social Manipulation

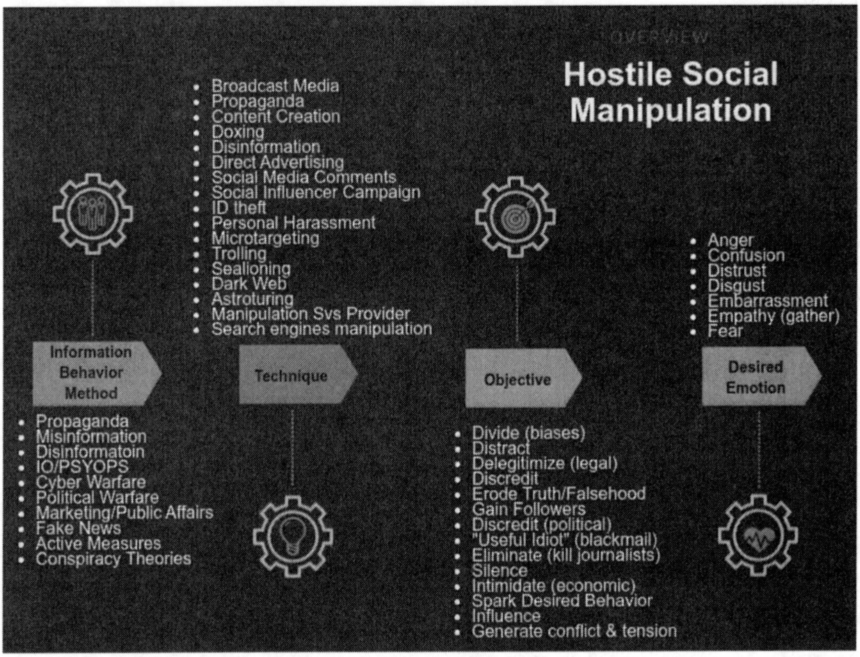

Source: RAND Corporation.

Recent Examples

ISIS in Iraq. Abu Musab al-Zarqawi became the "Bin Laden of the Internet". It is an example of the weaponisation of social media by non-state actors. Zarqawi's jihadist network, al Qaeda in Iraq (AQI), weaponised YouTube by creating content depicting their successes in killing U.S. soldiers and civilians to a musical soundtrack. By 2006, AQI named itself as the Islamic State of Iraq with its own IW/media arm tasked with professionalising the development of the content with a message of fear, action and blood to recruit and shape public opinion.

ISIS used the internet successfully to convince numerically superior Iraqi forces to abandon posts and weapons out of fear. This resulted in the rapid conquer of Mosul and large swaths of territory in Iraq and Syria. In addition, ISIS carried out its military offensive like a virtual marketing tour that recruited over 30,000 people from nearly a hundred countries to join its cause.

A column of approximately 1,500 ISIS fighters rolled into northern Iraq. They were equipped with dirty pickup trucks and second-hand AK-47s. They also broadcast their offensive. If you're launching an invasion in conventional military operations, you don't want the enemy to know about it. They wanted everyone to know about it. So they had countless fans and botnets on Twitter that conjoined around a hashtag, #AllEyesOnISIS.

The effect on Iraqi soldiers was devastating. The Iraqi army was much larger, far better equipped with tanks and helicopters, was better trained, backed by the U.S., most powerful military in the world. They were looking down at their smartphones and see what seemed like an ISIS victory playing out. It made 30,000 defenders run away, leaving much of their equipment for ISIS to claim and later broadcast using all the American equipment. What was playing out on social media changed the dynamics of the battlefield.

Things were reversed. By 2016, Iraqi forces understood the weaponisation of SMPs. They used ISIS Tactics, Techniques, Procedures (TTPs) against them in its SMP-enabled IW efforts using portable cellphone towers and its own #FreeMosul tag. The U.S. State and Defence Departments joined Iraqi forces in the offensive in cyber and social media. The result was there for all to see.

Syria. In 2015, after Iranian-backed offensive by the beleaguered Syrian regime failed to regain control of the city of Aleppo, members of Islamic Revolutionary Guard Corps-trained brigades started posting photos of the experience on Facebook, Twitter and Instagram. These photos divulged the aircrafts they boarded, the geolocation of fighters, the identity of their comrades and commanders, the weapons they carried and the airports the Iranian regime used for its logistical efforts.

When fighters died, militias took to social media to create remembrance pages and posted photos of funerals and martyrdom videos. Their friends responded with likes and comments, in the process revealing their identities. This wealth of open-source information helped real-time intelligence gathering. For example, selfies taken onboard Iran Air aircraft proved that the Iranian commercial carrier was being employed to support the fighting. As a result, it helped the U.S. to sanction Iran Air.[39]

Israel Strikes in Gaza in 2011. A significant online viral campaign complemented eight days of Israeli airstrikes in Op Pillar of Defense operation. The campaign in 2012 started with the assassination of a high-level Hamas militant. That was not unusual. What was remarkable is that the drone strike video was up within a few hours. The official Twitter account of the Israeli Defense Forces was announcing it out time and again. Immediately Hamas Twitter proxies responded, threatening war.

It was not the social media operatives of these two sides only, but millions and millions of Twitter messages also exchanged back and forth by the proxies of one side or another. There were 10 million of them, 90 per cent of which were outside the region. This was a representation of a limited military campaign that became a global war for public opinion.

Significantly, it was not just winning out online, but it was also affecting the battlefield decisions. The generals and politicians were making battlefield decisions while watching what was playing out on their smart phones.

Initially, the Israeli military was caught napping. They were losing this battle of narrative. Like a professional military, they reorganised and learnt. They created organisations within Israeli universities where Israeli students and students from around the world can participate in this battle of narrative.

Hamas Israel Conflict in Gaza, May 2021. The recent conflict in Gaza has revealed some fascinating aspects of the use of social media in a conflict scenario and maybe harbinger to future warfare. In the 11 days of conflict in May, when Hamas launched rockets at Israel and Israel replied by bombing targets in the Gaza Strip, social media turned into a battlefield. Moreover, it showed that social media has come to play an increasingly significant role in any conflict today.

This was a military conflict and psychological warfare was conducted in the media and on social networks. It aimed at influencing public opinion both domestically and internationally. Throughout the conflict, a storm of misinformation on social media was observed. Misinformation has flourished on Facebook, Twitter, TikTok and other social media about the violence between Israelis and Palestinians. False claims have been widely shared worldwide, at times with misidentified or mischaracterised photos and videos or fake rumours about Israeli troop movements or Palestinian threats. As per the analysis by *The New York Times*, the lies were amplified as they have been shared many times on Facebook and Twitter, spreading to WhatsApp and Telegram groups that have thousands of members. The effect of the misinformation is potentially deadly when suspicions and distrust have already run high.[40] Both sides are likely to continue trying to use the internet to marshal global opinion in their favour.

The Israeli Defense Forces (IDF) has a strong presence online. It has 1.3 million followers on Twitter and more than 70,000 on TikTok, where it has been posting videos of its forces in action and scenes from inside Israel. The Israeli government used its Twitter accounts to counter Hamas propaganda and defend its military campaign. For example, the IDF Twitter account provided regular operational updates and broadcast video of the Iron Dome antimissile system intercepting rockets from Gaza. The Chinese-owned site TikTok has a vast, mostly younger audience, with an estimated 700 million active monthly users worldwide. An Israeli analyst told the BBC, "Maybe because nobody thought that TikTok would be a powerful or important platform in Israel.[41]"

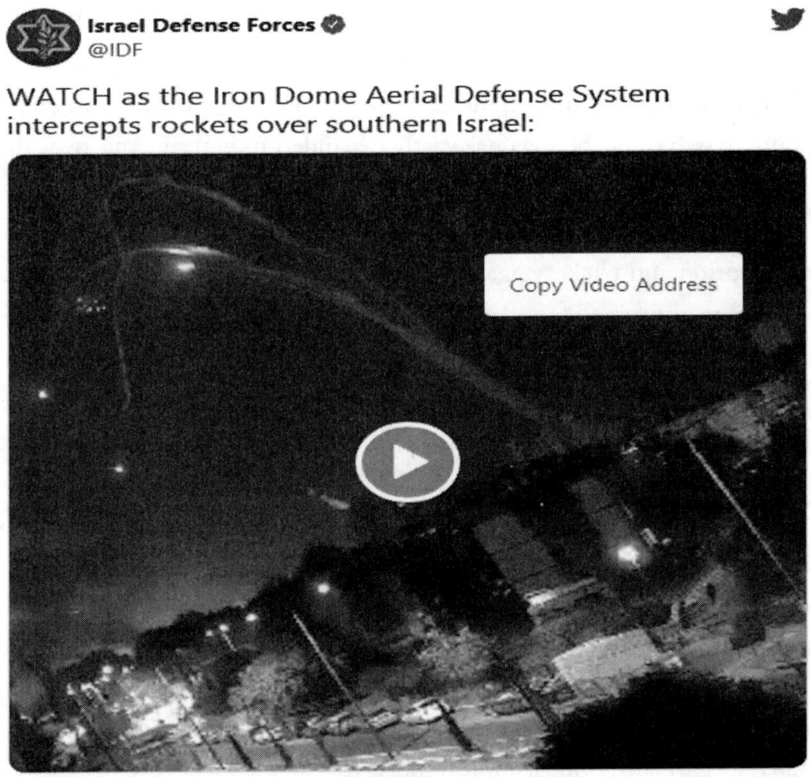

Both sides committed mistakes while trying to put up videos due to extreme time pressure. A 28-second video posted on Twitter by Ofir Gendelman, a spokesman for Prime Minister Benjamin Netanyahu of Israel, showed Palestinian militants in the Gaza Strip launching rocket attacks at Israelis from densely populated civilian areas. It was shared hundreds of times as the conflict between Palestinians and Israelis escalated. However, this was not from Gaza. This particular video could be found on many YouTube channels and other video-hosting sites from 2018. And according to captions on older versions of the video, it showed militants firing rockets not from Gaza but from Syria or Libya.

Arabic and Israeli news outlets shared many misleading or blatantly deceptive videos spread on YouTube and Facebook. For example, TikTok users boosted false claims that Israeli forces had set the Al-Aqsa Mosque on fire.

In the use of social media, the IDF has been highly proficient at doing it for many years. But Hamas has vastly expanded its skills at this over the past decade.

Use of Media for Military Deception. Militaries around the world have used deception and trickery against their enemies since long. For example, two years ago, the Israeli army reportedly faked soldiers' injuries at the scene of a Hezbollah missile strike, evacuated them in bandages to a hospital in a helicopter. It was reported then that the army orchestrated the injuries to trick Hezbollah into thinking that it had inflicted casualties and so agree to a cease-fire.

After days of airstrikes, late on May 13, 2021, Israel announced it was calling up its reservists and concentrating troops along the border before a possible ground invasion. Israel began firing artillery shells across the border at targets inside Gaza. Finally, Israel started to scramble forces along the border in what looked to be final preparations for an invasion. Then came the statement to the media, issued simultaneously in Hebrew and Arabic on Twitter, that invasion is underway.

Just after midnight, the Israeli military sent out a warning statement to the media: "IDF air and ground troops are currently attacking in the Gaza Strip." The vaguely worded statement set off frantic speculation that Israel had launched a ground invasion of Gaza. This would cause a bloody escalation of the operation against Hamas militants.

Military officials assured most Israeli journalists that no ground invasion had been put in motion. However, several reporters from foreign news outlets, were told categorically that IDF troops had entered the Palestinian territory. They reported that information accordingly, leading several leading media houses around the world, including Washington Post, The New York Times and AFP to publish articles stating that an Israeli ground assault on Gaza had begun. They cited the IDF's English-language spokesperson Jonathan Conricus.

Hours later, the IDF issued a "clarification." There were no troops inside Gaza. By then, several major news outlets had reported the ground offensive was underway. NBC News did not report that a ground invasion had taken place.

This led to broad speculation that this false report was made to convince Hamas that an Israeli ground invasion was occurring in northern Gaza. This prompted the terror group to send out some of its reconnaissance troops and anti-tank guided missile teams to confront the Israeli troops, where they were struck by the infantrymen, tanks and artillery cannons that were positioned inside Israel. The Israeli actions sent Hamas fighters rushing into defensive positions in an underground network of tunnels known as "the Metro". Israel sent in 160 warplanes and bombarded the tunnels for 40 minutes. It was reported that scores of militants had been killed, though it was impossible to say the exact numbers. Hamas did not comment on the incident.

The IDF officially denied that it had misled the foreign press intentionally about the non-existent ground invasion. It said that the incident was the result of an internal miscommunication. However, Conricus told reporters he took "personal responsibility" for the incorrect information.

The IDF did not explain the extended amount of time between it becoming aware of the significant error and officials issuing a correction. Ground invasions of Gaza are extremely rare, and such a major step would not be taken at the drop of a hat. While the IDF attempted to play down the incident as a misunderstanding, Israeli military commentators stated that the media had been used as part of an elaborate ploy to lure Hamas militants into a trap that may have killed dozens of fighters. Or Heller, a veteran military correspondent on Israel's Channel 13 TV said, "What we saw tonight was a very sophisticated operation that had a media aspect to it. They didn't lie. It was a manipulation. It was smart and it was successful." Heller said veteran Israeli correspondents knew that there was no chance of Israel sending troops across enemy lines at this stage. Military correspondents even gave statements on Twitter, assuring the public that there was no ground operation.

This incident caused a furor in western media. Based on its analysis of the army's statement and on the ground reporting in Gaza the Associated Press concluded that there was no ground incursion. it did not report there was one. However, others said the military had misled them or even lied when asked to clarify the initial statement and its ambiguous use of the word "in". It was felt that the foreign media had been turned into an accessory of sorts.

Daniel Estrin, NPR's correspondent in Jerusalem, said, "If they used us, it's unacceptable. And if not, then what's the story and why is the Israeli media widely reporting that we were duped?"

Felicia Schwartz, a correspondent for The Wall Street Journal, said she alerted news of a ground offensive after receiving explicit confirmation from Lt. Col. Jonathan Conricus, a military spokesman. In a statement posted on Twitter, she said Conricus "told me directly, `There are ground troops in Gaza.' That was the basis for a first story saying so. He retracted that statement two hours later and I changed the story to reflect that, and that is noted in the text and will be corrected."

Speaking to reporters on May14, 2021, Lt Col Conricus blamed an "internal miscommunication." He said, "These things can sometimes happen in the midst of a complex operation with many moving parts and with an unclear picture of what was happening. As soon as I understood that I had the wrong information, I updated the relevant people with a clarification. Yes. As it's written in the statement: Indeed, ground forces are attacking in Gaza. That is that they are in the Strip." On the same day, IDF spokesperson Hidai Zilberman told Israeli military correspondents explicitly that no soldiers, tanks or cannons entered Gaza during the assault but had instead been positioned within Israeli territory on berms located along the border.[42]

The misleading statement of May 14, 2021 further strained a rocky relationship between the IDF and the foreign media. A former military spokesman to the foreign media, Peter Lerner, said that the Israeli public, in general, has long felt the international media focus too heavily on the Palestinian side of the story while minimising Israeli concerns and suffering. The army is similarly inclined. Lerner said he felt it was unlikely the military intentionally lied, but the damage was done regardless. He added, "Your currency is credibility. I think this is a crisis of that credibility in the way it's being portrayed."[43]

The possibility that the military had used the international media for deception purposes in Gaza generated sharp questions for Colonel Conricus in a conference call. The representatives of The Wall Street Journal, The Times, The Washington Post, National Public Radio and Agence France-Presse, all of which had reported a ground invasion, peppered Colonel Conricus with questions about whether they had been turned into accessories to the military, why it had taken hours for the invasion report to be reversed, and how they would be able to trust the military's statements going forward.[44]

Colonel Conricus, a veteran officer and spokesman, said there had been no "attempt to try to fool anybody or to cause you to write anything that isn't true. I can understand that it may look differently." He called it "frankly embarrassing".

This prompted objections from several correspondents, saying it put them at greater risk. A military analyst for the Israeli newspaper Haaretz, Amos Harel, said that involving the office in a pattern of duping journalists would be an alarming development. He stated, "It's a very dangerous place for the IDF to be, to be suspected of misleading the international press, especially when we're on the verge of an escalation with Hamas, and Israel depends so heavily on trying to explain itself with the international media. It's risky for journalists, too. The Israeli Army may be forgetting that foreign journalists are on both sides of the fence, and it could be dangerous for them if they're suspected of being used for Israeli psychological operations.[45]"

To add to the confusion about the specific Gaza deception issue, Israel's Channel 10 has reported that a General Staff Deception Unit had been created recently. It was activated to cause Hamas to think that a ground invasion was underway.

Use of Kinetic Power against Cyber Power. It was reported that two Israeli airstrikes against targets in Gaza were intended to hit Hamas cyber operations centres. A strike on May 14th is stated to have hit what Israeli Air Force sources called "a cyber-equipment storage site in the northern Gaza Strip belonging to Hamas military intelligence." The site was apparently also serving as a data centre. The building also housed civilian media offices of NPR, the Associated Press and Al-Jazeera.

In a second airstrike on May 19, the Israeli military said it hit a "hideout apartment that was used by the terror operatives for offensive cyber activity against Israeli targets."

This was not the first example of using kinetic means against cyber means. The IDF carried out the first attack in May 2019. It bombed a building it believed to be the Hamas cyber unit's headquarters. This was described by the security experts as the first kinetic response to a cyber-attack.[46]

Israel Defense Forces
@IDF

CLEARED FOR RELEASE: We thwarted an attempted Hamas cyber offensive against Israeli targets. Following our successful cyber defensive operation, we targeted a building where the Hamas cyber operatives work.

HamasCyberHQ.exe has been removed.

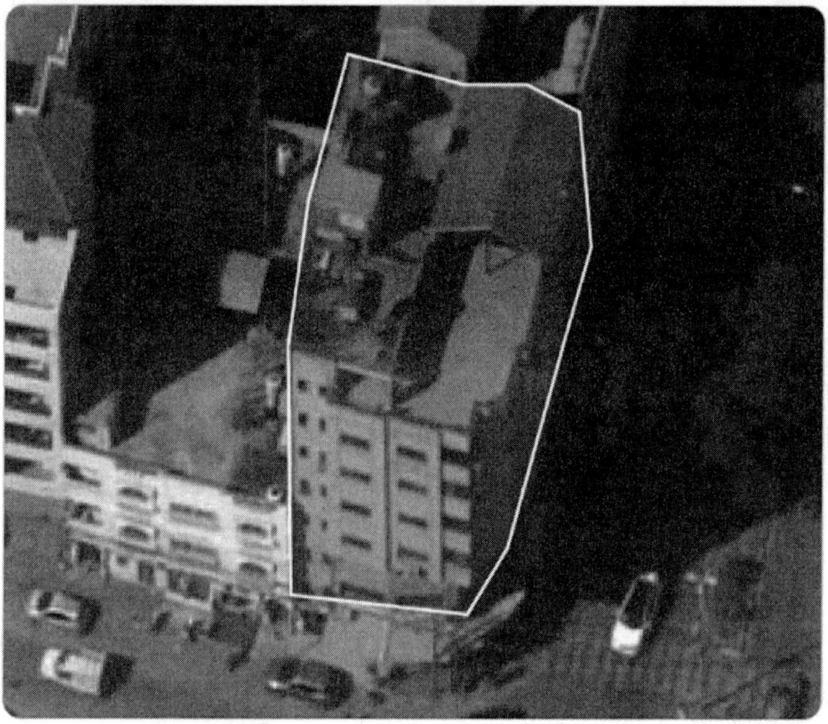

Role of Social Media Companies. The sophisticated algorithms that social media companies like Facebook, TikTok, Twitter and Instagram employ ensure that the user sees only the kind of content they want to see. The objective on both sides is not to change people's minds but to reinforce the people's views whose minds are already made up and provide them with talking points and content that they can share among their own networks. The power of this tool is so powerful that it cannot be ignored or characterised just as a facilitator.[47]

Social media platforms maintain that they have been vigilant in policing inaccurate content and incitements to violence. Policing misinformation can be a double-edged sword, particularly in political conflicts where the truth is sometimes subjective. Even if platforms have the best intentions, being too heavy-handed in flagging and correcting information might have the opposite of the intended effect. Applying moderation policies consistently and efficiently pose huge logistical challenges. Few users on either side of the conflict appear to be satisfied with the results.

Efforts to remove inflammatory content have also spurred allegations of prejudice and overreach. Instagram and Twitter blamed technical glitches after posts mentioning the eviction of Palestinians from the Sheikh Jarrah neighbourhood were wrongly deleted.

Benny Gantz, Israel's Defense Minister, told Facebook and TikTok executives that extremists were spreading disinformation about the conflict. He urged them to take action to prevent violence. According to Israel National News, the executives of both companies promised to "act quickly and effectively to prevent incitement on their networks".

On the other hand, Pro-Palestinian activists have cited many instances of their content being taken down by Facebook and Instagram.

Facebook. Facebook set up a 24-hour "special operations centre" to monitor hate speech and misinformation flowing from the region as violence flared, similar to emergency actions taken surrounding contested elections in other countries. The company's executives were also in contact with top Israeli and Palestinian officials.

Monika Bickert, Facebook's vice president for content policy said that Facebook established a task force of Hebrew and Arabic speaking monitors to identify and moderate disinformation. All of these people are real-time communicating with one another so they can quickly spot and respond to the changing landscape. The aim is to find out the interplay between those trends and our content policy, get updated guidance to reviewers and ensure that we're implementing that guidance very quickly. The work is labour intensive and Facebook hasn't said how long this targeted moderation effort would continue.[48]

Bickert did not share details about what trends Facebook sees in the misinformation on the violence on the ground.[49] Since Hamas is designated as a terrorist organisation by the U.S. State Department, some social platforms' rules, mainly Facebook's, bar posts by the group.

TikTok. A spokesperson from TikTok told the BBC in an emailed statement, "Our teams have been working swiftly to remove misinformation, attempts to incite violence, and other content that violates our Community Guidelines, and will continue to do so."[50]

WhatsApp. Representatives from WhatsApp said they did not have access to messages being shared in private chats. However, they would ban accounts they believed were involved in violence. The application had put a limit on how many times someone could forward messages to try to prevent misinformation from spreading. However, it is unclear how effective that was.

Russia

In Estonia 2007, Russia used IW to sow division by amplifying historical angst over efforts to move the Bronze Soldier statue. Russian information strategy against Estonia was a multifaceted information operation approach through[51]:

- Timely diplomatic messaging from President Putin against the North Atlantic Treaty Organization (NATO) expansion.
- Social media manipulation to spread disinformation.
- Malicious cyberattacks to disrupt its government, media and banking institutions.

RAND's research team refers to this approach as the disinformation chain that is driven by leadership (Putin), proxies (Kremlin-backed hacker) and amplification channels (social media, news outlets) to target the consumer (Estonians).

RAND Disinformation Chain

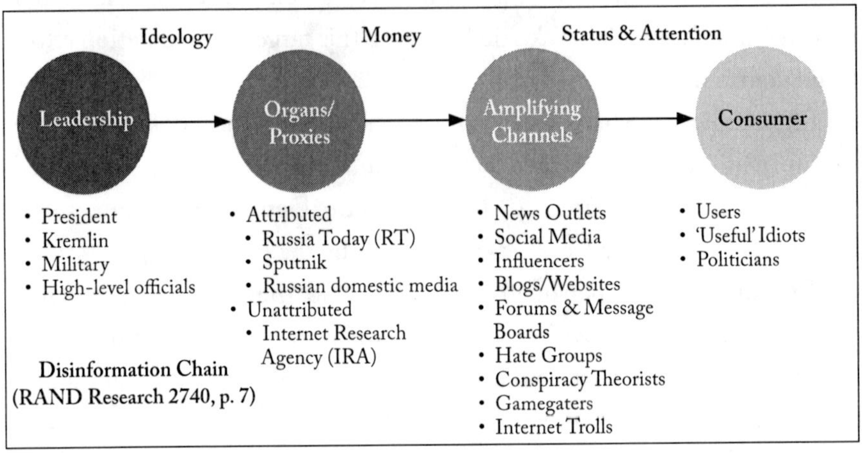

Source: RAND Corporation

Russia continued to improve its Techniques, Tactics and Procedures (TTPs) against other nations. During the 2014 Ukraine conflict, Russia integrated cyber warfare, electronic warfare, media outlets and social media by collecting indications and warnings on soldiers positioning by sending fake social media posts to their family's page. Russia used Ukrainian soldiers' reliance on mobile technology to adjust target sets designed to create fear, confusion and chaos.

During the 2016 U.S. presidential elections American polarisation was exploited by Russia to achieve its objective by fomenting confusion, chaos and distrust. The Mueller report of 2019 documented how the Internet Research Agency (IRA) paid about $100,000 for over 3,500 advertisements that specifically campaigned against some candidates and benefitted others during the 2016 U.S. presidential elections. 470 IRA-controlled Facebook accounts made more than 80,000 posts, between 2015 and 2017, resulting in targeted social media manipulation and IW messaging. These reached at least 29 million U.S. persons before deactivation.

Russia is leveraging social media warfare to unrelentingly attack the U.S. to erode the public's belief in the democratic system to return to its former status as a Great Power.

Social Manipulation across U.S. Instruments of Power

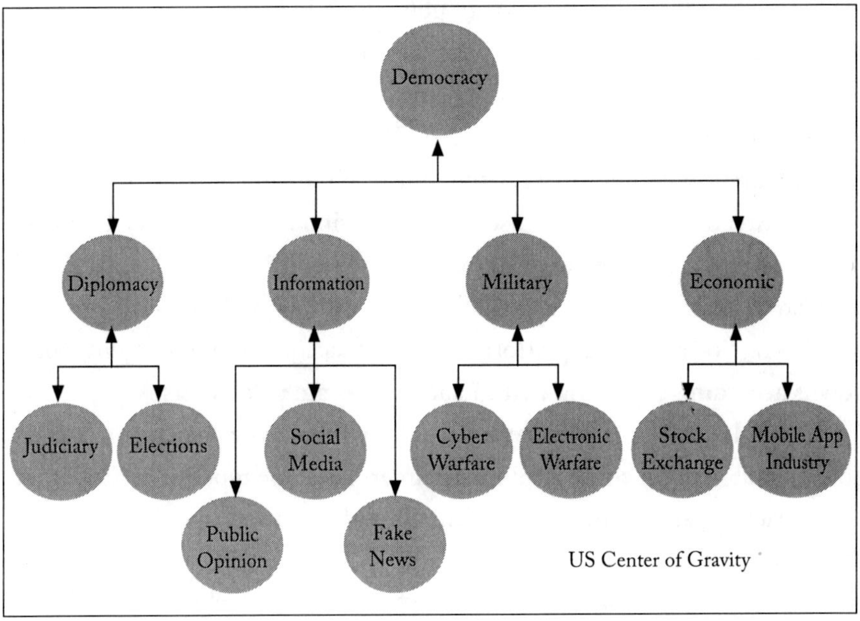

Source: RAND Corporation

The dichotomy between Freedom of Speech in Social Media and National Security Concerns

Social Media. Social media platforms are private players. The largest actors, like Facebook, Google, Twitter and Microsoft are global corporations. They have no public accountability. There is no regulatory oversight. Social media platforms are the vehicle. They are not the wrongdoer that is making false narratives. They hold data that could aid in uncovering the perpetrators. However, they are not law enforcers. They do not have mandate to address issues of national security.

There is a sheer scale of the challenge. On any given day, between 0.5 per cent to 1.5 per cent of all tweets qualify as violent or hate speech. This means hundreds of millions of posts a year that are encountered by the same number of users. Problems on the other platforms are similar. For example, on Facebook, websites promoting corona virus conspiracy theories have more than ten times the engagement of public health organisations.

According to the law they do not police their platforms. They do it as per their internal policies. For identifying disinformation material, it becomes problematic. It is usually context-sensitive and not always clear what is and is not in the category to be taken down. It is tough for a platform to know what is intentionally false, with the aim of either influencing a country's politics directly or by sowing discord and division in that country. Figuring that out needs a complex understanding of the political, social and cultural context. A platform requires a definition to know what to seek out and takedown. Social media platforms make decisions about content take-downs according to criteria that include corporate risk factors.

Recently, platforms like Facebook and Twitter have taken actions to ban political ads, hateful content and disclaimers on some types of content that is far-reaching and verifiably false. This shows that social media companies can make changes for the better.

Social media companies are reluctant to let intelligence and law enforcement agencies look behind the privacy walls of active accounts. This would cause a public outcry as user privacy is at stake. However, making those walls impenetrable prevents those same agencies responsible for keeping us safe from doing their job.

National Security Concerns. Due to the very structure of the internet, no western nation has yet found a solution to stop or deter malicious foreign cyber activity. It's near impossible to know quickly and with certainty if a foreign government is behind a disinformation campaign, ransomware implant or data theft. With uncertain attribution, the government's hands are tied.

The design of the platforms is to tie their profit to our psychology. In a system that monetises clicks, hate speech fueled by disinformation can quickly gain attention and engagement. It confirms pre-existing biases and plays out in a structure that rewards trends. The harmful and conspiratorial beliefs are spread via the proliferation of disinformation on social media by adversarial foreign actors seeking to harm national security.

The approach of social media platforms to curb this menace is not encouraging for security professionals. It is usually characterised by an ex-post response, lack of sustained action and an inadequate sense of urgency. Moreover, the mechanisms put in place by the platforms to identify what is termed fake news are unsuitable for this task. They rely on an obscure fact-checking exercise, whereas hostile states use highly sophisticated techniques.

For greater transparency, security agencies should be made aware of how such decisions are made and how a platform's algorithms make recommendations and curate what we see and hear.[52]

There is the sensitive issue of the state demanding to see data, without being intrusive into individual rights. However, one must understand Big Brother is no longer the state. The tech giants have taken that position, who misuse privacy protections based on their own politically driven algorithms rather than submitting themselves to the government's due process. Recent data shows that requests by the governments to access user data are growing.

The challenge for both social media platforms and government agencies is to devise mechanisms and implement regulations that make accounts linked to terrorist groups accessible to law enforcement agencies in real-time. Protecting communications between traffickers and terrorists should not be taken as privacy. Platforms know who these people are and can see what they are posting, even if it lies behind privacy settings.

Owners of social media must understand that freedom and privacy are not all-or-nothing. A balance has to be struck as our safety depends on it.[53]

Way Ahead

Today we live in a world where our national well-being depends not only on the government but also on the social media through which we lead our digital lives. While thinking about national security, we consider concrete threats. We spend a lot of money preparing to meet those traditional threats. However, it's online disinformation that poses the biggest threat to our country. Mostly we stand defenceless. We worry that controlling the flow of online information might violate the principle of free speech. We use the products made by tech companies. We are reluctant to regulate their industry.

We have to use technology itself. The very technology that is cause of the problem, can be used to correct it too. AI can help social media platforms spot lies, identify doctored videos and photographs and track the dissemination of falsehoods by domestic and foreign users. Social media companies can be persuaded, covertly or overtly, to cooperate with the national security apparatus.

A typical offensive strategy against a target population might consist of several steps:[54]

- Take the population and break it down into communities based on number of criteria like hobbies, politics, interests, concerns, needs etc.
- Determine the social dynamics of communication and flow of ideas within each community.
- Determine who in each community is most susceptible to given types of messages.
- Determine what narratives of different types dominate the conversation in each community.
- Use all of the above to design and push a narrative likely to succeed in displacing a narrative unfavourable to you with one that is more favourable.
- Use continual monitoring and interaction to determine the success of your effort and adjust in real-time.

Today technologies exist that can perform each of these steps continuously and at a large scale. However, while current technologies support the manual application of psychological research results, they do not fully automate it. This would be the next stage in technology development.

The same technologies can be used for defensive purposes. For example, one can use the techniques to break down the communities described above to detect adversary efforts to push a narrative and examine that narrative's content. The technology can help researchers concentrate while searching through massive amounts of social media data.[55]

Use of Artificial Intelligence (AI) in Information Warfare

The emergence of new threats like AI-supported disinformation campaigns has added a new dimension to information operations. The real power of AI in information warfare derives from several factors like societies' reliance on social media, unlimited access to and ability to spread information rapidly through cyberspace, dependence on cyberspace as a trustworthy information resource and human difficulties in distinguishing between fake and genuine media reliably and a lack of authentication or validation capabilities online.[56]

AI can psychologically alter the operational environment by changing the perceptions of both military and civilian personnel. AI is a tool that helps to accelerate the process of identifying, changing and generating information. False storylines based on AI-manipulated information and media can originate from anyone, anywhere. It then spreads fast with a harmful effect on trust. This degradation of trust works both ways. The soldier will not trust the crucial information for decision-making and combat performance, and civilians are not believing the Army's actions.

AI can be used to spread mischievous rumours influencing international will and public opinion. It would be extremely difficult to deny the alleged incident if audio and video recordings show it. The computer programmer could even use AI to create computer-generated people "on camera" giving false eye-witness accounts.

AI gives the Army with many strategic and tactical assistants by providing machine-speed analysis and decision-making. But it can work against the Army's goals and initiatives also. AI-generated information may significantly impact the future operability and trust of warfighters.

The increasing availability of manipulation software and advances in AI have made the generation of convincing fake audio and video material relatively easy. The rapid spread of such material through social media and a lack of sufficient validation methods in cyberspace has led to the emergence of a potentially powerful weapon for information operations.[57]

There are three specific AI/Machine Learning (ML) applications that could provide the death knell to authenticity:

- **Deepfakes.** Videos are created to make a person appear to say or do something that they never said or did.
- **AI-Generated Bodies and Faces.** AI-driven Generative Adversarial Networks (GANs) are being utilised to produce original and fake faces and even whole bodies. Troll and bot armies are of growing concern to military and government officials.
- **AI Writing.** A text generation tool created by OpenAI, a research institute based in San Francisco, can now compose original text in realistic prose. The tool continues to improve, generating convincing headlines, posts, articles, and comments, entirely free from human input.[58]

The convergence of these three technologies could cause the death of authenticity. How will the people struggle with being overloaded with a flow of AI-generated deepfakes constantly conveying mixed messages and troll armies that cannot be identified from their fellow citizens and soldiers?

There is an added risk of actual events being falsely claimed to be fake. Proving a falsely claimed fake to be genuine will be even more challenging than the opposite. The capabilities available to bad actors are increasing at a phenomenal rate, while states and others developing defensive or protective countermeasures are struggling to keep pace.

PLA in Information Domain

The Chinese strategy of information warfare focuses on what China calls "strategems" to build and maintain information superiority. These strategems help China to create cognitive errors and to influence the contents, process and direction of thinking of an adversary.

People's Liberation Army (PLA) of China believes that future wars will be contests to exploit information with the rise of the information age. Controlling the information domain is a prerequisite for achieving victory in a modern war. The Chinese do not use the word cyber as regularly as in the West. Cyber warfare takes place in the electromagnetic spectrum. China's military thinkers view cyber and network operations occur in an "information domain" which includes network, psychological, media operations and electronic warfare.

In 2015, China centralised space, cyber, electronic warfare, psychological warfare under the Strategic Support Force (SSF) to prioritise and execute its IW efforts. The creation of SSF highlights China's understanding of the information domain as a strategic resource in contemporary warfare.

China feels that controlling the information spectrum in the modern battlefield is a critical enabler and a fundamental prerequisite in a conflict. PLA assesses "information blockade" or "information dominance" is necessary to seize the initiative and set the conditions required to gain land, sea and air superiority.

China is of the opinion that warfare has also become informationised. Information itself is a new domain. It connects other domains such as the land, sea and air with each other. Warfare "under informatised conditions" refers to the application of IT to all aspects of military operations, including sensors and electronics on weapons systems and platforms, automated command and control systems and information operations including cyber, electronic, public opinion, psychological and legal warfare.

Along with these technical aspects of information operations, the PLA's combination of psychological warfare; the manipulation of public opinion or media warfare and the manipulation of legal arguments to strengthen China's diplomatic and security position or what China calls "legal warfare", join together in a comprehensive information operations doctrine.

Psychological Warfare

Historically in China, psychological operations involved the use of stratagem and deception. In its psychological warfare operations, the PLA may target an enemy's values, its motivation for fighting, peacetime or wartime, the logic of an adversary's foreign policy, security policy or national decisions. Psychological operations may target an adversary's civil populace and its leaders, as well as military personnel. The PLA's objectives were to cause an adversary's allies to take a neutral position or become disaffected from the ally. This is still the focus of psychological operations today.

According to Chinese thinking, psychological warfare is an integral part of information warfare. PLA's psychological warfare aims to weaken the enemy's will, shape international public narratives, from diplomatic and political stories and advance the PRC's interests through all phases of conflict. PLA intellectuals have emphasised the importance of both psychological and political operations in shaping the strategic situation ahead of conflict.

Chinese psychological operations are integrated into broader military operations and incorporated into the earliest stages of military planning. The Strategic Support Force (SSF)'s psychological warfare mission is performed by the 311 Base. This base is the only organisation in the PLA that is openly known for performing psychological warfare operations.[59] The 311 Base is a content creating unit. It performs missions and tasks associated with the PLA's concept of "Three Warfare" which comprises psychological warfare, public opinion warfare and legal warfare.

The 311 Base is closely associated with the Liaison Bureau within the Political Work Department. The Network Systems Department (NSD) of SSF is in complete command of the full spectrum of information operations including cyber, electronic and psychological warfare. The SSF's responsibility for psychological warfare could enable the PLA to exploit its cyber and psychological warfare capabilities together, learning from the success of Russia's efforts.

Influence Operations. The author has carried out a detailed analysis of China's influence operations in a paper[60] published by Vivekananda International Foundation.

The Communist Party of China's (CPC) propaganda apparatus continues to adapt and modernise as the cyber domain grows in importance, seeking to promote 'positive energy' online and to 'tell China's story well'. China has been trying to influence foreign thoughts and opinions for long. China's influence activities have moved from their focus on diaspora communities to target a far broader range of Western societies' sectors. They are stretching from universities, think tanks and media to national government, state and local institutions.

These Chinese inference and influence operations come in various forms like the following:[61]

- Manipulation of leading former European politicians working to promote Chinese interests.
- Penetration of regional organisations (Interpol, the Council of Europe) to orient their activities to align with Chinese interests.
- Manipulation of diasporas and Chinese communities living abroad, which United Front Work Department (UFWD) of the Central Committee of the Chinese Communist Party agents can mobilise during diplomatic visits.
- Pressure on researchers and the academic research apparatus using the issue of visas and financial programmes.
- In exchange for remuneration, distribution of a news supplement (China Watch) in major European daily papers creates economic dependence and stimulates self-censorship in the treatment of news about China.
- Be in charge of the majority of Chinese-language European media.
- Retaliatory measures against governments that are critical or judged to be "unfriendly".

Along with the technical aspects of information operations, the PLA combines psychological warfare in manipulating public opinion, media warfare and legal warfare that influences legal arguments to strengthen China's diplomatic and security position. China calls this Three Warfare. China effectively integrates this Three Warfare in a comprehensive information operations doctrine. Media warfare is the control and exploitation of communications channels for disseminating propaganda. It sets the circumstances for dominating communications channels for the conduct of psychological and legal warfare. Psychological warfare uses propaganda, deception, threats and coercion to affect the adversary's decision-making. It conducts military operations through perception management and deception while countering opponent psychological operations. Legal warfare uses international and domestic laws to claim the "legal high ground", sway target audiences, gain international support, manage political repercussions and assert Chinese interests. The PLA uses online influence activities to support its overall "Three Warfares" concept and undermine an adversary's resolve in a contingency or conflict.

Chinese Investment in the Media. The U.S.-China Economic and Security Review Commission's report to Congress in 2011 noted that *China Daily*, a Communist Party-affiliated state-owned newspaper, paid for inserts in newspapers such as *The Washington Post* and *The New York Times*.

A U.S. scholar has estimated that the Chinese government is spending $10 billion per year on propaganda in foreign countries. The government has paid to place news like propaganda supplements in prominent international newspapers. China has been playing propaganda videos on billboards in New York City's Times Square since 2011, costing millions of dollars.

Since 2012, China has increased foreign direct investment in U.S. entertainment, media and education from nearly zero to some $9 billion. A 2015 Reuters investigation reported that China state-run media employed a series of shell companies to obscure its ownership of 33 radio stations in the United States and 13 other countries. These radio stations actively sought to influence U.S. listeners' perceptions of critical topics, from the South China Sea to democratic elections in Hong Kong.

Mobile applications of its media organisations, including China Global Television Network (CGTN) brings out another aspect of China's propaganda outreach. It has delivered over 1 million downloads on the Android platform.

A New York Times report confirms that the Chinese government pays to deliver its propaganda to foreign audiences. China "spends hundreds of thousands of dollars" on Facebook advertising alone to promote its content on the network. It was observed that Xinhua's Twitter followers were growing at an unnatural rate. It was felt that other Chinese propaganda organisations might also be buying influence and followers on Western social media. *The New York Times* investigated in January 2018 and found that Xinhua had bought social media followers and reposts from a "social marketing" company called Devumi. The Chinese Government is ready to exploit U.S. social media companies for its propaganda purposes.

It was reported that *China Daily*, a mouthpiece of the CCP, paid $19 million to American newspapers in advertisement and printing charges alone between 2016-2020. In its report to the U.S. Department of Justice, *China Daily* stated that it had spent $11 million in advertising in prominent U.S. newspapers like *Chicago Tribune*, *The Los Angeles Times*, *The Houston Chronicle*, etc. It disclosed that it spent $2,65,822 on Twitter advertisements. The U.S. President Trump found propaganda ads in various newspapers by China, including *The Wall Street Journal* and *The Washington Post*, disturbing.

Role of The People's Liberation Army. Chinese military thinkers have propagated a theory of "cognitive domain operations" to defeat the enemy by employing the method of "mind superiority". According to the PLA, the next evolution of warfare will be cognitive warfare. The CCP realises that subsets of information warfare, such as cyber, electronic and psychological, are a new way to win without kinetic war.

The PLA conceives and executes influence operations through the use of social media. The PLA's plans for foreign social media include: enhance and defend the PLA's image, address adverse reporting, correct misperceptions, communicate deterrence signals, communicate resolve and undermine enemy resolve.

PLA authors have argued that by leveraging propaganda spread through email, short messages, cell phone communications and other interpersonal communications, including social media,[62] China can do all of the following:

- Seize the initiative.
- Bolster the debilitating psychological and morale-killing effects of kinetic attacks.
- Deceive enemy intelligence operations and degrade adversary understanding of the battlespace, making it "hard for people to distinguish the true from the false and thus more easily drive the enemy into a trap."

- Target enemy leadership more precisely and at lower costs.
- Defend one's morale and decision-making autonomy.
- "Sow discord in the enemy camp . . . to perplex, shake, divide and soften the troops and civilians on the opposing side."

In a paper on China's recent psychological operations against India, Lt Gen VK Ahluwalia, former Director CLAWS, has succinctly brought out China's probable Psyops strategy against India.[63]

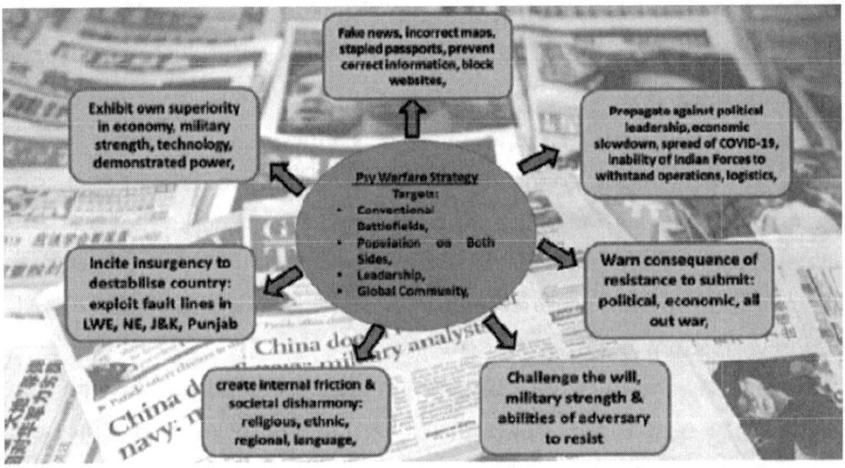

V. K. Ahluwalia, 'Psychological Warfare: Call out Adversaries' Designs', *CLAWS Journal*, Winter 2020.

Information Operations and India

The doctrine of Information Warfare (IW)

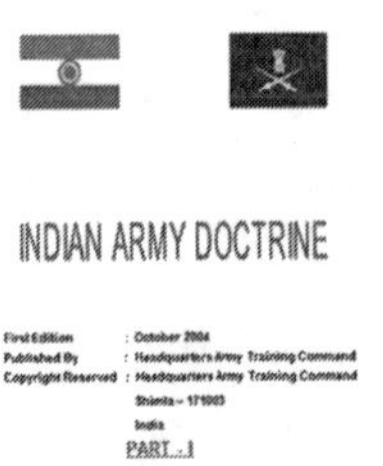

Indian Army's Doctrine published in October 2004 gave out different forms of IW on page 20 as:

- Command and Control Warfare (C2W)
- Intelligence Based Warfare
- Electronic Warfare
- Psychological Warfare
- Cyber Warfare
- Economic Information Warfare

- Network Centric Warfare

The details given as part of IW had a remarkable similarity to a similar document written by Marin C Libicki and published by the National Defense University of U.S. in1995.

Indian Army doctrine was revised and published in November 2010. In page 53 of the doctrine, it states, "IW battlespace deals with physical, information infrastructure and perceptual realms. From IA's perspective, IW will comprise Cyber Warfare, Psychological Warfare and Electronic Warfare."

Indian Army's Land Warfare Doctrine was published in 2018.[64] It states, Indian Army will develop capabilities to prosecute Information

Warfare Operations over the entire spectrum of conflict as well as in 'No War No Peace' scenario, with the aim to achieve full spectrum information dominance over the adversary. It will have the following components: Cyber Warfare (CW), Electronic Warfare (EW) and Psychological Warfare (Psy W).

Joint Doctrine for Perception Management and Psychological Operations

Joint Doctrine for Perception Management And Psychological Operations, JP-9 was published by Headquarters Integrated Defence Staff in March 2010.[65]

It was brought out earlier how U.S. has a lot of confusion regarding various terms used for information operations, psychological operations, influence operations and other terms. The same observations are applicable for this doctrinal publication.

Perception Management. The Doctrine talks about Perception Management. It says Perception Management comprise the following operations:

- Public Diplomacy.
- Public Information.
- Information Operations.
- Psy Ops.

Some highlights of the joint doctrine are given below:

Perception Management is basically undertaken against the foreign audience.

Psy Ops are conducted against friendly forces and civil population as well as adversary's forces and hostile people. Psy Ops are public presentation of the truth (not mis-information or propaganda).

The effectiveness of Psy Ops may be enhanced if they support and are supported by other similar activities like IO and Public Information (PI).

PI. PI differs from Psy Ops in that PI convey their messages through uncontrolled public media whereas Psy Ops uses media controlled by own forces and agencies. PI provides accurate and timely information without attempting to influence or sway the audience. PI and Psy Ops products should provide a timely flow of information to external and internal audience. PI and Psy Ops must be separate and distinct.

The following is observed:

- Normally service doctrines should follow joint doctrine. This is not the case here.
- The term Perception Management has not been used much after the publication of this doctrine.
- IO and Psy Ops are shown as subsets of Perception Management. Normally, Psy Ops is a subset of IO.
- Mix-up between Perception Management, Psy Ops and PI.

The views of our joint doctrine are exactly opposite to the U.S. joint doctrine on Psychological Operations.[66] U.S. Joint Doctrine states: PSYOP is intended to "convey selected information and indicators to foreign audiences to influence their emotions, motives, objective reasoning, and ultimately the behaviour of foreign governments, organisations, groups, and individuals. The purpose of psychological operations is to induce or reinforce foreign attitudes and behaviour favourable to the originator's objectives."

It further states that there is a "requirement that U.S. PSYOP forces will not target U.S. citizens at any time, in any location globally, or under any circumstances."[67]

This doctrine also dictates that the term "perception management" shall be eliminated from the DoD lexicon.

The author, while posted in HQ Northern Command in 2007-08, found that the term Perception Management was used to influence people affected by Counter Insurgency/Counter Terrorism Operations (CI/CT Ops) within our own country. For people across the border, it was Psychological Operations. There is a clear cut division of responsibility. It is recommended that the same two terms i.e. Perception Management and Psy Ops be used for CI/CT Ops and foreign audience respectively.

Organisation

Ministry of External Affairs has the Public Diplomacy Division, which was established in May 2006 to "educate and influence global and domestic opinion on key policy issues and project a better image of the country commensurate with its rising international standing." Public Diplomacy Division also partners with major domestic and international universities, think tanks and research organisations to organise seminars and conferences. Ministry of Information and Broadcasting lends support to the public diplomacy initiative with the ministry's strategic use of the media. However, currently, this org lies dormant and low key.

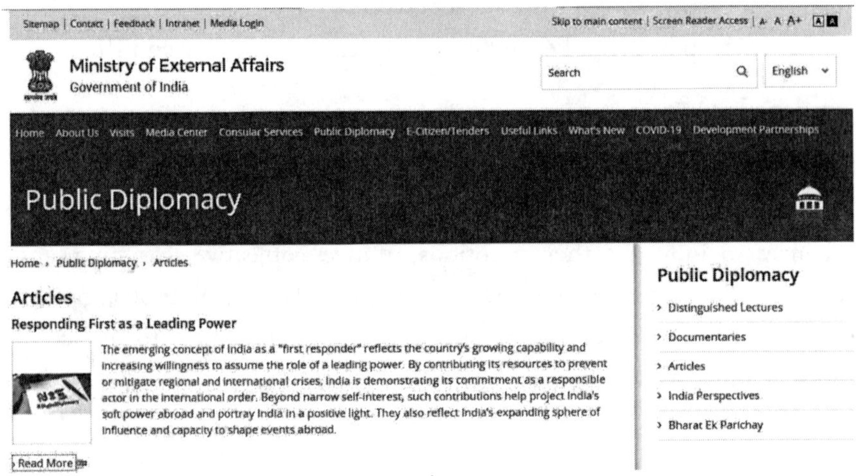

Armed Forces and other agencies have some sort of organisation for cyber warfare. However, no such organisation exists specifically for psychological operations.

Ministry of Defence has an old organisation named the Directorate of Public Relations.

Army. Respective service headquarters have their own organisation for PI Operations. In the army, the Additional Directorate General of Public Information (ADGPI), now renamed as ADG Strategic Communications (Strat Comn) comes under the Directorate General of Military Intelligence. It deals with Public Relation Activities, Media Relations and Monitoring,

Info release, Publicity, Image Projection and Perception Management. It aims to establish conditions that lead to confidence in our army and its readiness to conduct ops in peacetime and war.[68]

Recently there has been some reorganisation in this field. A new post of Director General of Information Warfare has been created under the Deputy Chief of Army Staff, Strategy. He will function as the 'single-point advice' person to the Vice Chief of Army Staff (VCOAS). He will have Directors General of Military Operations, Intelligence, Perspective Planning and Strategic Communication reporting to him. From outside, it looks an additional layer has been included in the chain of processing. But it is too early to judge the efficacy of the organisation.

Recommendations

> In traditional international conflicts, the side with the stronger military force tended to win. In today's information age, it is often the party with the stronger story that wins.
>
> —Joseph S. Nye, Jr.

Who is Responsible?

The most important issue is, who is in charge of Information/Psychological/Influence operations? In UK it is the foreign ministry. In U.S. the DoD takes the lead for the simple reason that they have got the funds. In recent times, the state department is being given importance, and funds are being transferred from DoD to the state department to carry out psychological operations. However, the cyber part for the delivery of content is still with DoD.

In the case of India, it is not clear who is overall responsible. For the allotment of budget and ability to prevail over the home ministry, foreign ministry and intelligence agencies, MoD definitely cannot be considered as the lead agency. At the most, MoD can lead in influence activities in CI/CT Ops within the country. The army in operational and tactical levels do a good job. However, there is no formalised mechanism. It is the personality of the commander on the ground which drives this operation.

In CI/CT environment, the army, intelligence agencies of both central and state governments, local police, CAPF and paramilitary organisations where applicable, concerned ministries etc., all come together and carry out influence operations, including winning hearts of minds (WHAM) of the population. Invariably they do a good job taking a "jugad" approach.

For information operations the various stakeholders in this operation are—the Ministry of Home Affairs and the intelligence agencies, Ministry of Defence, Ministry of External Affairs, Ministry of Information and Broadcasting, Ministry of Electronics and Information Technology, Ministry of Communications, Ministry of Education, Ministry of Law and Justice among others. Close coordination between these ministries will be needed to carry out information operations against an adversary. However, as of now, there is no central agency to coordinate and direct such a task.

For carrying out psychological operations at strategic level, the central government has to take a whole of government and whole of society approach. The strategy has to be chalked out at the highest level. The lead agency, in Indian circumstances, cannot be MoD. It should be MHA or a specific organisation under NSA working within NSCS. The National Security Council Secretariat is the appropriate agency to be made responsible for information operations, given India's notoriously stove-piped bureaucracy. The organisation should have experts from psychology, sociology, media, area specialists, language experts, legal, armed forces, political science specialists, foreign affairs, country experts, communication and social media.

Find the Right Term

Currently, the Indian armed forces and strategic community blindly follow U.S. jargons. Like the U.S. DoD, as brought out earlier, we also seem to be confused. If you want to influence people's minds across the border and the leaders of the adversary, what terminology should be used? Is it information operation, psychological operation, strategic communications, influence operations, perception management, public information operations, public field diplomacy or other similar terms? These terms are being used interchangeably, but they are not synonyms. The Indian armed forces must coin their own common terms and take appropriate actions to develop concepts, tactics, techniques and procedures. It is recommended that for operations across the border, the term Psychological Operations should be used. For people within the country in CI/CT Ops the term Perception Management would be appropriate.

Strategy and Doctrine

Indian government must enunciate a formal integrated strategy for Psychological Operations encompassing all facets of Psychological Operations at international, national, concerned ministries and armed forces. The armed forces should then chalk out their own tactics, techniques and procedures for this operation in their respective service domain. Indian Army should take the lead role in CI/CT Ops infested areas.

Organisation and Tasks at Apex Strategic Level

At the apex level establishment of a Center for Cognitive Security may be considered which will bring together experts working in fields such as computer science, cognitive science, social science, engineering, political campaigning, security, marketing, public policy and psychology to advance a theoretical and an applied engineering methodology to manage the full spectrum of information environment security issues. It should have close ties with government, industry, academia, think tanks, and public interest groups. It should have the following functions:[69]

- Bring together experts in various fields to develop Cognitive Security strategies, policies and implementation methods.
- Create clear and practical technology objectives in support of the policies and strategies developed.
- Identify and evaluate suitable commercial technologies.
- Identify and evaluate pertinent research results and develop and execute strategies for transitioning them into practice.

- Work with end-users from all communities to develop techniques, tactics and procedures to apply technologies identified and developed to policies and strategies.
- Create a research schedule for strategy and policy formulation, implementation and supporting technologies.
- Progress education and training materials and conduct workshops and conferences.
- Maintain a response team that will coordinate with all communities to identify influence campaigns and distribute alerts and warnings.

Coordination. The organisation at the apex strategic level should:

- Link executive leadership and implementation officers across departments and agencies.
- Explain the intent to work together.
- Understand existing efforts rather than creating new ones.
- Create an understanding of departmental and agency authorities and capabilities.
- Appreciate permissions to apply authorities.
- Reduce the emphasis on differences and credit for successes.

Adversary information operations span the responsibility of multiple government agencies. The concerned ministries must break out of siloed national security thinking, coordinate more effectively and provide space for cross-sector cooperation. Hard security and defence as well as cultural activity and media and many other realms of society which are not generally addressed are potential targets for an opponent to exploit. Normally the governments find it difficult to work effectively across traditional departmental boundaries. This bureaucratic vulnerability can lead to poor information flow, competition for resources and influence or the exclusion of key stakeholders.[70]

These shortcomings underline the need to work more effectively across government. Newly built capabilities required for monitoring, detecting and understanding the multiple elements of hostile information activities must be integrated to advance a shared view of what adversaries are doing, whom they are targeting and whether these activities are effective.[71]

Factors to be Considered at Strategic Level

The following factors may be considered at the strategic level:[72]

- What are the current objectives? Are current objectives likely to be achieved? If not, what outcomes are most likely under present or plausible conditions? Which actors or groups are most influential in political-military results?
- What strategies (e.g., force or negotiation) are most likely to influence the targeted groups and yield desired outcomes?
- How much authority/influence do targeted group leaders have over their supporters/followers?
- Which sources and information channels do target audiences use and find most credible?
- How are target audiences' attitudes structured, and how stable are they?
- What messages are they already receiving?
- What message sources, content and formats are most likely to be accepted and to foster change?
- How many messages need to be sent to them? What other actions need to be taken to achieve influence objectives?

The use of social media by our adversaries, both external and internal, has to be checked. The most obvious tool is the law. The present action by the government against Twitter is a case in point. There will always be difficulty in deciding what's sufficiently objectionable and require removal. Though challenging, it has to be done.

The government should promote international coordination to stop the opponents' disinformation campaign and bring cross-border cybercriminals to justice. It may consider setting up a national disinformation centre within the intelligence community, just like we've successfully done with the national counterterrorism centre.

As a part of the Three Warfare strategy China is likely to launch a robust Psychological Warfare campaign aimed at "generating dissent and discord in the enemy's camp, creating friction and fracturing links between the population and the leadership, between allies and between the military and civilian leadership." The campaign may be crude and heavy-handed in form. India should have its own mitigation strategy to thwart any such Psychological Operations campaign and should be able to launch its own Psychological Operations campaign with due subtlety. The preparation, themes, delivery mechanism and other details should be worked out well in advance.

The government may even consider joining Chinese social media platforms like Weibo and WeChat to reach most of the Chinese population and put forward India's viewpoints.

At the MoD Level

The MoD or the HQ IDS currently does not have an established definition for information warfare, nor does it have concepts of operations. No one is in charge here. Though with the raising of the Defence Cyber Agency, initial steps are being taken for cyber warfare. But no organisation exists for information warfare, a superset of cyber warfare. As mentioned earlier, presently, U.S. Army cyber command is thinking of including psychological operations aspects in the cyber command. MoD may think of leapfrogging and consider tasking Defence Cyber Agency the same. At least the pros and cons may be discussed and analysed.

MoD should immediately:

- Define information warfare.
- Develop an information warfare operational concept.
- Subordinate select organisations under a designated leader for information warfare.

Information warfare in armed conflict is a threat to morale of service personnel, command and control of forces and relations with local people in the area of operations. MoD must acknowledge that service members are being targeted in unconventional and subtle ways by our foes. These new tactics are effective at changing the narrative and views of our service people. MoD should:[73]

- Initiate action to defend its service members and their families.
- Initiate an anti-disinformation training program to educate and minimise the reach and impact of foreign agents online.
- Coordinate with intelligence agencies.
- Put in place the necessary people, policies, programs and partnerships to defend against these new threats in the information environment.

Indian Army

Talent Management. There is a general shortage of talent in this critical field. It is the same for all armies of the world. We must study how others are trying to solve this problem and improve our system. Talent management is not a key result area of Military Secretary (MS) branch. The rule, 'do what you are good at, and do not try to be something you are not,' applies. Government agency professional development systems deliberately cultivate generalists, leaders and decision-makers to manage organisations and produce and implement policy. This system is simply incapable of maturing talents in critical capabilities and maintaining the talent not just to be competitive but also to win.

Industry experts possess a perspective vastly different from professionals within the government or the army. Deputing junior officers to the industry would expose individuals to leading technology and bring their experiences and relationships back to the army. In some cases, hiring from traditional government contractors is a solution.

Intelligence Organisation. We have intelligence organisations and staff at every level. They already have well-developed doctrine and analytic processes honed over a period of time. They must be part of the information warfare battlefield and not a fringe player. Intelligence people also should get well acquainted with the requirements for OIE and provide adequate support for these operations in the form of data collection, analysis and intelligence products focused on the IE. Training in OIE should be formalised and expanded. Cross-functional analytic teams should be created to integrate intelligence functions better and increase attention to the IE.

CI/CT Ops. Indian Army should be the lead agency for carrying out perception management activities in J&K and North Eastern States within India.

The following is recommended in no particular order:

- Generously resource information power and information related capabilities (IRCs).
- Give greater emphasis and priority to information effects in operational planning and execution.
- Increase the prestige of information related capable personnel.
- Integrate physical and information power.
- Use information power extensively in operations below the threshold of conflict.
- Carefully record and document own operations.
- Produce high-quality video, digital and other information products.
- Focus on maintaining the support of domestic audiences by any means necessary.
- Standardise the processes associated with the IE to be consistent with and part of other routine staff processes.
- In coordination with the MoD seek expanded authorities to operate in the IE short of declared hostilities and in CI/CT Ops.
- Increase education and training to reflect the increasing importance of these capabilities and their role in future conflicts.
- Take steps to close capacity gaps in key capability areas, including cyber, influence, operations security and military deception.

Some factors to be considered for planning purposes.[74]

- IO is not well understood in the force.

- Success in IO requires prioritising intelligence support for IO.
- IO objectives must be clear and precise.
- Consider the information environment from the population's perspective.
- Things do not always happen for the reasons you think; causation can be complicated when behaviours, perceptions, cognition and culture are involved.
- Every operation is an information operation.
- IO can deliver effects on enemy forces and commanders and on civilian populations.
- Adversaries can do things that you cannot. Be prepared for them.
- Information-related capabilities that are not well integrated with operations are vulnerable to being overwhelmed.
- It can take years to build credibility but only minutes to tear it down.
- Effective information operations cannot be an afterthought. If IO is part of planning, it is more likely to be part of the plan.
- If effects in and through the information environment are important to the commander, they should feature prominently in the commander's intent.
- Manoeuvre and fires generate effects in the information environment, too.
- Plan for friendly-force mistakes and adversary propaganda.
- All communications are potentially global. What you do and say here can have effects elsewhere and vice versa.
- IO is like fire-support coordination; it is an integrating function, not itself an information-producing/affecting capability.
- Information-related capabilities can have lengthy timelines for both execution and results.
- Events do not always unfold according to plan, prepare IO branches and sequels.
- Warfare, including information warfare, involves trade-offs.
- The efforts planned and coordinated by IO need to be monitored and assessed; otherwise, you are shooting in the dark.[75]

In the end, we need to remember that the secret to getting ahead is to get started.

Conclusion

> In the information age, it's not just whose army wins, but whose story wins.
>
> —Joseph Nye

Over the past few decades, the global information environment (IE) has seen major changes driven by evolving technology, including merging the wired and wireless worlds and the continuous expansion of the cyberspace domain. The IE can be characterised by its unmatched breadth, depth and complexity, ubiquity, connectivity and exponential growth. Emerging technologies like artificial intelligence, big data analytics, Internet of Things, quantum computing promise greater changes.

The armed forces must become a potent and agile strategic actor. They should be effective in constantly evolving sensing and shaping activity against adversaries. This will require better integration of information and physical activity across multiple domains of land, maritime, air, cyber and space to leverage own national security capabilities.[76]

Today influence can be achieved only with a clear and persistent focus on audiences and effects. All activities in all domains must be focused on the information strategy to gain influence. Armed forces with information at their core and explicit knowledge of freedoms and constraints should try to contribute effectively as part of national and military strategy.[77]

However, information warfare will be a critical core competency in future armed conflicts. The battlefield is shifting from kinetic effects toward networked and information-driven outcomes. We must define its terms, develop operational concepts and doctrines for information warfare and transfer leadership and resources to empower its forces to fight and win in the information age.[78]

Social Media and the Internet have produced a revolution that has connected all aspects of human engagement where cognition ideas and perceptions are almost instantaneously available. While this connectivity has been a powerfully beneficial global change agent, it has also amplified human weaknesses and biases. Humans are social creatures that tend to drift into like-minded groups. We "Like" and share things online that echo with our own beliefs. We also like to believe what resonates with our community of friends and us.

The use of AI will change the information battlespace in a very big way. Future IO systems will be able to individually monitor and influence tens of thousands of people at the same time. The content can be algorithmically mass-produced. It is easy to use them to create disinformation. AI can create fake video. *The New York Times* maintains about a dozen Twitter feeds and produces around 300 tweets a day. Still, Russia's Internet Research Agency (IRA) regularly puts out 25,000 tweets in the same twenty-four hours. Next-generation bot armies will employ far faster-computing techniques and profit from an order of magnitude greater network speed when 5G services are fielded.

Notes

1. Zalmay Khalilzad, 'Strategic Appraisal: The Changing Role of Information in Warfare', RAND Corporation, 1999, at https://b-ok.cc/book/1117897/25906d
2. Catherine A. Theohary, 'Information Warfare: Issues for Congress', Congressional Research Service, March 5, 2018, at https://fas.org/sgp/crs/natsec/R45142.pdf
3. Kennan, George F., 'On Organizing Political Warfare', National Security Council Policy Planning Staff document, April 30, 1948.
4. Catherine A. Theohary, n. 2.
5. Joint Publication 3-13, Information Operations, Defense Technical Informational Center, November 27, 2012, Incorporating Change 1, November 20, 2014.
6. Gary Brown, Addressing Cyber-Enabled Information Operations, RU.S.I Newsbrief, May 2020, Vol. 40, No. 4, at https://rusi.org/sites/default/files/20200501_brown_web.pdf
7. Jen Weedon, William Nuland and Alex Stamos, 'Information Operations and Facebook', April 27, 2017, at https://about.fb.com/wp-content/uploads/2017/04/facebook-and-information-operations-v1.pdf
8. Catherine A. Theohary, n. 2.
9. Ibid.

10. Department of Defense, 'Summary of the 2018 National Defense Strategy of The United States of America'; Sharpening the American Military's Competitive Edge.
11. Eric V. Larson et al., 'Foundations of Effective Influence Operations: A Framework for Enhancing Army Capabilities', RAND Corporation, 2009, at https://www.rand.org/pubs/monographs/MG654.html
12. Isaac R. Porche III et al., 'Redefining Information Warfare Boundaries for an Army in a Wireless World,' RAND Corporation, 2013, at https://www.rand.org/pubs/monographs/MG1113.html
13. Matt Field, 'Congressional Testimony: How the Pentagon can Fight Information Warfare', *The Bulletin*, May 4, 2021, at https://thebulletin.org/2021/05/congressional-testimony-how-the-pentagon-can-fight-information-warfare/
14. Gary Brown, Addressing Cyber-Enabled Information Operations, RU.S.I Newsbrief, May 2020, Vol. 40, No. 4, at https://rusi.org/sites/default/files/20200501_brown_web.pdf
15. Ben Quinn, 'Revealed: The MoD's Secret Cyberwarfare Programme', *The Guardian*, March 16, 2014, at https://www.theguardian.com/uk-news/2014/mar/16/mod-secret-cyberwarfare-programme
16. Statement of Glenn S. Gerstell* Before the Subcommittee on Cyber, Innovative Technologies, and Information Systems of the U.S. House of Representatives Committee on Armed Services Hearing on Technology and Information Warfare: The Competition for Influence and the Department of Defense April 30, 2021.
17. U.S. Marine Corps, Changing The Term Psychological Operations to Military Information Support Operations, December 12, 2011, at https://www.marines.mil/News/Messages/MARADMINS/Article/887791/changing-the-term-psychological- operations-to-military-information-support-oper/
18. Cole Livieratos, Bombs, Not Broadcasts, Joint Forces Quarterly, Number 90, 3rd Quarter 2018, pp. 60-67, at https://ndupress.ndu.edu/Portals/68/Documents/jfq/jfq-90/jfq-90.pdf
19. Matt Field, n. 13.
20. Herb Lin, 'On the Integration of Psychological Operations with Cyber Operations', Lawfare (blog), January 9, 2020, at https://www.lawfareblog.com/integration-psychological operations-cyber-operations
21. Ellen Nakashima, 'U.S. Cybercom Contemplates Information Warfare to Counter Russian Interference in 2020 Election', *The Washington Post*, December 25, 2019, at https://www.washingtonpost.com/national-security/us-cybercom-contemplates-information-warfare-to-counter-russian-interference-in-the-2020-election/2019/12/25/21bb246e-20e8-11ea-bed5-880264cc91a9_story.html
22. Herb Lin, 'Doctrinal Confusion and Cultural Dysfunction in the Pentagon Over Information and Cyber Operations', Lawfare, March 27, 2020, at https://www.

lawfareblog.com/doctrinal-confusion-and-cultural-dysfunction-pentagon-over-information-and-cyber-operations

23 FM 3-05.30, MCRP 3-40.6 Psychological Operations, April 2005, at https://irp.fas.org/doddir/army/fm3-05-30.pdf

24. Ibid.

25. Maj Gen P K Mallick,VSM (Retd), 'Strategic Communications Opportunities and Challenges', March 18, 2018, at https://www.vifindia.org/sites/default/files/SC%20PPT%2018%20mar.pdf

26. 'U.S. Advisory Commission on Public Diplomacy, Public Diplomacy and The New "Old" War: Countering State-Sponsored Disinformation', September 25, 2020, at https://www.state.gov/public-diplomacy-and-the-new-old-war-countering-state-sponsored-disinformation/

27. Ibid.

28. Maj Gen P K Mallick,VSM (Retd), n. 25.

29. Ibid.

30. FM 3-13, Information Operations, December 2016.

31. ATP 3-13.1, The Conduct of Information Operations, Headquarters, Department of the Army, October 2018.

32. Isaac R. Porche III et al., 'Redefining Information Warfare Boundaries for an Army in a Wireless World,' RAND Corporation, 2013, at https://studylib.net/doc/12165232/the-rand-corporation-is-a-nonprofit-institution-that-rese...

33. Nowhere to Hide: Information Exploitation and Sanitization, The Mad Scientist Laboratory, March 7, 2019, at https://madsciblog.tradoc.army.mil/126-nowhere-to-hide-information-exploitation-and-sanitization/

34. Schwille, Michael, Anthony Atler, Jonathan Welch, Christopher Paul, and Richard C. Baffa, 'Improving Intelligence Support for Operations in the Information Environment,' RAND Corporation, 2020, at www.rand.org/t/RB10134

35. P. W. Singer and Emerson T. Brooking, 'LikeWar: The Weaponization of Social Media', Houghton Mifflin Harcourt, October 2, 2018.

36. Sara Fischer and Ashley Gold, 'Israeli-Palestinian fight spills over into social media', Axios, May 18, 2021, at https://www.axios.com/israeli-palestinian-fight-social-media-ab745237-3141-4eb7-96aa-8c19d5842477.html

37. Dave Davie, 'The 'Weaponization' Of Social Media—And Its Real-World Consequences', October 9, 2018, at https://www.npr.org/2018/10/09/655824435/the-weaponization-of-social-media-and-its-real-world-consequences

38. Eddy Gutierrez, 'Connect to Divide: Social Media in 21st Century Warfare, Over the Horizon', April 13, 2020, at https://othjournal.com/2020/04/13/connect-to-divide-social-media-in-21st-century-warfare/

39. Emanuele Ottolenghi, 'Social Media Is an Intel Gold Mine. Why Aren't Governments Using It?', Foreign Policy, March 26, 2021, at https://foreignpolicy.

com/2021/03/26/social-media-big-tech-facebook-twitter-intelligence-sharing-law-enforcement/

40. Sheera Frenkel, 'Lies on Social Media Inflame Israeli-Palestinian Conflict', *The New York Times*, May 14, 2021, at https://www.nytimes.com/2021/05/14/technology/israel-palestine-misinformation-lies-social-media.html
41. Toby Luckhurst, 'TikTok: How Israeli-Palestinian conflict plays out on social media', The BBC, at https://www.bbc.com/news/world-middle-east-57112614
42. 'Israeli military accused of using media to trick Hamas', NBC News, May 15, 2021, at https://www.nbcnews.com/news/world/israeli-military-accused-using-media-trick-hamas-n1267500
43. Josef Federman, 'Israeli military accused of using media to trick Hamas', The Associated Press, May 15, 2021, at https://apnews.com/article/hamas-middle-east-israel-media-4d942411c64c8ae1e919ae93401f8919
44. David M. Halbfinger, 'A Press Corps Deceived, and the Gaza Invasion That Wasn't', *The New York Times*, May 14, 2021, at https://www.nytimes.com/2021/05/14/world/middleeast/israel-gaza-disinformation.html
45. Ibid.
46. Catalin Cimpanu, 'Israel bombed two Hamas cyber targets', The Record, May 19, 2021, at https://therecord.media/israel-bombed-two-hamas-cyber-targets/
47. Keren Setton, 'Social Media Intensified Latest Hamas-Israel Conflict', The Media Line, May 25, 2021, at https://themedialine.org/life-lines/social-media-intensified-latest-hamas-israel-conflict/
48. 'Operational disinformation in Israel and Gaza. Hacks as blowback, and implausible finger-pointing. What was that name, again?', CyberWire, V3, Issue 20, at https://thecyberwire.com/newsletters/disinformation-briefing/3/20
49. Shannon Vavra 'Misinformation on Israel-Gaza violence prompts Facebook 24-hour tracking program', CyberScoop, May 19, 2021, at https://www.cyberscoop.com/misinformation-israel-gaza-violence-facebook/
50. Sheera Frenkel, 'Lies on Social Media Inflame Israeli-Palestinian Conflict', *The New York Times*, May 14, 2021 at https://www.nytimes.com/2021/05/14/technology/israel-palestine-misinformation-lies-social-media.html
51. Eddy Gutierrez, 'Connect to Divide: Social Media in 21st Century Warfare, Over the Horizon', April 13, 2020, at https://othjournal.com/2020/04/13/connect-to-divide-social-media-in-21st-century-warfare/
52. Glenn S. Gerstell, 'The National-Security Case for Fixing Social Media', *The New Yorker*, November 13, 2020, at https://www.newyorker.com/tech/annals-of-technology/the-national-security-case-for-fixing-social-media
53. Statement of Glenn S. Gerstell* Before the Subcommittee on Cyber, Innovative Technologies, and Information Systems of the U.S. House of Representatives Committee on Armed Services Hearing on Technology and Information Warfare: The Competition for Influence and the Department of Defense, April 30, 2021.

54. 'The Weaponization of Information—The Need for Cognitive Security', The RAND Corporation, April 27, 2017 available at: https://www.bibliotecapleyades.net/sociopolitica/sociopol_internet261.htm
55. Christopher Paul and Miriam Matthews, 'The Russian "Firehose of Falsehood" Propaganda Model', Santa Monica, Calif: RAND Corporation, PE–198–OSD, 2016.
56. Kim Hartmann and Keir Giles, 'The Next Generation of Cyber-Enabled Information Warfare', Conflict Studies Research Centre, May 2020 at https://www.researchgate.net/publication/341580088
57. John S. Davis II, et al., 'When Cyber Attacks Occur, Who Should Investigate?', RAND Corporation, December 6, 2018, at https://www.rand.org/blog/2018/12/when-cyber-attacks-occur-who-should-investigate.html
58. 'The Death of Authenticity: New Era Information Warfare', The Mad Scientist Laboratory, May 30, 2019, at https://madsciblog.tradoc.army.mil/149-the-death-of-authenticity-new-era-information-warfare/
59. Office of the Secretary of Defense, Annual Report to Congress: Military and Security Developments Involving the People's Republic of China, China Military Power, 2019, May 2019, pp. 48-49.
60. Maj Gen PK Mallick, VSM (Retd), 'China's Cyber-Influence Operations', May 15, 2021, at https://www.vifindia.org/paper/2021/may/15/China-s-Cyber-Influence-Operations
61. Jeangène Vilmer, A. Escorcia, M. Guillaume and J. Herrera, 'Information Manipulation: A Challenge for Our Democracies', report by the Policy Planning Staff (CAPS) of the Ministry for Europe and Foreign Affairs and the Institute for Strategic Research (IRSEM) of the Ministry for the Armed Forces, Paris, August 2018, at https://bg.ambafrance.org/IMG/pdf/report_information_manipulation.pdf?10364/0ced9e06f6ba84738088accbf0928cbc809ef42f
62. Mark Stokes and Russell Hsiao, 'The People's Liberation Army General Political Department: Political Warfare with Chinese Characteristics', Project 2049 Institute, October 14, 2013, at https://project2049.net/wp-content/uploads/2018/04/P2049_Stokes_Hsiao_PLA_General_Political_Department_Liaison_101413.pdf
63. V. K. Ahluwalia, 'Psychological Warfare: Call out Adversaries' Designs', *CLAWS Journal*, Winter 2020.
64. Indian Army, 'Land Warfare Doctrine 2018', at https://www.ssri-j.com/MediaReport/Document/IndianArmyLandWarfareDoctrine2018.pdf
65. Joint Doctrine for Perception Management And Psychological Operations, JP-9, Headquarters Integrated Defence Staff, March 2010.
66. Psychological Operations, Joint Publication 3-13.2, January 7, 2010, at https://fas.org/irp/doddir/dod/jp3-13-2.pdf

67. Steven Aftergood, DoD "'Clarifies" Doctrine on Psychological Operations, Federation of American Scientists', January 19, 2010, at https://fas.org/blogs/secrecy/2010/01/psyop/
68. Manvendra Singh, 'Army has a New Head of Information Warfare'. The Print, December 7, 2020 at https://theprint.in/opinion/army-has-new-head-of-information-warfare-but-stop-hiding-facts-from-indians/561524/
69. Prepared Statement by Dr. Rand Waltzman, The Rand Corporation.
70. European Center of Excellence for Countering Hybrid Threats, Tackling the Bureaucratic Vulnerability: An A to Z for Practitioners, European Center for Countering Hybrid Threats, 2020.
71. Statement of NINA JANKOWICZ Woodrow Wilson International Center for Scholars Science and Technology Innovation Program before the United States House of Representatives Armed Services Committee Subcommittee on Cyber Innovative Technologies and Information Systems Concerning "Technology and Information Warfare: The Competition for Influence and the Department of Defense" April 30, 2021
72. Eric V. Larson, et al., 'Foundations of Effective Influence Operations', RAND Corporation, at https://www.rand.org/content/dam/rand/pubs/monographs/2009/RAND_MG654.sum.pdf
73. Herb Lin, 'On the Integration of Psychological Operations with Cyber Operations', January 9, 2020, at https://www.lawfareblog.com/integration-psychological-operations-cyber-operations
74. Christopher Paul, et al., 'Lessons from Others for Future U.S. Army Operations in and through the Information Environment', RAND Corporation, 2018, at https://www.rand.org/pubs/research_reports/RR1925z1.html
75. Christopher Paul and William Marcellino, 'Dominating Duffer's Domain', RAND Corporation, at https://www.rand.org/content/dam/rand/pubs/research_reports/RR1100/RR1166z1/RAND_RR1166z1.pdf
76. Christopher Paul, et al., n. 74.
77. Harvard Kennedy School / Defending Digital Democracy/Version 1.0: February 7, 2019.
78. UK, MOD, Information Advantage, Joint Concept Note JCN 2/18.

4 Cyber Domain

Introduction

We are facing a future where security challenges will be less predictable; situations will evolve and change swiftly; and, technological changes will make responses more difficult to keep pace with. The threats may be known, but the enemy may be invisible. Domination of cyber space will become increasingly important........ When we speak of Digital India, we would also like to see a Digital Armed Force

-- PM's address to the Combined Commander's Conference, October, 2014

Today, computers and networking play a significant role in almost every facet of our lives. A substantial percentage of our life and activities depend greatly on information infrastructure. Though the use of computer and computer systems improves organisations' ability to conduct activities in a cost-effective and efficient manner, it brings in vulnerabilities. Those vulnerabilities can be used to damage our critical infrastructures.

The developers of the internet and IT in the previous generation did not give much thought to security. Internet was designed as an open service to afford access to information, facilitate sharing and enable collaboration. Open networks have propelled the digital revolution. However, it gave us an ecosystem where the price of entry for free, web-based services was the surrender of personal data. This makes us vulnerable. Protecting user-friendly systems are found to be much more difficult. Restrictive networks for the sake of security are less useful for users.[1]

While a huge amount of money is being spent on cybersecurity, it has not kept pace with increasingly sophisticated hacking. Investment in cybersecurity has risen from $3 billion in 2004 to $124 billion in 2019. This trend is going to increase. Whether lines of code written, in time spent, people employed or funds expended, the expense and effort required to protect, detect, patch, workaround and recover from attack far surpass those of hacking. The return on investment in cybersecurity is generally discouraging.

Because of the pandemic, growth in internet use to enable distributed work as work from home will continue even after the pandemic. Sensitive information like chip designs, drug formulas and patent applications will be exchanged online. Many unclassified but critical government business will be done remotely. The FBI has reported that cybercrime has increased by 300 per cent during the pandemic.

The internet and information technology have advanced to such a level that they have become a major element of national power. Nation-states are preparing themselves for the cyber battlespace. Many states are creating offensive cyberwar capabilities, developing national strategies and engaging in cyber attacks regularly.

The digital world has brought about a new type of war: cyberwar. Cyberspace is increasingly used as a theatre of conflict. Attacks can rapidly go international as covertly acquired or hacked computers and servers throughout the world are pressed into service, drawing in many nations. Across the levels of conflict, from insurgency to conventional warfare, cyber power has become a crucial element of modern technology-based military capability.

Strategic leaders must think carefully about what they could expect of conventional military operations in cyberspace. Armed forces would be expected to defend in cyberspace. This will not be an easy task. Most of the malicious activity that occurs in cyberspace is at a level below the threshold at which military force would traditionally have been justified.

Cyber Space

Cyberspace is one of five domains of air, land, maritime and space. These five domains are interdependent. Unlike the other domains, cyberspace is not geographically constrained. Cyber is a man-made domain. Cyberspace simultaneously occupies the space of the other strategic domains. Activities in cyberspace can enable freedom of action for activities in the different domains, and activities in the other domains can also create effects in and through cyberspace. Cyberspace includes the internet, computer systems, telecommunications networks including routers, switches, fibre-optic cables and wireless communications and embedded processors and controllers that allow critical infrastructures to work. Cyberspace operations (CO) is the employment of cyberspace capabilities where the primary purpose is to achieve objectives in or through cyberspace.[2]

Cyberspace is the only domain in which all instruments of national power—diplomatic, informational, military, and economic—can be concurrently exercised through the manipulation of data and gateways. As a result, cyberspace has turned out to be the centre of gravity for the globalised world. For nation states it is the centre of gravity not only for military operations but for all aspects of national activity.

The figure below presents the five strategic domains.

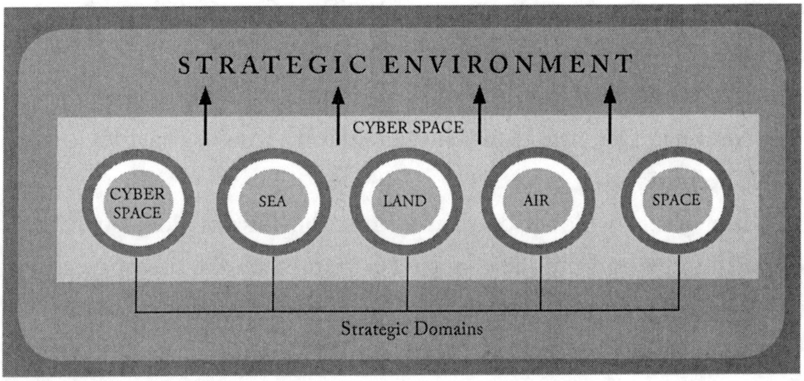

Cyberspace has three unique properties:

- It has no physical boundary.
- It occupies the same space as the other four domains.
- It can generate activity as a dimension and instrument of national power.

This means that actions in cyberspace can:

- Occur solely in the cyberspace domain.
- Move to one or more of the other traditional domains.
- Simultaneously affect activity in one or more of the other domains, either through human action or automation.

Definition. U.S. Department of Defense (DoD) in Joint Publication 1–02: DOD Dictionary of Military and Associated Terms defines cyberspace as:

Cyberspace is a man-made global strategic domain, dimension of national power, and instrument of the dimension of national power within the information environment, consisting of the interdependent network of information technology infrastructures and resident data—including the Internet, telecommunications networks, computer systems, and embedded processors and controllers—for the production and use of information by individuals and organisations.

This definition does not include the Electro-Magnetic Spectrum (EMS), which is not man-made. However, it is necessary for the physical movement of code through the domain. Therefore, it fails to recognise human use.

Former Director of the Information Strategies Concentration Program at the National Defense University, Daniel T. Kuehl, provides such an inclusive definition:

Cyberspace is a global domain within the information environment whose distinctive and unique character is framed by the use of electronics and the electromagnetic spectrum to create, store, modify, exchange, and exploit information via interdependent and interconnected networks using information-communications technologies (ICT).

A UN Security Council Resolution defines, "Cyber warfare is the use of computers or digital means by a government or with explicit knowledge of or approval of that government against another state, or private property within another state including: intentional access, interception of data or damage to digital and digitally controlled infrastructure. And production and distribution of devices which can be used to subvert domestic activity."[3]

Layers of Cyberspace. Cyberspace can be viewed as three interrelated layers: physical, logical and social made up of five components of geographic, physical network, logical network and cyber persona. Each layer represents a different focus from which Cyberspace Operations (CO) may be planned, conducted and assessed.[4]

- The physical network layer consists of the information technology (IT) devices and infrastructure in the physical domains that provide storage, transport and processing of information within cyberspace. It includes data warehouses and the connections that transfer data between network components. The physical network components include the hardware and infrastructure.
- The logical network layer consists of those elements of the network related to one another in a way that is abstracted from the physical network, based on the logic programming (code) that drives network components.
- The cyber-persona layer is a view of cyberspace created by abstracting data from the logical network layer using the rules that apply in the logical network layer to develop descriptions of digital representations of an actor or entity identity in cyberspace (cyber-persona). The cyber-persona layer consists of network or IT user accounts, whether human or automated and their relationships to one another.[5]

The Three Layers of Cyberspace

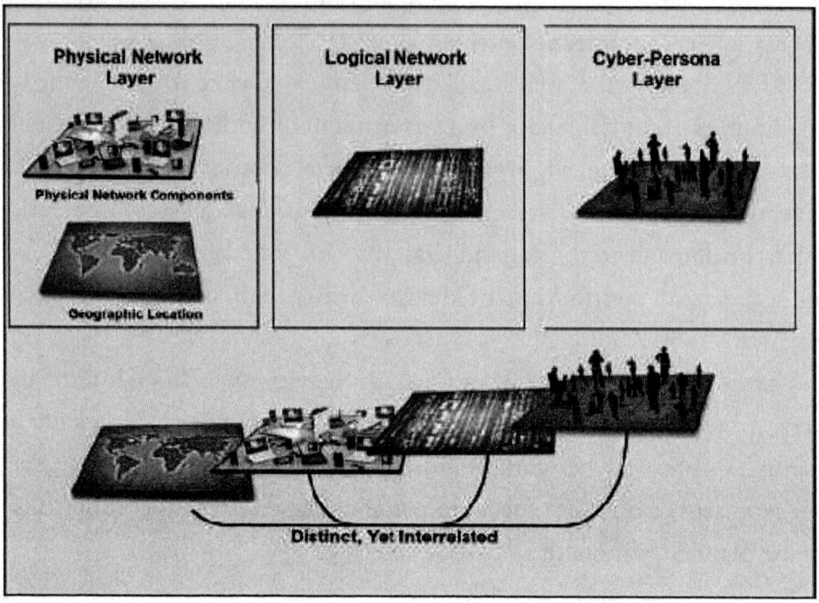

Source: https://irp.fas.org/doddir/army/pam525-7-8.pdf, p. 8.

Availability of cyber capabilities is necessary for the effective planning, and execution of CyberOps. It is depicted in the following diagram.

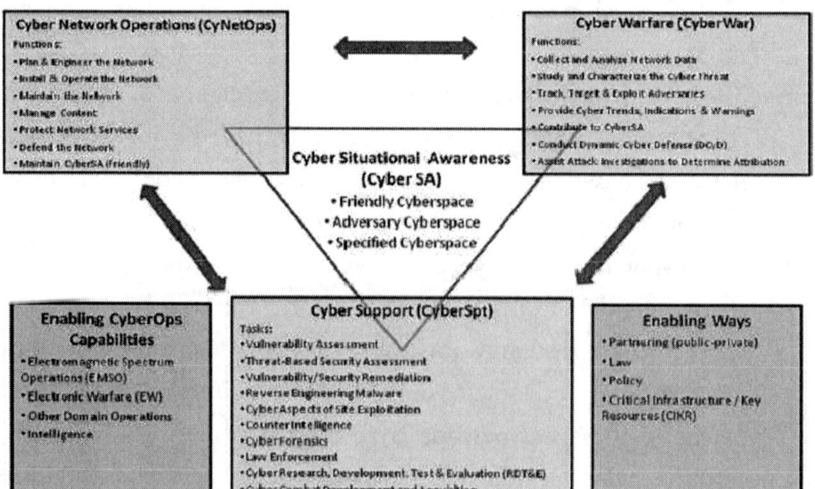

Source: https://irp.fas.org/doddir/army/pam525-7-8.pdf, p. 24.

Cyberspace Characteristics

Cyberspace helps in dynamic information exchange which affects all aspects of life. It also allows opponents to access this information and disrupt critical operations from any location. From a military perspective, cyberspace activities rarely require the movement of forces, allowing engagement from extended standoff ranges. It can influence the opinion of populations that are inaccessible through the other domains. Some of the characteristics are given below.

EMS. Cyberspace cannot exist without being able to exploit the existing EMS. Without the EMS, information and communications technologies (ICT) would be unable to communicate with each other and ICTs themselves would not function.

Man-made objects. Cyberspace requires man-made objects to exist.

It can be reverse-engineered. Cyberspace actions including codes and algorithms can be analysed and recoded for use. Cyber operations can be turned against the originator or other targets through reverse engineering.

It can be constantly replicated. Due to inexpensive and readily available hardware, IT systems and networks, damaged systems can be quickly repaired and reconstituted.

No Single National/International Ownership. Cyberspace is not under any single nations' or entities' complete control. This enables free information flow but hampers global accountability, standardisation and security.

Lack of Cooperation/Collaboration. The lack of international laws and regulations complicates responses to actions. The difficulty in the attribution of a cyber attack makes them easily deniable. No cyber Rules of Engagement for conflicts between nation-states exist.

Low Cost. Cyberspace is the most affordable domain through which attack can take place. Malware and training are readily available over the internet at no cost. Enemies can develop, edit and reuse current tools for network attacks. Inexpensive tools and training allow an adversary to compete without costly ships, aircraft or missiles.

Volatile. The success of cyberattacks depends on vulnerabilities within the adversary's network. If the opponent finds out the vulnerability of their networks and closes it, the cyberspace attack technique becomes useless. Therefore, great care must be taken to prevent alerting opponents.

Speed. Cyberspace operations can take place at the speed of light. However, preparation for those operations can take a lot of time.

Unintentional cascading effects. There is always a danger of unintended cascading consequences. Though offensive cyber capabilities are developed and evaluated in computer labs and cyber ranges, there is no surety how a capability will behave when introduced to cyberspace.

Dominant offensive action. As of now, the offence is dominant rather than the defence in cyberspace. This is because an attacker has to be successful only once, whereas the defender has to be successful all the time.

Range. The range is not a factor in cyberspace. Attacks can take place from anywhere in the world.

Attribution. Attribution of attacks is very difficult. It complicates possible responses.

Society's overpowering reliance on cyberspace. Today's society's irresistible reliance on cyberspace provides attackers a target-rich environment.

Cyber Threats

Many countries, including India, are under constant assault in cyberspace. The term Advanced Persistent Threats is used for targeted, sophisticated hacking attacks aimed at governments by state actors or agents connected with nation-states. Such attacks have targeted governments, energy, global petrochemical companies, science and technology sector, mining sector, military contractors, critical infrastructure and many others.

Threats, dangers and risks because of adverse action in cyberspace have three general characteristics:

- **They are broad.** Anything dependent on the cyber domain is potentially at risk.
- **They are embedded.** Threats arise from inherent vulnerabilities, from malicious hardware or from malware placed in complex software operating systems.

- **They are diverse.** Potentially hostile actors include nation-state actors, terrorist organisations, criminal gangs and all kinds of state-sponsored, mercenary or individual hackers.

Cyber Threat Spectrum. We are facing threats from individual hackers to Nation-state cyber-enabled kinetic attack. These have already manifested themselves in different situations and places. The Level of Danger Vs Cyber Threats is illustrated below:

Cyber Treat Spectrum

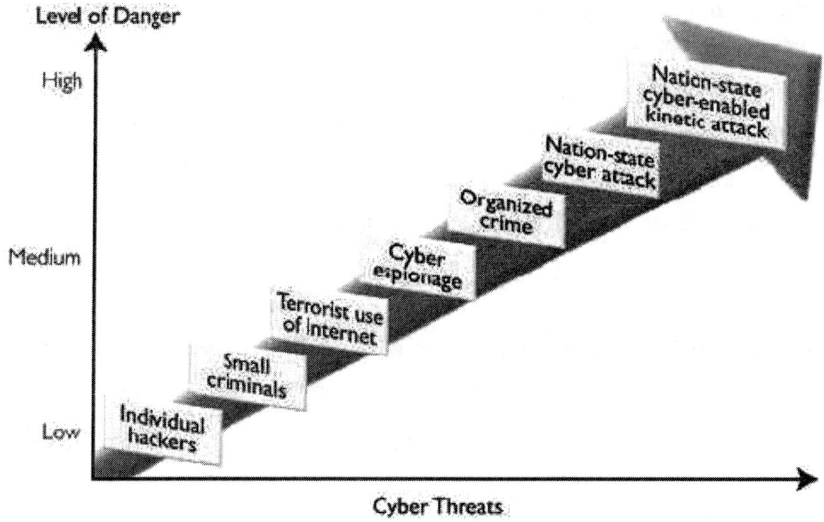

There is a fundamental difference between security threats in cyberspace and those existing in the real world. The factors which contribute to this difference are[6]:

- The global span of cyberspace creates conflicting and overlapping jurisdictions of control by nation-states with differing legal and cultural approaches and distinct strategic interests.
- Dependency on the cyber domain makes disassociation is impossible. Our reliance on cyberspace for national security functions cannot be undone.

- Cyber hardware and software products from different countries makes it virtually impossible to provide reliable supply chain assurance.
- The scalability of the cyber domain makes it different. We deal with a mechanism by which operations on a global scale are controlled.
- Few people control operations within the domain. Everyday users cannot modify or control the software and hardware they use.
- Due to the interconnectedness and interoperability of cyberspace, no locus of positive control is feasible. It will require close international cooperation.
- Changes in the cyber domain happen fast. Unfortunately, each change creates a new cycle of vulnerabilities.
- The distribution of cyber assets extends to all types of organisations, each with different resources, capabilities and concerns.
- Technical ability to attribute actions with a sufficient degree of confidence is lacking. Anonymity is achieved easily.

Cyber Risk

Cyber risk can be defined as a function of the following parameters: threat, vulnerabilities of the systems you need to protect and consequences of losing the systems. The threat can be broken into two categories: adversary intent and their capabilities. Vulnerabilities are described as either inherent or operationally introduced and consequences either fixable or fatal to the impacted systems.[7]

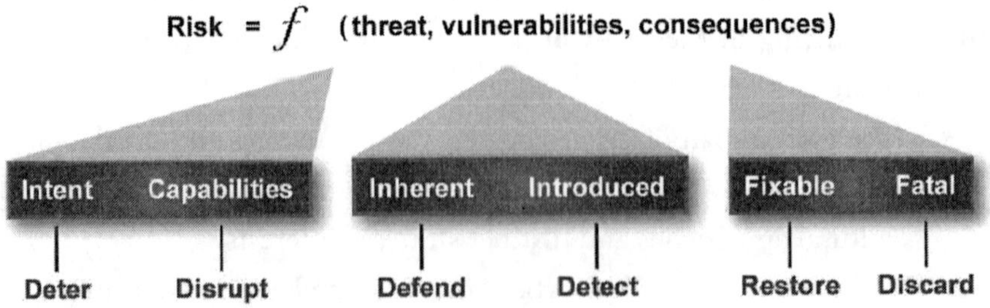

Source: Resilient Military Systems and the Advanced Cyber Threat, U.S. Department of Defense, Defense Science Board (DSB) Task Force Report January 2013, p. 14.

Lowering any of the three variable factors will reduce the risk. Therefore, concerned policymakers and cybersecurity experts should execute their roles to decrease the threat, vulnerability and adverse consequences associated with the risk factors.

Information Infrastructure

Components. The global, national and defence Information Infrastructures comprise the following distinct interdependent components:

- Hardware.
- Software applications.
- Information itself.
- People.
- Power supply.

Connectivity. The broad, instantaneous and seamless connectivity and reach across Global, National and Defence Information Infrastructure networks contributes considerably to infrastructure functional efficiency. Real-time communications are critical in many businesses, government, and defence areas, including sensor to shooter configurations during combat operations.

Bandwidth. Demand for bandwidth by clients has outstripped bandwidth availability. In defence, it is an essential feature for real-time delivery of surveillance and reconnaissance imagery and the immediate accessibility of intelligence databases.

Functional Interdependence. It is a significant factor for the operational efficiency and security of any information infrastructure. Failure of any component of an interdependent system can impact the functionality of another part or the whole system.

Ownership and Control. Ownership of the networks varies between the government and private sector. In most countries, the major telecommunications service providers are privately owned. In the globalised world, those services may be owned or partly owned by foreign private corporations. Defence Information Infrastructure exists primarily at the tactical level. The diverse and distributed ownership of infrastructure presents enormous security challenges.

Cyber Power

Joseph Nye defines cyber power as "The ability to use cyberspace to create advantages and influence events in other operational environments and across the instruments of power."[8] Cyber power is the capability to control IT systems and networks in and through cyberspace.

The following factors shape cyber power:

- Technology.
- Organisation.
- Information.

Cyberspace is transforming how information is created and the connectivity used to transmit and exchange that content. Influence is exercised by employing soft power and smart power in the pursuit of strategic goals. The crucial elements of cyber power are the use of the electromagnetic spectrum, electronics technology and integrated man-made infrastructure. The vital aspect of cyber power is its capability to manipulate a target's cyber infrastructure via exploitation and attack.

Cyber power depends on hardware and software. Malware is malicious software that interferes with computer and internet-based applications. It is a key weapon in cyber warfare.

Cyber power has three main characteristics:

It is ubiquitous. It can be stealthy. Land, sea, air and space power can create a strategic effect on each of the other domains. Cyber generates a strategic impact on all domains simultaneously.

It is complementary. It is indirect. Though cyberattacks can be damaging and disruptive, their coercive ability is still limited. Till the time cyber power can prove its coercive ability, it will be considered a complementary instrument.

It can be stealthy. It is attractive as it can be used clandestinely on a global scale without it being attributable to the wrongdoer. Databases can be accessed for classified or proprietary information or changing the data sets. Malicious software can be put in adversary IT systems and networks until these weapons are activated and cause their intended damage.

Harvard Kennedy School of Government in a recent study of cyber power of various countries, has ranked U.S. as the most powerful cyber power nation.

2020 National Cyber Power Index (NCPI) Rankings[9]

Belfer Center **National Cyber Power Index 2020 "Top 10"**			Specific Rankings	
#	Country	Overall score	Capability	Intent
1	United States	50.24	1	2
2	China	41.47	2	1
3	United Kingdom	35.57	3	3
4	Russia	28.38	10	4
5	Netherlands	24.18	9	5
6	France	23.43	5	11
7	Germany	22.42	4	12
8	Canada	21.50	11	9
9	Japan	21.03	8	14
10	Australia	20.04	16	8

Cyber Deterrence

Deterrence theory in cyberspace differs from classic nuclear deterrence and conventional deterrence in the aspects of actors and means. Cyber deterrence is a result of states' desire to avoid being attacked in or via cyberspace. Potential targets include their military networks, critical infrastructures like finance, industrial sector, communication lines, power grid and transportation. The state also needs to understand the interdependencies of critical infrastructure to societal continuity and the psychological impact an attack could have on the public psyche as indirect impacts of a cyberattack.

The defence of cyber elements should not be treated differently to efforts to defend against conventional attacks. The most significant difference when comparing nuclear to cyber deterrence is that the effects of a strike in cyberspace are far from being as absolute as in nuclear warfare.

Deterrence is a state of mind. The efficacy of cyber deterrence relies on the ability to impose or raise costs and deny or lower benefits related to a cyber attack in a state's decision making calculus. Credible cyber deterrence is equally dependent on a state's willingness to use these abilities and a potential aggressor's awareness that these abilities and the will to use them exist.

For cyber deterrence to work effectively, it will have to consist of a comprehensive scheme of offensive and defensive cyber capabilities, supported by a robust international legal framework.

Deterrence in cyberspace is more challenging to achieve than deterrence in conventional domains. Cyberattacks are cheaper to execute compared to the cost of defence of entire networks. The ability to identify the assailant and view his cyber activity as an act of war, followed by a response according to the rules of war, is highly challenging. In cyberspace, an attacker has the advantage in that he is to succeed only once. One cannot defend everything. Maintaining and updating defence systems are costly. It is difficult to distinguish between a cyberattack and computer malfunction. Retaliation in cyberspace is difficult to execute because:

- Attribution is challenging in cyberspace. Complexities include the time it may take to technically or politically attribute an attack to a specific actor, difficulties raised by false flags, plausible deniability by proxy actors and reliance in some instances on private actors for forensic attribution. Attribution of a cyberattack necessitates time intensive, all source information, often spanning numerous networks and actors.
- Reliance on cyberspace is asymmetric. Some states and non-state actors have relatively smaller attack surfaces than others, limiting the potential scope and scale of retaliation in kind. Potential adversaries may not be equally vulnerable to cyberattacks.

- The difficulty of signalling. It is tricky given the secrecy of cyber operations. Cyber capabilities are less visible than their kinetic counterparts and have limited life spans.
- Retaliation requires proper categorisation of an incident and making a proportional response after that. In the cyber domain, the purpose and scale of an attack are often ambiguous.
- Difficulty of discerning between offensive and defensive behaviour.
- Deterrence through punishment in cyberspace is nearly impossible. An overwhelming campaign to deliver devastating pain and suffering on an enemy population is not yet feasible. However, this may change as technology changes.
- Deterrence through denial is difficult due to the perceived ease of offensive operations. Also, there are vulnerabilities an attacker can exploit.
- A diversity of actors in cyberspace complicate deterrence. It may not be clear who needs to be deterred and difficult to identify what they value to affect their cost-benefit calculus. Many actors are actively engaged in this domain, ranging from nation-states to criminal organisations, individual hackers, patriotic groups, private corporations, terrorist organisations, etc.

The assumption that all actors in cyberspace, including individuals, non-state hacking groups, state intelligence agencies and military operators, would act rationally may not be true.[10]

Deterrence is primarily about messaging or the ability to communicate boundaries and consequences. Martin Libicki renders the core message of deterrence as "if you do this then that will be done." The ability to send that message requires the following:

- **Attribution.** The state must be able to define the target of retaliation.
- **Thresholds.** The state must be able to consistently distinguish between acts that merit retaliation and those that do not.

- **Credibility.** The state's will to retaliate must be believed.
- **Capability.** The state must be able to pull off a successful response.

Attribution. In earlier days, attribution was difficult. But over the past decade process of attribution has improved considerably. Prompt, high-quality attribution is costly but possible today. As Rid and Buchanan note, "The larger a government's technical prowess, and the larger the pool of talent and skills at its disposal, the higher will be that state's ability to hide its own covert operations, uncover others, and respond accordingly.[11]"

Despite the technological advancement, attribution still has the following issues:

- Attribution remains uncertain due to states' plausible deniability and false flag attacks. Moreover, the collaboration between the attackers and the state is difficult to prove.
- Establishing collaboration with a state is a problem. It is feasible to track attackers and their geographic location. It isn't easy to establish any formal government role in the cyberattack.
- Attribution can never be sure. Accused states will disagree about their complicity from their government with the attackers. This requires prior intelligence to argue with certainty that the actors were complicit.

Defensive capabilities play an equally important role in deterring cyberattacks. They make sure that essential services and functions of society continue unchanged. They deny or reduce the benefits an attacker may get via cyberattacks. Defensive cyber capabilities increase a state's resistance to attacks, enable the state to strengthen the security of potential targets, reduce the consequences and limit or eliminate an aggressor's ability to threaten the state through cyberspace.

Deterrence by denial is the more defence-orientated, reactive form of deterrence.[12]

Deterrence by Denial

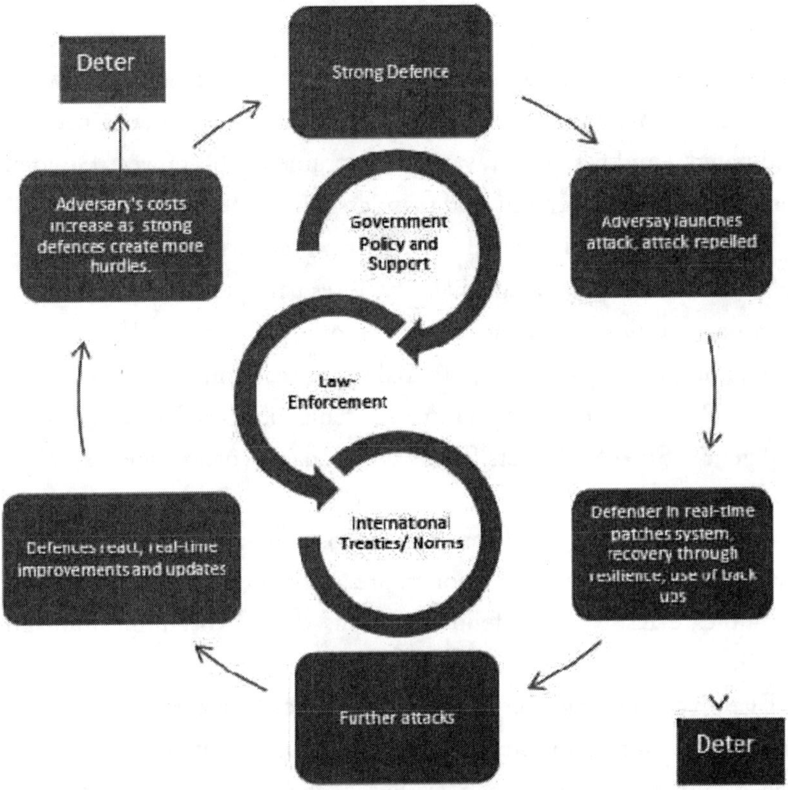

Over and above offensive and defensive capabilities, a robust international legal framework that addresses cyber aggression is the most critical component of a comprehensive approach to deterrence.

Today battle in cyberspace is in the grey zone between war and peace. Nation-states have to spend more time pre-empting adversaries and degrading their ability to do so and less time trying to persuade its competitors that it is not worth hacking. In cyber warfare, the best defence is a good offence. Deterrence by punishment in the cyber domain has many risks. It can never be known exactly whether it was the threat of punishment that led to the change in adversary behaviour or whether there were other reasons for it. Deterrence integrates both worlds of cyber and kinetic into one equation of the balance of power.

Signalling is vital in cyberspace because the intent of cyber operations can be challenging to discern. Signalling is also essential for escalation management so that actions taken in support of defending forward are not unintentionally perceived as escalators. Signalling should necessitate coordinated employment of various instruments of power. Diplomatic efforts should be deliberately and seamlessly integrated.

When deterrence by denial fails, the next recourse is deterrence by cost imposition. There is a strategic liability in resorting to that course of action as a response action, i.e., an accumulation of incurred costs. These costs can include but are not limited to potential exposure/compromise of a valuable Internet-Protocol (IP)-based, Human Intelligence (HUMINT) or Signals Intelligence (SIGINT) assets. These assets enable covert cyber exploitation activities.

Successfully applying deterrence by cost imposition requires effective signalling. If an adversary is not aware of an attempt in cyberspace to communicate resolve to defend the status quo, a cost-imposition effort will fail.

Effective signalling after imposing costs in cyberspace requires revealing its identity. Cost imposition in cyberspace requires that an effect be visible. Once a vulnerability has been exploited and revealed through a visual impact, a well-resourced adversary promptly will mitigate or remediate associated risks and pursue a full forensic investigation to know who is behind exploitation. The techniques used will lose their potential value for future employment.

U.S. Example

Report of the U.S. Defense Science Board (DSB) Task Force on Cyber Deterrence[13]

In February 2017, Final Report of the U.S. Defense Science Board (DSB) Task Force on Cyber Deterrence was published. It defines cyber deterrence as "the use of both deterrence by denial and deterrence by cost imposition to convince adversaries not to conduct cyberattacks or costly cyber intrusions

against the United States." Eight guiding principles for the DoD and U.S. government were:

- Deterrence by cost imposition requires understanding what key adversary decision-makers value, holding that they value at risk, and communicating the credible will and capability to respond.
- Deterrence by cost imposition requires credible response options at varying levels of conflict.
- In the event of a cyberattack on the United States (i.e., a failure of cyber deterrence), the question should not be whether to impose costs in response, but how and when to do so against the attacker and connect the response to the attack.
- The United States must clarify that it seeks to deter and will aim to impose countervailing costs in response to some forms of costly cyber intrusions.
- Responding to adversary cyberattacks and costly cyber intrusions carries a risk of escalation and intelligence loss, but not responding carries near-certainty of suffering otherwise deterrable attacks in the future.
- Reducing the vulnerability of U.S. critical infrastructure is essential to deterrence by denial. It also reinforces the credibility of U.S. threats to impose costs on attackers.

- Cyber arms control is not viable, though norms and rules of the road may be both viable and highly valuable.

Planning for cyber deterrence operations will have the following challenges:

- In widely varying contexts from peace, an adversary might conduct cyberattacks to "grey zone" conflict, to severe crisis to war.
- Campaign planning must be an integral part of a broader political-military campaign and other diplomatic and military actions.
- Effects of cyberattacks can be highly uncertain and attribution may be difficult in some cases.
- Planning must engage senior national security leaders to make complex judgments under tremendous ambiguity about a range of issues, including adversary leadership views, the risks of escalation in varying contexts and the specific impacts of both adversary and own cyber actions on the strategic interests of the state.

The Cyberspace Solarium Commission (CSC)[14]

In the U.S. the Cyberspace Solarium Commission (CSC) was established to "develop a consensus on a strategic approach to defending the United States in cyberspace against cyberattacks of significant consequences."The Cyberspace Solarium Commission published its final report on March 11, 2020.

The Chairman, in his forward note, outlined the following big ideas:

- Deterrence is possible in cyberspace.
- Deterrence relies on a resilient economy.
- Deterrence requires government reform.
- Deterrence will require private sector entities to step up and strengthen their security posture.
- Election security must become a priority.

U.S. National Cyber Deterrence—Current Policy Focus

Cyber Themes of Current U.S. National Cyber Deterrence Policy
• Balanced combination of deterrence by denial and deterrence through cost imposition.
• Whole-of-government approach leveraging full range of national instruments of power: diplomatic, informational, military, economic, intelligence, and law enforcement.
• Tailorable to a specific situation and adversary; not "one-size-fits-all."
• Extendable to international allies and partners.
• Part of a larger U.S. deterrence posture that includes a foundation of nuclear deterrence.
• Includes explicit declaratory statements in some U.S. cyberspace strategy documents.
• Widespread availability of cyberspace capabilities requires deterrence of nonstate actors in cyberspace.

Cyber deterrence poses difficult questions. Some of them are:[15]

- Should we expect both traditional deterrence denial and punishment components to operate with equal emphasis and equal effect in cyberspace?
- Will denial, a passive feature of cyber deterrence, be dominant?
- How active and responsive should we expect cyber deterrence to be?
- Does the Cold War model of strategic deterrence leave us expecting that cyber deterrence should be mainly a national military concern?
- How can we mitigate that tendency and ensure that we take the complete account of a state's cyber deterrence capability? Most of these capabilities will be non-military, much of which will not even be owned by the government?
- How can we ensure that the private and public sectors collaborate to best effect?
- If the public sector cannot be expected to be solely responsible for cyber deterrence, what is reasonable to expect from the government?
- If the malicious activity falls below the threshold of the use of force, what should be a more nuanced position?

Latest Thinking

Gen. Paul Nakasone, Director of the NSA and Commander of the U.S. Cyber Command, during a hearing on April 15, 2021 in Washington, D.C. stated that traditional military deterrence "is a model that does not comport to cyberspace." Traditional deterrence is a binary world of yes or no in regards to conflict. But those rules don't hold in cyberspace, where much of the nefarious activity; whether by nation-states, cybercriminal ransomware gangs or other threat actors; plays out non-stop in an ambiguous strategic gray zone.

Nation-states, keep cyber activities below a level justifying a kinetic response. Cyberespionage activities like SolarWinds and the Microsoft Exchange hacks do not justify a traditional military response.

Ransomware gang REvil conducted a number of high-profile ransomware attacks in recent years. CYBERCOM worked with an unnamed foreign government to "shut down" the ransomware gang. In spite of the setback, REvil is unlikely to stop operations permanently. The group will most likely reemerge in the future with a new online identity before resuming its lucrative ransomware attacks. The group is unlikely to be totally deterred.

In October 2021, Microsoft revealed that the Russia's Foreign Intelligence Service (SVR) has not been deterred from hacking U.S. infrastructure and companies since being ousted and sanctioned for the SolarWinds campaign in April, 2021. The SVR has continued operations, merely changing its targets and some tactics.[16]

Military Domain

Cyberwar is a conflict in virtual space with means of information and communication technology (ICT) and networks. Cyberwar aims at influencing the will and decision making capability of the enemy's political leadership and armed forces in the theatre of Computer Network Operations (CNO).[17]

There are three forms of Computer Network Operations:

Computer Network Attack (CNA). CNA is deliberate actions and operations over an extended period of time to alter, disrupt, deceive, degrade or destroy adversary computer systems or networks or the information and programs resident in or transiting these systems or networks. A cyberattack seeks to cause the adversary's computer systems and networks to be unavailable or untrustworthy and less valuable. It is destructive in nature.[18]

Computer Network Exploitation (CNE). CNE uses actions and operations to obtain information that would otherwise be kept classified and is resident on or transiting through an adversary's computer systems or networks. Cyber exploitations are usually covert in nature. They do not seek to disturb the normal functioning of a computer system or network. The best cyber exploitation is one that a user never notices. It is non-destructive.

The fundamental difference between a cyberattack and cyber exploitation is the payload's nature to be executed. A cyberattack payload is destructive, whereas a cyber exploitation payload acquires information non-destructively.

Computer Network Defence (CND). It involves all measures necessary to protect own ICT means and infrastructures against hostile Computer Network Attack and Computer Network Exploitation.

CND is the most essential activity for the armed forces in cyberspace. The vast majority of attacks frequently apply to internet-connected computers. Victims of cybersecurity lapses and cyberattacks include many civilian systems. The armed forces have a significant role in protecting their own systems. The armed forces must think innovatively as they make their cyber defence goals, architectures, policies, strategies and operations.

The continuum of cybersecurity and cyber operations is explained in the following diagram.

Continuum of Cyber Security and Operations

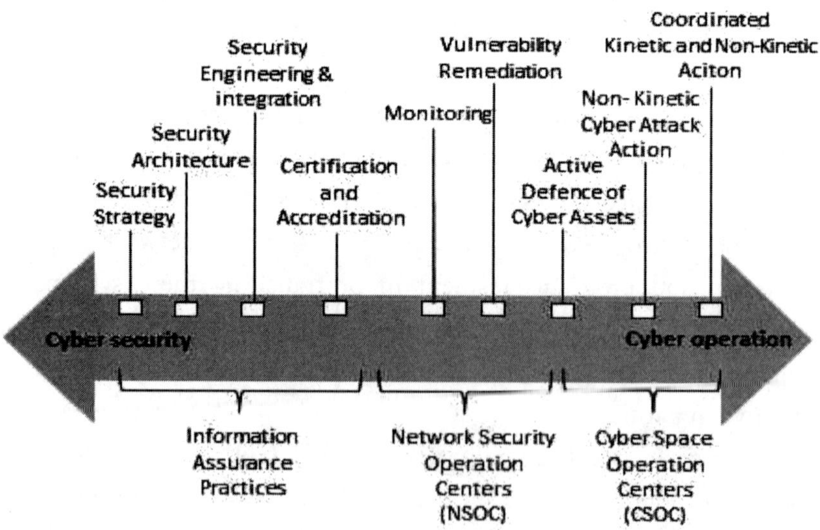

Vulnerability of military systems to cyberattacks. Computers managing the logistics on desktops or weapons systems having embedded hardware or software are vulnerable. It is possible to make a tank fail to start up or a sophisticated missile retargets in mid-air. Many military weapon systems contain the same foreign chips and code that commercial systems do. Similarly, military software is vulnerable to the same cyberattacks as commercial software. Military supply chains have many of the same risks.

Militaries worldwide are now exploiting these vulnerabilities in weapons systems to carry out operations. For example, in 2007, Israel bombed a Syrian nuclear reactor. The air attack was preceded by a cyberattack on Syrian air defences that resulted in radar screens showing no change as bombers struck with impunity.

It's not military bases will be blown up. However, some bases will lose power data and communications. Therefore, cybersecurity aspects must be taken seriously in military procurement, from weapons systems to logistics and communications contracts.

In U.S., a GAO report of 2018 expressed concern regarding the lack of secure and patchable U.S. weapons systems. The report observed that "in operational testing, the Department of Defence routinely found mission-critical cyber vulnerabilities in systems that were under development. In addition, DoD is still learning how to contract for cybersecurity in weapon systems, and selected programs we reviewed have struggled to incorporate systems' cybersecurity requirements into contracts."

The point is simple. If your weapons and systems aren't secure, don't even bother bringing them onto the battlefield.[19]

Different type of vulnerabilities are explained below:

Details of Vulnerabilities

Vulnerabilities	Description
Software	Applications or system software may have accidentally or deliberately introduced flaws the use of which can subvert the intended purpose for which the software is designed.
Hardware	Vulnerabilities can be found in hardware, including microprocessors, microcontrollers, circuit boards, power supplies, peripherals such as printers or scanners, storage devices and communications equipment such as network cards. Tampering with such components may secretly alter the intended functionality of the component or provide opportunities to introduce malware.

Vulnerabilities	Description
Seams between hardware and software	An example of such a seam might be the reprogrammable read-only memory of a computer (firmware) that can be improperly and clandestinely reprogrammed.
Communications channels	The communications channels between a system or network and the 'outside' world can be used by an adversary in many ways. An adversary can pretend to be an authorized user of the channel, jam it and thus deny its use to the adversary or eavesdrop on the channel to obtain information intended by the adversary to be classified or kept secret.
Configuration	Most systems provide a variety of configuration options that users can set based on their own tradeoffs between security and convenience. Because convenience is often valued more than security, many systems are configured insecurely.
Users and operators	Authorized users and operators of a system or network can be tricked or blackmailed into doing the bidding of an adversary or sell their services.
Service providers	Many computer installations rely on outside parties to provide computer-related services, such as maintenance or internet service. An adversary may be able to persuade a service provider to take some special action on its behalf, such as installing attack software on a target computer.

The potential for damage that cyberwar can inflict on national and economic security could be immense. Unfortunately, not much knowledge about Computer Network Attack capabilities is available. There are very few case studies. Most information lies outside the public domain.

This weaponisation of cyberspace also has adverse consequences. WannaCry and NotPetya attacks of 2017, which caused massive economic harm, spread autonomously to computer systems across dozens of countries and hundreds of enterprises in a matter of hours. These are perfect examples as nation-state developed exploit software was leaked and repurposed in these attacks. WannaCry disabled the United Kingdom's National Health System, putting lives at risk in the process.

As of now, cyber alone is unlikely to win wars. There is considerable risk for an attacking state of uncontrollable blowback effects in the highly networked virtual space. The states that are most likely to develop the technology for strategic cyberwar are also most dependent on their ICT infrastructures, making them highly vulnerable in a cyberwar. It is unlikely that there will ever be a pure cyberwar fought exclusively with cyber weapons.

Generally, cyberwar is seen as a new kind of war that is cheaper, cleaner, with less or no bloodshed and less risky for an attacker than other forms of armed conflict. So this looks as if cyberwar is attractive.

The elements that make cyberwar attractive are:[20]

- Cyberwar is cheaper since it does not require large numbers of troops and weapons.
- The entry costs are low. With a computer and Internet access, anyone can engage in cyber warfare.
- Cyberwar is easy to deliver by stealth via global connectivity from anywhere.
- Tools for attack are cheap and openly available on the Internet.
- The proliferation of such tools happens without any control.
- There are no technological, financial or legal hurdles to overcome against that proliferation.
- There is an advantage for the attacker who can profit from the latest and newest innovations.
- Cyberspace offers the attacker anonymity because it is very difficult to trace the origin of an attack.
- Cyberspace gives disproportionate power to small and otherwise relatively insignificant actors.
- Operating behind false IP addresses, foreign servers and aliases, attackers can act with almost complete anonymity and relative impunity, at least in the short term.
- Cyberwar may help to avoid the need to engage in combat operations and thus saves lives.
- Cyberwar leads to the ability to disrupt the adversary rather than destroy his forces.
- Blurred traditional boundaries: Cyberwarfare creates its own fog and friction of war.

- Inherent in cyberwar are the difficulties of tactical warning and attack or damage assessments.
- Cyberwar enables actors to achieve political and strategic goals without the need for armed conflict.
- Cyberwar skips the battlefield. Systems that people rely upon, from banks, the electric power grid, to air defence radars, are accessible worldwide from cyberspace and can be quickly taken over or knocked out without first defeating a country's traditional defences.
- Cyberwar happens at almost the speed of light. As photons of attack packets stream down fibre-optic cables, the time between the launch of an attack and its effects is barely measurable, thus creating more risks for decision-makers, particularly in a crisis.
- The victim of an attack has to invest considerable resources into neutralising the threat, which requires teams of dedicated software and hardware experts with specific skill sets. Unfortunately, such persons are difficult to recruit and retain as the private industry offers more attractive terms for their talent.
- The vulnerabilities of countries increasingly dependent on complex, interconnected and networked information systems increase over time, thus providing adversaries with a target-rich environment.

Like other elements of the modern military, cyber forces are likely to be integrated into the overall battle strategy. Cyberweapons will be used individually, in combination, blended simultaneously with conventional kinetic weapons as force multipliers.[21]

Cyber Kill Chain[22]

The term kill chain is used by the U.S. military to describe the steps or stages an adversary takes to attack. Lockheed Martin applies the same concept to cybersecurity and explains the Cyber Kill Chain in its paper Intelligence-Driven Computer Network Defense Informed by Analysis of Adversary Campaigns and Intrusion Kill Chains.[23] The cyber kill chain model is a helpful construct for understanding the steps that an attacker must go through to launch a successful cyber operation. The cyber kill chain is defined as "a systematic process to target and engage an adversary to create desired effects." A cyber intrusion requires an aggressor to develop a payload, breach a trusted boundary, establish a presence within a trusted environment and take actions within that environment. The attacker must accomplish the following seven steps in the cyber kill-chain:

- **Reconnaissance.** The attacker starts by researching, identifying and selecting targets. Reconnaissance may also involve examining vulnerabilities and exploits for possible use in later steps of the kill-chain.
- **Weaponisation.** Malware is coupled with an exploit and payload to create a cyber weapon.
- **Delivery.** This step consists of transmitting a weapon to its target. Delivery can be accomplished via several means, including phishing emails and the use of infected USB drives.
- **Exploitation.** After the weapon has been delivered to the target system, code is activated that enables the weapon to take advantage of the particular exploit it was designed to use.
- **Installation.** After the exploitation code has been run, the weapon installs the payload into the target system. The code is now embedded in the trusted environment, often without the defender knowing that this has occurred.
- **Command and Control.** The installed code is inside the target system, and most often, it will beacon back to let the attacker know that it is in place. The attacker can then send instructions to the malware.
- **Actions on Objectives.** The attacker is now in a position to take actions within the target environment. These actions could focus on denial, degradation, disruption, destruction or manipulation of data.

Organisations worldwide have adopted this model to help them better defend against more advanced/targeted threats.

The seven steps of the cyber kill chain can be grouped into three broad phases: pre-launch, launch and post-launch. The pre-launch phase includes intelligence gathering and reconnaissance, planning, weaponisation and testing. The second phase focuses on the delivery of the weapon via a propagation method. The third phase consists of post-intrusion activities: installing the malware on the target system, command and control of the malware and actions on objectives. The attacker may also attempt to assess the damage of the operation.[24]

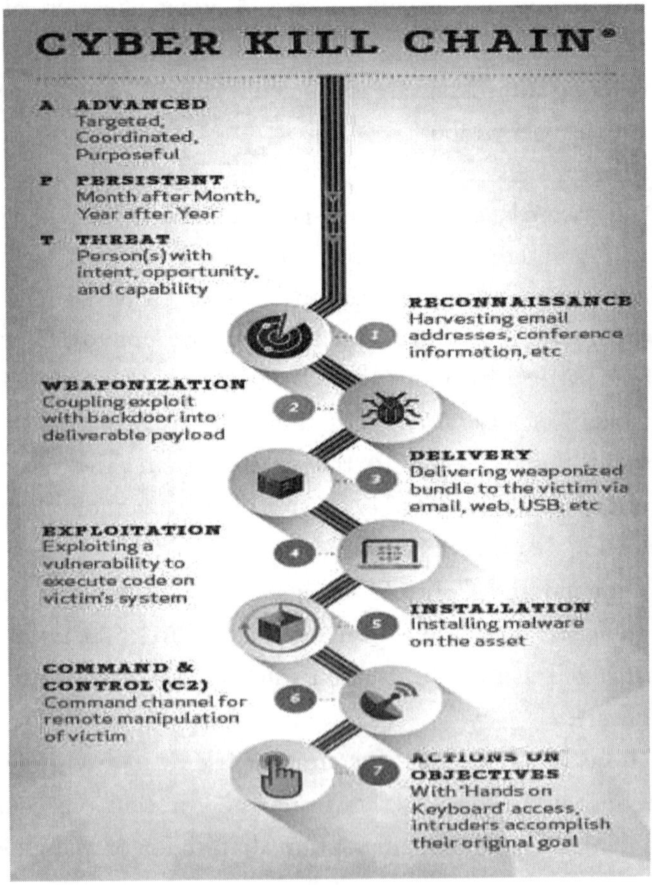

Source: Intelligence-Driven Computer Network Defense Informed by Analysis of Adversary Campaigns and Intrusion Kill Chains, available at: http://www.lockheedmartin.com/content/dam/lockheed/data/corporate/documents/LM-White-Paper-Intel-Driven-Defense.pdf

"Hack-back"

Hack-back is the practice of victimised actors, often via some expert service provider hired to help mitigate the costs of an attack, undertaking their offensive cyber operations to find and delete stolen information, monitor an attacker after the fact and minimise the chance of a future assault. In practice, hack-back often occurs in several stages, which are illustrated in Figure below.

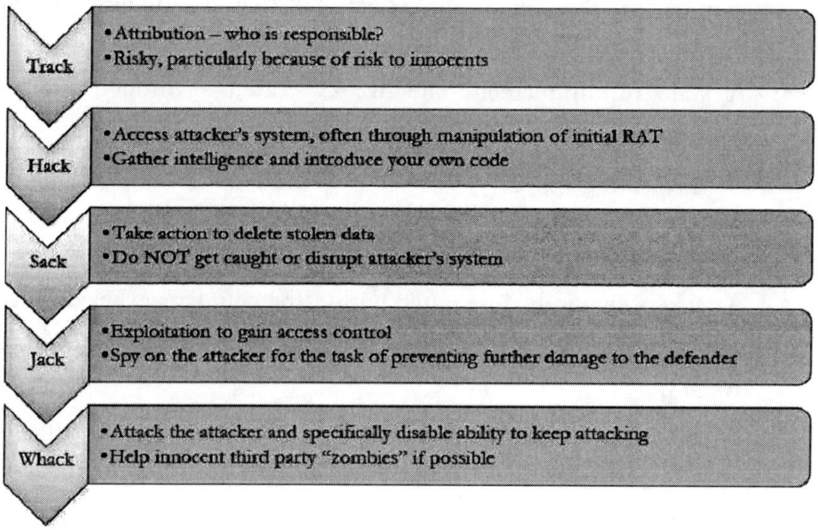

Hack-back is not legal. In the U.S., it cannot be done without a special court warrant which has rarely been issued. In Europe, it violates the Council of Europe Cybercrime Convention. However, a niche industry exists that use proxy servers in foreign countries and personnel based overseas to bypass legal restrictions.

Guidelines for formulating an attack strategy.[25] A broad guideline for formulating a cyberattack strategy can be summarised as under:

- In both emergency and routine situations, security organisations should be required to integrate tools for cyberattacks in their operative plans and the actual use of force in battle.
- Cyberattack ability should not stand alone but should be part of a general plan to influence a comprehensive, overt conflict.

- If integrated within a general plan, an effective cyberattack may be implemented against a focused target through a superficial, rapid, broad attack of objectives other than "gold targets" (military targets, state infrastructure).
- An effective attack need not be a sophisticated attack. A cyberattack can significantly harm a target that is not "cyber rich" and technologically developed. A highly developed technological state may be more vulnerable to cyberattack than an underdeveloped one because it has fewer defence abilities.
- A state can implement effective cyberattacks through proxies without taking responsibility as part of an overt war, while the state accepts responsibility for the kinetic aspect.
- A significant cyberattack requires a build-up of force, knowing the target and advance planning.
- Attackers should be integrated within the country's cyber defence system as part of the regular planning and operation of the defence system.
- A cyberattack can serve as a layer in interstate dialogue, with the attack's goal being to send a message, usually a warning.

Features of Offensive Cyber Operations (OCO)

OCO can be carried out in times of peace and war in conflicts with different intensity with and without kinetic force. It can influence the activities of all other domains of warfare and lead to escalation or de-escalation. The exact nature and utility of usage fundamentally differ for counter value and counterforce capabilities, as evident in conventional operations.

Cyber operations should not be considered in isolation. States respond to cyber intrusions using the threat of military force, legal charges, sanctions and a host of other mechanisms they can muster. In democratic countries, 85 per cent of critical infrastructure is with the private sector. A state cannot go on the offence unless private networks are sufficiently secure and resilient. After a major cyber incident, the state has to ensure that continuity of the economy and other measures required to bring networks back online. Layered cyber deterrence, therefore, focuses on deterrence by denial to protect the connectivity we all rely on in the 21st century.[26]

OCO can be taken for defensive purposes for the following:

- Before the adversary attack.
- Forestall offensive cyber action about to be undertaken by the adversary.
- Provide early warning of adversary cyberattack. For this defender must penetrate adversary networks before a tactical threat emerges.
- During the adversary attack.
- Disrupting a cyberattack in progress by disabling the attacking computers.
- After adversary attack.

OCO can be undertaken for following purposes:

- Traditional military operations.
- Suppression of adversary weapons (e.g., air defences).
- Interference with adversary command and control.
- Disruption of logistics chains.
- Non- traditional operations like covert action.
- Influencing the outcome of a foreign election like hacking voter registration, destroying pension records, conducting information warfare.
- Destabilising a nation through attacks on the financial system.
- Damaging an adversary's nuclear weapons production facilities.
- Damaging personal reputation of adversaries, manipulating perceptions.
- Attacks on critical infrastructure like Power grid, Transportation, Financial infrastructure, Communications, etc.

Military Cyber Strategy on OCO:

- OCOs will be conducted as per the laws of war.
- Targets of OCOs include opponent's command and control networks, military-related critical infrastructure and weapons capabilities.

- OCOs may be conducted before the outbreak of outright hostilities.
- Offensive capabilities with significant effects for disruption of an adversary's military-related networks or infrastructure so that the own military can protect self-interests in an area of operations.

Integration of Cyber Warfare in a Conventional Military Operations

Armed conflict takes place at the strategic, operational and tactical level. These are hierarchically organised and mutually supporting. In an ideal Clausewitzian, linear model of warfare, all of these levels are directed toward attaining a political objective. The policy directs the strategy employed to achieve it.

With the emergence of cyberspace, tactical and operational questions have taken precedence over strategic ones. Cyber operations and tactics are different from conventional ones due to the battlefield's unique nature and scope. In conventional warfare, the battlefield is clearly defined within the various domains.

At the tactical level, attacks are defined by singular engagements. These may include disruptive attacks against critical infrastructures, such as DDoS attacks against critical infrastructure like the financial sector. At the operational level, destructive attacks against command and control and various communication systems may shift an opponent's capability. The effect may be measured based on repeated attacks that yield leverage in the form of knowledge or reduced willingness to fight.

The cyber operation is likely to be a part of any conventional military campaign in future. For example, it can disrupt an air defence system, enabling an aircraft in performing its mission. Cyber warriors may require the support of others to facilitate their operations like cyberattack against air-gapped or otherwise isolated systems. The rival country's political will can be adversely affected by aerial attacks, naval blockade and cyber operation.

Any decision to conduct cyber warfare against an enemy will be decided at the highest strategic level. A cyberattack can disrupt the lawful operation of foreign governments, industry and society. Armed forces worldwide face a unique set of issues to develop appropriate rules of engagement for interactions with the security elements of opponent states. There is an argument with valid reasons that the nature of the cyber domain suggests that all attacks are potentially strategic in nature. The fundamental interconnectedness of networks would not allow the effects to be meaningfully limited, controlled or known beforehand. No matter how discretely intentioned any given cyberattack, it would have substantial unintended consequences. This would cause unknown but potentially significant political risk.

Military forces must determine:

- Conditions under which the undertaking of cyberattacks is permissible.
- Specific profile of targets that can be attacked.
- Duration of an assault.
- Necessary communications surrounding an attack.
- Lines of communication within the government necessary to authorise different forms of action.

Integrating cyber effects

Military cyber operations should be coordinated, synchronised and integrated with all other military capabilities across the strategic, operational and tactical levels of operations. The problem with the armed forces is they do not yet understand how to conduct cyberspace operations. They do not have strategies to implement agile command and control system to face the complex dynamics presented by the cyber domain. Admiral Mike Rogers, then Commander of U.S. Cyber Command, in 2015, stated, "Our traditional command and control and organisational constructs do not enable the speed and agility required to keep pace with change in the cyber domain. We must adapt, and soon!" The armed forces have to think about cyberspace afresh to meet new challenges.[27]

Force Multiplier. Another significant characteristic of cyberwarfare is using cyberweapons as a force multiplier for conventional military operations. Cyberweapons are well suited for attacks on logistical networks, command and control facilities and reinforcements to "induce operational paralysis, which reduces the enemy's ability to move and coordinate forces in the theatre."[28] Cyberweapons may not have a direct kinetic effect on an adversary's weapon systems like tanks and aircraft. But cyberattacks can render some of these weapons useless.

Strategic effects. Cyber is not affected by physical geography. Cyber's virtual and flexible properties can create various impacts in terms of complexity and severity and at a scale that can be controlled. It may offer options to hold strategic target sets at risk that otherwise would be unreachable. The 2008 Stuxnet attack against the Iranian nuclear programme is an excellent example of cyber enabling operations for strategic effect.

Operational effects. Integrating cyber capability into operational level planning in military operations is a new and evolving process. A high degree of integration and cooperation is needed with units and organisations that routinely operate at the strategic level to create cyber effects successfully. It is entirely plausible that cyber operations would have been taking place for some time before conventional forces are deployed.

Tactical effects. It takes time to develop access and invest in capability. At the tactical level, this may mean that creating high-end cyber effects is reserved for early or essential actions that have a high pay-off. However, lower-level attacks may increasingly be seen in operations. The Israeli integration of cyber operations into the conventional bombing of a Syrian nuclear installation in Operation Orchard is an excellent example of the operational/tactical use of cyber.

Time. Cyber accesses take years to develop. This knowledge of specific accesses and capabilities, understandably, will be held at the highest classification levels and tightly controlled. While the preparatory phase can take years, the execution phase may take only seconds.

Strategic level

The Strategic level of warfare is the level of warfare at which a nation determines national strategic security objectives and guidance, then develops and uses national resources to achieve its objectives.[29] In conventional warfare, strategic operations can be carried out by long-range strikes against rear areas or the opponent's heartland, including against civilian targets. Cyberattacks can be used to disrupt services and degrade morale rather than cause mass destruction. Enemy's critical infrastructure, including electrical power grids and power generation facilities, telecommunications and financial systems, transportation systems and government networks, are attractive targets for cyberattacks supporting military operations.

Cyber Conflict Issues.[30] Many issues have to be discussed, debated and resolved at the highest level before a policy on the use of cyber operations at the strategic level can be arrived at. Some of these issues are:

- Will cyberwarfare constitute an effective form of coercive power?
- What type of large-scale effects be achieved through cyberattacks?
- Could cyberwar be used to conduct economic coercion, sanctions, blockades, etc.?
- Can cyberwarfare be used for deterrent purposes?
- What factors will govern the capacity of a state or organisation to deter cyberattack?
- What characteristics of cyberwarfare capabilities will constitute the most effective deterrent means versus what sorts of adversaries?
- What are the thresholds for a response to be established?
- How will adversaries signal intent/communicate in situations involving cyber warfare capabilities?
- How would coercive and deterrent uses of cyberwarfare forces likely fail or fall short?
- How can states and organisations establish the most effective defences?
- How will cyber defence effectiveness interact with the effectiveness of other coercive means, particularly economical or military?
- Will cyberwarfare influence regional security dynamics?
- How will disadvantaged groups or states view opportunities and risks?
- How will strategic culture influence its adoption and use?

- How would cyberwarfare impact crisis stability and crisis management considerations?
- Will threats of decapitation or paralysing communications substantially change crisis dynamics?
- What types of events are most likely to exacerbate crises involving cyberwarfare?
- How do difficulties of attribution and the possibility for "spoofing" particularly influence these considerations relative to cyberwarfare?
- What are the possibilities for collateral damage and/or unintended effects from the use of specific cyberwarfare capabilities, particularly malicious code?
- How should command and control arrangements be orchestrated?
- How would cyberwar influence war termination dynamics?

Operational level

At the level of operational and tactical military commanders. Rules of Engagement (ROE) for operational commanders to respond with latitude to enable action like in other domains should be clear. In conventional war, these are clear. Written orders are issued. This allows commanders to organise their forces as needed to counter adversary action.

Commanders on the ground should understand the cyberspace domain to include human interaction that spans the entire spectrum from competition to conflict. They should recognise that the defence ministry and intelligence agencies are in continuous engagement with adversaries.

Speed is of the essence in the cyber domain. Measurement of risk in cyberspace is important. Assessment of risk at the tactical level and providing timely and relevant information to operational commanders is essential. Do we have the ability to do that? The intelligence process has to include cyber factors.[31]

Cyber Capabilities at Operational and Tactical Levels (Corps HQ and Below). OCO conducted to support Corps and below can temporarily disable enemy weapon systems and critical infrastructure to minimise death and destruction on the modern battlefield. Alternatively, it could open wide a digital Pandora's Box of unforeseen and unexpected events released at the speed of light. It can have significant negative strategic, operational and tactical ramifications. These unintended consequences can include the loss of the capability, adversary network access in other geographic combatant commands, risk of digital fratricide and risk of adversary retaliation. Given the tremendous resources needed to develop and procure OCO capabilities by nation states there is a requirement for extensive analysis and study before getting into such activities at the tactical level.[32]

Operational Military Issues in Cyber Conflict.[33] Cyberwarfare plays a role at the tactical, operational and strategic levels of war: from impacting engagement systems at the tactical level, to the adversary's ability to mass and synchronise forces at the operational level, to the ability of senior leadership to maintain clear situational awareness of the national security environment at the strategic level.

OCOs are conducted against strategic targets. They have typical mission time frames lasting weeks, months or even years. Strategic targets require long lead times to identify vulnerabilities, develop capabilities to exploit these vulnerabilities and execute missions against these targets. This allows extensive testing and confirmation of these payloads to minimise collateral damage.

At the tactical level of operations in Corps and below level, the rapid pace of operations does not allow extensive detailed planning. Targets at the Corps and below level are typically opportunistic or time-sensitive. The cyber kill chain of reconnaissance, weaponisation, delivery, exploitation, installation, command and control and actions on objective must be much faster. Military commanders and their staff below the national command level cannot assess risks for conducting OCO. The leadership of armed forces lacks the fundamental understanding of not only the technical aspects of cyberspace activity but also the political, economic, social implications and are unprepared to answer questions associated with what cyberspace is or how to conduct cyberspace operations. This could lead to unanticipated and unintended consequences.

The following issues need to be looked into critically:

- How can we measure/evaluate cyber warfare capabilities?
- What considerations will influence targeting strategy to achieve coercive, deterrent and defensive objectives with cyber warfare capabilities?
- How can cyber warfare capabilities be best integrated with other military forces?
- How will they affect evolving operational concepts?
- How do they influence the development of advanced C4ISR or space capabilities?
- How can leaders and personnel for conducting cyber warfare be trained, educated and grown?
- How can conflict scenarios involving cyber warfare be evaluated?
- What are the relative strengths and weakness of modelling, simulation, gaming and exercises?
- How will cyber warfare capabilities factor into evaluating conflicts involving other forces?
- How can capabilities enhance transparency related to cyberwarfare capabilities and operations be developed?
- How can actors more quickly attribute the sources of attacks/disruptions?
- Will international cooperation play a key role?
- How can visualisation, collaboration and information discovery technologies enhance situational awareness and decision making in cyber conflict?

Tactical Level

In February 2014, then Chief of Staff of the U.S. Army, Gen Ray Odierno stated that: "We have to be able to do that and potentially be able to conduct tactical offensive cyber operations, because I think in the future, that'll be another way for us to maneuver in the battlespace that we might be in. So I think we have to develop those techniques."

Cyber actions at the tactical or operational level can be used against deployed forces and their support echelons. The most probable form of attack is against command and control systems, including sensors and computer networks, against the software that runs advanced weapons such as Surface to Air Missiles or fighter aircraft. All offensive cyber capability is not practical at the tactical echelon. There are four key factors that determine whether Army cyber operations are suitable at the tactical level:

- **Proximity** refers to how physically close a soldier needs to get to a target to employ OCO.
- **Frequency** refers to how often a tactical unit is expected to perform OCO.
- **Expertise** refers to the degree to which highly trained experts are required to perform OCO.
- **Containment of effects** refers to the ability to keep OCO effects within a bounded area for a predetermined duration.

Disadvantages of the Tactical Environment. Tactical networks have limited bandwidth. They also have high bit error rates, high latency and intermittent connectivity. Both the users and the infrastructure are mobile. Command and Control data pass through these channels. Additional security measures cause data flow challenges. The distributed nature of Army tactical networks, combined with adversary proximity, makes it easier for an adversary to intercept communications. This problem is aggravated when tactical units are within an adversary's radio line of sight. However, the adversary is also vulnerable in this situation.[34]

The drawback with tactical cyber operations is that cyberspace is not tied to the same geographic boundaries as in conventional operations.[35] The potential impact of cyber operations at the tactical level may be on the diplomatic, information, military, economic, financial, intelligence and legal (DIMEFIL) situation. Cyberspace's lack of geographical constraints may make any deconfliction process too long and complicated. It makes cyberspace effects outside of a controlled battle space too unresponsive to be relevant to a tactical operation.

Tactical military commanders nowadays are aware of the potential of OCO. They want to control cyber capabilities on the battlefield, given the nature of the trajectory of future wars.[36] They are looking for the following:[37]

- Enabling warfighters to utilise cyber at the tactical level, use commercial smartphones, tablets and laptops to securely access classified information over Wi-Fi and Long Term and Evolution (LTE) technology.
- To shut down the enemy's communication in a critical phase of the battle.
- To deny a local insurgent group access to a social media service they have been using for communication or shut off a video camera to blind the adversary during an operation to the targeted infrastructure.
- In tactical formations of advances armed forces like the U.S., many systems already exist to help a commander gain intelligence in cyberspace. It includes the ability to map adversary networks, identify potential vulnerabilities and perform counter reconnaissance operations to either confuse or deny hacking attempts. This requires augmentation.

Goals and Objectives for Tactical Cyber Operations. The recommended goals and objectives for cyber operations at the tactical level may be:[38]

- Defend Tactical Assets and Key Cyber Terrain.
- Enable Effects Through Tactical Offensive Cyber Operations.
- Provide the Means to Enable Cyber Derived Intelligence to support the Tactical Commander. Data and information made available through social media or shared through cyberspace have value to military planners. The armed forces need to develop capabilities to process and analyse these data for use by tactical organisations.

Problem Areas. There are issues that need to be resolved before OCO is attempted at the tactical level. Some of them are:

- There is a severe shortage of trained cyber specialists available to combat threats in real-time on the battlefield. This is not merely a manpower issue.
- There is confusion and gaps at the organisational and cultural levels. Changing the cyberspace organisational structure to align responsibilities with proper authorities is a challenging task.
- Apparent lack of knowledge at the decision-maker's level in the utilisation of tactical cyberspace operations employment.
- There are challenges for integrating cyberspace operations at the tactical level due to lack of knowledge, training, capability, authority, policy and approval.

There are two fundamental cyber capabilities which are required at the tactical level:

- Defending tactical assets and key terrain, including command and control systems, weapons systems and vehicles.
- Enabling effects through tactical OCO.

DOTMLPF-P Model[39]

DOTMLPF-P is the acronym for the U.S. DoD model methodology for Doctrine, Organisation, Training, Materiel, Leadership Education, Personnel, Facilities and Policy. This model represents categories of solutions required to create an operational capability from Information Technology (IT) and other technology products. This is an authoritative intellectual tool in DoD's efforts to improve efficiency and effectiveness.[40] To develop OCO capabilities for military applications, attention must be paid to Doctrine, Organisation, Training, Materiel, Leadership Education, Personnel, Facilities and Policy.

DOTMLPF-P[41] is defined as:

- **Doctrine**. The way we fight, e.g., emphasising manoeuvre warfare combined air-ground Campaigns.
- **Organisation**. How we organise to fight in the Air, Land, Maritime, Space and cyber domain.

- **Training**. How we prepare to fight tactically; basic training to advanced individual training, various types of unit training or joint exercises.
- **Material**. All the items are necessary to equip the forces, that is, weapons, spares, and communication, so the force can operate effectively.
- **Leadership and education**. How we prepare and educate our leaders to lead the fight from squad leader to 4-star General or equivalent.
- **Personnel**. Availability of qualified people for peacetime, wartime and various contingency operations.
- **Facilities**. Real property, installations and cyber range facilities that support own forces.
- **Policy**. Common approaches and procedures.

Questions. Several questions on important aspects of DOTMLPF-P need to be critically analysed. This is meant for the Army. Issues are similar in the Air Force and Navy. Some of them are:

Doctrine Questions

- How will the Army concurrently develop Cyber Operations doctrine with the evolution of the cyberspace domain and cyber commands? Joint and Army Cyber Operations concepts and doctrine should be on the same wavelength.
- Does current Army doctrine adequately address Army Cyber Operations capabilities and integration with the other Army operations and functions and with joint operations throughout a joint campaign?
- How does emerging joint Cyber Ops doctrine influence the conduct of Army operations?
- Does joint and Army doctrine adequately address the joint interdependence in the area of cyberspace and Cyber Ops?
- What are the impacts of national and international law on joint and Army Cyber Ops doctrine?

- Are cyberspace and Cyber Ops adequately addressed in Army doctrine for the theatre, corps, and division (and below) doctrinal publications?
- Are current Tactics, Techniques and Procedures adequate to execute required Army Cyber Ops?
- What emerging Cyber Ops technologies, processes and capabilities need to be codified in Army doctrine?
- What types of joint command and control and battle command operations may be impacted by Army Cyber Ops doctrine?
- Does the Cyber Ops doctrine help the commander on the ground?
- Does the Cyber Ops doctrine provide the commander with an ability to affect operations?

Material Questions

- How will compatibility and interoperability, as well as operational effectiveness, be achieved for Cyber Ops systems?
- What technologies are critical to consider and invest in to develop effective and capable Cyber Ops material solutions.
- Given the crowded nature of the Electromagnetic Spectrum (EMS), how can the Army effectively operate in cyberspace and the EMS?
- Given the technical nature of Cyber Ops systems, how will the Army develop personnel and organisations capable of effectively executing Cyber Ops planning, command and control, operations and maintenance?
- How will the Army effectively integrate Cyber Ops capabilities given the highly interdependent and interrelated nature of other operations like Electronic Warfare?
- Since Cyber Ops capabilities often have a short shelf life, what is the most effective and efficient way to use Research, Development, Test & Evaluation (RDT&E) and acquisition processes to gain and maintain advantage?

Leadership and Education Questions

- How does the Army develop adaptive leaders who understand cyberspace and Cyber Ops, know how to integrate and employ Cyber, and recognise and adopt advanced technologies into an operational advantage?
- How do we provide collaborative, distributed training aids that support commanders and staff during planning, preparation, rehearsal, and execution of cyberspace exercises and integration?
- How can Cyber Ops be incorporated into training exercises and leader development to develop Cyber Ops planning and operations?
- How does the Army best educate leaders and Soldiers to understand the complex and ever-changing future Operational Environment?

Military Leadership

Military commanders and their staff are generally ill-prepared to assess risks for conducting offensive cyber operations (OCO). The man-made cyber domain exhibits following unique traits that differentiate itself from the traditional military domains:

- A lack of permanence exists for objects within the domain as they appear, disappear or change at rapid speed.
- The domain lacks measures of effectiveness for operations. The view of the virtualised battlefield is limited and an accurate feedback loop for actions and effects does not exist.
- Actions within this domain occur at computational speed or near the speed of light.
- The ability of an attacker to remain anonymous or even to masquerade as another entity. Proxy servers and The Onion Router (TOR) make attribution of an attack difficult, if not impossible.
- Cyber operations are characterised by a lack of detection by the targets for intelligence gathering and destructive effects until it is too late to defend themselves.

Because commanders and their staff lack experience, education and expertise in cyberspace operations, the decision-makers cannot assess the risks involved in OCO. Cyber operations have the potential to be considered mixed gambles, where both gains and losses may coincide. This is more vital in cyberspace operations as a superbly executed operation may still not yield the desired end-state of the commander as they will lack perfect knowledge of a target configuration or hardware.[42]

Personnel Questions

- How do we recruit and retain the personnel necessary to perform Army Cyber Ops functions?
- What skill sets are required in Army civilian and contractor support personnel?
- What are the best means of selecting Army Cyber Ops officers?
- Should the Army pre-commissioning programs include a Cyber Ops component?
- What is the right mix of personnel between Cyber Ops professionals and other personnel selected to serve in Cyber Ops related positions?
- What will be the Cyber Ops personnel impacts as they relate to other proponents?
- What will be the personnel end strength impacts as related to required Cyber Ops capabilities?

Concept of Operations

Since OCO, especially in the cyber domain, is highly classified, not much informations is available about even the concept of operations. United States Cyber Command (USCYBERCOM) was established in June 2009. During the raising of the organisation, the concept of cyber operations was debated extensively. U.S. Cyber Command developed a Concept of Operations which was released in November 2010. It lays out broad roles and responsibilities for cyberspace operations. This generally meets joint guidance. The concept of operations must have changed over the last decade. However, the Concept of Operations, Version 1.0 (September 21, 2010) gives valuable input about the thinking behind it.

U.S. Cyber Command's Concept of Operations. U.S. Cyber Command's Concept of Operations recognises that a majority of cyber operations will originate at the theatre and local levels, thereby placing them under the immediate control of the geographic combatant commanders and their components and recognises that nearly all cyberspace operations can simultaneously affect the global theatre and local levels because cyberspace operations can be virtually unconstrained by geography.

When a cyberspace operation is confined to the area of responsibility of one geographic combatant command, U.S. Cyber Command will act as a supporting commander to the geographic combatant commander.

When the cyberspace operations impact global functions or create effects across the borders of more than one geographic combatant command's area of responsibility, the geographic combatant commanders may support U.S. Cyber Command, as directed.

DoD Global Information Grid operations, USCYBERCOM Concept of Operations, Version 1.0 (September 21, 2010)

- Actions taken to direct and provide guidance and unity of effort to support efforts to design, build, configure, secure, operate, maintain, and sustain DOD networks to create and preserve availability, integrity, authentication, confidentiality and non-repudiation information.
- Proactive Network Operations, the major operational method by which U.S. Cyber Command will conduct this line of operation, anticipates vulnerabilities and takes actions to preserve availability, confidentiality, integrity, and non-repudiation prior to discovering threats and intrusions.

U.S. Cyber Command. Offensive cyberspace operations USCYBERCOM Concept of Operations, Version 1.0

- Proactive Network Operations, the major operational method by which U.S. Cyber Command will conduct this line of operation, anticipates vulnerabilities and takes actions to preserve availability, confidentiality, integrity and non-repudiation before discovering threats and intrusions.

- Creation of various enabling and attack effects in cyberspace, to meet or support national and combatant commander's objectives and to actively defend DoD or other information networks, as directed.
- The primary U.S. Cyber Command offensive operational method will be effects-based operational planning and execution, maximising leveraging and coordination across DOD and the interagency to meet objectives.
- Offensive targeting will be conducted using the guidance, apportionment and tasking process.[43]

Cyber Weapons

Intelligence Community and militaries worldwide have developed new tools for exploiting, subverting, degrading and destroying adversaries' informational assets. This category of capabilities is loosely described as 'cyber weapons'. There is no single definition of Cyber Weapons. Rid and McBurney define cyber weapons as "computer code that is used, or designed to be used, to threaten or cause physical, functional, or mental harm to structures, systems, or living beings."

Cyber weapon is the combination of three factors:

- **Vulnerability**. A weakness or flaw in hardware or software that can be taken advantage of by an attacker. Vulnerabilities are properties inherent in the systems (hardware or software) that one seeks to "hack."
- **Exploit**. Programs are written to take advantage of a vulnerability and cause a specific effect, such as gaining access to a system or shutting down a piece of hardware.
- **Propagation Method**. In this, an exploit is delivered to a target, such as a phishing email.

The payload of a missile is the warhead with some explosive. In case of a cyber weapon, the payload could be a software program that copies information from the computer and sends it back to an external source. It can also be a program that alters and manipulates information stored in the system. It can allow remote access so that the computer can be controlled or directed over the Internet.[44]

Cyber weapons are written in computer code. They can infiltrate whole networks or infect individual computers. They rely on software vulnerabilities, poor cyber hygiene and people who inadvertently open attachments infected with malware. They can confuse the enemy, shut down military attacks before they occur and baffle communication systems. A lot of hard work has to be done beforehand to figure out what targets to hit and maintain access.

Cyber weapons can be installed in hardware also. Backdoors can be embedded in hardware and installed at any point in the supply chain, from initial fabrication to the process of shipping a finished system to an end-user. If the payload causes data exfiltration, we call this cyber exploitation. If the payload causes damage, destruction, degradation, or denial, the use is called a cyberattack.

Cyberattacks often create cascade effects that were outside the original intentions of the attacker. Reverse-engineering and analysis of malicious code used in recent sophisticated cyberattacks have revealed four common characteristics that help provide a more precise and practical definition for a cyber weapon:[45]

- A campaign that may amalgamate multiple malicious programs for espionage, data theft or sabotage.
- An attacker with intimate knowledge of details for the workings of the targeted system.
- A stealth capability that facilitates undetected operation within the targeted system over an extended time period.
- Special type of computer code to circumvent protective cyber security technology.

Cyber weapons will be used individually, in combination or simultaneously with conventional kinetic weapons as force multipliers. Cyber weapons have the following advantages:

- Easier to obtain and use.

- The cost to develop this new class of weapons is within reach of many countries, extremist or terrorist groups and individuals. Cybercrime organisations have been reported to develop cyber weapons.
- The raw materials in terms of hardware, software and skilled personnel needed to make cyber weapons are widely available.
- Cyber weapons are low-cost, low-risk, highly effective and easily deployable worldwide.
- Funding, timelines for procurement and sustainment costs will be much lower than those incurred by conventional weapons systems such as tanks and aircraft.
- Easier to use with plausible deniability and a higher degree of anonymity, making them well suited for covert operations.
- May operate on time scales ranging from a second to years. It can function anywhere from next door to anywhere in the globe.
- The weapons may initially act in a non-lethal manner. Subsequently, they may well have lethal effects.
- A larger range of options and possible outcomes.

Problem Areas. Employment of cyber weapons has the following disadvantages:[46]

- The outcome of cyberattacks is uncertain. It is difficult to estimate deliberate and collateral damage.
- Cyber weapons can be copied and their proliferation cannot be controlled. Stuxnet-inspired weapons and technology may soon be in the hands of rogue nation-states, terrorists, organised crime and hackers. These weapons may soon look different from the original.
- Their effects are global and cannot be limited to a specific geographic theatre.
- They are strategic in nature. Once used, they lose their deterrent value and effectiveness as knowledge of their specific capabilities may quickly spread across the Internet.
- They are not generally destroyed during an attack. Once released, such a weapon is relatively easy to capture. Cyber forces can analyse

and deconstruct its code to make suitable countermeasures for future attacks. The same may be used as a weapon against its sender.

- The conventional weapon systems including sensors, communication systems and control systems, are becoming vulnerable to cyber weapons as they become more automated and networked.
- Though the systems are embedded with highly advanced security, there is also a vulnerability to foreign access whenever there is an opportunity for interconnection.
- The life expectancy of any cyber weapon is only as good as the life of the vulnerability that the cyber weapon is designed to exploit. A program that can continually develop newer and more sophisticated methods to exploit anticipated emerging vulnerabilities is needed.

Use of Cyber Weapons. The use of cyber weapons on targets during a conflict or in peacetime can have disastrous consequences. However, there is a growing tendency of their use on the battlefield or in peacetime. U.S. has publicly acknowledged using cyber weapons in its fight against the Islamic State of Iraq and Syria (ISIS). In February 2016. Secretary of Defense Ash Carter said that the U.S. Cyber Command is conducting offensive cyber operations to cause ISIS to "lose confidence in their networks, to overload their networks so that they can't function, and do all of these things that will interrupt their ability to command and control forces."

There has been no reported loss of life directly linked to cyberattacks till date.[47] There is no international agreement on how cyber weapons should be regulated. There is an increasing temptation for nations to view cyber weapons as a form of warfare favouring or even replacing traditional negotiations that can be prolonged or frustrating. The danger is, the next generation of cyber weapons will increasingly target and destroy physical equipment in industrial and military facilities. Human casualties will not be too far.

In today's interconnected world, there is a danger of cyber weapons spilling into the open. Such spillage and a black market for malware create new risk vectors. In 2017, the National Security Agency of U.S. lost control of a cyber weapon known as EternalBlue. It was leaked online by a group known as 'the Shadow Brokers.

As states spy on each other, the malware used by them can be repurposed to attack commercial interests, support authoritarian domestic spying campaigns and compromise individual privacy.

In cyber operations, rules of engagement are not clear. The policies and laws governing the use of cyber weapons are still under development. Cyber warfare has blurred the line between nation-states and non-state actors and even between traditional notions of sovereignty and loyalty.

Cyber Weapon Market. Malicious code is available and can be traded and sold on the Dark Web by those with the resources to purchase it or exchange for illicit products and services. Cyber weapons are cheap and widely available in the market at a price for nation-states, criminals and harmful actors.

Non-state developers of cyber weapons are engaged continuously in research and development, creating new exploits. It is easy to buy malware to support blatant cyberattacks. Traditional arms control methods are difficult to enforce as cyber weapons are not in the exclusive control of nation-states.

There is a rising demand for offensive cyber tools and systems. It is predicted to rise as much as 39 per cent by 2027. This trend has led cyber experts to call it a 'cyber arms race', which is expected to expand shortly. Finnish IT expert Mikko Hypponen stated that "we might very well be spending the next 60 years in a cyber arms race." The most advanced companies like BAE Systems, CISCO Systems or Israeli Aerospace Industries(IAI) in this field are mainly located in the United States, Israel and Europe.

About a hundred nations have cyber organisations of some kind, on the lines of U.S. Cyber Command. The funding, number and quality of human resources, organisation, technical capability, willingness to use the weapon, policy, etc. may vary. Use of the beyond government resources are different for different countries. The U.S. tends to rely on private contracting companies. Russia has made use of criminal networks. China is linked to its cyber militia.

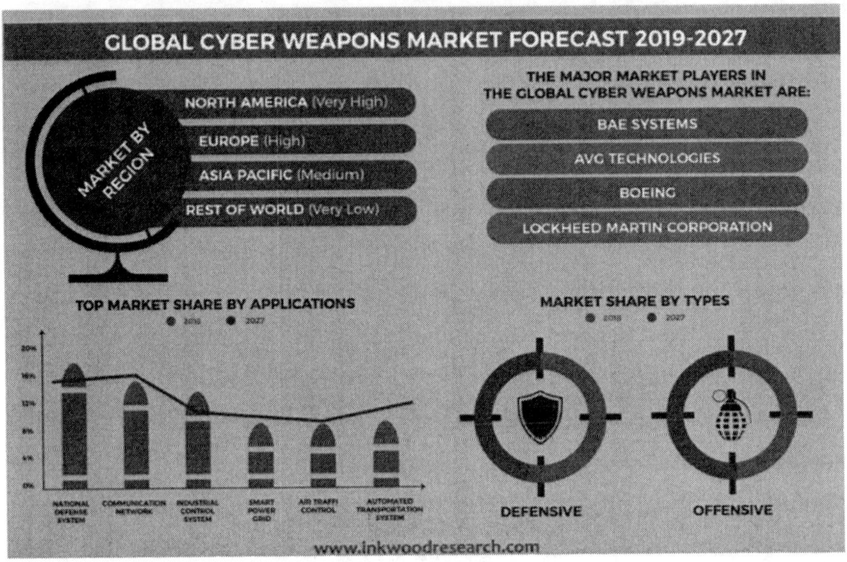

Source: 'Cyber Weapons: The New 'Arms Race'?', September 3, 2019, at https://finabel.org/cyber-weapons-the-new-arms-race/

The uncertain effects of cyber weapons, coupled with the availability of defences and the need for secrecy and surprise, reduce their ability to serve as a strategic deterrent in their own right. Available defences and the potential for network evolution to mitigate the effects of an attack given early warning requires cyberattackers to rely on the surprise for much of their effectiveness. To achieve surprise, secrecy is required, reducing the ability of a state to make credible threats without compromising its cyber warfare capabilities. Credible threats regarding specific means of attack or targets invite the vulnerable state to take protective actions that could blunt the threat's deterrent value.

Rules of Engagement (RoE)

As cyber operations are getting integrated with conventional warfare, policymakers, military planners and field commanders will increasingly face a fundamental issue: how to formulate the Rules of Engagement (RoEs) for armed forces. Military leaders act within a complex network of authorities derived from law, policy and regulation. Authorities provide commanders necessary permissions needed to conduct military operations. It includes the power to use force, of which RoEs are one crucial component.

The cyber-world is not an isolated battlefield. It is part of a larger overall conflict. Responses to the cyber are not always in the cyber field. It can be kinetic or a combination of both, among others.

Typically armed forces tend to apply the same principles that govern the use of kinetic weapons to use cyber weapons while recognising the unique characteristics of the cyber domain and cyber weapons. However, this has proven to be a difficult challenge.

If a military unit comes under cyberattack, it takes passive defence measures within the systems or networks for which they are responsible. They may use anti-virus systems, firewalls, intrusion detection systems (IDS), intrusion protection systems (IPS), deleting malware found on the systems or dropping connections that could be used for malicious purposes. However, the unit or the headquarters would not be allowed, on its own authority, to conduct a cyberattack or kinetic attack in response. It would require separate authority.[48]

Very few cyberattacks come in the military domain. If a cyberattack against the electrical grid causes a large-scale blackout resulting in thousands of death, what type of a response a nation-state will make? Should action to thwart an election include sending fighter aircrafts? Is that the proper response? What is the sliding scale of launching military offensives in cyberspace? Should it be in the cyber domain, or a kinetic reply or a combination of both?

In the case of physical attacks, the rules of engagement are clear and well-established. The challenge for military professionals is that incoming attacks are not predictable. There is a tendency to assume that the laws of conventional war extend to cyberspace also. Cyber warfare does have rules. These rules are not intuitive to Generals used to fighting conventional wars.

The U.S. Department of Defense (DoD) defines RoEs as "directives issued by competent military authority that delineate the circumstances and limitations under which U.S. forces will initiate and/or continue combat engagement with other forces encountered."[49] U.S. forces operate under three types of RoE:

Standing Rules of Engagement (SRoE). It provides a general set of always-operative rules related to self-defence for forces in peacetime and a template for operation-specific RoEs.

Supplemental RoEs. Also known as mission-specific RoEs, these are tailored for a region, a mission or a specific operation and may elaborate on and/or interpret the SRoEs for a given mission without contradicting them.

Standing rules for the use of force (SRUF). It governs military actions inside the U.S.

Difficulties of Comprehending Rules of Engagement for Cyberwar. Many aspects of the cyber conflict are revolutionary in nature. The following merits consideration:[52]

- The internet is an artificial environment that can be shaped in part as per national security requirements.
- The proximity of adversaries is determined by connectivity and bandwidth, not terrestrial geography.
- The blinding proliferation of technology and hacker tools makes it impossible to be familiar with all of them.
- Software updates and network reconfigurations increase the unpredictability of the battlespace of cyber conflict with little or no warning.
- Cyberattacks are flexible to be effective for information warfare and propaganda, espionage and critical infrastructure destruction.
- Cyber conflict favours the attacker.
- The difficulty of obtaining reliable attack attribution lessens the credibility of deterrence, retaliation and prosecution.
- The shortage of expertise and evidence can make victory, defeat and battle damage assessments a highly subjective undertaking.
- The nature of cyber conflict means a significant battle could take place with only the direct participants knowing about it.
- There are limited moral inhibitions to cyberattacks because they relate mainly to the use and abuse of data and computer code. Up to now, there is little perceived human suffering.

It will take many years to integrate all the revolutionary aspects of cyber conflict into military doctrine and formulate the RoEs. Developing appropriate rules for the use of cyber weapons is very difficult. RoEs are supposed to be developed before using these weapons so that proper guidance under operational conditions is available to the warfighters. Various contingencies must be anticipated in advance. However, it is not possible to imagine all possible contingencies before they happen. The following issues need solving:[51]

- RoEs must be developed to cope with the fact that several dimensions of cyberattacks span a more comprehensive range than those encountered in the classical warfighting domains.
- Cyberattacks may range from being non-lethal to destructive on a society-wide scale.
- The potential targets that may be adversely affected by cyberattacks are likely more extensive than the equivalent set of potential targets for other weapons.
- The impacts of cyberattacks may be easily predicted in some cases but may have a higher uncertainty than the impacts of kinetic weapons in other cases.
- A cyberattack conducted for offensive purposes may well require authorisation from higher command levels than a technically similar cyberattack conducted for defensive purposes.
- The adversary may range from being an individual hacker to a well-funded nation-state.
- The adversary might not react at all to a cyberattack or might even respond with weapons of mass destruction.

It is unrealistic to make a single RoE that would cover all aspects of cyberattack. Instead, it will be better to create a range of RoEs that apply to specific kinds of cyberattack for probable particular circumstances. The following issues elucidate the complexity of developing RoEs in advance by looking at the question under what circumstances a retaliatory cyberattack might be launched to neutralise an ongoing threat:

- Who should influence and who should develop RoEs for active threat neutralisation?
- What level of impact must an incoming cyberattack have to justify active threat neutralisation?
- How far are the intent and the identity of a cyberattacker relevant?
- How does the proportionality principle apply to active threat neutralisation?
- How far down the chain of command should delegation of authority for neutralisation be carried?
- How should the scope, duration and intensity of a neutralisation action be calibrated?

A further level of complication in developing RoEs is that the factors above cannot be assessed independently.

The factors described below create difficulties for formulating RoEs in the cyber domain:

Ambiguous intent. Determining the purpose behind cyber activity can be confusing. For instance, differentiating between enemy preparation for an imminent attack and enemy reconnaissance in cyberspace is very difficult. Yet, from a technical perspective, both operations involve essentially the same activities.

Differentiating between reconnaissance and routine intelligence collection is more complicated. The majority of adversary objectives in cyberspace are to create access to systems and data, maintain a persistent presence on those systems and steal information and intellectual property. Distinguishing hostile intent from other activities is a challenge for applying RoEs promptly.

The need for speed. In the conventional war reacting quickly is necessary to eliminate an immediate threat. Illuminating an aircraft with a fire-control radar indicates that a missile is about to be launched against it. Delaying the destruction of that radar will enable the aircraft to be attacked. In cyberspace, a response action is needed very quickly to eliminate or disrupt. Cyber RoEs should account for likely combination of enhanced machine-based indications and warning, careful automated responses and human decision making.

Hostile acts in cyberspace may cross national boundaries. The physical distance between the origin of the attack and where it has its effects may be considerable. The same is applicable for any defensive response action.

Cyberspace RoEs should cater for these geographic realities of cyberspace. In addition, coordination between armed forces and intelligence agencies will be needed when jurisdictions overlap.

An important question for anticipatory self-defence is the degree and nature of the evidence needed to determine an imminent attack. It could be based in part on information provided by human intelligence, technical intelligence or signals intelligence. In cyberspace, signals intelligence could include information derived from sensors that have been pre-positioned inside adversary networks.

While exercising the right of anticipatory self-defence the factor of necessity and proportionality has to be kept in mind.

Law

Some experts believe that current civilian and military laws can be the foundation for a future set of cyber warfare rules of engagement. However, many gaps exist that could confuse responses at the national level.

Technology and cyberspace are changing at a rapid speed. Usually, law is unclear to define what constitutes an illegal cyber act as opposed to regular computer activity by information security researchers. It makes obsolete the internally and externally negotiated legislature that countries make.

In 2017, Microsoft proposed a digital Geneva Convention, which outlined to constitute a multi-national effort to define the rules of engagement for cyberspace. One year later, UN Secretary-General Antonio Guterres called for the establishment of international rules of conduct for cyber warfare.

No definition can be adequate without international legitimacy. If a group of experts actually did convene to create binding digital Geneva

Conventions, it is not clear from what source it would derive its authority. In the absence of a binding global accord, the world will remain vulnerable to a diverse mix of hackers, warriors, intelligence operatives, criminals and angry teenagers.

NATO sponsored the Tallinn conference to address these issues. The Tallinn Manual Tallinn 2.0 was released in February 2017. The document presented scenarios that were designed for the most destructive and disruptive of cyber operations. International laws like those regulating telecommunications, diplomacy and war were applied. The document's 13 authors, known as the International Group of Experts, contributed legal commentary and made recommendations that could serve as a framework to create future rules of engagement. But the document was not widely adopted or seen as actionable. In the fog of a cyber war, this exercise using a web of laws was found to be too complex to understand and apply. Moreover, it is nonbinding and was not an official NATO publication. NATO is now on shaky ground. There is no assurance that the U.S. would abide by any agreement.

However, Michael Schmitt, Tallinn Manual project director and University of Exeter professor, believes that the trick is getting nations to acknowledge that the development of rules of engagement is happening in real-time, on a case-by-case basis. He says, "We act as if we can make up the rules of the game as we go along because there is nothing out there." Schmitt proposes that the next step should be to get like-minded countries and industry leaders together to start defining their rules and boundaries and build from there.

While creating a formal set of widely-understood rules of engagement in cyber warfare is a highly complex undertaking, experts are optimistic that they can be defined. They point towards the Law of the Sea as an example of a framework of laws defining how countries interact outside of defined national borders. This mentality can also be valid within the cyber domain. The international community has to see it that way. And that time is now.[52]

The international community must follow NATO's tentative footsteps in Tallinn and convene digital Geneva Conventions that produce a few deep, well-enforced rules regarding the conduct of the war in cyberspace. Without a global accord on what constitutes cyber war, the world will be left in a lawless state governed by contradictory laws and norms and exposed to the possibility of a shocking war launched by a few anonymous keystrokes.[53]

China and Cyber War

China's President Xi Jinping has stated clearly that his objective for China is to emerge as a 'cyber superpower'. China wants to be one of the world's most powerful nation in cyberspace. The information technology revolution has produced both significant opportunities and vulnerabilities for china. China hosts some of the world's most vibrant and successful technology companies. It also remains a major victim of cybercrime.

Chinese People's Liberation Army (PLA) believes that future wars will be contests in the ability to exploit information. The outcome of the war will be decided by the side that is better to generate, collect, transmit, evaluate and manipulate information.

In Informationised warfare, the lines between peacetime and wartime get blurred. In the information age, a nation cannot wait for the hostilities to break out to collect intelligence, carry out influence operations, develop anti-satellite systems or design computer software weapons. This warfare will include peacetime activities aimed at civilian and commercial entities and operations against rival military systems in war.

The "comprehensive national power" is the measurement of a state and society's power, It includes economic, military, diplomatic, political, science and technology and cultural components. Now it is measured in terms of information. The middle kingdom has emerged as a cyber superpower. It has enormous economic and military capabilities that augment its overall national power. It aggressively pursues emerging technologies like Artificial Intelligence (AI), big data, robotics, quantum computing and 5G technology.

In the unfolding fourth industrial revolution, this would enable China to flourish. China's cyber power is a critical component of its comprehensive national power. Recently in a study of cyber power of several countries, Harvard Kennedy School of Government has ranked China as the second most powerful nation after U.S.[54]

Cyber Exploitation Activities

Chinese hackers have done cyber espionage at emerging high-technology advanced manufacturing companies of industries, like semiconductors, biotechnology and aerospace in the U.S., Japan, Europe and Southeast Asia. They were interested in the financial information and negotiation strategies of companies in the banking, energy, law and pharmaceutical sectors. Keith Alexander, a former NSA Director, said that the Chinese operations enabled the "greatest transfer of wealth in history."

The Washington Post reported that Chinese hackers stole critical files relating to missile defence, including "the advanced Patriot missile system, ... an Army system for shooting down ballistic missiles, ... and the Navy's Aegis ballistic missile defence system." The hackers also gathered information on planes, helicopters, and ships, including "the F/A-18 fighter jet, the V-22 Osprey, the Black Hawk helicopter and the Navy's new Littoral Combat Ship, which is designed to patrol waters close to shore." These were the weapons on which the United States would rely in a fight with China.

Concept of Warfare

The PLA differs substantially from its Western counterparts in its approach to cyber operations. It does not use the word cyber as extensively as the West. PLA identify everything related to cyber advancements as the process as informatisation. PLA does not consider cyber power as a distinct capability like land, sea, air and space. PLA's experts view cyber operations as occurring in an information domain. This domain includes network, electronic warfare, psychological and media operations.

PLA theorists believe that 'network-electronic operations' will be vital to combat effectiveness as a new means of warfare. Cyber and network operations can be an 'indispensable method for deterring powerful enemies' with the potential to enable winning without fighting under certain conditions.

China's 2015 defence white paper emphasised that the PLA should be able to fight and win 'informationised local wars'. It stated: "integrated combat forces will be employed to prevail in system vs. system [i.e. C4ISR] operations featuring information dominance, precision strikes, and joint operations" to meet the offensive and defensive operational requirements of modern warfare.

The Science of Strategy, PLA's Current View of Warfare, published by the China's National Defence University (NDU) in 2017 explains that wars will represent a "system of systems confrontation." The PLA envisages warfare will be conducted on the tangible and intangible battlefields. The tangible battlefield includes land, sea, air and space domains, whereas the intangible battlefield includes the cyberspace, electromagnetic spectrum and psychological cognition. Operations are characterised as highly dynamic, decentralised, blurring between the front and rear areas and rapid transitions between offence and defence. Characteristics include non-contact, non-linear and asymmetric operations.

The PLA's information warfare strategy emphasises overcoming a militarily superior adversary by exploiting the adversary's reliance on critical nodes in the electronic, space, cyber, and psychological domains. Three of these four warfare areas are now centralised under the SSF's Network Systems Department.[55]

Intelligentised Warfare. The CCP announced in October 2020, that modern warfare is evolving to include intelligentisation and incorporated the concept into its 14th Five-Year Plan. China expects that advanced technologies like AI, cloud computing and big data analytics will be changing the future of warfare quickly.

PLA strategists have stated that operationalisation of AI will be necessary to improve the speed and quality of information processing by reducing battlefield uncertainty and providing decision making advantage over potential adversaries. The PLA is also exploring next-generation operational concepts like intelligentised warfare, cross-domain mobile warfare, attrition warfare by intelligent swarms, AI-based space confrontation and cognitive control operations.[56]

Strategic Support Force (SSF)

The Strategic Support Force, raised in 2015, has consolidated and integrated China's previously disparate cyber, electronic, space and psychological warfare units under a unified command structure. The PLASSF's Network Systems Department has combined technical reconnaissance bureaus (TRBs) responsible for cyber espionage and signals intelligence, as well as elements of the former GSD Fourth Department (4PLA) responsible for electronic countermeasures and offensive cyber operations. The structure of the PLASSF incorporates the concept of 'integrated network and electronic warfare'.

The Strategic Support Force is responsible for collecting and managing technical intelligence, including from cyber and space assets; supporting joint operations and carrying out attacks against an adversary's command network.[57]

The PLA's cyber capabilities of defence, offence and reconnaissance have been centralised under the SSF. The PLA wants to use offensive cyber operations to disrupt, degrade or damage opponent systems, including critical infrastructure, preceding and during various stages of a conflict and in a range of conflict scenarios. PLA would use defensive cyber operations to defend against the same ability from a rival. Reconnaissance includes cyber espionage against military, civilian or commercial targets and theft of military technological know-how, intellectual property etc. In some cases, espionage and reconnaissance intrusions can be leveraged for destructive capability later.

As a strategic organisation, the SSF comes directly under the Central Military Commission (CMC), but may report to the theater commands in wartime. The SSF provides information support derived from space, cyber and terrestrial-based means to all PLA services and the five joint theater commands.[58]

Network Systems Department. The SSF Network Systems Department is responsible for information warfare with the tasks that include cyber warfare, electronic warfare (EW), technical reconnaissance and psychological warfare. The integration of cyber and EW elements under one organisation is an important step to realise the operational concept of integrated network and electronic warfare. The Network Systems Department gives intelligence support to the theater commands by taking advantage of a diverse suite of ground based technical collection assets to provide a common operating picture to geographically dispersed operational units.[59]

Evolution of Cyber Warfare

Cyber space is a relatively new domain which is man-made. However, due to fast advancements in ICT technology, cyber warfare is evolving continuously within a very short span of time. We have already seen how cyber is being utilised in conflicts worldwide.

Some of the conflicts in the last 15 years will show how cyber was used. A brief chronology of important interstate cyber conflict events is given in the following figure.

Attack name	*Date*	*Target*	*Effect*	*Suspected sponsor*
Trans-Siberian Gas Pipeline	June 1982	Soviet gas pipeline (civilian target)	Massive explosion	United States
Estonia	April–May 2007	Commercial and governmental web services (civilian target)	Major denial of service	Russia
Syrian Air Defense System as part of Operation Orchard	September 2007	Military air defense system (military target)	Degradation of air defense capabilities allowing kinetic strike	Israel
Georgia	July 2008	Commercial and governmental web services (civilian target)	Major denial of service	Russia
Stuxnet	Late 2009–2010, possibly as early as 2007	Iranian centrifuges (military target)	Physical destruction of Iranian centrifuges	United States
Saudi Aramco	August 2012	State-owned commercial enterprise (civilian target)	Large-scale destruction of data and attempted physical disruption of oil production	Iran
Operation Ababil	September 2012–March 2013	Large financial institutions (civilian target)	Major denial of service	Iran
Sony	November 2014	Commercial networks and data (civilian target)	Large-scale disruption of access to networks and loss of confidentiality of information due to public disclosures	North Korea
Ukrainian Power Utilities	December 2015	Civilian critical infrastructure (civilian target)	Temporary loss of power for 230,000 civilians, permanent damage to SCADA systems	Russia

Estonia, May 2007

Estonia is one of the most electronically advanced countries in Europe. In April 2007, the relocation of a Soviet-era war memorial sparked protests and riots among Estonia's Russian minority in capital Tallinn. After two nights of violent clashes and riots, the first cyberattacks began. There was a barrage of coordinated distributed denial of service (DDoS) attacks on the Estonian Parliament, ministries, banks and media institutions. As a result, the websites of the Ministries of Foreign Affairs and Justice had to shut down, Prime Minister Andrus Ansip's Reform Party's website was defaced, banks in Estonia were shut down, save a few, but it came at great monetary costs and affected international banking also. Russia denied any involvement in the attacks, but Estonian officials have reiterated that Russia was certainly behind the attacks.

Despite some more bizarre claims made at the time, it is now generally accepted that the attacks were more a cyber dispute than a cyber war. Estonia's computer emergency response team (CERT) esponded quickly

and competently to the attack, using well-established successful techniques. The Estonia cyberattacks were aimed at disrupting and degrading civilian services. The attack did not result in permanent damage and did not destroy any critical infrastructure. This was not a sophisticated attack technically. It was a precursor of much more severe and devastating future battles.

Following the attack, NATO, of which Estonia is a member, established the NATO Cooperative Cyber Defence Centre of Excellence (CCD COE) on May 14, 2008 at Tallinn, the capital of Estonia.

Robert Giesler, Pentagon's former Director of Information Operations, had an interesting observation. He said, 17 per cent of the computers that attacked Estonia were in the United States. Did the Estonians have the right to attack the U.S. in response, and what responsibility did the U.S. bear?

Operation Orchard—Attack on Syrian Nuclear Plant by Israel, September 2007

In September 2007, Israeli F-15 and F-16 aircrafts assaulted a suspected nuclear reactor in Syria in an operation known as Operation Orchard. This incident is perhaps one of the finest examples of the use of network intrusion to support a kinetic military action.

Israel employed a computer program designed to attack computer networks and alter the data being provided by a sensor system to either human or linked machine observers. Israel disrupted Syrian air defence systems and fed them false radar and other sensor information to mask the transit of Air Force jets into Syria.

Some other reports stated that Israeli cyber warriors were able to attack the computer networks controlling Syrian air defence systems and use a built-in kill switch, a piece of code incorporated during the production phase and designed to allow unauthorised control of a system. It was said that a malware was inducted into a laptop of a high Syrian official in a hotel clandestinely.

Whatever the case, one of Russia's most sophisticated air defence systems did not show any aircraft in their scopes when F-16s were creating havoc.

Russian attack on Georgia, July 2008

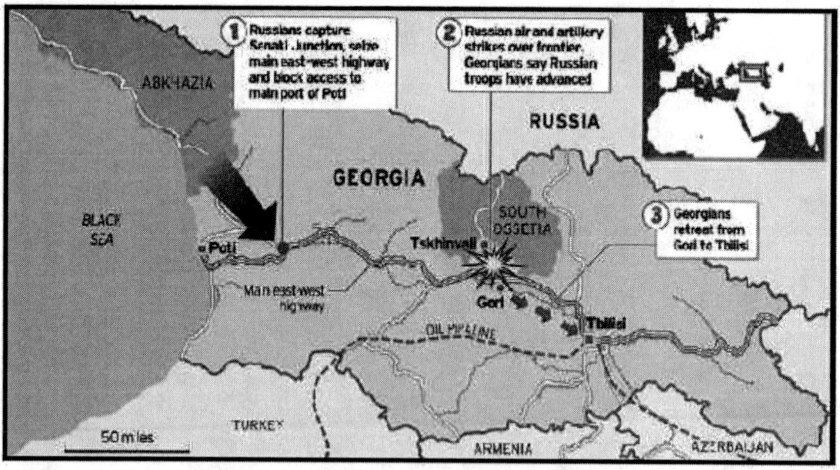

Russian—Georgian Conflict, August 2008

The cyberattack on Georgia was the first online assault carried out in conjunction with a military offensive. A large scale DDOS attack began on July 20, 2008, before the military invasion of Georgia by Russian forces, shutting down Georgian servers. This was about two months before the five-day war between Russia and Georgia over Georgia's breakaway region of South Ossetia. It is an example of using cyber weapons as a force multiplier for conventional military operations. As the invasion began, the attacks increased and spread to other targets. Small-scale DDoS attacks started in June 2008.

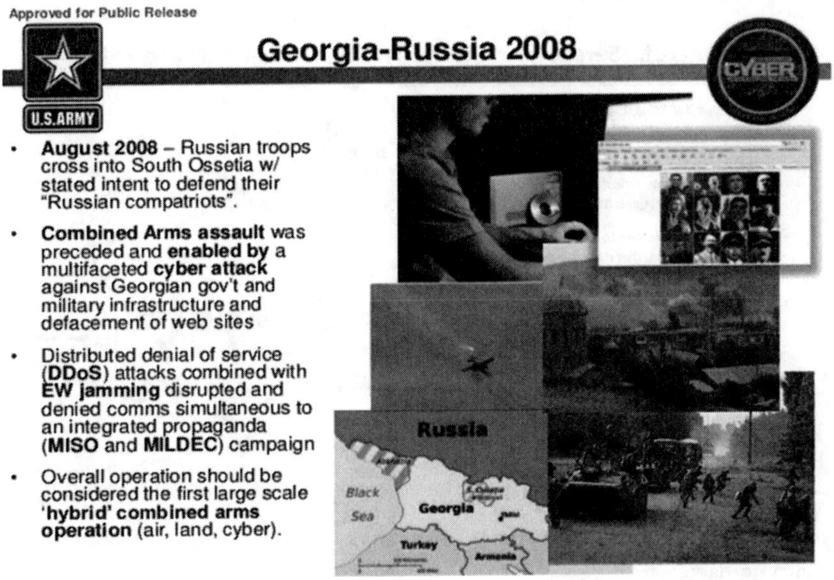

This forced the Georgian government to move critical communication services to commercial U.S. sites as their own services were shut down. Russian online hacker groups effectively disrupted the dissemination of information by the Georgian government at a crucial stage in the conflict.

The cyberattacks inflicted minor damage because much of Georgia's economy and critical infrastructure were not integrated into the internet.

Black Energy, late 2015

In December 2015, a sophisticated attempt to interfere with the Supervisory Control and Data Acquisition (SCADA) systems that controlled electrical grid functions in Ukraine was reportedly made by Russians.

This attack successfully disrupted the functions of electricity distribution companies across Ukraine. About 1.4 million people were left without power for a few hours. This may not seem particularly significant. However, this incident was the first time that a foreign actor had successfully achieved a real-kinetic effect in a cyber only attack on critical infrastructure. Black Energy thus highlights the increasing relevance of infrastructure vulnerabilities to national security considerations.

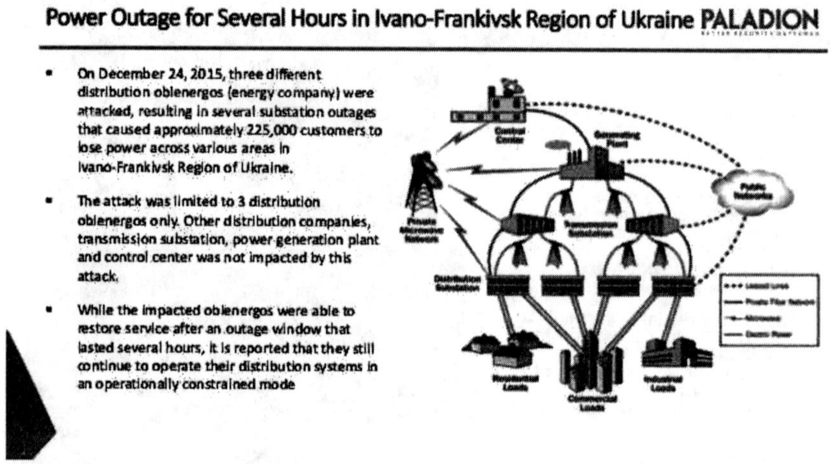

Source: https://www.slideshare.net/PaladionNetworks01/black-energy-pushing-the-country-to-darkness

Operation Cast Lead, December 2008

Israel began a military assault on Hamas's infrastructure in Gaza on December 27, 2008, called "Operation Cast Lead". A cyber backlash by Arabic hackers targeted thousands of Israeli government and civilian Web sites. Unlike other instances of cyber conflicts, this conflict involved both State (Israel and possibly Iran) and Non-State hackers.[60]

Most of the Non-State Arabic hackers involved did not have the technical skill to carry out sophisticated network attacks, opting instead for small to midscale denial of service attacks and mass website defacements.

No zero day vulnerabilities were exploited in these attacks. Most attackers focused on old Web site vulnerabilities that had not been patched. This is the first instance of a voluntary botnet ("Help Israel Win") used in a Cyber conflict where individuals voluntarily passed control of their own computers to the botnet host server.

STUXNET, Cyberattacks against Iranian Nuclear Facilities, 2009-2010

A cyber worm called 'Stuxnet' reportedly developed by American and Isreali cyber experts and released in 2009, damaged number of Siemens of Germany made centrifuges in a highly protected site at Natanz, in Iran. Stuxnet is a sophisticated cyber weapon. It attacks and disables nuclear centrifuges that operate with a SCADA system of the Siemens type, overriding the proprietary software and overloading the centrifuges. The damage to the nuclear plant was deemed as substantial. It had put the nuclear weapons development program off track for some years.

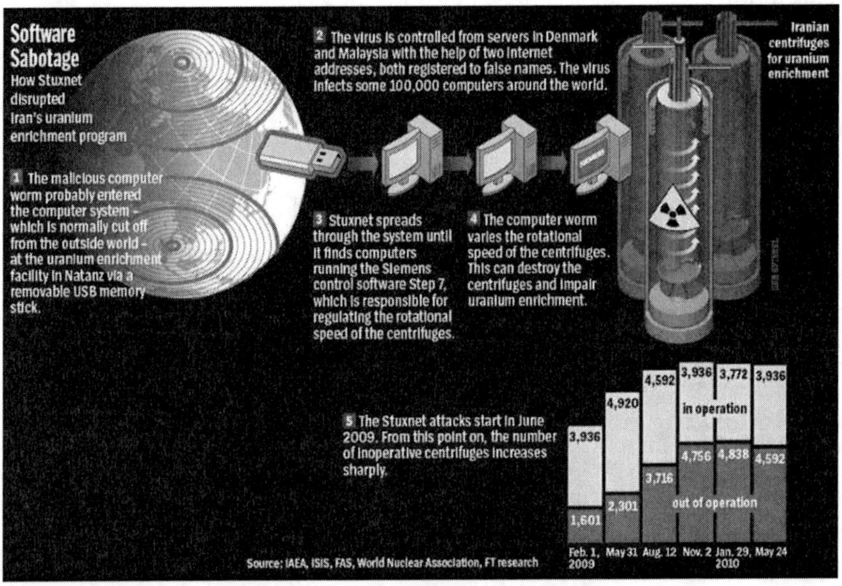

Source: https://cyberhoot.com/cybrary/stuxnet/

Stuxnet showed that cyber weapons can be designed to be effective, discriminate and to inflict proportionate damage on their targets instead of attacks with conventional weapons.

Indian Cyber Space

Over the last 15 years or so, India has slowly but steadily taken several actions to secure its cyber domain. The Government of India has been studying the model of U.S. on cyber security, and has tried to adopt some of their organisations and policies. Organisations like the National Technical Research Organisation (NTRO), the National Critical Information Infrastructure Protection Centre (NCIIPC) and National Cyber Security Coordinator were modelled on U.S. National Security Agency (NSA), National Cyber security and Communications Integration Centre (NCCIC) and The U.S. Cyber security Coordinator respectively. There are dichotomies in the U.S. Systems as they are in Indian organisations.

The national division of responsibilities for cyber security in the U.S. are as follows:[61]

- The Justice Department would, among other things, investigate, attribute, disrupt and prosecute cyber crimes, lead domestic national security operations and conduct the domestic collection, analysis and dissemination of cyber threat intelligence.
- Department of Homeland Security (DHS) would, among other things, coordinate the national protection, prevention, mitigation of and recovery from cyber incidents; disseminate domestic cyber threat and vulnerability analysis and protect critical infrastructure.
- DoD would defend the nation from attack, gather foreign threat intelligence and determine attribution and secure national security and military systems.

Indian has put policies and organisation in place for cyber security. Things are moving in the right directions. The observations on USA are equally applicable here. We need to learn from others and adopt the

Best Practices from all over the world as there is no one single solution available.

Institutionalised cyber security in India is a relatively new phenomenon wherein the security structures have been created post proliferation of threats beyond the purely 'cyber crime' domain to threats with potential to affect economic growth and impact national security. Ministry of Electronics and Information Technology (MeitY) has been a pioneer in creating security structures and implementing security measures in the country. The National Cyber Security Policy was released in July 2013.

India has taken several steps to strengthen its cyber defence capabilities. In a keynote address, delivered in 18th Asian Security Conference on 10 February 2016, the then Deputy National Security Advisor of India, stated that:[62]

- A National Cyber Security Policy has been announced and is being implemented.
- An elaborate National Cyber Security assurance framework is under implementation.
- The National Cyber Security Coordinator was appointed in 2015.
- Coordination amongst various agencies has improved.
- A National Critical Information Infrastructure Protection Centre (NCIIPC) has been set up. There is a regular dialogue with the key sectors of the economy.
- Public-private partnership is being developed. There is an active dialogue between the government and the private sector.
- A National Cyber Coordination Centre (NCCC) is being set up.
- Efforts are being made to develop cyber security skills in the country. New cyber security curricula are being introduced in the colleges.
- Cyber security Research and Development (R&D) policy has also been under active consideration by the government.
- The Indian Computer Emergency Response Team (CERT-In), an organisation set up in 2004, has done significant work in dealing with cyber incidents and spreading awareness.

- India is pursuing active cyber diplomacy by setting up cyber security dialogues with several countries and is participating in several international fora including the UN on cyber security.

Since then, rapid progress has taken place. Some of them are:[63]

- IT Act 2000 was amended in 2008. Further addition have been done.
- A National Cyber Security Policy has been implemented.
- An elaborate National Cyber Security assurance framework is under implementation.
- Coordination amongst various agencies has improved.
- A National Critical Information Infrastructure Protection Centre (NCIIPC) has been set up. There is a regular dialogue with the critical sectors of the economy.
- Public-private partnership is being developed. There is an active dialogue between the government and the private sector.
- A National Cyber Coordination Centre (NCCC) has been set up to generate necessary situational awareness of existing and potential cyber security threats and enable timely information sharing for proactive, preventive and protective actions by individual entities. Phase-I of NCCC has been made operational.
- Efforts are being made to develop cyber security skills in the country.
- Cyber security Research and Development (R&D) policy has also been under active consideration by the government. Research and development is carried out in the thrust areas of cyber security including Cryptography and cryptanalysis, Network & System Security, Monitoring & Forensics and Vulnerability Remediation & Assurance through sponsored projects at recognised R&D organizations.[64]
- Public-Private Partnership has been developed for cooperation and collaboration for responding to cyber security incidents.

- The Indian Computer Emergency Response Team (CERT-In), an organisation set up in 2004, has done significant work in dealing with cyber incidents and spreading awareness.
- Cyber security exercises are being conducted regularly to enable assessment of preparedness of organisations in Government and critical sectors.
- Guidelines have been issued for Chief Information Security Officers (CISOs) regarding their key roles and responsibilities for securing applications/infrastructure and compliance.
- Cyber Swachhta Kendra (Botnet Cleaning and Malware Analysis Centre) has been launched for the detection of malicious programs and provide free tools to remove the same.
- All the new government websites and applications are audited before their hosting and on a regular basis after hosting.
- CERT-In conducts regular training programmes for network/system administrators and Chief Information Security Officers (CISOs) of Government and critical sector organisations to secure the IT infrastructure and mitigate cyberattacks.
- Information Security Education and Awareness (ISEA) Project is being implemented with the objective of capacity building in Information Security, training of Government personnel and creation of mass Information Security awareness. The project aims to train 1.14 lakh persons under Academic activities (formal and non-formal courses) by 2020 through 52 academic and training institutions.
- Cyber forensics training labs in all north eastern states, CBI Academy Ghaziabad and cities such as Mumbai, Pune, Kolkata and Bangalore have been setup and more than 28,000 state police from North Eastern States, Maharashtra, West Bengal and Karnataka have been trained for dealing with cybercrime.
- Cyber Crisis Management Plan (CCMP) for countering cyber threats and cyber terrorism has been developed and workshops have been conducted for Central Government Ministries/Departments, States/Union Territories and other organisations.

- Under Cyber Crime Prevention for Women and Children (CCPWC) Scheme, Government of India has released grants to States/UTs to set up a Cyber Forensic cum Training Laboratory and organise capacity building programme on cyber awareness and cyber crime investigation.
- A Division has been established under the Ministry of Home Affairs to deal with Cyber and Information Security.
- The Indian Computer Emergency Response Team (CERT-In) has entered into a Memorandum of Understanding (MoU) with its overseas counterpart agencies/Computer Emergency Response Teams (CERTs) for information exchange and collaboration for cyber security incident response.

But in the cyber domain, things move very fast. Most government organisations, because of the bureaucracy, are always in the catch-up mode. The various organisations responsible for different aspects of cyber security are discussed below. The principal security structures in India are as follows.

National Cyber Security Policy. Government of India published The National Cyber Security Policy-2013 on July 2, 2013. The salient aspects of the policy are:[65]

- Creating a secure cyber ecosystem.
- Creating an assurance framework.
- Encouraging Open Standards.
- Strengthening the Regulatory framework.
- Creating mechanisms for security threat early warning, vulnerability management and response to security threats.
- Securing E-Governance services.
- Protection and resilience of Critical Information Infrastructure.
- Promotion of Research & Development in cyber security.
- Reducing supply chain risks.
- Human Resource Development.
- Creating Cyber Security Awareness.
- Developing effective Public-Private Partnerships.

- Information sharing and cooperation.
- Prioritised approach for implementation.

The National Cyber Security Policy, however, lacked the following key elements:

- Milestones and performance measures.
- Cost and resources.
- Roles and responsibilities.
- Linkage with other key strategy documents.

It is time now to review the National Cyber Security Policy. There is a subtle difference between policy and strategy.[66] A National Cyber Security Strategy is under preparation and is expected to be published shortly.

National Information Centre (NIC). National Informatics Centre (NIC) was established in 1976 and has since emerged as a "prime builder" of e-Government/e-Governance applications up to the grassroots level and a promoter of digital opportunities for sustainable development. NIC, through its ICT Network, "NICNET", has institutional linkages with all the Ministries/Departments of the Central Government, State Governments/ Union Territories and about 625 District administrations of India. NIC has been involved in steering e-Government/e-Governance applications in government ministries/departments at the Centre, States, Districts and Blocks, facilitating improvement in government services, wider transparency, and promoting decentralised planning and management in better efficiency and accountability to the people of India. The following major activities are being undertaken:[67]

- Setting up of ICT Infrastructure.
- Implementation of National and State Level e-Governance Projects.
- Products and Services.
- Consultancy to the government departments.
- Research and Development.
- Capacity Building.

CERT-IN. The Computer Emergency Response Team-India (CERT-IN), which operates under the MeitY, is the nodal agency for responding to computer attacks. While coordination of cyber security among various sectors of economy and departments of government remains under the ambit of CERT-IN, the charge of protecting critical information infrastructure has been given to National Technical Reconnaissance Organisation (NTRO), a specialised intelligence-gathering agency. While the National Critical Information Infrastructure Protection Centre (NCIIPC) protects assets in vital sectors of Indian economy such as energy, transport, banking, telecommunication and space, the CERT-IN looks after the rest. CERTs have been created in all departments of the government and various economic sectors with the charge of implementing the guidelines issued by CERT-IN and responding/reporting such attacks.

Broad Categories of Attacks Handled by CERT-IN are Identity theft-Spoofing, Phishing, Malicious Code-Virus, Trojans, Root Kits, Bots, Spam —Open Proxy Servers, Defacement of websites, Malware Propagation through compromised websites, Network Scanning/Probing, DoS attacks, Exploitation of Hardware and Software vulnerabilities, Social Engineering, Spyware and Adware, Emerging threats—RFID threats, VoIP threats, Embedded OS vulnerabilities.

National Cyber Coordination Centre (NCCC). Union Ministry of Electronics and Information Technology (MEITY) has operationalised the first phase of the National Cyber Coordination Centre (NCCC). It scans internet traffic metadata coming into the country detecting cyber threat in real-time and alert various organisations.

Key Facts. The critical tasks of NCCC are:[68]

- NCCC is a multi-stakeholder cyber security and e-surveillance agency.
- It comes under the Indian Computer Emergency Response Team (CERT-IN), Union Ministry of Electronics and Information Technology.
- It has powers under the Indian constitution with the provision of section 69B of the Information Technology Act, 2000.

- It will be India's first layer for cyber threat monitoring and all communication with the government as well as the private service providers will be monitored round the clock.
- Its mandate is to scan internet traffic and communication metadata (which are little snippets of information hidden inside each communication) coming into the country to detect real-time cyber threats.
- The system will then alert various organisations as well as internet service providers (ISPs) for timely action against the threats.
- NCCC also will coordinate across multiple intelligence agencies.
- It will virtually be in touch with the control room of all ISPs, flowing at the point of entry and exit, including international gateways.
- Apart from monitoring the internet, the NCCC will also look into various threats posed by cyberattacks.
- It will have top experts from the cyber security fields and will run like similar organisations in other countries like the U.S., UK, Germany, France, etc.

The government has authorised the Director of NCCC in the Ministry of Information Technology as the designated officer for issuing requisite directions on blocking online content according to provisions specified in the IT Act and blocking rules, as per a gazette notification.

Section 69 A of the IT Act pertains to the power to issue directions for blocking for public access of any information through any computer resource, in the interest of sovereignty and integrity, defence of India, security of the state, friendly relations with foreign states or public order or for preventing incitement to the commission of any cognisable offence. The procedure and safeguards subject to which such blocking can be carried out are specified in rules issued in 2009.[69]

Indian Cyber Crime Coordination Centre (I4C)

The scheme to set up I4C was approved in October 2018 at an estimated cost of Rs 415.86 crore to deal with all types of cyber crimes in a comprehensive and coordinated manner. It has seven components viz., National Cyber Crime Threat Analytics Unit, National Cyber Crime Reporting Portal, National Cyber Crime Training Centre, Cyber Crime Ecosystem Management Unit, National Cyber Crime Research and Innovation Centre, National Cyber Crime Forensic Laboratory Ecosystem and Platform for Joint Cyber Crime Investigation Team. At the Union Ministry for Home Affairs (MHA) initiative, 15 States and UTs have given their consent to set up Regional Cyber Crime Coordination Centres at respective States/UTs. It will be set up under the newly created Cyber and Information Security (CIS) division of the MHA.[70]

Union Home Minister inaugurated Indian Cyber Crime Coordination Centre (I4C) in New Delhi on January 10, 2020.[71]

Overview of the I4C Scheme

- An outlay of Rs 415.86 crore.
- To act as a nodal point in the fight against cyber crime.
- Identify the research problems/needs of Law Enforcement Agencies (LEAs) and take up R&D activities in developing new technologies and forensic tools in collaboration with academia/ research institutes within India and abroad.
- To prevent misuse of cyber space for furthering the cause of extremist and terrorist groups.
- Suggest amendments, if required, in cyber laws to keep pace with fast-changing technologies and International cooperation.
- To coordinate all activities related to the implementation of Mutual Legal Assistance Treaties (MLAT) with other countries related to cyber crimes in consultation with the concerned nodal authority in MHA.

National Cyber Crime Reporting Portal (www.cybercrime.gov.in) is a citizen-centric initiative that will enable citizens to report cyber crimes online through the portal. All the cyber crime related complaints will be accessed by the concerned law enforcement agencies in the States and

Union Territories for taking action as per law. This portal enables the filing of all cyber crimes with a specific focus on crimes against women, children, particularly child pornography, child sex abuse material, online content pertaining to rapes/gang rapes, etc.[72]

Centralised Monitoring System (CMS)

Minister of State in the Ministry of Communications and Information Technology on February 19, 2014 in reply to a question in Lok Sabha stated, Government has decided to set up the Centralised Monitoring System (CMS) to automate the process of Lawful Interception & Monitoring of telecommunications.[73]

Government of India
Ministry of Communications and IT
Department of Telecommunications
(Access Service Cell)
Sanchar Bhawan, 20, Ashok Road, New Delhi-110001

File No: 800-12/2013-AS.II — **Dated:** 11th October' 2013

To

All Unified Licensee(s)

AMENDMENT 2 OF 2013

Subject: Amendment to the Unified License agreement regarding Central Monitoring System.

The Government has decided to set up Centralized Monitoring System (CMS) for lawful interception and monitoring of communications. For the implementation of the same, LICENSEE's Lawful Interception System needs to be connected to the CMS at Regional Monitoring Centre (RMC) through Interception Store and Forward (ISF) server placed in LICENSEE's premises.

For this purpose, kindly find hereby enclosed the amendment to the condition 8.2 of Part-II of the Unified License agreement.

(P.C.Sharma)
Director(AS-II)

Copy to:

1. Secretary, TRAI
2. Sr. DDG, TEC
3. Sr. DDG (TERM), DoT
4. DDG (Security), DoT
5. All DDsG TERM.
6. Director (AS-I)/ Director (AS-III)/ Director (AS-IV), Dir(AS-V), DoT
7. DDG(IT) for website.

A project prepared with an estimated cost of Rs 400 crore for CMS has been approved by the Government. The execution of the CMS project has been entrusted with the Centre for Development of Telematics (C-DOT). The envisaged salient features of CMS are as follows:

- Electronic provisioning of target number by a Government agency without any manual intervention from Telecom Service Providers (TSPs) on a secured network, thus enhancing the secrecy level and quick provisioning of the target.
- Central and Regional Centres which will help Central and State level Law Enforcement Agencies in Interception and Monitoring.
- Research and Development (R&D) in related fields for continuous up-gradation of the CMS.

Centralised Monitoring System has been planned to be implemented in phased manner in about three years.

In a Lok Sabha session in May 2016, Union Telecom Minister said that the system is for the "process of lawful interception", adding that regional monitoring centres in Delhi and Mumbai had been operationalised.

The C-DOT Annual Report of 2018 talks about a Centre of Excellence for Lawful Interception being set up, which would use high-end technologies, such as open-source intelligence, image processing and search engine tools to scan Twitter and Facebook for surveillance.

The Ministry of Home Affairs, in December 2018, released a notification, authorising ten central agencies to intercept, monitor and decrypt any "information generated, transmitted, received or stored in any computer."

National Intelligence Grid (NATGRID)

The necessity for the NATGRID came after India's worst terror attack in its commercial capital in 2009 exposed the deficiency that security agencies have no mechanism to look for vital information in real-time.

On August 11, 2015, Minister of State in the Ministry of Home Affairs in Lok Sabha stated, The NATGRID is conceived to be a framework that will leverage Information Technology to connect approved User Agencies (security/law enforcement) with designated Data providers (Airlines, Banks, SEBI, Railway, Telecom, etc.) to enhance the country's counter-terrorism capability. The platform envisages approved operating procedures and oversight mechanisms to facilitate access between users and providers to enable them to analyse and disseminate information/

intelligence for synergising efforts to counter terrorism related activity. The total expenditure up to March 31, 2015 on NATGRID project is Rs 98.14 crore. Work on both the physical infrastructure and a technical component is in progress.[74]

The NATGRID will have data related to all immigration entry and exit, banking and financial transactions, credit card purchases, telecom, individual taxpayers, air flyers, train travellers, besides others to generate intelligence inputs.

In the first phase, ten user agencies and 21 service providers will be connected with the NATGRID, while in the later stages, 950 organisations and in subsequent years another 1,000 organisations will be connected with it.

The ten agencies which will be able to access the NATGRID data on real-time basis are: Intelligence Bureau (IB), Research & Analysis Wing (R&AW), Central Bureau of Investigation (CBI), Enforcement Directorate (ED), Directorate of Revenue Intelligence (DRI), Financial Intelligence Unit (FIU), Central Board of Direct Taxes (CBDT), Central Board of Excise and Customs (CBEC), Directorate General of Central Excise and Intelligence (DGCEI) and Narcotics Control Bureau (NCB).[75] Interestingly MoD or any of its intelligence organisations cannot access NATGRID.

NETRA

NETRA (NEtwork TRaffic Analysis) is a real-time software network developed by the Centre for Artificial Intelligence and Robotics (CAIR) at the Defence Research and Development Organisation (DRDO). It is mainly used by the Intelligence Bureau (IB) and the Research and Analysis Wing (RAW) with some capacity being reserved for domestic agencies under the Home Ministry.[76]

The software is meant to monitor Internet traffic on a real-time basis using both voice and textual forms of data communication, especially social media, communication services and web browsing.

National Critical Information Infrastructure Protection Centre (NCIIPC)

With the advancement of convergent communication technologies and shared Information system in India, Critical Sectors are becoming more dependent on their Critical Information Infrastructures (CIIs). These CIIs are interconnected, interdependent, complex and distributed across various geographical locations. Various inherent threats exist to CIIs, ranging from terrorist attacks to organised crimes to espionage, malicious cyber activities, which are proliferating. Protection of CIIs and hence CIs of the nation is one of the paramount concerns of the government.[77]

India has designated National Critical Information Infrastructure Protection Centre (NCIIPC) of the National Technical Research Organisation (NTRO) as the nodal agency under Section 70A(1) of the Information Technology (Amendment) Act 2008 for taking all measures including associated Research and Development for the protection of Critical Information Infrastructures (CIIs) in India.

NCIIPC is driven by its mission "To take all necessary measures to facilitate the protection of Critical Information Infrastructure, from unauthorised access, modification, use, disclosure, disruption, incapacitation or destruction, through coherent coordination, synergy and raising information security awareness among all stakeholders" and with a vision "to facilitate safe, secure and resilient Information Infrastructure for Critical Sectors in the country.

The NCIIPC started with several sectors but has now truncated them into five broad areas that cover the 'critical sectors'. These are:

- Power and Energy.
- Banking, Financial Institutions and Insurance.
- Information and Communication Technology.
- Transportation.
- E-governance and Strategic Public Enterprises.
- Health.

While defence and intelligence agencies have also been included under the CII framework, these have been kept out of the purview of the NCIIPC's charter. Balance of the sectors is now the responsibility of CERT-IN. However, CERT-In does not have any executive authority and is known to issue advisories.[78]

Key Responsibilities of NCIIPC

- National Nodal Agency to protect NCII.
- Deliver advice to reduce vulnerabilities.
- Identify all CII elements for notification.
- Provide strategic leadership and coherent Government response.
- Coordinate, share, monitor, collect, analyse and forecast threats.
- Develop plans, adopt standards, share best practices and refine procurement processes.
- Evolve protection strategies, policies, vulnerability assessment and auditing methodologies and plans for CII.
- Undertake R&D to create, collaborate and develop technologies for the growth of CII protection.
- Develop training programs for CII protection.
- Develop cooperation strategies.
- Issue guidelines, advisories, etc., in coordination with CERT-IN and other organisations.
- Exchange knowledge and experiences with CERT-IN and other org.
- NCIIPC may call for information and give directions to CII.

National Cyber Security Coordinator. First National Cyber Security Coordinator was appointed in April 2015 in the National Security Council Secretariat (NSCS) under National Security Advisor (NSA). This is not a Secretary level appointment, but a Special Secretary level post. In the fierce bureaucratic set up it was a bit let down, as the importance of cyber security is well known. He is supposed to work under one of the Deputy NSAs. Starting from a scratch, lot of important work has been done. Since it works directly under PMO, it can push through many projects or initiatives, bypassing the labyrinth of bureaucracy. Protected from routine interferences, the office has virtual independence. He can get things done at a faster pace.

Normally, responsibility for cyber security of the nation is not entrusted to an intelligence agency. Organisations like The National Security Agency (NSA) of the U.S. or the Government Communications Headquarters of the UK (GCHQ) or other such intelligence agencies help others with their expertise in niche technology areas. Responsibilities for cyber defence in India are distributed within the government among several organisations. There has to be coordination and collaboration on cyber issues between agencies and departments. Who coordinates cyber security activities between different ministries? Responsibility and authority must go together. A National Cyber Security Coordinator has no authority over anybody. He draws his strength from his proximity to the National Security Advisor and the Prime Minister's Office. Surely there has to be an institutional mechanism for coordinating such vast and diverse agencies.

There are shortcomings in this organisation National Cyber Security Coordinator.

- Does not have any executive power since it is not under any Ministry.
- Not in the loop for cyber operations undertaken by the intelligence agencies. Intelligence agencies carefully avoid him. Today, in the cyber domain, defence and offence are complimentary.
- Staff for National Cyber Security Coordinator is meagre, given the plethora of issues the office handles.
- No ministerial or legislative control over their functioning. It cuts both ways.
- Danger of getting overboard and taking unnecessary risks with grave consequences when there is no control over them.

The U.S. has abolished the post of National Cyber Security Coordinator as it was found that this post has become an extra-constitutional authority and was interfering with the routine functioning of the respective ministries responsible for the respective cyber security tasks.

Public-Private Partnership (PPP)

A Joint Working Group with Data Security Council of India (DSCI) and National Security Council Secretariat (NSCS) went into various aspects of Public-Private Partnership (PPP) in India. The salient guiding principles and objectives on the Public-Private Partnership (PPP) are as under:[79]

- Given the diverse stakeholders in cyber security, institutional mechanisms should be set up to promote convergence of efforts both in public and private domains.
- Use existing institutions and organisations to the extent possible in both private sector and government and create new institutions where required to enhance cyber security.
- Set up a permanent mechanism for private public partnership.
- Identify bodies that can play a broader role in funding and implementation in the public and private sector.
- Identify areas where both the private and public sector can build capacities for cyber security.
- Put in place an appropriate policy and legal frameworks to ensure compliance with cyber security efforts.
- Promote active PPP cooperation in international forums and in formulating India's position on global cyber security policies.
- Establish India as a global hub of development of cyber security products, services and manpower.
- Promote indigenisation and work on joint R&D projects to meet the cyber security needs of the country.

Except for few exceptions, there has hardly been any progress on the PPP model. Indian IT industry is worth $150 billion. They have some well-established cyber security procedures. What is the process of exchanging the best practices with this civil sector and the government sector? Indian IT industry, showing huge profits in their balance sheets must be goaded into participating in national cyber security efforts.

There is a serious mismatch of understanding between the civil sector and the government agencies dealing with cyber security. The government agencies feel that the private sector is only interested in grabbing the order but is not serious enough to develop Indian solutions. They don't put adequate effort into research and development (R&D) and are unwilling to invest in the country's cyber security infrastructure.

On the other hand, the private industry feels that there is very little understanding of cyber security in the top echelons of government agencies. Procedures are too bureaucratic, rigid, long and time-consuming. The vendors are usually treated shabbily. They feel that since they provide cyber security solutions across the globe, they have the expertise. If the government wants, then they should approach the private industry and not the other way around. They quote the recent example of U.S. Secretary of Defence, visiting the Silicon Valley and interacting with the behemoths for providing support to DoD cyber activities.

Surely, there has to be a middle ground where the sharply divergent views can be met.

The private industry is very sensitive to any cyber breach in their respective organisations. They always do the damage control first and would not like to share the information because of commercial reasons. What can NCCIPC and CERT-IN do to develop mutual trust and ensure that this information of compromise is shared immediately so that mitigation action across the sectors can be initiated? In a hypothetical scenario a big Indian IT giant has been compromised and data has been stolen, and that affected company is reasonably certain from where the attack has come and carries out a hack back against the party. What should be the role of government agencies? Though the private industry is duty-bound to report any breach of cyber security to government agencies, many such incidents go unreported. What is the mechanism by which punitive action is taken against the defaulters?[80]

Though Joint Working Group has advocated Public-Private Partnership we need to be careful. What is the definition of the private sector? There are a lot of Multi-National Corporations (MNC) involved. Most American Companies are major snooping partners of the U.S. Intelligence Agencies, specially NSA and are governed by the U.S.

domestic laws. The PRISM gives out in graphic details how NSA obtains intelligence from these agencies:

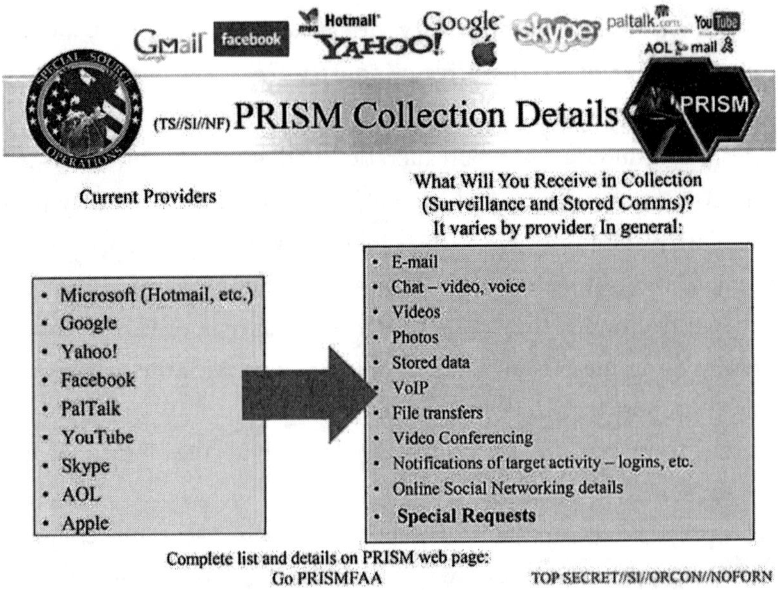

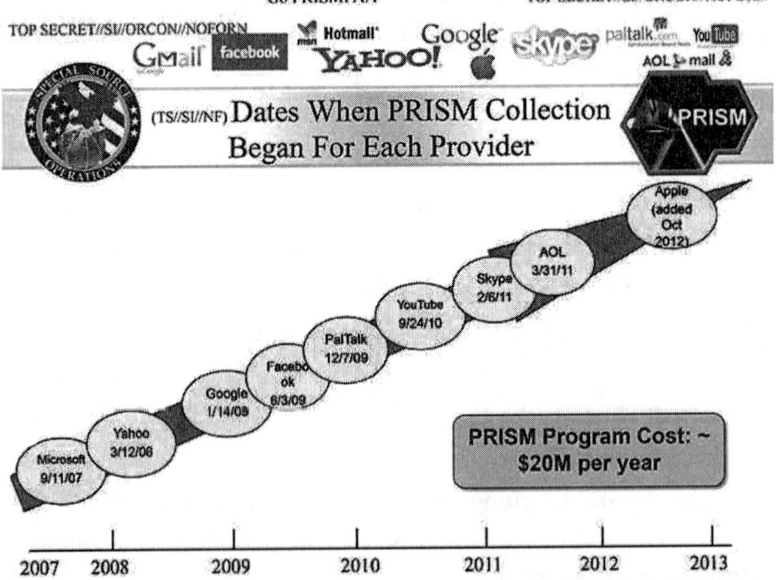

Source: https://www.washingtonpost.com/wp-srv/special/politics/prism-collection-documents/

When we talk about Private should we include MNCs? Today Google India and other are treated like Indian companies. They represent India in international high tables as Indian companies. Indian IT companies are doing a lot of good work. However, can they all be trusted? What happens if some insider like Edward Snowden gets compromised?

There are some issues with hardware. We have a lot of apprehension about using Chinese Company Huawei switching equipment in our networks, especially in critical infrastructure. Because of their lower cost, in most cases, Huawai gets selected as the lowest bidder. However, it has never been proved that there are embedded hardware or softwares in their equipment. The same question can be asked for CISCO equipment. If we are so paranoid about Huawei, why not CISCO?

Today MNCs manage most of our telecommunication networks. ICT hardware is mostly from them. FDI limit in Telecom sector has been increased to 100 per cent. We cannot shut out MNCs. In today's environment with COTS equipment, it is very difficult to identify totally indigenous equipment. Chips will be from all over Taiwan, China, Hong Kong, Singapore, etc. How do we ensure their correctness of not having any malicious code? All the countries face the same dilemma.

We have to prioritise our work on critical infrastructure. The nuclear, power, railways, dams, the Supervisory Control and Data Acquisition (SCADA) System controlling them should be our first priority.

In the U.S. Department of Defence (DoD) NSA has much more cyber capability than the Department of Homeland Security (DHS). DoD is responsible for protecting .mil domain and DHS for .gov domain. However, for .com network which is used by 85 to 90 per cent of all internet users, there is no governmental organisation specially responsible. The same situation in India exists.

We need to place particular emphasis on building adequate technical capabilities in the areas of cryptology, digital signatures, testing for malware in embedded systems, operating systems, fabrication of specialised chips for defence and intelligence functions, search engines, artificial intelligence, routers, SCADA systems, etc.

Security Standards and Audits

Given the role of security standards and audit in enhancing the level of preparedness and assurance in cyber security, the private sector should be an active partner in undertaking the following activities:

- Define baseline security standards and practices/guidelines for the critical sector organisations in the public and private sectors. The standards may be developed by a MCIT led body with the active involvement of the industry and academia.
- Define enhanced standards and guidelines for organisations that fall in the high risk category, i.e., the critical information infrastructure organisations.
- Laying down security standards and guidelines for acquisition of IT products and services.
- Develop protection profiles, capture users' cyber security concerns, aid the procurement of IT products, and comply with IT products' compliance before deployment.
- Work jointly towards the establishment of Institute of Cyber Security Professionals of India (similar to ICAI for CAs). This could be an autonomous institution under the patronage of MCIT.
- Make cyber security audit mandatory by an appropriate amendment in the listing requirements under the Companies Act.

Testing & Certification

The following measures may be taken for enhancing testing & certifying facilities to address the growing concerns relating to supply-chain vulnerability:[81]

- Establishment of National Testing and Certification Schemes under the supervision and oversight of appropriate empowered entities under the MCIT.
- While the action is underway for the establishment of Telecom Testing and Certification Centre in the telecom sector, there is a need to establish an independent government certification body

for IT products under the MCIT. The certification body should be separate from the testing facilities. In the interim, Standardisation Testing and Quality Certification (STQC) may be authorised as a certificate issuing body for IT products.

- Development of skills and competence of evaluators, validators and certification body personnel for successfully running the National Testing and Certification Scheme.
- Establishment of private owned testing labs, duly accredited by the certification body. Government may provide the necessary incentives for the private sector for opening testing labs.
- Encourage active participation in the communities of interest for defining protection profiles for addressing the security requirements of specific sector.
- Take necessary steps to transition from a 'Common Criteria Certificate Consuming Nation' to a 'Common Criteria Certificate Authorizing Nation.'

In U.S. National Institute of Standards and Technology (NIST) is responsible for improving the cyber security of critical infrastructure. It established the voluntary NIST Framework to help critical infrastructure owners and operators reduce cyber risks. NIST Framework for Improving Critical Infrastructure Cybersecurity, version 1.0, 12 February 2014 gives out a fair idea how this organisation helps in cybersecurity efforts.

India does not have any such organisation. Should we have such organisation in India? Strongly recommended.

Capacity Building

The following is recommended:[82]

- A concerted effort to increase the number of cyber security professionals and equip them to efficiently meet the challenges of cyber security.
- Ministry of Communication and Information Technology (MCIT) and Ministry of Human Resource Development (MHRD) and

the private sector may jointly establish a cyber security capacity-building framework.

- Establishing a competency framework to assess skills required, identify gaps, engagement with private sector on cyber security and devise strategies and programmes for capacity-building.
- Work towards establishing a multi-disciplinary Centre of Excellence (CoEs) in cyber security areas including best practices, forensics, cyber crime investigation, studies, research and international frameworks/ institutions.
- MCIT and the private sector should jointly run cyber security awareness campaigns for the general public, teenagers, children, etc.
- Ministry of Home Affairs (MHA) and MCIT may set up training facilities for training of Law Enforcement Agencies (LEAs) in cyber crime investigations and cyber forensics. The private sector may be associated with establishing training facilities and providing basic and advanced level training to the LEAs.
- Government and private sector may fund research & development for the development of indigenous cyber security products and solutions that meet international standards and address the global market.

Standards and Protocols

We need to have uniform standards, protocols and norms across the country. The agencies involved are Ministry of Electronics and Information Technology (MeitY), Indian Standards Institute (ISI), Bureau of Indian Standards (BIS) and NCCIPC. We can think of a central agency like National Institute of Standards and Technology (NIST) of the USA functioning under the Department of Commerce.

Indian Solutions

Bhaba Atomic Research Centre and Indian Space Research Organisation have developed world class indigenous security solutions as they had to undergo international restrictions and strict security requirements.

BARC developed an excellent network security solution called Secure Network Access System (SNAS). Electronic Corporation of India Limited was made the designated agency for servicing and maintenance. In armed forces classified networks this is not being utilised.

It was expected that for armed forces own classified networks switching equipments from manufacturers like Huawei and ZDNet would be excluded, and the armed forces would take the lead. This has not happened, and because of L1 syndrome, the Chinese manufactured IT equipments are now part and parcel of armed forces classified networks.

International Institute for Strategic Studies (IISS) study. IISS has carried out a Net Assessment on Cyber Capabilities and National Power of various countries. The IISS Report observations on India are interesting:[83]

- India has made only moderate progress in developing its policy and doctrine for cyberspace security.
- India's approach towards institutional reform of cyber governance has been slow and incremental. The key coordinating authorities for cyber security in the civil and military domains were established only in 2018 and 2019, respectively.
- In promoting national cyber security the private sector has moved more quickly than the government.
- India is visible and active in cyber diplomacy. It is not among the leaders on global norms, preferring instead to make productive, practical arrangements with key states.
- India's offensive cyber capability is Pakistan focused and regionally effective. It is not tuned towards China.
- India's best chance of advancing to the second tier is by harnessing its great digital industrial potential and adopting a whole-of-society approach to upgrade its cyber security.
- Prime Minister Narendra Modi, in a speech on Independence Day in August 2020, devoted a paragraph to the new cyber security strategy, promising it would soon emerge. More than one year down the line, it has not been published yet.

- Since the early 2000s India's cyber command-and-control structure has been under development but remains decentralised.
- Cyber security powers are spread across various agencies, with reports of overlapping competencies and bureaucratic turf wars.
- The IB, RAW and DIA each represent a part of India's cyber intelligence capability. They are all heavily reliant for core capability on the technical-intelligence agency, the NTRO. Various parts of the Ministry of Home Affairs, including the Cyber Crime Wing and Central Forensics Science Laboratory, are also important sources of cyber intelligence.
- India's cyber-intelligence reach is weak. It relies on partnerships with the U.S., the UK and France for a higher level of cyber situational awareness.
- The infrastructure at the heart of India's digital economy is built largely from imported equipment.
- Almost all the country's most popular mobile apps were designed abroad. One exception is Aarogya Setu, the Indian government's COVID-19 contact-tracing app.
- India has been the victim of cyberattacks frequently, including on its critical infrastructure. A significant proportion of them has been attributed to China or Pakistan. CERT-IN reported that there were more than 394,499 incidents in 2019. 2020 saw an upswing in attacks from China.[84]
- The majority of the cyber incidents flagged by CERT-IN appear to have been attempts at espionage. Yet they could have resulted in severe damage to the integrity of Indian networks and platforms.
- India had the second-highest number of ransomware attacks in the world in 2020.
- Because of stringent guidelines from the Reserve Bank of India (RBI), the financial sector is more secure than other areas of the Indian economy.

Cyber Security. In spite of all the complexities India has done reasonably well in the field of cyber security. The Global Cyber security Index (GCI) is an initiative of the International Telecommunication Union (ITU), the UN specialised agency for ICTs. The Global Cyber security Index (GCI) is a trusted reference that measures the commitment of countries to cyber security at a global level. GCI is assessed along five pillars of Legal Measures, Technical Measures, Organisational Measures, Capacity Development and Cooperation , and then aggregated into an overall score.

India was ranked 47th out of 175 countries in the International Telecommunication Union's 2018 Global Cyber security Index, well behind its geopolitical rival China (27th).[85]

However, remarkably in the latest 2020 Global Cyber Security Index India is ranked tenth whereas China is ranked at 33.[86]

GCI results: Global Score and Rank

Country Name	Score	Rank
United States of America**	100	1
United Kingdom	99.54	2
Saudi Arabia	99.54	2
Estonia	99.48	3
Korea (Rep. of)	98.52	4
Singapore	98.52	4
Spain	98.52	4
Russian Federation	98.06	5
United Arab Emirates	98.06	5
Malaysia	98.06	5
Lithuania	97.93	6
Japan	97.82	7
Canada**	97.67	8
France	97.6	9
India	97.5	10

Critical Issues to be Addressed in the Indian Context

Command and Control Set-up. There should be no ambiguity in the responsibility of organisations for cyber security. In the U.S. National Security Agency and the Cyber Command comes under the DoD. In the UK, GCHQ comes under the Foreign Ministry. In Israel, National Cyber Bureau, directly under the Prime Minister, regulates activity in the Cyber Space. Responsibilities for cyber defence in India are distributed within the government among several organisations. There has to be coordination and collaboration on cyber issues between agencies and departments. Who coordinates cyber security activities between different ministries? Responsibility and authority must go together. In the Indian context, NTRO doesn't come under any ministry and operates directly under Prime Minister's Office (PMO). The interplay between the Ministry of Defence (MoD), the Ministry of Home Affairs (MHA), the Armed Forces, and the intelligence agencies, both internal and external, needs to be clearly demarcated. Who will carry out offensive cyber operations in a conflict scenario? Can an intelligence agency do it keeping in mind the rules of engagement or the laws of armed conflict?[87] A National Cyber Security Coordinator has no authority over anybody. Surely there has to be an institutional mechanism for coordinating such vast and diverse agencies.

National Critical Information Infrastructure

National Critical Information Infrastructure Protection Centre (NCIIPC) was formed under National Technical Research Organisation (NTRO). For some selected critical infrastructures, NCIIPC takes the lead role. For other non-critical structures, it is the responsibility of the CERT-IN. The National Disaster Management Authority (NDMA), under the MHA, also has the responsibility for the protection of critical cyber infrastructure. Though NDMA has done very little on this issue.

CERT-IN is an advisory body and not an implementation agency. Responsibility and authority for all the sub-sectors of critical information infrastructure should be demarcated and made accountable. The lead agency to formulate National Cyber Security Policy is the Ministry of Electronics and Information Technology (MeitY). This ministry does not have control over powerful ministries and departments like MoD, MHA and NTRO. The way our ministries work in the stovepipe systems, the interaction, sharing of information, earmarking of specific roles and assignment of responsibility suffer.

Regulatory bodies for each sub-sector of critical infrastructure must be identified and made responsible and accountable for respective sub-sectors. For example, if a severe breach in a nuclear power plant occurs with the potential to the great loss to life and property, who should be made accountable. The introduction of private players in nuclear power sectors will make the issue more complicated. Similarly, who is responsible for cyber security of the huge defence industrial base of Defence Public Sector Undertakings (DPSUs) and factories under the Ordnance Factory Board (OFB)? With the recent participation of private industries, the cyber security aspects will take more relevance. Who is responsible for the cyber security of the private players of the defence industry?[88]

In the recent past, two incidences of breach of cyber security and cyber exploitation activities of foreign actors have come to light. One is cyber attack in India's largest civil nuclear facility, the Kudankulam Nuclear Power Plant (KNPP) in Tamil Nadu[89] and the other is reported Chinese penetration of India's power grid at multiple load dispatch points causing power outage at Mumbai.[90] Some critical issues which have come out of these two incidents merit immediate action. Some of them are:

- How come cyber security of Nuclear power plants, malfunctioning which can cause millions of people in cities like Chennai, are not in the mandate of NCIIPC?
- In both cases, the incidences were reported by western cyber security companies. How come our own systems fail to detect these?
- Does the Government of India have the capability to attribute to the perpetrators of these actions and nail them comprehensively?
- Does India have the capability to take offensive action as a measure of deterrence? North Korea has been active in cyber crime-related activities in India.

- What are the options for diplomatic action available to India?

Role of Regulators. Questions must be raised about the core competencies and resources of the regulator. The following questions are relevant regarding cyber security regulators:

- What is the process of appointment and evaluation of regulators?
- How are their competencies assessed?
- Do regulators have a proficient process? Do they possess the technical know-how?
- Do they have the practical experience to relate to challenges faced by the respective sector?
- Are the regulators consulting vertically and horizontally with other regulators of critical information infrastructure? Who organises these interactions?
- What control does National Cyber Security Coordinator have on the regulators?

Audit Considerations

The following questions arise in the context of Audit:

- In the case of Kudankulam Nuclear Power Plant (KNPP) which audit standard was followed by both internal and external auditors? Was it latest version of IEC 62645 standard?
- Who are the internal auditors of nuclear power plants, how are they selected?
- In the last audit, was the cyberattack detected?
- Auditors check particular following of instructions. Were they capable of detecting the sophisticated attack if it was not reported from outside?

Code Breaking

India does not have any credible code-breaking capability. The introduction of the 128 or the 256 bits keys has made the issue of code-breaking extremely difficult. However, this capability exists in NSA of U.S., GCHQ of UK and probably in Russia and China. If we do not have this capability, we must make efforts to develop these capabilities. Academia, industry and expertise from countries like Ukraine, Belarus and such other East European countries and South Africa can be explored.

R&D in the Field of Cyber Security

We have no choice but to have our own software and hardware in niche technology areas as no country shares these. Wikileaks and Edward Snowden have already revealed the capability of the U.S. As an initial effort, Indian researchers should be tasked to develop the same kind of capabilities.

We should take a policy decision to use Indian made switching equipment in our selected critical infrastructure. Indian manufacturers like 'Tejas Networks' should be encouraged. The human resource development policies must be suitably modified to attract the right kind of talent to train and nurture them. Despite the huge budget the NSA has, NSA is most vulnerable to insider's threat. Manning and Edward Snowden are the prime examples. The most secret cyber weapons developed by the NSA have been put on the internet which can be used by anybody in the world for cyber operations. What is the policy to thwart insider threat in our cyber security organisations?[91]

In September 2015, the Indian government released a draft National Encryption Policy that sought to set encryption standards and lay down conditions for decryption of information for the lawful investigation. This was hastily withdrawn under pressure from the media. It is time now to catch the bull by the horn. The national security interests must be supreme.

Defence Research and Development Organisation (DRDO)

In the recent past, Defence Research and Development Organisation's (DRDO) mandate has been widened to support national cyber security architecture, which includes testing capabilities, security solutions, networking systems and cyber defence tools. In this process, it has also established national infrastructure, enhanced defence industrial capability and developed committed quality human resources. We must make all organisations accountable. We should ask for Return on Investment from the DRDO to be verified by the stakeholders.

It was expected that for armed forces own classified networks, switching equipments from manufacturers like Huawei and ZDNet would be excluded and the armed forces would take the lead. This has not happened. Because of L1 syndrome, the Chinese manufactured IT equipment are now part and parcel of armed forces classified networks. We need to place particular emphasis on building adequate technical capabilities in the areas of: Cryptology, Digital signatures, Testing for malware in embedded systems, Operating systems, Fabrication of specialised chips for defence and intelligence functions, Search engines, Artificial intelligence, Routers, SCADA systems.[92] DRDO should be made responsible for developing these in a strict time frame.

Armed Forces Domain

Any outside agencies including NCIIPC do not audit the cyber security of the three services of the armed forces. At least, the three services should audit each other. Respective services certify themselves as cyber secure. This is not acceptable. Cyber security of the IT network of the three services must be audited by some external agency. In U.S. professional hackers are called in a big bounty programme and challenged to hack DoD classified networks and award huge prize money. This is how they find out vulnerabilities in their networks. The Indian Armed Forces must also do something like this.

Within the U.S. Department of Defense, there is an organisation called Defense Information Systems Agency (DISA). DISA provides, operates and assures command and control and information-sharing capabilities in direct support to joint warfighters, national-level leaders and other missions across the full spectrum of military operations. Should we have an organisation like DISA in MoD?

There should be clarity as to what is to be constituted as an act of war in the cyber domain. Factors like loss of life and property, economic impact, and diplomatic and political effects can be considered an attack of significant consequences.

Who will permit offensive cyber operations? What are the rules of engagement? India procures a huge amount of Defence equipment from foreign countries. What is the mechanism to check whether there is any malware in the increasingly sophisticated technology areas? No country shares the codes. What is the mechanism in the procurement of equipment procedure and supply chain management system to ensure that bugs are not present?

The human resource development policies for the armed forces in the cyber domain will require drastic changes to attract and keep talents in such niche technology areas. Present policies are inadequate. Armed forces must initiate R&D efforts on their specific requirements, especially for the battlefield. Can they compromise the adversary's classified military network, interfere in the command or data link of the Unmanned Aerial Vehicle (UAV)/drones, task the Special Forces with appropriate wherewithal to compromise the adversary's Optical Fibre Communication (OFC) network? Can we de-anonymise the Darknet. It has been done by the three leading universities of three different countries.[93]

Cyber Capabilities at Operational and Tactical Levels (Corps Headquarters and Below)

What is our policy to provide cyber capabilities at operational and tactical level? In the U.S., for carrying out sophisticated cyber operations in operational and tactical battlefields where proximity to the target is essential, teams from the most elite and niche technology cyber warfare experts of Tailored Access Operations (TAO) of NSA are embedded with appropriate level in the battlefield. Do our armed forces have similar arrangements with NTRO? We may follow the example of the U.S. Marine Corps and its efforts to get SIGINT and Cyber support from NSA.

India must enunciate its cyber strategy for both cyber security and offensive cyber operations. A part may be classified, but the relevant aspects must be made known to the people concerned about their tasks and responsibilities. On cyber-related issues projects have to be implemented on the fast track, and no delay is acceptable. The responsibility and accountability of different agencies must be clearly defined. The huge approximately US$ 150 billion IT industry should be made a partner in national cyber security efforts as government alone cannot do this job. There is no alternative to indigenous cyber security solutions. Snowden revelations have shown what the revered multinational companies do for U.S. government agency like NSA.

Defence Cyber Agency. In the end 2019, the Government of India raised a Tri-Service Organisation, Defence Cyber Agency (DCA) for looking after all cyber-related issues concerning armed forces. DCA will build on the already existing Defence Information Assurance Research Agency (DIARA) under HQ Integrated Defence Staff. Probably it is a precursor to the establishment of a Cyber Command. All three services have their individual CERTs and defensive mechanisms in place. DCA will be instrumental in coordinating training, research and development, most important funding if applicable, liaison with all other agencies outside defence domain. There is a command and control issue here. The components of the three services do not come under DCA. Armed Forces work strictly in command channels. If there is a divergence of opinion between DCA and services, the services components will follow their own hierarchy.

Recommendations

Cyberspace has no boundaries. It encompasses all other domains. Any action at the national level may have grave repercussions at the international level. Responsibilities for cyber operations at the national, ministry of defence or services levels are not strictly specific to the particular level. They are overlapping and affect each other.

Given below are recommendations at the national, ministry of defence and Indian army level.

National Level

We must have a small Group of Minister for giving leadership and strategic direction.

We should appoint a Deputy National Security Adviser for Cyber at the secretary-level directly under NSA. The whole range of issues like cyber security, cyber diplomacy, capacity building, espionage and offensive cyber operations are too big and important a national security portfolio not to have a dedicated senior official steering the wider national effort.

Priority and allocation of resources for offensive and defensive actions should be clear. Plans should be for long, medium and short term.

Develop a comprehensive cyber strategy which should have:

- Tactics that are actionable, reliable and precise on short notice.
- Strategic effects as measured by direct and timely impact to digital systems of interest.
- Strategic outcomes as measured in terms of the advancement of national objectives.
- Conduct cross-government audit across defence, security and intelligence agencies under the arrangement of the Cabinet Secretary.
- Cooperation with friendly countries. The exchange of technologies with countries like Israel, Taiwan, Japan, Australia, Ukraine, Belarus, South Africa, Sweden should be explored.
- Through cyber diplomacy, demonstrate to the international community our adherence to international law.
- Should continuously review and assess the effectiveness of ongoing operations within a clear legal and ethical framework.
- Give clear signals to adversaries, both state and non-state actors and cybercriminals, about punitive actions by the government if they transgress boundaries.

Develop an operations approval framework incorporating the concept of a small standing cadre of National Security Council and interagency "approvers" to streamline decision making for both offensive and defensive cyber operations. The current approval process is too long and bureaucratic.

Should support bilateral and multilateral activities for the development and operation of an International Cyber Stability Board of like-minded nations and industry partners to protect cross-border critical infrastructure and create common standards.

The vulnerabilities equities process must be coordinated at the government level. This process helps the security agencies decide when to remain quiet about a vulnerability so that own people can exploit it and divulge it so that it can be patched, enhancing everyone's cyber defences.

The government should lead in developing and implementing standards and best practice in emerging niche technology areas. Public key cryptography, quantum computing, and artificial intelligence are some fields the government should lead in research and development.

India is increasingly becoming a space power. There are a lot of vulnerabilities in the space sector. Our space assets and support infrastructure must be protected from cyberattacks. The cyber security aspect should be embedded ab initio.

Cyber activities of criminals, state and non-state actors, need to be curbed. Offenders have to be apprehended and prosecuted. Cyber laws and procedures have to be suitably strengthened/amended to combat transnational cybercriminal activities. This should be done in consultation with the private industry.

Critical Infrastructure. Though a lot of work has been done to identify critical information infrastructure and responsibilities for cyber security of respective sectors, a lot remains to be done. In all such sectors, regulators have to be appointed, and clear-cut responsibilities have to be given. Computer Emergency Response Teams (CERT-IN) and NCIIPC can issue advisories but cannot enforce implementation.

Exchange of Information. Exchange of information about any breach of security and mitigation measures must be strengthened between the private and the public sectors. Institutional mechanisms have to be put in place. Trust has to be developed between them. The industry does not trust intelligence agencies easily.

Research and Development. Funds for research and development have to be spent judiciously and prioritised. The private sector must contribute to cyber-related research and development.

The Private Sector. A vast majority of our cyber infrastructure is owned and operated by the private sector like the internet service providers. The government usually would not want to maintain a long term, active presence on private-sector networks to provide defensive capabilities. The government, however, should closely work with the private sector in three areas:

- Setting the conditions for a truly secure cyber infrastructure.
- Significantly empowering private sector defensive capabilities.
- Providing for interoperable capabilities and joint exercises in the event that a national crisis requires the government to assist the private sector more directly or to respond directly against a threat to the nation.

There is a need for an India version of the Information Sharing and Analysis Centers (ISACs) and Information Sharing and Analysis Organisations (ISAOs) of the U.S. The Government of India should assist the private sector in their cyber security efforts and help facilitate critical cyber security information sharing, both among private sector actors and between the government and the private sector. NCIIPC has taken some welcome steps, introduced standard operating procedures (SOPs) and formats for reporting incidents. But a lot more is required to be done. The private industry must, therefore, come forward for sharing information.

Entities such as Infosys, Tata Consultancy Services (TCS) or Wipro may be aware of a particular vulnerability or threat. It can take a long time before relevant information spreads throughout the cyber eco-system and results in the deployment of patches, installation of new technologies, changes in network architecture, or the adoption of new policies that adequately counter the threat. Sharing of such information must be done quickly. The government should have programs that provide the private sector with threat information data and other forms of assistance designed to help private organisations improve their cyber security postures. It is difficult for the private sector to access the wealth of information and assistance that the government, particularly the NTRO and the CERT-IN could provide.

Threat information sharing is significantly more efficient when automated, relying on standardised feeds and formats to communicate key pieces of data. The NCIIPC and the CERT-IN should encourage automated sharing of threat information and push for greater interoperability between such initiatives, including the incorporation of confidence levels in the sharing of cyber threat indicators (such as IP addresses and MD5 hashes).[94]

Ministry of Defence (MoD)

The role of armed forces for the protection of critical information infrastructure, including the private sectors, should be clearly defined. What happens when the armed forces are called in an aid to civil authority in case of some cyber calamity? The armed forces should:

- Should extensively use cyber training ranges. Preferably Indian Army should take the lead.
- Should develop and implement professional development courses to build leaders and elite forces in the cyber branches of all services.
- The MoD and the Army should leverage appropriate expertise outside the military from academia, industry and individuals to augment their cyberspace planning, operation and capability development.
- Should establish a Centre of Excellence (CoE) for cyber. The Indian Army can be the lead agency as it has already a CoE at Military College of Tele communication Engineering (MCTE), Mhow.
- Coordinate with the services and integrate cyber operations and related activities.
- Should develop theories of cyber operations at strategic, operational and tactical levels.
- Should encourage open discussion regarding the future evolution of military cyberspace in terms of tasks, authorities and organisational structures.

- Should consider raising an organisation like U.S. Department of Defense, Defense Information Systems Agency (DISA) which provides, operates and assures command and control and information sharing capabilities in direct support to war fighters, national level leaders across the full spectrum of military operations.
- Should create a mechanism to ensure that bugs are not present in the procurement of equipment and supply chain management system.
- Should define Rules of Engagement for armed conflicts.
- Should lay down human resource development policies for the Armed Forces in the cyber domain. It will require drastic changes to attract and keep talents in such niche technology areas. The RM should direct the Chiefs of the Army, Navy and the Air Force to direct their military secretary branch and its equivalents to treat the cyber career field as a national security priority, where promotion boards must understand the cyber mission as a priority and facilitate recruitment, retention and career-long professional development in cyber expertise.
- Create a red team for performing operations on MoD critical systems and critical infrastructure.
- RM should get regular updates on identified challenges, plans and progress.
- Direct DCA to develop cyber capabilities/effects, focused on adversary military targets, which would include:
- Development of infrastructure and tools to support his forces.
- Ensure operational experience and an appropriately skilled workforce.
- Create agility to respond to dynamic situations/opportunities.
- Develop a deliberate plan and acquisition strategy that leverages existing infrastructure and identify where new infrastructure and tools are required.

- Develop a plan for joint training, exercises and ultimately operations with and alongside other national cyber organisations operating as joint teams.
- Ask DCA to establish and enlarge professional military education opportunities at all levels, allowing military personnel to work in cyber-related private sector positions. Should encourage greater commercial exchange opportunities to improve skills and operational understanding.
- Create a mechanism to coordinate national cyber priorities and private-public collaboration across the spectrum of peace, no war no peace and war. DCA should play a key and unique role in this.
- The Office of Net Assessment in HQ IDS should institute a continuous strategic net assessment process to support its own operations. This process should leverage the intelligence community, industry and academia and integrate red team assessment activity for measuring our effectiveness in cyberspace.
- Should coordinate with MHA, Ministry of Law and Intelligence Agencies to review existing laws governing action in cyberspace. Should update or draft replacement language to protect own people and promote national interests in cyberspace.

The incident of the recent compromise of widely used enterprise IT systems (SolarWinds), reportedly by Russian intelligence and Russian cyberattacks against Ukraine's critical infrastructure are well known. In case of such happening in India, what should be our action? What offensive cyber capabilities should we develop? Should war game all these likely eventualities and take action accordingly.

The responsibilities should be made clear. For example, who should take action against ransomware crime group, terrorist operation online or state actors like China or Pakistan?

Cyber Security Audit of MoD Organisations and Defence Industrial Base. Currently, NTRO does not carry out a cyber security audit of MoD organisations. Armed forces networks must be audited by some independent agency like NCIIPC. Similarly, Defence Research and Development Organisation (DRDO) networks and organisations, Defence Public Sector Undertakings (DPSUs) and Ordinance Factory Board (OFB) organisations must be audited. Under the 'Make in India' campaign, several private sector organisations have become a part of the defence industrial base eco-system handling sensitive equipments and accessories. Some responsible agency like the NTRO must carry out their cyber security audit.

War Gaming of Probable Events. Probable scenarios in a realistic environment should be war-gamed to determine the vulnerabilities in our systems and take appropriate remedial measures. For instance, just before a conflict in India's Northeast, the power grid and railways communications network fails, adversely impacting the large-scale movement of men and material of the armed forces. War-gaming scenarios like these will help identify and plug weaknesses.

Though there has been improvement in the cyber defence of power networks, the efficacy varies. The NTPC and other public sector undertakings may be well off in cyber protection. The same cannot be said about the arrangement in a state-owned hydroelectric plant that is also connected to the national power grid. A hacker could easily get into the national power grid through this poorly protected power plant and create mayhem at a time of their choosing. What can India do to prevent this incident?

Development of Crypt Analysis Capability. India does not have any high-grade decrypting capability. The introduction of 128 or 256 bits key has made code-breaking extremely difficult. However, the U.S's National Security Agency (NSA) and the UK's Government Communications Headquarters (GCHQ) already possess this capability, as do perhaps Russia and China. India must start the process of developing this capability. Cryptographers, mathematician and analysts with the power of super computers must get together to develop this capability. Collaboration with countries like Ukraine, Belarus, South Africa, Iran and Russia can be explored.

Forensic Labs for Embedded Hardware and Software. India is the world's biggest importer of military equipment, with plenty of electronic hardware and software components. But no country shares its codes. There is always a chance of embedded hardware and software in these weapons platforms. What is the mechanism to check whether there is any malware in the increasingly sophisticated technology areas? What is the mechanism in the procurement of equipment procedure and supply chain management system to ensure that bugs are not present? While procuring, some legal and business clauses can be incorporated. But there is no getting away from India having its testing facilities. This is extremely niche technology and costly, but it needs to be developed.

Command and Control Set-up. There should be no ambiguity in the responsibility of organisations for cyber operations. For offensive cyber operations, the interplay between the Ministry of Defence, the armed forces, Ministry of Home Affairs and intelligence agencies (internal and external) and NTRO needs to be clearly demarcated. Who will carry out offensive cyber operations in a conflict scenario? Can an intelligence agency do it, bearing in mind the rules of engagement or the laws of armed conflict?

Collaboration with Friendly Countries. India should actively collaborate and exchange information with friendly countries like Japan, Taiwan, Vietnam and Australia. For developing niche technology, counties like Israel, Ukraine, Belarus, Romania and South Africa can be approached.

Indian Army

The utilisation of cyber training ranges, training and development of human resources are the same as given above for MoD.

Cyber Capabilities at Operational and Tactical Levels. Indian Army's policy of use of cyber capabilities at operational and tactical level should be clearly enunciated. Due to the characteristic of terrain features and target equipments in operational and tactical battlefields, proximity to the target is essential for cyber operations at operational and tactical levels. In the U.S., to carry out sophisticated cyber operations in operational and tactical battlefields, the most elite and niche technology cyber warfare experts from the NSA's Tailored Access Operations are embedded at the appropriate level in the battlefield. They carry out the tasks and fall back to the headquarters. IA should make similar arrangements with NTRO.

Development of Deterrence Capability. Though this is a highly classified domain, the armed forces and intelligence agencies must develop these capabilities in close cooperation. These should be tested in peacetime so that they can be employed in the event of a war. Projects that can be undertaken as part of capability development could include:

- How to penetrate the adversary's classified military networks.
- How to isolate a built-up area electronically and in the cyber domain before carrying out any kinetic operation.
- The kind of tasking to be given to Special Forces operating deep inside enemy territory. For instance, can they puncture the enemy's optical fibre cable network and obtain data?
- Develop malware in pen drives to be inserted in the enemy's classified network with the help of intelligence agencies so that information is sent back undetected at appropriate times.
- Develop cyber exploits to be planted in the enemy's key military infrastructure like telephone exchanges, main servers of classified networks or radar installations to explode electronically at an appropriate time to make them non-functional.
- How to influence the minds of opposing operational, strategic commanders and leaders, especially of our northern neighbours.
- The security of the tactical data link from India's extremely costly airborne early warning and control system to the other flying aircrafts or to the bases. India must develop its own solutions for such highly classified links and not rely on foreign technology for this.
- How to overcome electronic and cyberattacks by swarm of drones.
- How to develop a malware that can be flown into an adversary's dense radar coverage, homed onto the radar beam and inserted to make the Air Defence Command and Control Systems malfunction, like in Operation ORCHARD.

Removal of Chinese Network Equipment. Earlier, there was no national policy on the use of Chinese network equipments and hardware. The audit authorities have no concern for national security and insist on the least price. Chinese companies always have the advantage of low prices. Although commanders at every level have the authority to overrule the audit observation on the grounds of security and procure equipment, this is not done. This has resulted in large-scale Chinese network devices in India's many sensitive and classified networks. Efforts should be made now to take out the Chinese equipments from these networks.

Cyber operations capabilities in the tactical battle area could include the following:

- Collect intelligence by rapidly exploiting captured digital media.
- Counter and exploit adversaries' unmanned aerial systems by exploiting data feeds.
- Protect friendly unmanned aerial systems functioning in the area of operations.
- Gaining access to closed networks in or near the area of operations, including extracting and injecting data.
- Using electronic warfare systems as "delivery platforms for precision cyber effects."
- Exploiting new devices emerging from new trends and opportunities.
- Conducting cyberspace intelligence, surveillance and reconnaissance operations.
- Engaging in offensive social media operations.
- Should develop theories of cyber operations at strategic, operational and tactical levels.
- Should encourage open discussion regarding the future evolution of military cyberspace in terms of tasks, authorities and organisational structures.
- Develop a deliberate plan and acquisition strategy that leverages existing infrastructure and identify where new infrastructure and tools are required.

Procurement of Equipment. China generally follows Russian concepts and equipments for electronic warfare. Russia showed its superiority in electronic warfare on the battlefields of Ukraine and Syria. In a military parade to celebrate the 70th anniversary of its founding in October 2019, China showcased its latest equipment, including electronic warfare. Even as India procures the latest MiG 29 fighter jets and Sukhoi Su-30 MKI aircraft, it is worthwhile to consider acquiring the latest electronic warfare equipment from Russia that suits the country's requirements.

Conclusion

The internet and global connectivity are expanding at an astonishing speed. Cyberspace is now the new platform for political, economic, military, and cultural interactions and engagements. Computers have revolutionised the function of the world. Cyberspace domain will control national security, economic development, social stability and cultural communication.

While artificial intelligence, quantum computing and cloud computing are revolutionary technologies that will affect cyber conflict, they are not the only upcoming innovations. Internet of Things (IoT) will connect everything we own, from cars to toasters. Smartphones will be used to collect information or forcing control of autonomous machines. Many of these revolutionary technologies could be made by private corporations, obliged to no one, granting them cyber superiority over the world's greatest powers.

There are no rules within cyberspace that cannot be changed. Greg Conti and David Raymond have eloquently defined cyberwar in their book, On Cyber:

Cyber brings new capabilities to bear and will fundamentally alter warfare. However, at its heart, war will remain war. War is ugly, despicable, and something that will remain with us.... Just as airpower alone cannot solve all problems, nor can cyber. Cyberspace operations, however, will play an increasingly important role in all future conflicts.[95]

Cyberspace blurs the boundaries of time and geography that have long constrained military operations. While cyber warfare is currently limited to information networks and network- systems, it will drastically expand shortly. Rather than decide between kinetic and non-kinetic effects, threat actors and cyber warriors will choose the impact that will produce the desired outcome. Cyber-based effects will not be limited only to networks of computers and infrastructure. They will encompass all electronic information processing systems across land, air, sea, space and cyberspace domains.

Cyberspace is now being treated as a warzone where armed conflicts occur between states and sometimes with non-state actors, without proving to be decisive.

Military operations in cyberspace, should be fought as part of a comprehensive, integrated civil-military approach in which civil and military efforts are interdependent and more effective.

Conflict in the cyber domain raises the following questions:

- Is cyberwar replacing conventional warfare? Is the face of a battle getting fundamentally changed? What will be the implications for armed forces, intelligence services and law enforcement agencies?
- Is technological change outpacing regulatory efforts and the initiative for democratic control?
- Can cyberspace be an environment where war begins, fought and concludes decisively?
- Does the prospect of conflict in cyberspace transform or revolutionise the thinking about strategy and tactics of military operations which have evolved over centuries?
- In the era of cyber operations is this hierarchy of strategic, operational and tactical levels still relevant? Or will all military activity in cyberspace at all levels become more homogeneous, with cyber activity running as a single thread from bottom to top?

Cyber Deterrence. The purpose of cyber deterrence is to convey the message that the benefits expected from adventurism or aggression will be outweighed by the costs and/or punishments imposed. It poses difficult questions:

- Should both components of traditional deterrence of denial and punishment operate with equal emphasis and equal effect in cyberspace? Or one of them will be dominant.
- How active and responsive will be cyber deterrence?
- Should cyber deterrence be mainly a national military concern? How can we ensure that when much of the capabilities are non-military and may not even be owned by the government? The private sector is no longer the provider of deterrence capability. It is a deterrent factor in its own right with its interests to protect and its conflicts to prevent.

Cyber Weapons. A cyber weapon is a combination of opportunity and technology, followed by action and effect:

- Opportunity is the discovery of a bug, flaw or vulnerability in an ICT system.
- Technology is a combination of exploit and malware.
- Action involves the deployment of the exploit in the right place and at the right moment to infiltrate the malware.
- Effect involves everything from loss of personal data to temporary network disturbance, industrial espionage, election manipulation, network collapse and indirect physical damage.

Leadership. It is essential for the leaders to "get dirty" with their troops. There are teams of technically oriented operators that are far removed from the higher echelons of command that are doing the work. If those troops do not understand why their actions matter and how they are part of the survivability and prosperity of the organization, they will suffer from disenchantment. For effective command and control, the leaders in cyber warfare need to be ready to sit next to their operators and learn from "on-keyboard" actions. There is no better exposure that they can get than helping their cyber warriors execute the mission.

Jointness. The military operations in cyberspace will be conducted as a joint, inter-service and collaborative effort. There is a robust command and control set-up requirement if that joint effort is to be coherent, timely and effective. There will be a necessity for a doctrinal framework to guide training and preparation and a system of joint 'battle damage assessment' to review operations, identifying successes and failures to inform future operations.

Concept of Victory. A cyber conflict in itself may not produce decisive victory as is expected in traditional military operations. Whenever armed forces are deployed operationally, the first step in the evaluative process should remind the higher strategic aim. Then only ask how the different components of a military operation would serve that aim.

This can be seen in Coalition operations against Da'esh. It resulted in victory in that the proto-state was largely defeated militarily. That defeat of Da'esh was achieved through a form of attrition warfare, steadily reducing the number of fighters available to the Da'esh leadership. Cyber operations made little direct contribution to the campaign of attrition. However, they contributed significantly to the campaign against the Da'esh ideology which in turn helped to undermine the Da'esh fighting spirit.

Rules of Engagement. National policy on cyberspace dictates the aims and rules of engagement for cyber capabilities and the organisation and execution of operations. However, these rules apply only to the nations and fighters that are willing to abide by them. No Geneva Convention exists for cyberspace. In cyberspace, a nation-state like North Korea or Iran can have the same devastating effect on earth's most powerful nations. The use of digital space has effectively levelled the playing field.

AI. Bad actors aim to manipulate the truth using DeepFake videos and other approaches. The more accurate and realistic a fake appears to be, the more likely it is to be accepted as truth. With the spread and scale of online means and in combination with social media avenues to help spread the disinformation, almost any message could be shared and placed into the target audience's decision-making process. Thanks to the availability and power that AI and automation offer, things can go from bad to worse in seconds. Knowledge, a running inventory and a planned response to fake items are a must. AI can beat AI, but the crux of the response remains on humans.

Amos Yadlin, Executive Director of Tel Aviv University's Institute for National Security Studies (INSS) and former IDF's chief of Military Intelligence, succinctly summed up the issue. Yadlin noted that although, as a fighter pilot, he has a great deal of respect for air power, it cannot determine the battle on its own and neither can the cyber realm. It is an important realm, but not one that can replace the physical dimension or combat. "With all due respect to the cyber realm," he explained, "at the end of the day, we need soldiers on the mountaintops to finalise matters.... As to the future of the cyber realm, it may be that 'winter is coming,' or a Pearl Harbor, but we aren't there yet." Yadlin asked how it could be if the cyber realm is such a powerful dimension, that the Russians "have already been fighting in Syria for three years and have not yet decided the campaign? How have the Americans been fighting in Afghanistan for 17 years?" He said that the threat of intervention in the democratic process by means of the cyber realm, as it is claimed was perpetrated during the U.S. presidential elections, is concrete and extremely dangerous. "Look at what the Russians did, and I send you home with this thought: for 70 years, they tried to topple the United States economically by means of the nuclear threat, planes, submarines, and tanks. And on one day in November 2016, they rigged the elections in America. They did not do it secretly. They simply supplied information to Wikileaks and thereby influenced public opinion and moved voters from one place to another. But that is not all. In doing so, they also divided the United States in a way it has not been divided since the Civil War and struck at Americans' confidence in their president, in Congress, in the legal system, and in their societies."

Notes

1. Martin C. Libicki, David Gompert, 'Quantum Communication for Post-Pandemic Cybersecurity', at https://ccdcoe.org/uploads/2021/05/CyCon_2021_Libicki_Gompert.pdf
2. JP 3-12.

3. UN Security Council, Resolution 1113 (2011), March 5, 2011.
4. TRADOC Pam 525-7-8, The United States Army's Cyberspace Operations Concept Capability Plan 2016-2028, February 22, 2010.
5. 'USAWC Information Operations Primer Strategic Cyberspace Guide', at https://usermanual.wiki/Document/StrategicCyberspaceOperationsGuide. 29560538/html
6. National Security Threats in Cyberspace, a Workshop of the National Strategy Forum, Part of the McCormick Foundation Conference Series, September 2009.
7. 'Resilient Military Systems and the Advanced Cyber Threat', U.S. Department of Defense, Defense Science Board (DSB) Task Force Report January 2013, p. 14.
8. Joseph S. Nye, 'Cyber Power', Cambridge, Harvard Kennedy School, Belfer Center for Science and International Affairs, May 2010, p. 3.
9. Julia Voo, et al., 'National Cyber Power Index 202', Harvard Kennedy School of Government, September 2020, at https://www.belfercenter.org/publication/national-cyber-power-index-2020
10. Max Smeets, 'Cyber Deterrence Is Dead. Long Live Cyber Deterrence!', February 18, 2020, CFR, at https://www.cfr.org/blog/cyber-deterrence-dead-long-live-cyber-deterrence
11. Thomas Rid and Ben Buchanan, 'Attributing Cyber Attacks', Journal of Strategic Studies, (2015) 38:1-2, pp. 4-37, at https://www.academia.edu/11253168/Attributing_Cyber_Attacks
12. A A Ghionis, 'The Limits of Deterrence in the Cyber World', University of Sussex.
13. Report of the U.S. Defense Science Board (DSB) Task Force on Cyber Deterrence, at https://apps.dtic.mil/dtic/tr/fulltext/u2/1028516.pdf
14. Senator Angus King, 'Cyberspace Solarium Commission', March 11, 2020, at https://www.solarium.gov/
15. Haley, C. A Theory of Cyber Deterrence The Front Page 6/2/13 available at: http://journal.georgetown.edu/2013/02/06/a-theory-of-cyber-deterrence-christopher-haley/
16. Brad D. Williams, 'Nakasone: Cold War-style deterrence "does not comport to cyberspace"', Breaking Defense, November 4, 2021, at https://breakingdefense.com/2021/11/nakasone-cold-war-style-deterrence-does-not-comport-to-cyberspace/
17. NATO Allied Joint Publication (AJP) 3.10, Allied Joint Doctrine for Information Operations, November 23, 2009. Joint Publication 3-13 Information Operations, Joint Staff, Department of Defense, February 13, 2006.
18. Herbert S. Lin, 'Offensive Cyber Operations and the Use of Force', at https://jnslp.com/wp-content/uploads/2010/08/06_Lin.pdf
19. Bruce Schneier and Tarah Wheeler, 'Hacked drones and busted logistics are the cyber future of warfare', Brookings, June 4, 2021, at https://www.brookings.edu/techstream/hacked-drones-and-busted-logistics-are-the-cyber-future-of-warfare/
20. Fred Schreier, 'On Cyberwarfare', DCAF Horizon 2015 Working Paper No. 7.

21. Peter Sommer and Ian Brown, 'Reducing Systemic Cybersecurity Risks', OECD, OECD/IFP Project on Future Global Shocks, January 14, 2011, pp. 6 and 13.
22. Lance Spitzner, 'Leveraging the Human to Break the Cyber Kill Chain', SANS, January 12, 2016, at https://www.sans.org/security-awareness-training/blog/leveraging-human-break-cyber-kill-chain
23. Eric M. Hutchins, et al., 'Intelligence-Driven Computer Network Defense Informed by Analysis of Adversary Campaigns and Intrusion Kill Chains', at http://www.lockheedmartin.com/content/dam/lockheed/data/corporate/documents/LM-White-Paper-Intel-Driven-Defense.pdf
24. A "Kill Chain" Analysis of the 2013, Target Data Breach, Majority Staff Report for Chairman Rockefeller, Committee On Commerce, Science And Transportation, March 26, 2014, at https://www.commerce.senate.gov/services/files/24d3c229-4f2f-405d-b8db-a3a67f183883
25. Gabi Siboni and Ofer Assaf, 'Guidelines for a National Cyber Strategy', Institute for National Security Studies, Memorandum No. 153, March 2016, at https://www.inss.org.il/wp-content/uploads/systemfiles/INSS%20Memorandum%20153%20-%20Guidelines%20for% 20a%20Nat ional %20 Cyber%20Strategy.pdf
26. Mike Gallagher, 'State of Deterrence by Denial', The Washington Quarterly, Volume 42, Issue 2, June 28, 2019, at https://tnsr.org/2020/03/one-war-is-not-enough-strategy-and-force-planning-for-great-power-competition/
27. Kallberg, J. and Cook, T. S., 'Unfitness of Traditional Military Thinking in Cyber', IEEE Access, Volume 5: 8126-8130, 2017, at https://cyberdefense.com/wp-content/uploads/2018/09/Unfitnesstraditionalthinking.pdf
28. Robert A. Pape, 'Bombing to Win: Air Power and Coercion in War,' Foreign Affairs, May/June 1996, at https://www.foreignaffairs.com/reviews/capsule-review/1996-05-01/bombing-win-air-power-and-coercion-war
29. Joint Publication JP 3-0, 2017, at https://www.jcs.mil/Portals/36/Documents/Doctrine/pubs/jp3_0ch1.pdf?ver=2018-11-27-160457-910
30. James Mulvenon, 'Toward a Cyberconflict Studies Research Agenda', at https://ieeexplore.ieee.org/stamp/stamp.jsp?arnumber=1492343
31. 2018 Cyberspace Strategy Symposium Proceedings, USCYBERCOM, at https://www.cybercom.mil/Portals/56/Documents/USCYBERCOM%20Cyberspace%20Strategy%20Symposium%20Proceedings%202018.pdf?ver=2018-07-11-092344-427
32. Michael Klipstein and Michael Senft, 'Cyber Support to Corps and Below: Digital Panacea or Pandora's Box?', October 19, 2016, at http://strategicstudyindia.blogspot.com/2016/11/cyber-support-to-corps-and-below.html
33. Trey Herr and Roberta Stempfley, 'Tactical and Operational Dynamics of Cyber Conflict, School of International and Public Affairs. Columbia University, 2017, at http://static1.1.sqspcdn.com/static/f/956646/28023288/1541728849813/

SotF+2017+CCSA+SIPA+Tactical++Operational.pdf?token=nQneu8vdiiGmV4VhOjyGWR2uySw%3D

34. Kristen Kushiyama, 'Army to Focus on Cyber Strategy in Tactical Environments', CERDEC Public Affairs, May 11, 2015, at https://battle-updates.com/us-army-to-focus-on-cyber-strategy-in-tactical-environments-by-kristen-kushiyama-cerdec-public-affairs/
35. Andrew, et al., 'Computer therapy for the anxiety and depression disorders is effective, acceptable and practical health care: An updated meta-analysis', 2018, at https://www.ncbi.nlm.nih.gov/pubmed/29422409
36. Kawasaki, C. '4 ways to deliver tactical cyber to the battlefield', April 3, 2018, at https://www.fifthdomain.com/opinion/2018/04/03/4-ways-to-deliver-tactical-cyber-to-the-battlefield/
37. Andrew, Metcalf, and Barber, 'Tactical Cyber: How to Move Forward', Small Wars Journal, September 14, 2014, at http://smallwarsjournal.com/jrnl/art/tactical-cyber-how-to-move-forward
38. Isaac R. Porche III, Christopher Paul, Chad C. Serena, Colin P. Clarke, Erin-Elizabeth Johnson and Drew Herrick, 'Tactical Cyber Building a Strategy for Cyber Support to Corps and Below', RAND Corporation, Santa Monica, California 2017, at https://www.rand.org/pubs/research_reports/RR1600.html
39. Guidance for Developing and Implementing Joint Concepts, at https://www.jcs.mil/Portals/36/Documents/Doctrine/concepts/cjcsi_3010_02e.pdf?ver=2018-08-01-134826-593
40. Doctrine, Organization, Training, Materiel, Leadership and education, Personnel, Facilities and Policy, at http://www.e-mapsys.com/DOTMLPFP(3).pdf
41. JP 1-02, 2016 The Joint Publication (JP) 1-02, Department of Defense Dictionary of Military and Associated Terms, As Amended Through 15 February 2016 available at: https://fas.org/irp/doddir/dod/jp1_02.pdf
42. Major Michael Klipstein, 'Seeing is Believing: Quantifying and Visualizing Offensive Cyber Operations Risk', SPRING 2019, Cyber Defense Review, at https://cyberdefensereview.army.mil/Portals/6/8_KLIPSTEIN_CDR_V4N1.pdf?ver=2019-04-30-105200-547
43. More Detailed Guidance Needed to Ensure Military Services Develop Appropriate Cyberspace Capabilities, Justia, GAO Reports, GAO-11-421, Defense Department Cyber Efforts, May 20, 2011, at https://gao.justia.com/department-of-defense/2011/5/defense-department-cyber-efforts-gao-11-421/
44. Fred Schreier, 'On Cyberwarfare, DCAF Horizon 2015 Working Paper No. 7, at https://studylib.net/doc/14933410/on-cyberwarfare-fred-schreier-dcaf-horizon-2015-working-p...
45. Clay Wilson, 'Cyber weapons: 4 defining characteristics', GCN, June 4, 2015, at https://gcn.com/articles/2015/06/04/cyber-weapon.aspx

46. Eric D. Trias and Bryan M. Bell, 'Cyber This, Cyber That…So What?', *Air & Space Journal*, Vol. XXIV, No. 1, Spring 2010.
47. Clay Wilson, 'Cyber weapons: 4 defining characteristics,' GCN, June 4, 2015, at https://gcn.com/articles/2015/06/04/cyber-weapon.aspx
48. C. Robert Kehler, Herbert Lin* and Michael Sulmeyer, 'Rules of engagement for cyberspace operations: a view from the USA', *Journal of Cybersecurity*, 3(1), 2017, 69–80, at https://academic.oup.com/cybersecurity/article/doi/10.1093/cybsec/tyx003/3058505
49. Department of Defense, Joint Publication 1-02, Department of Defense, Dictionary of Military and Associated Terms, 2016.
50. Kenneth Geers, 'The Art of Cyberwar', Internet Evolution, January 24, 2012.
51. Fred Schreier, n. 46.
52. Patrick Mallory, 'The Time Has Come for Rules of Engagement for Cyberwarfare', Infosec Resources, August 28, 2018, at https://resources.infosecinstitute.com/topic/the-time-has-come-for-rules-of-engagement-for-cyberwarfare/
53. Tarah Wheeler, 'In Cyberwar, There are No Rules,' Foreign Policy, September 12, 2018, at https://foreignpolicy.com/2018/09/12/in-cyberwar-there-are-no-rules-cybersecurity-war-defense/
54. Maj Gen P K Mallick, VSM (Retd), 'The PLA's Developing Cyber Warfare Capabilities and India's Options, Strategic Study India', at https://indianstrategicknowledgeonline.com/web/PLA%20CYBER%20CAPABILITIES%20AND%20ITS%20ADAPTION%20IN%20WARFARE.pdf
55. Caitlin Campbell, 'China's Military: The People's Liberation Army (PLA)', Congressional Research Service, June 4, 2021, at https://www.everycrsreport.com/files/2021-06-04_R46808_848c9c293ea2f76c1b766d917401751eeefa03a5.pdf
56. Military and Security Developments Involving the People's Republic of China, Annual Report to Congress, Fiscal Year 2000, Office of The Secretary of Defense, at https://media.defense.gov/2021/Nov/03/2002885874/-1/-1/0/2021-CMPR-FINAL.PDF
57. Maj Gen P K Mallick, VSM (Retd), n. 56.
58. 'Military and Security Developments Involving the People's Republic of China', Annual Report to Congress, Fiscal Year 2000, Office of The Secretary of Defense, at https://media.defense.gov/2021/Nov/03/2002885874/-1/-1/0/2021-CMPR-FINAL.PDF
59. Ibid.
60. Maj Gen PK Mallick, VSM (Retd), 'War and Its Present Status Evolution of Cyber', at https://indianstrategicknowledgeonline.com/web/EVOLUTION%20OF%20CYBER%20WAR%20AND%20ITS%20PRESENT%20STATUS%20.pptx.pdf
61. Maj Gen P K Mallick, VSM (Retd), 'Cyber Security in India–Present Status', Vivekananda International Foundation, October 2017, at https://www.vifindia.org/sites/default/files/cyber-security-in-india-present-status.pdf

62. Ibid.
63. Cyber Security, Ministry of Home Affairs, December 18, 2018, at https://pib.gov.in/PressReleaseIframePage.aspx?PRID=1556474
64. Maj Gen P K Mallick, VSM (Retd), 'Cyber and Space Strategy for India', at https://indianstrategicknowledgeonline.com/web/1%20Cyber%20and%20Space%20Strategy%20for%20India.pdf
65. Maj Gen P K Mallick, VSM (Retd), n. 63.
66. Maj Gen P K Mallick, VSM (Retd), 'India's National Cyber Security Strategy: How to Go About It', Centre for Land Warfare Studies, Issue Brief No. 222, April 2020, at https://www.claws.in/static/IB-222_Indias-National-Cyber-Security-Strategy.pdf
67. http://www.nic.in/node/41
68. 'India now has a National Cyber Coordination Centre (NCCC) to monitor cyber threats', *India Today*, August 11, 2017, at https://www.indiatoday.in/education-today/gk-current-affairs/story/nccc-cyber-india-1029203-2017-08-11
69. 'National Cyber Coordination Centre Director to be nodal officer under IT Act for issuing directions to block online content', *The New Indian Express*, January 20, 2010, at https://www.newindianexpress.com/business/2020/nov/11/national-cyber-coordination-centre-director-to-be-nodal-officer-under-it-act-for-issuing-directions-2222439.html
70. Details about Indian Cybercrime Coordination Centre (I4C) Scheme, Ministry of Home Affairs, GoI, at https://www.mha.gov.in/division_of_mha/cyber-and-information-security-cis-division/Details-about-Indian-Cybercrime-Coordination-Centre-I4C-Scheme
71. Shri Amit Shah inaugurates Indian Cyber Crime Coordination Centre (I4C) in New Delhi; dedicates National Cyber Crime Reporting Portal to the Nation, Ministry of Home Affairs, GoI, January 10, 2020, at https://pib.gov.in/PressReleasePage.aspx?PRID=1599067
72. Indian Cyber Crime Coordination Centre (I4C)—A 7-Pronged Scheme to Fight Cyber Crime, Ministry of Home Affairs, GoI, July 17, 2019, at https://pib.gov.in/Pressreleaseshare.aspx?PRID=1579184
73. Unstarred Question No: 4181, Ministry of Communications and Information Technology, Lok Sabha, GoI, at http://loksabhaph.nic.in/Questions/QResult15.aspx?qref=150407&lsno=15
74. Unstarred Question No: 3493, Ministry of Communications and Information Technology, Lok Sabha, GoI, at http://loksabhaph.nic.in/Questions/QResult15.aspx?qref=22670&lsno=16
75. 'National Intelligence Grid to be ready by early 2020', India Today, September 22, 2019, at https://www.indiatoday.in/india/story/national-intelligence-grid-to-be-ready-by-early-2020-1601949-2019-09-22
76. Udbhav Tiwari, 'The Design & Technology behind India's Surveillance Programmes', Centre for Internet and Society, January 20, 2017, at https://cis-india.org/

internet-governance/blog/the-design-technology-behind-india2019s-surveillance-programmes

77. Executive Summary and Abbreviations, at https://www.cii.in/uploads/2Guidelines%20for%20Protection%20of%20NCII-%20Executive%20SummaryAbbreviations373.pdf
78. Maj Gen P K Mallick, VSM (Retd), n. 63.
79. Ibid.
80. Maj Gen P K Mallick, VSM (Retd), n. 39.
81. Recommendations of Joint Working Group on Engagement with Private Sector on Cyber Security, at https://cii.in/WebCMS/Upload/JWG%20report.pdf
82. Maj Gen P K Mallick, VSM (Retd), n. 39.
83. 'Cyber Capabilities and National Power: A Net Assessment', IISS, June 28, 2021, at https://www.iiss.org/blogs/research-paper/2021/06/cyber-capabilities-national-power
84. Indian Computer Emergency Response Team, Ministry of Electronics and Information Technology, 'CERT-In Annual Report (2019)', p. 3, at https://www.cert-in.org.in/Downloader?p ageid=22&type=2&fileName=ANUAL-2020-0001.pdf
85. International Telecommunication Union, 'Global Cyber security Index 2018', p. 58, at https://www.itu.int/dms_pub/itu-d/opb/str/D-STR-GCI.01-2018-PDF-E.pdf
86. https://www.itu.int/epublications/publication/global-cybersecurity-index-2020/en/
87. Maj Gen P K Mallick, VSM (Retd), n. 63.
88. Ibid.
89. Maj Gen P K Mallick, VSM (Retd), 'Cyber Attack on Kudankulam Nuclear Power Plant—A Wake Up Call', Vivekananda International Foundation, December 2019, at https://www.vifindia.org/sites/default/files/cyber-attack-on-kudankulam-nuclear-power-plant.pdf
90. Maj Gen PK Mallick, VSM (Retd), 'Chinese Cyber Exploitation in India's Power Grid—Is There a linkage to Mumbai Power Outage?', Strategic Study India, January 2021, at https://indianstrategicknowledgeonline.com/web/Chinese%20Cyber%20Exploitation%20in%20India%E2%80%99s%20Power%20Grid%20.pdf
91. Maj Gen P K Mallick, VSM (Retd), n. 63.
92. Ibid.
93. Ibid.
94. Maj Gen PK Mallick, VSM(Retd), U.S. National Cyber Strategy and Department of Defence (DoD) Cyber Strategy: An Analysis, VIF.
95. Gregory Conti and David Raymond, *On Cyber: Towards an Operational Art for Cyber Conflict*, New York: Kopidion, 2017, p. 274.

5 Space Domain

Introduction

Space was once called the "final frontier". Secure and stable access to space is a critical component of our everyday lives. The use of space for commercial purposes and exploration has expanded rapidly, with nearly 4987 satellites orbiting the earth. 382 objects were launched into space in 2018. While most of these satellites are used for communication, the rest have been used for Earth observation, technology development, navigation and scientific exploration. A substantial number of these satellites are also used by governments and militaries, with many having dual-use capabilities, such as the Global Positioning System (GPS) satellite constellation.

Currently, almost every country either owns a satellite or has a stake in space. About 70 countries and global organisations operate or own satellites. The U.S. Space Force tracks about 26,000 thousand objects including satellites and debris in space. This number is likely to proliferate. Access to and the use of space is a vital national interest. The domain is now "congested, contested, and competitive". The human activities dependent on space systems includes most of the major functions that are important to modern society, including trade and commerce, banking and financial transactions, personal, corporate and government communications, agriculture and food production and distribution, power and water systems, transportation, news gathering and distribution, weather assessment and prediction and health care and entertainment.

Today, a growing number of countries, including the U.S., Russia, China, India, Iran, South Korea, North Korea and the European Space Agency's member states, can build and launch a vehicle capable of reaching orbit. Space is more diverse, disruptive, disordered and dangerous than in the past. While 93 per cent of all space launches during the Cold War were by the U.S. and the Soviet Union, the majority of launches today are by other nations. Governments and their large budgets are no longer the only drivers of space activities. A new set of non-state space actors have become foundational and catalytic elements of space activity. 56 years after the launch of the first commercial satellite, Intelsat 1 (1965), the dynamics of space activity continue to shift towards the commercial use of space for consumers and businesses and traditional government customers. Approximately 90 per cent of satellites launched in 2020 were commercial rather than the government.

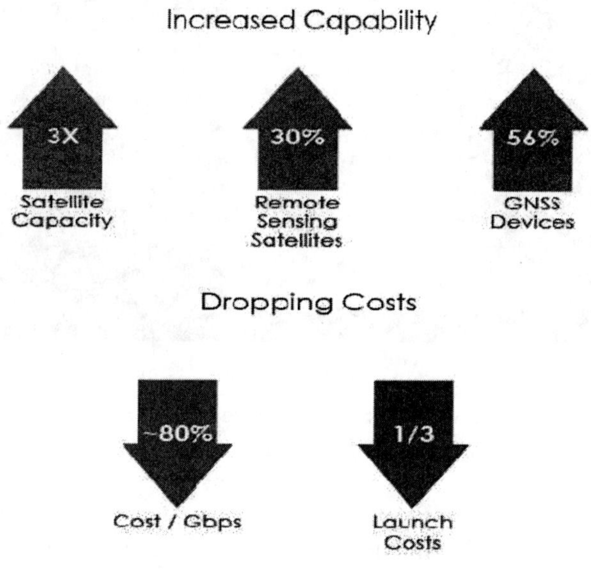

Source: Satellite Industry Association (SIA) and Bryce Space and Technology.
Note: Treands over the last ten years.

Space has become disruptive because many private companies pursue new space missions, such as on-orbit servicing of satellites and in-space mining and manufacturing. SpaceX, for example, plans to launch thousands of small Starlink satellites to provide global internet service. Other private firms are venturing into space missions that previously were the exclusive domain of nation-states, such as space-based radar and radio frequency (RF) monitoring. As a result, sorting out potential threats in a more crowded space environment may become increasingly difficult.

In 2019, the size of the core global space economy was approximately $366 billion comprising of government budgets and the revenues from satellite services, ground segment, launch, and manufacturing. The investment bank Morgan Stanley forecasts the space economy will grow to $600 billion by 2030.

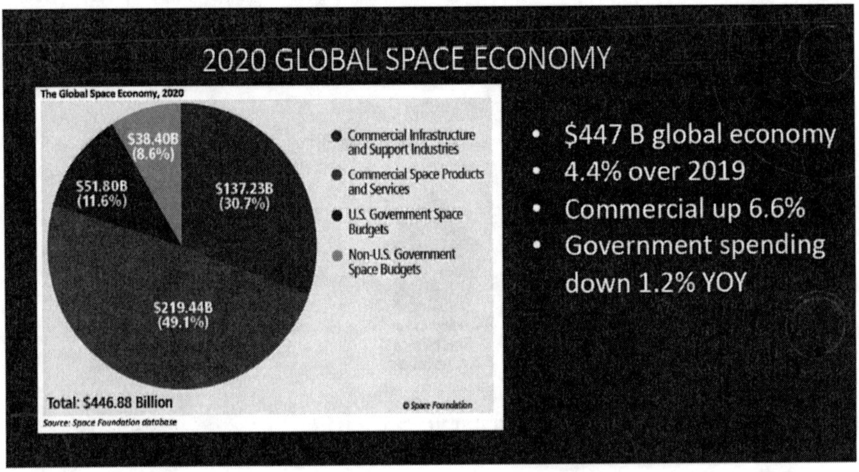

Source: Global Space Economy Hit $447B In 2020, Report Shows, Aviation Week Network, August 23, 2021, available at: https://aviationweek.com/aerospace/commercial-space/global-space-economy-hit-447b-2020-report-shows

Civil space activities include government-led efforts to explore space and advance human understanding. Commercial activities are those where companies provide services to make a profit, whether in the near or long term. Consequently, commercial space activities are designed to generate wealth from access to and use of space. The intelligence sector primarily includes intelligence, surveillance and reconnaissance missions conducted by government agencies for national security purposes. This sector may employ high-resolution imagery considered essential to the formulation and execution of foreign and defence policies.

Space Sectors of 2020

Sector	Examples of Activities	Examples of Actors
Civil Space	International Space Station, Hubble Telescope, Apollo Program, Artemis Human Lander Program	NASA, NOAA, FAA, FCC
Commercial Space	Launch industry, Earth observation, communications, broadband	SpaceX, ULA, Iridium, Maxar, Lockheed Martin, Boeing, Blue Origin
National Security: Military	GPS, communication, missile attack warning satellites	Space Force, Air Force, Army, Navy, Coast Guard
National Security: Intelligence	Signals intelligence, reconnaissance	Intelligence agencies

Source: https://aerospace.org/sites/default/files/2021-01/Gleason-Dickey_SpacePrimer2_20210118_2.pdf

Like the air, land, sea and cyberspace, space is also a domain within which military operations occur. Space is integral to the current way of warfare. Military space activities seek to achieve political objectives through offensive or defensive operations, whether into, through, or from space. Military space activities may include activities and effects to ensure access to and use of space for national purposes. There are a variety of military space capabilities and activities, including space situational awareness, space lift, space control, positioning, navigation, and timing; satellite communications, environmental monitoring, missile warning, space-based Intelligence, Surveillance and Reconnaissance (ISR) and nuclear detonation detection. Space capabilities have proven to be significant force multipliers when integrated into military operations.

SpaceX is an example of which way the space segment can move in the future. SpaceX has disrupted the launch market with its partially reusable Falcon 9 rocket. In addition, its Starlink constellation of satellites may disrupt the communications market. The Starlink constellation alone now has more operational satellites in orbit than China. The addition of about 900 SpaceX Starlink satellites to low Earth orbit (LEO), has brought the total constellation size to more than 1,200, as shown in figure below. This is the largest satellite constellation in history by a wide margin. It makes up approximately a third of all operating satellites in space[1] now.

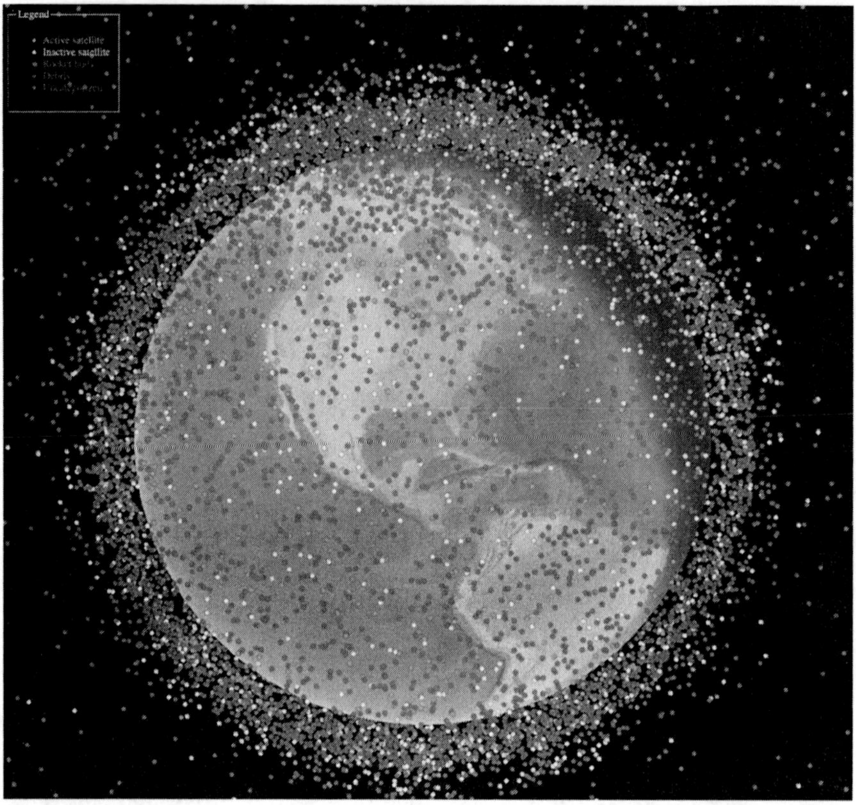

Source: Space Situational Awareness in Low Earth Orbit, IBM Space Tech - Space Situational Awareness, available at: https://ibm.github.io/spacetech-ssa/

Space Domain

The space domain is the area above the altitude where atmospheric effects on airborne objects become negligible. The U.S. has notified that area of responsibility (AOR) of its Space Command is the area surrounding the earth at altitudes equal to, or greater than, 100 km above mean sea level. There is a unique relationship between space and cyberspace. Many space operations depend on cyberspace and an important part of cyberspace can only be provided via space operations.

Space systems consist of three related segments: space, link, and ground.[2]

The space segment comprises the spacecraft, ground stations, and the data links connecting them

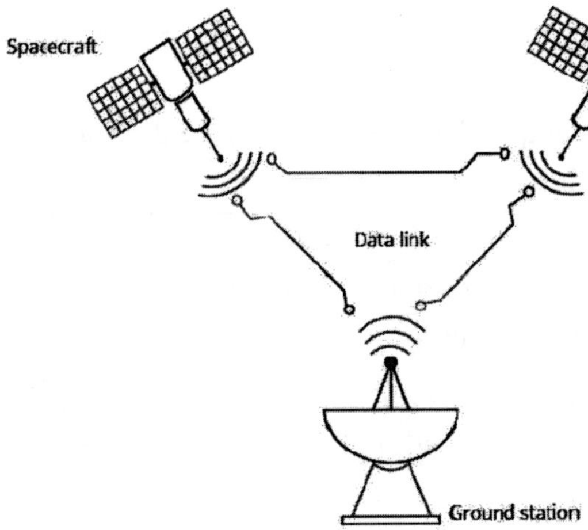

Source: Deloitte analysis.

The ground segment consists of ground-based facilities, antennas and equipment supporting command and control (C2) of space segment resources, ground-based processing equipment, space situational awareness (SSA) sensors and the interconnectivity between the facilities in which this equipment is housed. In addition, the ground segment incorporates the operational management planning hardware and software at a regional satellite communications support centre (RSSC) and the satellite command and control centres used to perform satellite, payload and transmissions control.

The link segment includes signals connecting ground and space segments through the electromagnetic spectrum (EMS). This includes telemetry, tracking, and commanding (TT&C) signals necessary to control the payload and spacecraft. Apart from the TT&C signals, the satellite payload signals, such as the SATCOM signal, enables communication between points on the ground or the Positioning, Navigation and Timing (PNT) signals that will allow navigation.

The space segment comprises the operational spacecraft within the space domain. In addition, the space segment comprises military and commercial satellites and SATCOM payloads in orbit.

Space Domain. The unique characteristics of space domain and its critical assessment are given below.

Space Domain	
Proposed Unique Characteristic or Capability	**Critical Assessment**
(a) There are no geographical boundaries in space. As a Global Commons, space overcomes the international law aspect of a nation's territorial sovereignty [emphasis in original].	**(a) Not Unique.** One can argue that geosynchronous orbit spots have some equivalence to sovereignty based on the location and frequency use of the satellite.
(b) Satellites are subject to the laws of orbital mechanics. Adjustments to orbits expend fuel and reduce asset life span.	**(b) Not unique.** All physical domains are subject to the laws of physics.
(c) Environmental considerations place demands on satellites' characteristics to include size, weight, and power, further hindering the spacecraft's performance and life span.	**(c) Not Unique.** The land domain section also tried to claim the environment as its unique trait. Each domain must consider environmental factors in operational planning.
(d) Though space is infinite in expanse, certain altitudes and orbital patterns are advantageous. These portions of space are becoming crowded.	**(d) Not a characteristic of capability.** The statement is an observation about the current construct and population of space objects.
(e) Electromagnetic Spectrum (EMS) access is vital to space operations because it is the sole medium for space-based assets to transmit and receive information and/or signals. Therefore, Joint Force Commanders must sufficiently control the EMS to interact with space systems.	**(e) Not unique.** Certainly use of the EMS enables space operations, but the EMS supports operations in all domains.
(f) Space is no longer a domain exclusively transited by state actors. Many non-state actors maintain assets in orbit and often military capabilities Iridium satellite phones, Virgin space tourism, etc. employ these non-state assets.	**(f) Not Unique.** Space has been used by non-state actors since 1961, four years after Sputnik 1. The evolution and proliferation of commercial and other non-state space assets has evolved with military use.

Orbital Characteristics of Space

Spacecraft orbit types and parameters are selected based on the purpose and capabilities of the satellite to provide the most significant benefit for the least cost. The most common orbit types used by the military are Geosynchronous Earth Orbit (GEO), Highly Elliptical Orbit (HEO), Medium Earth Orbit (MEO) and Low Earth Orbit (LEO).

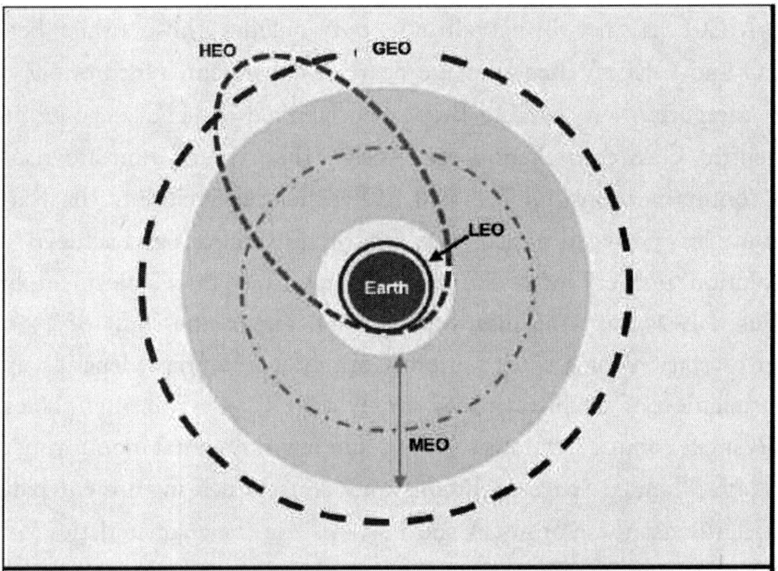

GEO – Geosynchronous Earth Orbit
HEO – Highly elliptical Orbit
LEO – Low Earth Orbit
MEO – Medium Earth Orbit

Source: FM 3-14, Army Space Operations, Headquarters, Department of the Army, October 2019

GEO satellites are synchronised to the Earth's rotation, orbiting at the same rate at which the Earth rotates upon its axis. A geostationary orbit is a distinct type of GEO placed directly over the equator, so that a satellite appears at a locked point in the sky to observers on the ground. It allows continuous line of sight (LOS) observations within a substantial footprint covering slightly over one-third of the globe. As a result, GEO is ideal for worldwide communications, surveillance, reconnaissance, observing large-scale weather patterns and missile warning.

HEO has the shape of a long ellipse. At their most distant points from Earth satellites HEO may be over 25,000 miles away. In the elliptical orbit, the satellite's closest point of approach could be only a few hundred miles above the Earth's surface. Set in phased orbits, two satellites can provide continuous high-latitude coverage, filling the polar coverage gaps of GEO satellites. As a result, HEOs are ideally suited for communications, scientific, surveillance and weather missions over higher latitudes.

MEO has no formal altitude but includes those orbits between LEO and GEO. When they are nearly circular semi-synchronous orbits are categorised as MEO. They are classified as HEO, when highly eccentric. GPS constellation uses MEO. This type of orbit are also used for communications. Objects in LEO are relatively close to the Earth. It can use less powerful transmitters for communications and achieve higher resolution imagery with similar-sized apertures than objects in higher orbits. LEOs have the disadvantage of being in the sight of a ground user or station for a short period. Continuous coverage depends upon a constellation of satellites spaced evenly around several orbital planes. For ISR, small communications satellites and environmental monitoring LEO is ideal. Manned space-flight missions and science instrument payloads frequently use these orbits. A short synopsis of the characteristics for each orbit type is given below.

Orbit Type and Characteristics				
Type	Description	Advantages	Disadvantages	Applications
Geosynchronous Earth orbit	Roughly circular ~23,000 miles above Earth's surface	Continuous coverage over specific area Coverage nearly hemispheric	Far from Earth- resolution and signal limitations Easier to jam signal latency	Communication Surveillance Reconnaissance Weather collection Missile warning
Highly elliptical orbit	Long ellipse ~600 miles at perigee (closest to Earth) ~25,000 miles at apogee (farthest from Earth)	Long dwell time over a large area Coverage of high North of South latitudes	Continuous coverage requires multiple satellites	Communication over high North or South latitudes Scientific Surveillance Reconnaissance Missile warning

More Earth orbit	Roughly circular Between ~1,000 miles above Earth's surface	Stable orbit Less signal latency	Highest radiation level environment	Positioning, navigation, and timing Communication
Low Earth orbit	Roughly circular Up to ~1,000 miles above Earth's surface	Near Earth - high resolution and signal strength	Small coverage area over Earth surface Limited coverage windows for any specific geographic region	Surveillance Reconnaissance Weather collection Manned space flight Communications

Environment Considerations

The space environment is a major limiting factor affecting every feature of a satellite's size, weight and power. It influences the performance and life span of any operational spacecraft.

Space Weather. Almost all natural hazards to space capabilities, except from the threat of meteoroids and cosmic rays, come from the Sun. The diverse phenomena resulting from the Sun's activity are collectively termed "space weather". It gets manifested as increased electromagnetic noise, solar flares, ionosphere interference or protracted impact by energetic charged particles. Cosmic rays, charged particles, the Van Allen radiation belts and other natural phenomena in space may disturb communications, navigation accuracy and sensor performance and may even lead to electronic failure.

Debris. Operational satellites remain under constant threat of impact of debris. Debris from satellite explosions or impacts, orbiting particulates left behind during a satellite's lifetime, trash such as rocket bodies and meteoroids may damage operational systems.

- **Debris Dispersal.** Usually, if an object separates from an orbiting body, it will begin with follow the same orbit irrespective of its size. Debris may take up to years to separate from its source. Depending on altitude and velocity, such objects may last in a stable orbit for tens or even hundreds of years.
- **Cascading Collisions.** The preferential use of some orbits compounds the collision risk. As the orbital space around the earth becomes

more overcrowded, a small collision may create a chain reaction, creating debris that renders some orbits unusable for centuries.

The number of objects in orbit will continue to increase rapidly with the broader availability of lower-cost, small satellites. The challenge of space congestion will grow. Space actors will need better capabilities to track and identify objects and prevent collisions in space.

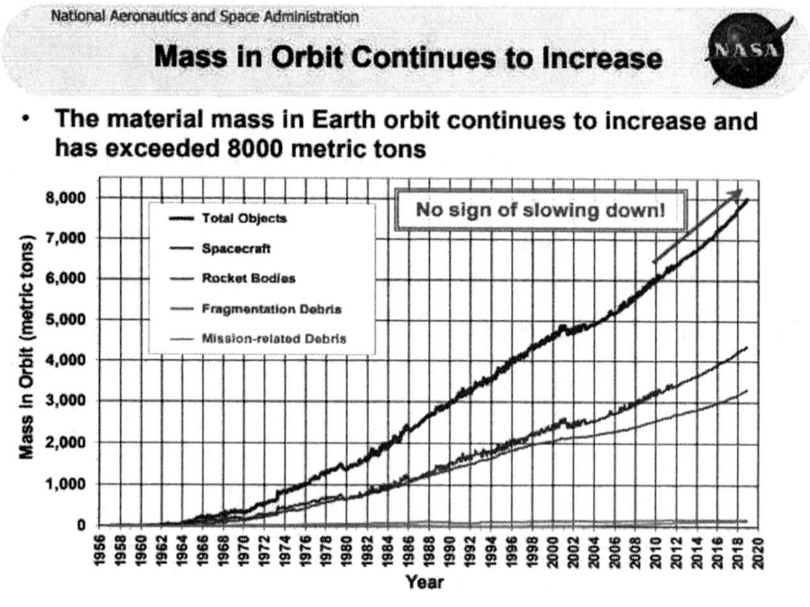

Source: NASA

Resilience. Most satellites face the drawback of having zero redundancy due to their size and cost. The development of microsatellites provides an alternative with the advantage of creating a network of lightweight, easily deployed satellites. In addition, they are more resilient than a single satellite. This type of satellite constellation would replace some systems that currently rely on lower numbers of larger, more expensive satellites.

The resilience of satellite arrays can be improved by upgrading ground-based infrastructure. Redundant ground-based systems and plans can be put in place if part of the satellite array goes down. This means to have an existing, less-capable ground-based infrastructure in reserve in case of a worst-case scenario. In addition, encouragement of the civilian space industry is necessary to continue and sustain military and civilian use of space.

Delta-V (ÄV): A Limiting Factor

As a satellite moves quickly, it has a lot of inertia. Repositioning or changing a satellite in its orbit, known as a manoeuvre, can require significant time and energy. Since space is vast and the tight natural relationship between a satellite's direction, speed and altitude, changing an orbit requires both time and ΔV.

Manoeuvring a satellite in space is very different from operating an aeroplane. Since the satellite travels at high speeds, attempting to change its course through space requires expending energy to generate ΔV. Maneuvers in space are measured by the extent of velocity change required. The magnitude of these velocity changes, provided almost exclusively by onboard propellants, is Delta-V (denoted: ÄV) and measured in meters per second. A satellite is designed with a specific ÄV budget. A satellite operator will plan satellite manoeuvres based on how much ÄV is left in the satellite's kitty. Unlike an aeroplane that can be refuelled, once a satellite is launched, it cannot increase its ÄV budget.

Space capabilities have become central to military operations like missile warning, geolocation and navigation, target identification, and tracking of adversary activities. In addition, the intelligence collection capabilities that commercial remote sensing satellites provide is reducing the ability of all countries to remain undetected while performing sensitive testing and evaluation activities or military exercises and operations.

All commanders should have a basic awareness of the fundamental advantages offered by space operations to employ space capabilities effectively. For example, authorised commanders may have satellite operators change a satellite's orbital parameters to meet mission requirements in certain circumstances. However, when doing so, the commander must understand this will deplete fuel, which may significantly degrade the performance and life span of a system.

Threats in Space

Space is an integral part of modern warfare. Space access and denial are critical components of a nation's national and military strategies. In addition, counter space capabilities can be used to reduce adversary's military effectiveness for winning future wars.

Threats in space can be broadly categorised into four distinct segments[3]:

- Lethal physical weapons to strike directly or create a detonation near a satellite or ground station. These include:
- Direct ascent anti-satellite weapons, a sub-orbital missile launched directly at a satellite.
- Co-orbital anti-satellite weapons launched into orbit and manoeuvred to the target at a time chosen by the owner.
- Attack on a satellite ground station using various weapons such as guided missile, rocket, artillery or improvised explosive device.

Non-lethal physical weapons such as electromagnetic emitters which may have physical effects on space systems without making physical contact.

- Lasers to temporarily dazzle or permanently blind mission-critical sensors on a satellite.
- High powered microwave weapons to disrupt a satellites' electronics or cause permanent damage to electrical circuits and processors.
- Electromagnetic pulse weapons to create high radiation levels and damage unshielded satellites in the affected and nearby orbits.

Directed energy attacks target how space systems transmit and receive data by electromagnetic jamming or spoofing radio frequency signals.

- Electromagnetic jamming is the deliberate radiation, re-radiation or reflection of electromagnetic energy to prevent or reduce an enemy's effective use of the EMS, and with the intent of degrading or neutralising the enemy's combat capability.
- Spoofing is a technique of broadcasting an emulated signal with false or misleading information to deceive a receiver or system into processing the fake data. Spoofing is designed to provide

incorrect results to mislead users, discredit the receiver or corrupt the data.

Cyberspace attack targets the data and the systems dependent upon the data rather than the radio frequency band in which the information is transmitted. Cyberattacks may target the ground stations, end-user equipment or satellites.

Space Threat Categories

Lethal - Physical Weapons (bullets, mortars, munitions) Example include: • Direct ascent anti-satellite • Co-orbital anti-satellite • Attack on ground facilities	Direct Energy Weapons (targets the means a systems uses to transmit/receive data) Example include: • Electromagnetic jamming • Spoofing
Non-Lethal – Physical Weapons (electromagnetic emitters) Example include: • Lasers • High-powered microwave • Electromagnetic pulse	Cyberspace Weapons (targets data and systems) Example includes: • Ground stations • End user equipment • Databases • Satellites

Electronic Warfare, Directed Energy and Cyberattacks

Kinetic attacks need to come close to a target, both on the ground and satellite. There are ways to attack from a distance also. The electromagnetic spectrum can be used to inflict temporary or permanent damage. Since the attacks occur from a distance, it adds to deniability and reduces the problem of getting physically close. Intentional jamming can be difficult to differentiate from unintentional interference, which makes attribution more challenging. Two major types of electromagnetic threats, that can be dispatched by satellites or ground or airborne units are:

- Electronic warfare includes using radio frequencies to overpower an opponent's signals with random noise called jamming and the purposeful simulating of an opponent's signals to send harmful commands or data called spoofing. Electronic warfare attacks are known as reversible attacks as they do not cause permanent damage to a satellite.

- Directed-energy weapons use concentrated radio frequencies like high-power microwaves or lasers to hamper a satellite's operations. Outcomes from directed-energy weapons can be either reversible or nonreversible. For example, lasers can be utilised to temporarily blind optical sensors and cameras or permanently damage sensitive onboard equipment. On the other hand, high-power microwaves obstruct the onboard electronics, with effects ranging from temporary unworkable to melting of critical components and other permanent damage.

There are some crucial points to understand how these effects could play in a conflict.

Intensity dissipation. The intensity of the electromagnetic signal decreases with the square of the distance from the source. Thus, for satellites in orbit, where distances are in hundreds or thousands of kilometres, a threat would need high-power levels to engage with electronic warfare or directed-energy weapons successfully.

Due to distance signals in a vacuum only lose strength. But, when a signal goes through the atmosphere, gases such as water vapour and oxygen absorb some of the intensity. Liquid water also degrades signal strength. Therefore, a ground-to-space or space-to-ground attack will require more power than a space-to-space attack of the same distance.

Precision. Electronic warfare requires a significant degree of precision to execute. For a successful jamming attack, the attacker has to send a jamming signal that matches the signal of the target's receiver. Matching a signal is a mix of achieving the right frequency, polarisation and signal strength. Signal strength is vital because a jamming signal must be at least equally strong as the targeted signal to cause interference. Furthermore, since satellites move in predictable paths, it is easier for an attacker to characterise a target's signal and adjust its jamming broadcast accordingly.

Spoofing. Spoofing attacks need greater precision. A spoofer should also broadcast the right type of information on the signal to match a signal's frequency, polarisation, and signal strength. The attacking spoofer, to be effective, has to understand thoroughly both the signal itself and how the targeted system interprets the signal.

Cyberattack. Although electronic attacks involve interfering with a satellite's radio frequency signals, cyberattacks target the data used and transmitted by a satellite. Cyberattacks on satellites require exploiting hardware or software weaknesses in the communications link between ground network and the satellite to either steal data or inject malicious code into the system. An attack by cyber on a satellite can result in loss of information needed to perform its mission or control of the vehicle itself.

A cyberattack on a ground station is similar to a cyberattack on any other land-based network. A satellite can also be targeted directly by a ground station set up by a bad actor instead of the ones it was designed to communicate with. On the other hand, a satellite can also be cyber attacked by another satellite. The attacking satellite has to be nearby. Closeness will depend on the specific capability of the attacking satellite.

Overview of Cyber Threat Vectors for Space Systems

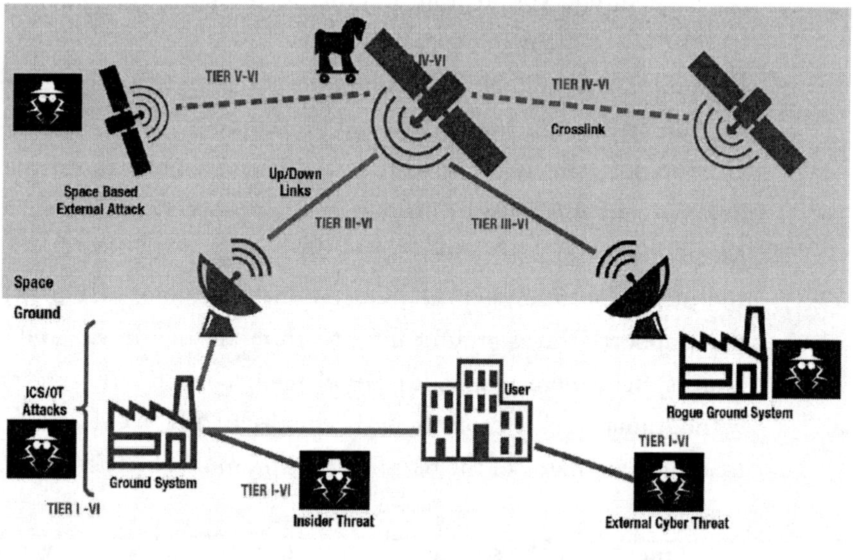

Source: Brandon Bailey, 'Establishing Space Cybersecurity Policy, Standards, and Risk Management Practices', Aerospace, October 2020, p. 5, available at: https://aerospace.org/sites/default/files/2020-10/Bailey%20SPD5_20201010%20V2_formatted.pdf

Electronic warfare, directed energy and cyberattacks significantly increase the number of attempts an attacker can take. They can deliver effects far faster than the deliberate pace of space-to-space engagements. Even though many of these outcomes are reversible, they can severely degrade capabilities during a fight.[4]

Cyber Gaps in Space Systems

From past Experiences based on audits, assessments and public disclosures, the following gaps have been identified across many space systems. These gaps are separated based on their position in the space system architecture (ground versus space).

Ground Segment. The gaps in the ground segment are:

- Insider threats are rarely considered.
- Cyber Defence and Incident Response are mostly poor.
- Network design and segmentation usually are lacking. It permits lateral movement once the boundary is penetrated.
- Shortage of encryption from internal to the perimeter boundary and the use of many insecure protocols.
- Endpoints lack suitable hardening, doesn't protect against many well-known Tactics Techniques and Procedures (TTPs).
- Ground software is the easiest attack vector as secure software development and software assurance is not properly implemented. Mostly use COTS software.
- Industrial Control System and Operational Technology (ICS/OT) that support critical ground infrastructure are highly vulnerable. These systems were designed and implemented much earlier and are without much cyber protections. Ground-based ICS/OT struggle to implement many of the best practices promoted by ICS-CERT.

Space Segment. For the spacecraft, most security is directed towards cryptography on the command link, Transmission Security (TRANSEC) and Telecommunications Electronics Materials Protected from

Emanating Spurious Transmissions (TEMPEST) controls. Some of the gaps identified are:

- Insider threats are rarely considered.
- Ground systems are vulnerable and are the most likely entry point.
- Spacecraft softwares are vulnerable if secure design and coding principles are not enforced and software assurance is not properly carried out.
- Due to the autonomy of a spacecraft, software availability and resilience is critical.
- Supply chain compromising of hardware and software could go undetected due to insufficient policies and procedures and absence of on-board monitoring.
- Deficient on-board monitoring, logging and alerting capabilities.
- Safe mode features can put spacecraft in a more vulnerable state (i.e., crypto bypass mode).

Protecting the Space System—Defense-in-Depth

Earlier space system design had an assumption that protection at the boundaries like the communications link and the ground system will be enough. However, little internal protection exists if the boundary is breached. Current and future space system designs should overcome the risk of an adversary breaching the boundary and operating unhindered inside the system.

A space system must have cyber security protections applied to both the ground and space segments. Unfortunately, the focus has been on the ground segment. Securing the spacecraft has been neglected. Defense-in-depth can be explained by using an onion as an example of the various layers of security.

Large traditional developments and modern, rapidly developed space systems should ensure that they have a cyber-hardened design with risk-based defence-in-depth throughout. An example of Ground Defense-in-Depth Principles is given below.

Space Defense-in-Depth Principles

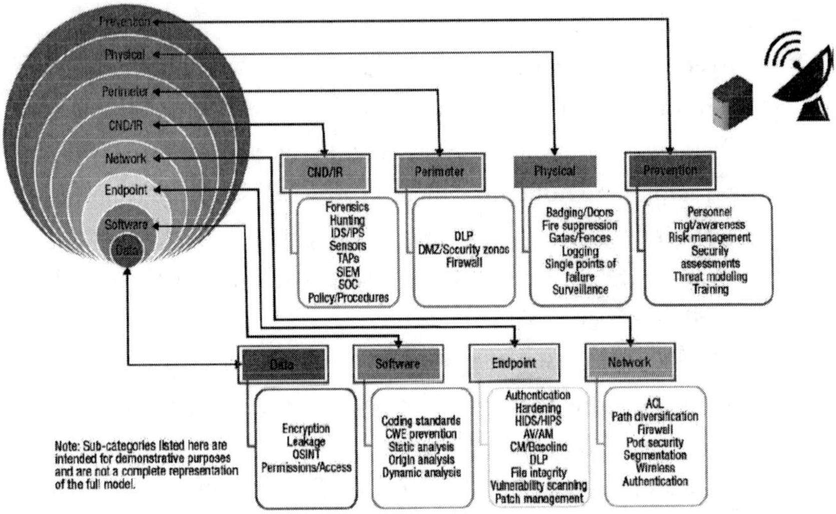

Source: Brandon Bailey, 'Establishing Space Cybersecurity Policy, Standards, and Risk Management Practices', Aerospace, October 2020, p. 8, at https://aerospace.org/sites/default/files/2020-10/Bailey%20SPD5_20201010%20V2_formatted.pdf

Space Weapons

Space has supported military planning and operations on earth since the beginning of the space age. For decades military satellites have been in use for military communications, ISR, PNT and other functions to allow terrestrial forces to operate more effectively. These passive uses of space are not considered weapons, although they provide intelligence and enable military operations.

Something could be considered a space weapon if it originates in space or has effects in space. Weapons that originate on earth and impact on earth are generally not considered space weapons, even if they transit through space. An example is intercontinental ballistic missiles. A space weapon is used to apply force directly against an adversary (force application) or to directly interfere with an adversary's ability to conduct military operations in, through, or enabled by space.

The Table below categorises potential space weapons by the domains in which they originate and have effects like earth-to-space, space-to-space, and space-to-earth and the physical means like kinetic and non-kinetic by which these effects are achieved.

Framework for Types of Space Weapons

	Kinetic	Non- Kinetic
Earth to Space	**Example** Direct ascent ASAT **How do they work?** A missile fires a warhead or projectile into space to directly strike or detonate near a target satellite. The warhead can be conventional or nuclear. **What are their effects?** A kinetic Earth-to-space weapon produces space debris that can affect the safe operations of other satellites in affected orbits. In addition, nuclear detonations in space increase the radiation exposure of other satellites and can significantly shorten their lifespan. **Have they been demonstrated?** Earth-to-Space kinetic weapon has been tested by the United States, Russia, China and India. In addition, the United States and Soviet Union tested nuclear weapons in space in the 1960s.	**Example** Uplink Jammer, Laser Dazzler/Blinder, Cyberattack **How do they work?** Non-Kinetic counter space weapons can be stationed on ground, maritime, or airborne platforms and used to affect the operation of satellites or the sensors they carry without making physical contact. **What are their effects?** Non-Kinetic weapons disrupt or degrade the ability of the satellite to function correctly. They can have temporary or permanent effects, but they do not generally produce orbital debris or other collateral damage. **Have they been demonstrated?** Multiple nations have demonstrated these capabilities, including Russia, China, Iran and others.
Space-to-Space	**Example** Co-orbital ASAT, Space-based Missile Defence Interceptors **How do they work?** A satellite is placed into orbit and manoeuvres to intercept its target by striking it directly or detonating a conventional or nuclear warhead in its vicinity.	**Example** Co-orbital Crosslink Jammer, Co-orbital High-powered Microwave **How do they work?** A satellite is placed into orbit and uses non-kinetic means (such as a high-powered microwave or jammer) to disrupt the operation of another satellite.

	Kinetic	Non- Kinetic
Space-to-Space	**What are their effects?** A kinetic space-to-space weapon would produce space debris that can affect the safe operation of other satellites in similar orbits. In addition, a nuclear detonation in space would increase the radiation exposure of other satellites and significantly shorten their lifespan. **Have they been demonstrated?** The Soviet Union tested co-orbital kinetic ASAT weapons repeatedly during the Cold War.	**What are their effects?** They can degrade, disrupt or destroy a target satellite without making physical contact, producing orbital debris or otherwise affecting other satellites. The effects can be temporary or permanent depending on the form of attack used and the protections on the target satellites. **Have they been demonstrated?** No open-source examples could be found of such a system being demonstrated although such tests could look like remote proximity operations to outside observers.
Space-to-Earth	**Example** Space-based Global Strike (e.g. "Rods from God") **How do they work?** Weapons are placed in orbit and, when commanded, deorbit and reenter the atmosphere and strike a target on the Earth. Damage can be inflicted using the weapon's kinetic energy, or a warhead can be deployed from the reentry vehicle (either conventional or nuclear). **What are their effects?** The effects depend significantly on the type of warhead used (conventional or nuclear). Still, they would be like terrestrial-based ballistic missiles in terms of their ability to hit targets anywhere on Earth with little warning. **Have they been demonstrated?** While the U.S. military has contemplated the idea of using space-based weapons for the prompt global strike, there are no open-source examples of such a system being tested.	**Example** Space-based Downlink Jammer, Space-based High-powered Laser **How do they work?** A Satellite equipped with a non-kinetic weapon could target forces on Earth, such as a laser used to intercept missiles or aircraft in-flight or a jammer used to interfere with radars or satellite ground stations. **What are their effects?** When used, the effects would be localised to the target area, but such a system could theoretically strike anywhere without warning. **Have they been demonstrated?** While the U.S. military has contemplated space-based lasers for boost-phase missile defence, there is no open-source example of such a system being tested.

One of the standard methods of attacking space systems is uplink jamming of satellite communications signals. Directed energy weapons, such as lasers designed to dazzle or blind the sensors on satellites, can be used to attack satellites in space from Earth. China has demonstrated the ability to dazzle a satellite with a laser from Earth. Russia is reportedly developing new land and airborne lasing systems to replace its older Sokol Eshelon airborne lasing aircraft.

Space-to-Space attack methods include a broad range of kinetic and non-kinetic co-orbital ASAT weapons and space-based missile defence systems. A kinetic co-orbital ASAT can crash into another satellite or detonate a conventional or nuclear explosive near another satellite. Non-kinetic space-to-space weapons could be challenging to detect because their use may not be readily observable from Earth. While not intended to target other satellites, space-based missile defence systems would also have an inherent space-to-space capability.[5]

Kinetic Space-to-Earth weapons can be armed with conventional or nuclear warheads, or they can use sheer kinetic energy to destroy targets. The "Rods from God" concept called for a constellation of satellites armed with tungsten rods that would deorbit and strike targets on Earth with explosive force, although no such system was ever developed or tested. Non-kinetic space-to-earth weapons include space-based jammers that could disrupt the downlink signals from satellites over large regions and space-based high-powered lasers that could target objects in the air or on the surface. However, the technology required for this remains challenging.[6]

Effectiveness of Space Weapons

Space weapons are designed as per the target they will be attempting to strike. If the intended target is in orbit, then it becomes more complicated. As a general rule, the higher the satellite's orbit, the harder it is to target. However, satellites with lower orbits have faster orbital speeds, which makes them more challenging targets. More satellites are required at lower altitude to provide continuous coverage of an area. Contrarily, fewer satellites are needed at a higher altitude to provide coverage. Satellites at lower orbits are more easily reached with weapons. They are not easily targeted and destroyed. Since the numbers are more to cover a target area, multiple strikes are needed. Imagery satellites, which typically orbit at about 1,000 km, are some of the easiest to target. Multiple satellites need to be knocked out through multiple successful strikes to create an actual effect. GPS satellites orbiting at about 20,000 km and communications and signals intelligence (SIGINT) satellites orbiting at 36,000 km are some of the hardest to target. Also, they are some of the most critical satellite infrastructures to target.

To locate and track a ground-based system, other space-based systems or some combination of the two are required. Between space and terrestrial targets, terrestrial targets are easier to locate and track. However, tracking satellites need global coverage and precise instruments to locate and continually track targets in space accurately. This key capability is lacking for many nations that have otherwise successfully used weapons such as ASAT missiles.

There is a requirement of a method or vehicle by which the strike is delivered. Ground and aircraft-based systems have been demonstrated. They do not attract the same controversy that surrounds placing weapons on spacecraft or satellites. The weapons spacecrafts would carry have the benefit of not being permanently stationed in orbit. They can operate above any country due to being outside of any country's airspace.

The strike methods can be divided into kinetic and non-kinetic weapons. Kinetic weapons can be categorised as nuclear and non-nuclear weapons. Non-nuclear kinetic weapons can be divided along the lines of projectile or ramming. Ramming specifically is separated due to the implication that it would sacrifice a system or satellite that was intended to be used for different purposes. A projectile is built and planned for strike purposes from the beginning.

Cyberattacks and electronic warfare (EW) have been separated from other Non-Kinetic weapons, such as lasers and particle beams, as they are not inherently intended to destroy the satellite.

Decomposition of different weapon strike methods

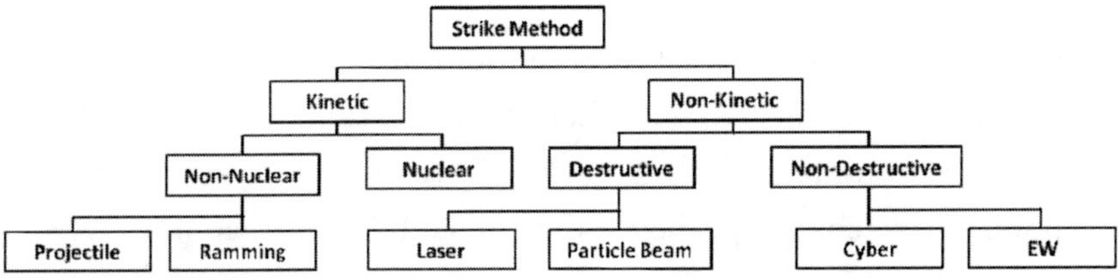

Anti-Satellite (ASAT) Operations

ASAT missiles are some of the most inefficient methods of conducting ASAT warfare. Larger and heavier rockets are needed to reach a satellite corresponding with its orbital height. Smaller and more mobile missiles cannot strike above low earth orbit. China's most powerful solid-fuel missiles cannot reach the orbit of GPS satellites.

The cost of launching a missile to strike a satellite is about the same launch cost of putting the satellite there. The designed missiles and projectiles are not sure to hit fast-moving, low-orbit satellites. Multiple kinetic projectiles are likely needed to guarantee a kill.

For space-to-space engagements, missiles and inert projectiles are less than ideal. The key benefit is that they can be placed in space at a relatively low cost as the primary technology is already reasonably advanced. Each of the projectiles would likely not be particularly massive or heavy. However, for propellant-based projectiles intended to be stationed in space, the extreme environment of vacuum and radiation will mean that new propellants will need to be developed that are more stable in space. It is likely they will still degrade over a more extended period of time. If one wanted to deploy non-propellent-based projectiles, more technological development would be required to field a system such as a rail gun.

Conventional Space-to-Earth orbital strike system's strike capability is limited and they are vulnerable to attack. The most frequently discussed version of Space-to-Earth kinetic weapons is the concept known as "Rods from God". As explained earlier, it involves placing tungsten carbide-uranium cermet rods in orbit to drop them to strike the globe at high velocities relying on their kinetic energy for terminal effect. The disadvantages are: the inert unguided projectile would be imprecise, have a long response time, have an uncertain terminal effect and are financially prohibitive to place in space in sufficient quantities.

Kinetic Ramming. Theoretically, all satellites in space could be weaponised by changing their orbit to collide with another satellite. Although satellite-to-satellite attack via ramming with any satellite is possible, it is constrained and very inefficient. There are a few problems with the ramming of satellites. First, the satellite should be close in orbit to its intended target. Second, the satellite being used is not inherently designed to ram. Instead, it is using its manoeuvring systems to create the crash. Third, it isn't easy to put a satellite in the same orbit at the same place as another satellite and expect to collide with it. It would require sensors to provide terminal guidance to the target. A satellite that would typically serve a functional purpose would have to be thrown away.

Nuclear. Nuclear weapons are the most practical weapons that can be used or stationed in space. Their effect is disproportionate to their size, which makes them economical to deploy. The area of effect is not only the blast of nuclear weapons, but also the effect of electromagnetic pulse. Nuclear weapons would create an enormous amount of collateral damage to the point of being undesirable. However, stationing them in space allows for an effective second strike capability. It is unlikely that nuclear weapons will be employed in space in future due to well-respected norms in space.

Laser. The term lasers here refers to lasers that are of sufficient strength to cause physical damage to a target. It excludes lasers used for targeting sensory equipment which comes under EW. Directed energy weapons travel at or near the speed of light, are easier to aim and require little or no lead for the target. Conversely, they do not have an unlimited range as the beam does diverge over distance. They distort and diffract if travelling through a medium such as air, losing energy over distance. For deploying lasers to or from space, a balance is required between using more energy and effort for transportation to position energy weapons closer to their target and utilising larger and more energy-intensive weapons to place them further away.

Ground-based lasers and particle beams do not easily pierce the atmosphere and are not suitable for striking satellites. The targeted spacecraft could blunt the ground-based instrument's effort to attack it through manoeuvres. A ground-based instrument can only cover a narrow area of space.

Energy beams meant to strike from Space to Earth have the same shortcomings as the terrestrial versions without any of the benefits. It would not have the ground-based infrastructure to support a powerful enough beam. With current technology, such a satellite launched into space would be massive and extraordinarily expensive. Space deployed lasers used as defence systems for satellites is likely to see the deployment of this system. France is pursuing installing these as defensive systems. It can be seen as a controversial and provocative move at the moment.

Particle Beam. Particle beams have some of the same characteristics and drawbacks as laser systems. However, particle beams are being preferred in some areas of development as they have the technical advantage of being far less energy-intensive for the same desired terminal effect. The U.S. is pushing for the development of particle beam weapons. One of the main benefits of a space-based directed energy weapon is in missile defence systems due to the little flight time. They could be reused and fire as many shots as their energy storage and production will allow.

Cyber. Cyber and EW are the most useful ground-based countermeasures to satellites as they require minimal investment compared to their ability to deny an expensive space-based system. Satellite designers are considering building encryption into their command and control systems to prevent hijacking. However, satellite cybersecurity has remained limited in scope and function. The ability to inexpensively co-opt and disrupt satellites makes cyber warfare a precious terrestrial tool for space warfare that avoids directly destroying satellites.

Electronic Warfare. Electronic warfare has just as much potential as cyberattacks for a ground-based system and substantial potential as even a space-based system. Uplink or downlink jamming effectively takes satellites entirely out of the fight. Satellites positioned in space can provide wide-area jamming capabilities. Uplink jamming is the more commonly available means of attacking space systems, which interferes with the signal received by satellite.

Beyond basic jamming, it is possible to use a lower-power laser deployed on Earth or even in space to dazzle or blind a satellite's sensors non-destructively. The primary use of this ability would be to locally blind imaging satellites passing overhead of a battlespace. It may be possible to influence satellites in higher orbits with sufficiently focused and powerful beams. This ability to negate satellites' advantage cheaply without destroying the satellite makes EW the preferred method of attacking space capabilities.

There are multiple technologies to counter ASAT operations without deploying space weapons as defence systems. Some of them are: increasing the capabilities of individual satellites, diversifying and deploying more satellites and enhancing ground-based installations.

Anti-jamming and cyber security must become vital aspect of satellite design. A change in the current mindset is required to understand protecting satellites effectively. From the critical analysis given above, the following insights can be obtained:

- An array of choices will be available for states to conduct offensive space operations.
- Non-state actors might be able to use micro and nano satellites to disrupt space operations.
- Certain kinds of attacks in space will not be easily attributable to any one state or non-state actor.
- Any offensive operation carried out in space must be done with caution as the danger of creating space debris could be catastrophic.[7]

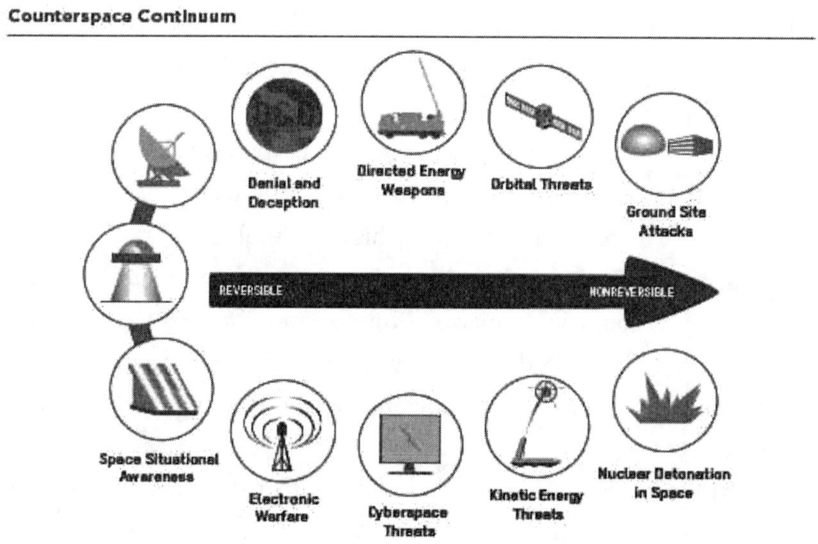

Source: 'Challenges to Security in Space, Committed to Excellence in Defense of the Nation', January 2019.

Advantages and Disadvantages of Space Weapons

Advantages. Space-based weapons have some advantages over weapons based on land, sea or in the air. The economic and technical feasibility of space weapons has considerably increased. Space surveillance capabilities have radically improved. It enables the ability to track, target and attack objects in orbit better than in the past. A new launch vehicle class is making it less complicated and less expensive to get objects to orbit. The arrival of extremely capable smallsats and CubeSats and new systems of propulsion imply that space-to-space kinetic weapons are less costly and less technologically risky than in the past. Lasers and high-powered microwave technological advances advocate the enhanced feasibility of space-to-space, non-kinetic space weapons. Space-to-Earth weapons remain the most hypothetical. However, with the introduction of proliferated Low Earth Orbit (LEO) constellations, even they may be more viable than in the past.

Space-based weapons offer tempting advantages in conflict. Space-to-Earth weapons can attack targets deep inside enemy territory without the risk of aircraft and cruise missiles getting shot down. In addition, states having such capabilities would have better ability to project power globally. Presently intercontinental-range missiles are the only weapon system with global reach and rapid response time.

Space-based weapons are less vulnerable to traditional, kinetic methods of attack than terrestrial-based systems. Tracking and targeting a satellite or a weapon in orbit is a complex, high technology work. Space-based weapons are relatively invulnerable to kinetic attack by less technologically sophisticated countries. Space-to-Space and Space-to-Earth kinetic weapons are difficult to defend because their high speeds and brief flight times provide a minimal window for warning and potential response options.

Disadvantages. Space-based weapons are vulnerable to non-kinetic attacks like jamming or laser attacks. Spacecrafts follow highly foreseeable orbits, diminishing their ability to surprise an adversary and making them vulnerable to countermeasures. Manoeuvring the space weapon reduces this weakness but decreases the weapon's ability to fulfill its primary mission as its fuel is exhausted, shortening its mission life. Creating the weapons less visible through techniques to reduce their visibility increases the cost of the weapon. In the foreseeable future, deployment, development, sustainment and reconstitution of space-based weapons will be expensive compared to terrestrial-based weapon systems.

It is debated that space weapons present broader geopolitical risks due to their potential deterrence and strategic stability. Space capabilities have a handy relationship to nuclear stability and the potential for escalation between great powers. Earth-to-Space weapons create concerns because targeting early warning satellites, strategic surveillance satellites and nuclear command and control communication satellites could also be recognised as the immediate prelude to a nuclear first strike by an adversary, triggering a response on the nuclear escalation ladder.

Space weapons might upset strategic stability in other ways. Space weapons provide a first-mover advantage for striking in space. Their speed could produce crisis instability since decision makers on both sides will have very little time to decide what to do in case of a sudden attack in space. It can create a high risk of rapid escalation due to misunderstanding, miscommunication and miscalculation.

The use of destructive, non-reversible kinetic Earth-to-Space or Space-to-Space weapons would leave a cloud of debris and produce a long-term hazard to all satellites. Using weapons with non-kinetic, non-permanent effects would mitigate this risk.[8]

Armed Forces in Space Domain

Introduction

Over the years constant improvements in technology, technology transfers and globalisation of services have led to the development and proliferation of advanced space systems across the commercial, civil and military sectors. Operations in the space domain are progressively contested, degraded and operationally limited.

The space domain is the area above the altitude where atmospheric effects on airborne objects become negligible. Space is a physical domain, like the land, maritime and air domains, within which military, civil and commercial activities are conducted. There are several distinct advantages to using space for operational purposes. These include freedom of action, overflight, global perspective and responsiveness. Now developing states and non-state actors can increase their influence by purchasing or leasing chosen space capabilities, products and applications easily.

Military planners have to coordinate further support from civil, commercial and foreign organisations. The armed forces all over the world are becoming increasingly dependent on the use of commercial space systems to provide communications; intelligence and other supports. Commanders have to understand how other government departments and agencies, friendly nations, international organisations, nongovernmental organisations (NGOs) and adversaries use space capabilities to facilitate their operations.

Space capabilities should be carefully integrated into every aspect of joint operational planning much before operations begin. Absence of integration increases the fog and friction of war.

Though space operations and cyber operations are different, operations in space require use of cyberspace. Cyberspace helps in satellite control and spacecraft data transport. The people responsible for defending the armed forces networks under cyber operations treats SATCOM payloads like a communications transport medium, like copper wire, microwave links or fiber optics do in other physical domains. The transport layer is critical. The linkages must be kept under observation during all phases of military planning and operations to ensure cyberspace concerns are met.

Benefits from Access to Space. Space assets provide commanders with coverage beyond the geographical areas and access to otherwise denied areas. There are no overflight restrictions for spacecraft in outer space. This characteristic makes space-based ISR, remote sensing, SATCOM, and PNT more responsive than terrestrial alternatives. The space domain provides a global vantage point from which large swaths of the land, maritime and air domains can be assessed for strategic, operational and tactical level applications.

Space operations provide the flexibility to rush capabilities like communications or ISR much faster than ground-based or airborne capabilities. As priorities change, some space resources can be rapidly reallocated to the areas where they are needed most.

The armed forces are getting more and more dependent on the use of commercial space systems. There are additional risks connected with using commercial services. These have to be balanced against the potential benefits.

Space-based assets utilise the EMS for transmitting and receiving signals. The electromagnetic frequency bands that space-based systems use have finite capacity. To ensure freedom of action for space assets it is crucial to achieve the required level of EMS control.

Threat to Space Operations

Space is a congested, contested, competitive and naturally hazardous environment. Space assets face natural and man-made threats. Natural threats to satellites include solar activity, radiation belts and natural orbital debris. Terrestrial weather like high winds, clouds and rain can adversely affect launch, SATCOM and overhead persistent infrared (OPIR) missile warning capabilities. Man-made threats can be unintentional like satellite debris or electromagnetic interference (EMI) or intentional like jamming, lasing, cyberspace attacks and anti-satellite (ASAT) weapons.

While developing plans and strategic estimates, concerned responsible people should consider the possibility of hostile actions from both state and non-state actors' intent to deny or disrupt own forces' use of space capabilities. Ground segment assets are vulnerable to physical attack and cyberspace attack. The space segment is susceptible to attacks from ASAT weapons, directed energy weapons, interference from laser blinding and exo-atmospheric nuclear detonations.

Space Mission Assurance

There are many methods to offer space mission assurance against the natural or man-made threat. These methods can be categorised as defensive operations, reconstitution and resilience.

Defensive Operations. These operations are carried out to neutralise or reduce the effectiveness of hostile action against own space systems. Own forces should be able to disrupt a threat's targeting or attacking of space systems. Examples of defensive operations can be synchronised and systematic maneuvers of on-orbit assets to confuse and overwhelm an enemy's targeting system. It includes active measures to deceive, degrade or destroy targeting systems and a space object surveillance and identification capability that provides warning and characteristic of the attack.

Reconstitution. It comprises of actions taken after severe degradation to restore functionality to an acceptable level. It includes launching additional satellites or activating extra ground stations, new signals and spectrum to augment the capabilities and capacity required for mission success.

Resilience. It is the ability of an organisation to ensure mission success against hostile action or adverse conditions with higher probability, shorter periods of reduced capability and across a wide range of scenarios, conditions and threats. Resilience may leverage alternate government, commercial or international capabilities. Resilience is an internally focused characteristic of an organisation. Resilient capabilities can be achieved through one or a combination of the following methodologies:

- **Disaggregation.** It is the separation of dissimilar capabilities into separate platforms or payloads like separating tactical and strategic protected SATCOM.
- **Distribution.** It is the utilisation of various nodes to perform the same mission or functions as a single node. For example, the highly resilient nature of the distributed GPS architecture allows for more gradual degradation and presents an adversary the problem of far larger number of targets than if the system relied on a singular node.
- **Diversification.** It is sharing the same mission using different platforms, different orbits or systems and capabilities of commercial, civil or international partners.
- **Protection.** It consists of active and passive measures to ensure space systems provide the required mission support in any operating condition. It includes EMI protection, nuclear hardening and maneuverability and other ASAT countermeasures. It also includes efforts to enable satellite operators to reinstate satellite functions, capabilities or capacity.
- **Proliferation.** It is deployment of larger number of the same platforms, payloads, or systems of the same types to perform the same mission.
- **Deception.** It is planned by commanders to ensure the survival and resilience of their space mission. Deception in space operations is intended to mislead a threat with respect to the location, operational status, capability, robustness or mission type of a national security system or payload.

Deterrence. Adversaries are deterred from attacking own space capabilities when they believe a credible threat of unacceptable counteraction exists and the cost of action overshadows the benefits.

Display of the resources and resolve to implement responses using all suitable instruments of national power could make an adversary believe that the cost of the attack is not worth the benefit. Protective measures and resilient architectures can reduce the likely advantages gained by an adversary.

Orbital Characteristics of Space

The four most common orbit types used by the military are GEO, highly elliptical orbit (HEO), medium earth orbit (MEO), and LEO. These have been explained separately.

Space Operations and Associated Capabilities

Space Situational Awareness (SSA)

Situational awareness is the most important aspect of conducting space operations. The U.S. Strategic Command defines SSA as "the requisite current and predictive knowledge of space events, threats, activities, conditions and space system (space, ground, link) status capabilities, constraints and employment—to current and future, friendly and hostile—to enable commanders, decision makers, planners and operators to gain and maintain space superiority across the spectrum of conflict."[9]

SSA requires detailed knowledge of the space domain, understanding of the Operational Environment (OE), intelligence on all foreign space systems, correlation of effects to a cause and proper distribution and sharing of SSA information. SSA supports the following key objectives:

- **Ensure space operations and spaceflight safety.** SSA provides the infrastructure to ensure space operators understand the conditions which could adversely impact successful space operations and spaceflight safety, such as collision avoidance of on-orbit assets.
- **Implement international treaties and agreements.** SSA is a means by which compliance can be verified and by which violations can be detected.

- **Protect space capabilities.** The ability to monitor all space activity enables protection of space capabilities, helps deter others from initiating attacks against terrestrial and space capabilities and assures allies of continuing support during peace, crisis and conflict.
- **Protect military operations and national interests.** SSA supports and enhances military operations

Space surveillance resources include a combination of space-based and earth-based sensors. SSA depends on integrating space surveillance, collection and processing, environmental monitoring, status of own satellite systems and analysis of the space domain. SSA should include understanding of the space capabilities and intent of adversaries.

As the space domain has become more congested and contested, the potential for intentional and unintentional threats to space system assets has increased. To mitigate these threats, a variety of initiatives is to be undertaken to enhance its network of sensors and systems to provide SSA, the current and predictive knowledge of space objects and the operational environment upon which space operations depend. SSA information can be used to find out the cause of space system failures, like environmental effects, unintentional interference or adversary attacks enabling decision makers to decide appropriate responses.

Basically there are Four Functions of SSA. These are:

- **Detect, Track and Identify.** It is the ability to search, discover and track space objects and monitor events to distinguish between objects and their type and use. Its primary role is in support of safety of flight and support of offensive counter space and defensive counter space missions. This capability is required to provide the data for creation of a user-defined operational picture and presentation to the decision makers.
- **Characterise.** It is the ability to determine strategy, tactics, intent and activity including characteristics, operating parameters of all space capabilities and threats posed by those capabilities. This provides the decision makers with the knowledge and confidence

to make assessments of space capabilities, objects, and events that may affect the mission.

- **Threat Warning and Assessment.** It is the ability to predict and differentiate between potential or actual attacks on or from space objects; predict space weather environment effects and space system anomalies and their potential impact and provide timely status of friendly forces. Its primary role is in direct support of offensive and defensive counter space operations. This capability provides the commanders with an assessment of events related to space capabilities and advanced warning of potential events or threats and their impacts to space capabilities or other capabilities dependent on space.
- **Data Integration and Exploitation.** It is the ability to fuse, correlate and integrate multi-source data into a single common operating picture and provide decision-level SSA information to the decision makers to enable decision-making for space operations.[10]

SSA Sensors. The data from U.S. DOD gives an idea about the number of sensors deployed for SSA. According to DOD, a potential of 375 sensors and systems are available for SSA across the commercial, civil, military and intelligence communities. Sensors include satellites, optical telescopes and radar systems. Most sensors used for SSA serve multiple missions, missile warning and missile defence. Ground-based sensors are located around the world to provide a global picture. The U.S. Strategic Command's Joint Space Operations Center (JSpOC) is responsible for analysing the data provided by the sensors and processing it into useable SSA information. For example, in 2014, JSpOC provided 671,727 collision warnings to satellite operators to alert them of a potential need to move their satellites to avoid a collision with another space object.[11]

While DOD provides most of these sensors and systems, other entities—such as NASA, National Oceanic and Atmospheric Administration (NOAA), the intelligence community and commercial companies also provide data used for SSA. For much of the core group of sensors, DOD is leveraging assets by using sensors that perform other missions as their primary functions, such as sensors used for missile defense and missile warning. The U.S. Strategic Command's Joint Space Operations Center (JSpOC) is responsible for analysing the data provided by the sensors and processing it into useable SSA information.

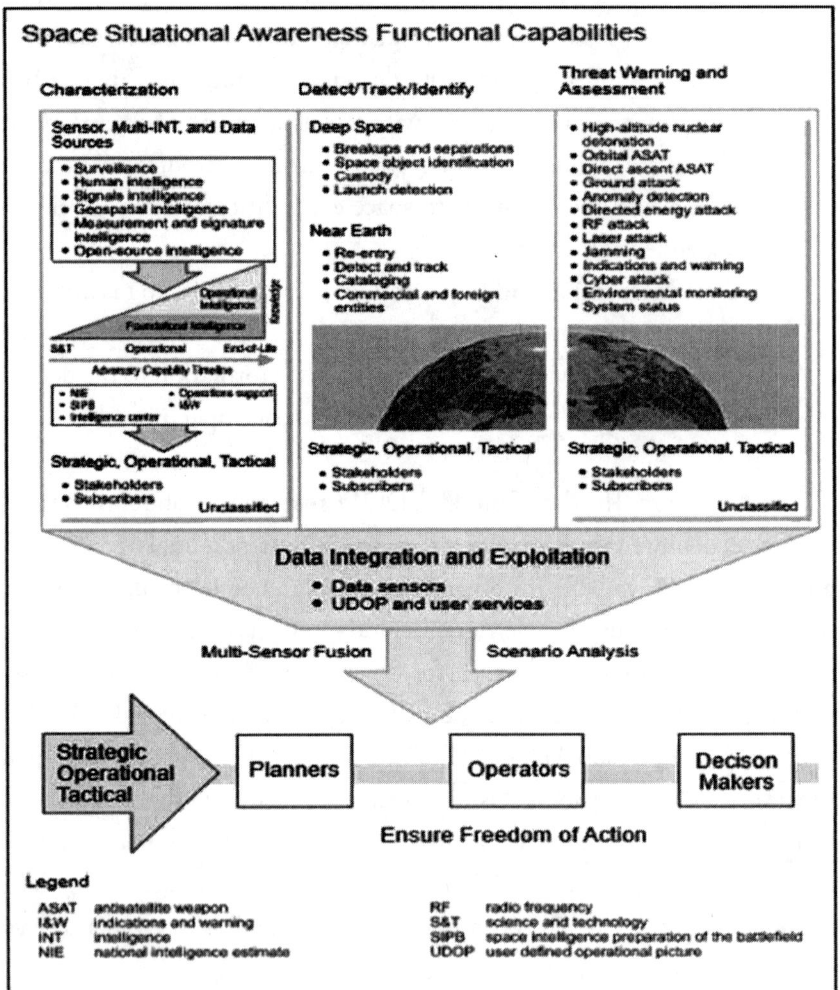

Source: Air Force Doctrine Publication (AFDP) 3-14 Counterspace Operations, Space Situational Awareness, available at: https://www.doctrine.af.mil/Portals/61/documents/AFDP_3-14/3-14-D04-SPACE-SSA.pdf

An example of how U.S. DOD functions will give an idea how this operation is done. The Joint Space Operations Center (JSPOC) provides a Common Operating Picture. The United States Space Command (USSPACECOM) plans, integrates, conducts and assesses global space operations and tracks all space objects using DoD certified space and Earth-based optical and radar systems, providing missile warning capabilities and space object orbital location information for the protection of space assets. These certified sensors make up the Space Surveillance Network (SSN). Currently USSPACECOM also has responsibility for notifications of potential impending near misses or collisions of space objects to commercial, government, domestic and international spacecraft operators. This includes maintaining a "catalog" of known positions of space objects available to operators and researchers via a global public service (https://www.space-track.org), although some information may be redacted for national security reasons. This catalog has a wide variety of domestic and international users to include industry, government and academia. Currently the orbital catalog only incorporates data from sensors certified by DoD, although USSPACECOM does have access to other sensor data. The DoD also has more than two dozen government-to-government agreements under which enhanced space object location data is provided beyond the publicly-available catalog.[12]

Environmental Impacts. The table below provides some examples of linkages between environmental cause, effect and its impact on warfighter.

Space Capability Joint Effect	Environment Cause	Environment Effects	Warfighter Impacts
Communications on the move	Lonospheric scintillation, ionospheric refraction	Degraded/broken communication link, anomalous radio wave propagation	Loss of command and control, lives/ missions at risk
Intelligence, Surveillance and Reconnaissance (ISR)	Upper atmospheric density change, ionospheric refraction and scintillation	Inaccurate space object identification and tracking	Space object collision (e.g. suttle), inaccurate enemy space force position

Space Capability Joint Effect	Environment Cause	Environment Effects	Warfighter Impacts
Missile Intercept	Aurora, upper atmospheric density change, ionospheric refraction and scintillation	Degraded warhead detection and tracking	Decreased probability of missile intercept, lives at risk
Precision Engagement	Ionospheric scintillation, ionospheric refraction	Degraded GPS system performance	GPS guided weapons miss target, increased collateral damage/ civilian casualties
Intelligence	Aurora, upper atmospheric density change, ionospheric refraction and scintillation	Decreased intelligence system performance	Inaccurate enemy position data
Spacecraft anomaly Assessment	Solar/Magnetospheric particle radiation, Upper atmospheric density change, ionospheric refraction and scintillation	Satellite system anomalies, Increased operational downtime of space system	Decreased operational space System utility (GPS, Space-Base-Infra-Red System (SBIRS), Space Radar (SR), etc.)
Attack Assessment	Solar/Magnetosphere particle radiation, auroral, upper atmospheric and ionospheric changes	Enemy and friendly weapon system performance degradation	Inability to meet attack assessment timelines, inability to distinguish hostile attack from natural effects

Figure given below is a high level view of the SSA architecture. It shows how the information from these SSA areas, supply actionable information required for the command and control of space capabilities to support the warfighter.[13]

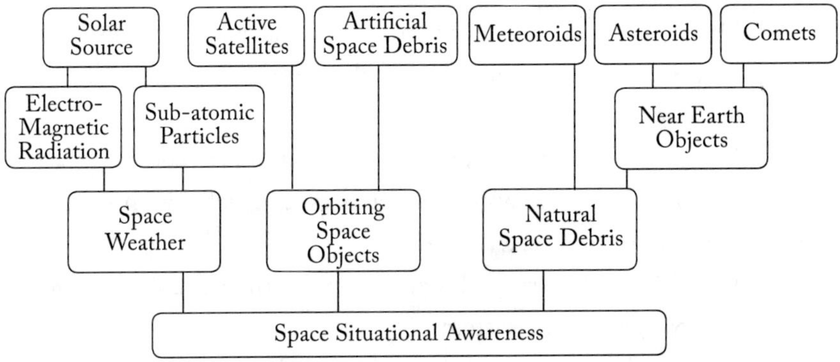

Source: https://www.spaceacademy.net.au/intell/ssa.htm

Space Control

Space control refers to the ability to freely use space to one's benefit while denying it to the adversary. Space control begins with defence like hardening command, control, communications and reconnaissance facilities to prevent enemy interference. It includes shielding satellite components, giving them the ability to maneuver to avoid collisions, disguising their location with decoys or stealth technologies and arming satellites or their escorts to destroy attackers.

Space control employs Offensive Space Control (OSC) and Defensive Space Control (DSC) operations to ensure freedom of action in space and defeat efforts to interfere with own space systems. Space control contributes to space deterrence by employing a variety of measures to assure the use of space.

OSC. OSC operations comprise offensive operations conducted for space denial, where denial involves methods to deceive, disrupt, degrade, deny or destroy enemy space systems or services. OSC actions targeting an enemy's space related capabilities and forces could employ reversible and nonreversible means as per the situation. Some of the means adopted are:

- **Deceive**. Measures to mislead an adversary by manipulation, distortion or falsification of evidence or information into a system to induce the adversary to react in a manner detrimental to their interests.

- **Disrupt.** Measures to temporarily loss of an adversary's use or access of a system for a period. Generally there is no physical damage to the target system.
- **Deny.** Measures to temporarily eliminate an adversary's use, access or operation of a system for a period, usually without physical damage to the affected system.
- **Degrade.** Measures designed to permanently damage the adversary's use of a system.
- **Destroy.** Measures to permanently eradicate the adversary's use of a system. Normally physical damage to the target system is done.

DSC. DSC operations include all active and passive measures to defend friendly space capabilities from attack, interference or unintentional dangers. DSC operations can apply to defence of space, link or ground segments of a space system. Some of the methods are:

- The ability to preempt and suppress attacks is part of successful DSC operations. DSC capabilities must be integrated with SSA elements. A strong DSC capability influences enemies' perceptions of own space capabilities.
- DSC employs a variety of measures that contributes to space deterrence.
- Active space defense consists of those actions taken to offset imminent space control threats to own space forces capabilities.
- Passive space defence measures include camouflage, concealment, dispersal of space systems, deception, evasion and hardening of links and nodes of space system.

Navigation Warfare (NAVWAR)

NAVWAR is careful offensive and defensive actions to guarantee friendly use and prevent adversary use of PNT information through coordinated employment of space, cyberspace and electronic warfare (EW) capabilities. NAVWAR is aided by supporting activities like ISR and EMS management.

Integrated offensive and defensive NAVWAR activities make sure friendly PNT information use is unhindered while simultaneously denying the adversary's use of PNT information.

Positioning, Navigation and Timing (PNT)

Armed Forces depend on assured PNT systems for precise and accurate geolocation, navigation and time reference services. PNT information is critical for almost every modern weapons system. GPS has provided the global community generally unchallenged access to space-based PNT services. Due to its free access, constant availability, high accuracy and modest cost of GPS receivers many armed forces of the world integrated GPS into their tactics, techniques and procedures (TTP). The growing availability of non-U.S.-based global navigation satellite systems (GNSSs) gives adversaries an option to leverage GPS. They can attempt to deny U.S. and its allies GPS through jamming, while preserving their own PNT capabilities. We must have assured PNT through the synergy of space, cyber and EW operations.

GPS provides two levels of positioning services. The normal positioning service is available to all users through the broadcast of an unencrypted signal. The precise positioning service, used by U.S. defence forces and its allies, uses an encrypted code broadcast over two frequencies. Precise positioning service users have a substantial advantage over standard positioning service users due to the relative robustness of the encrypted signal and the ability to correct for environmental conditions by accessing two frequencies.

Intelligence, Surveillance and Reconnaissance (ISR)

Space-based intelligence collection complements air and ground based information collection. Surveillance from the space domain enables the forces to overcome terrestrial line of sight restrictions and affords coverage of large area of interest. Advantages of space-based collection capabilities are their coverage where very little data is available from ground, maritime or airborne sensors. In certain specific cases the only early surveillance available will be from space assets. Space sensors can provide hyperspectral, multispectral, geospatial and signals intelligence, synthetic aperture radar imagery and other various capabilities of value to the ground forces commander.

Demands on individual space-based systems regularly exceed their capacity. Their related orbit requirements may limit the ability to meet operational requirements. Space-based ISR systems are operated by military, nonmilitary and intelligence community organisations. In a difficult scenario, it is essential to identify the effective demand of ISR in the space domain.

Space-based intelligence collection mechanism integrates and synchronises assets, sensors and systems for collecting data and information on an object or in an area of interest. This includes warning to ballistic missile activity, target analysis, threat capability assessment, situational awareness, battle damage assessment and characterisation of the Operational Environment.

ISR capabilities improve planning by providing latest information of terrain and adversary force dispositions. Space-based imagery, supports other intelligence activities including order of battle, current intelligence, targeting and combat assessments, scientific and technical intelligence assessments and operational planning and rehearsal.

Space-based ISR assets support targeting. In recent military campaigns, ISR for targeting has been increased by using satellites to provide accurate information on a single target with a high level of precision including impact points for attacks. Space-based ISR sensors play an important part in the Battle Damage Assessment process.

In military operations the critical part is not just to have enough data, but also to exploit and analyse the data and transpose that into reliable Intelligence. To analyse collected data from space and optimising data fusion requires highly qualified specialised analysts with experience. There is a critical shortage of this human resource.

ISR is a crucial process in operational planning in which information from satellites will play a noteworthy role to collect data. The use of commercial space data could improve the space-based ISR asset resiliency by acquiring new images in case of limited satellite availability.[14]

Chief of recently raised U.S. Space Forces (USSF) Gen. John W. "Jay" Raymond said that since small satellites have become more operationally relevant and the cost of launches has dropped, "there's a role here for the Space Force and tactical-level ISR." He said, U.S. Space Command and the Space Force's predecessor Air Force Space Command have not typically participated in this role, but now is the time to provide the service in a role that is "complementary" to what already exists.

Lt. Gen. John F. Thompson, head of Space and Missile Systems Center during a May 12, 2021 Mitchell Institute Space Power Forum, said, "We look forward to sharing details. There are many small and medium businesses, startups, and other organizations that have relevant capabilities already and we are confident that we can procure ... that data in a commercial way.[15]"

Satellite Communications (SATCOM)

Intrinsically SATCOM systems facilitate beyond Line of Sight connectivity. This helps national and strategic leadership to maintain situational awareness and tell their intent to the operational commanders responsible for conducting operations. SATCOM provides crucial connectivity for tactical maneuver forces. SATCOM systems provide voice and data connectivity.

The inherent capabilities of satellite systems provide significant advantages over other communications systems. Some of the advantages are:

- **Global Coverage.** Satellites can focus capacity in areas of special interest, if required.
- **Real-Time, Over-the-Horizon Transmission of Voice and Data.** Most SATCOM systems provide real-time connectivity for both voice and data. SATCOM can provide the tracking of force disposition and status.

- **Independence from Terrestrial Communications Architecture.** Some SATCOM links make long terrestrial communications links redundant. With these SATCOM links commanders can communicate without the need for physical connectivity or terrestrial LOS communication over relay infrastructure.
- **Flexibility.** Satellite systems provide global coverage and interlinking between frequency bands and systems. A few systems provide a relatively low probability of detection (LPD). Flexibility gives the commanders latitude in mixing and matching satellite systems to meet specific operational requirements. Selected waveforms and directional antennas afford LPD, wide bandwidths allow higher data rates, ground stations permit cross patching and satellite positions facilitates global coverage.
- **Support to Mobile Forces.** SATCOM systems provide the communications support required by fast paced tactical maneuver forces whose rapid movement and geographically dispersed deployments move them away from direct access to land lines and line of sight communication.

Satellite Operations

Satellite operations maneuver, configure, operate and sustain on-orbit assets. It is considered as either spacecraft or payload operations. Payload operations include monitoring and commanding of the satellite payload to collect data or provide capability in the OE. They are designed to deploy, operate and sustain systems in the space environment. Payload operations are critical to the communications, command and control, movement, maneuver, protection and sustainment of space assets.

Spacecraft operations include TT&C, maneuvering, monitoring state-of-health and maintenance sub-functions. TT&C is the process of monitoring spacecraft systems, transmitting the status of those systems to the control segment on the ground and receiving and processing instructions from the control segment. Satellite operations include protection mechanisms to ensure access to space assets.

Rendezvous and proximity operations (RPO) are specific processes where two resident space objects are intentionally brought close together. Servicing of space assets requires the capability to rendezvous, conduct close proximity operations and dock with the space asset. On-orbit servicing capabilities enable inspection, repair, replacement, and/or upgrade of spacecraft subsystem components and replenishment of spacecraft consumables.

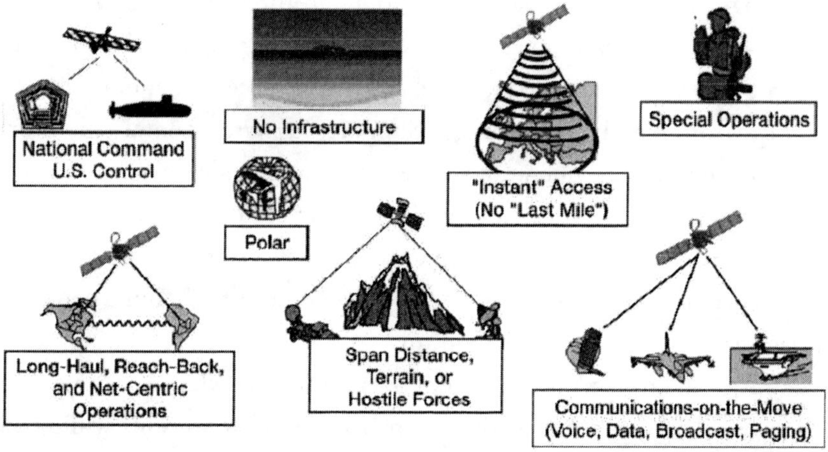

Source: FM 3-14, Army Space Operations, Headquarters, Department of the Army, October 2019.

Environmental Monitoring

Terrestrial Environmental Monitoring. Terrestrial environmental monitoring provides information on meteorological and oceanographic factors in the maritime, land and air domains that affect military operations. Environmental monitoring information includes data provided by non-military satellites. A major advantage of environmental satellites is their ability to gather data in remote or hostile areas, where little or no data is available. For example, space-based environmental data is critical over most oceanic regions, where terrestrially observed data is often sparse. Terrestrial weather can impact space-based surveillance and reconnaissance. Clouds, heavy rain or sand storms have an impact on imagery. Time of day and lighting conditions may affect electro-optical imagery quality. Adverse weather around a ground station can impact data reception.

Space Environmental Monitoring. Space environmental monitoring provides data that supports forecasts, alerts and warnings for the space environment that may affect space assets, space operations and their terrestrial users. Space-based monitoring of the space domain provides the ability to detect and mitigate the impacts of space weather on satellites, manned spaceflight and communications to, from and through space. Detection of solar events and measurement of the radiation environment allow operators to protect resources and deduce likely causes of spacecraft anomalies.

Environmental Monitoring Support. Environmental monitoring support to military operations gives the commander awareness of the OE. Imagery capabilities can provide planners with current information on subsurface, surface and air conditions, such as trafficability and land use, vegetation, beach conditions, cloud cover and moonlight percentage. Imagery may be used to monitor civil infrastructure during natural calamities and disaster management operations. Knowledge of these factors allows land forces to avoid adverse environmental conditions while taking advantage of other conditions to enhance operations.

Some factors related to weather analysis include, but are not limited to:

- Terrestrial weather, such as heavy precipitation can interfere with SATCOM reception.
- Cloud cover impacting collection of electro-optical imagery and data
    - o Interference with electro-optical, multispectral imagery and infrared collection.
    - o The high moisture content in cloud cover may hinder the infrared detection capability of missile warning sensors.
    - o Degradation of space-based infrared sensors due to cloud cover. If there is a missile threat, the cloud cover may inhibit detecting and reporting on hreat missile launches.

Missile Warning

Missile warning is based on detecting an event. Ground-based radars detect the movement of ballistic missiles and high energy infrared heat events such as the hot exhaust of an intercontinental ballistic missile. Theater missile warning reports these detections throughout the depths of the battlespace.

Missile warning provides known launch locations and predicted impact points when specific launches are detected. It gives timely threat warning of inbound missile. Well-placed forces help increase timely warning so that troops on ground have sufficient time to take protective measures to a threat missile event.

Missile warning tracking uses all available space and ground system data to provide senior leaders the requisite timely warning and description of ballistic missile events. Missile Tracking includes launch detection, mid-course tracking, terminal phase re-entry, impact prediction, nuclear detonations detection to support threat and non-threat determination and follow-on decision making.

The missile warning system uses a mix of space-based and terrestrial sensors. Space-based sensors usually provide the first warning of a missile launch. Ground based radars provide follow-on information on launches and confirmation of strategic attack. There is no room for error in missile warning. All information provided must be timely, accurate and unambiguous.

The missile defence system depends on satellites to track ballistic missile launches and help guide ground-launched kill vehicles. Technology that can bring down a ballistic missile in midflight could be used to destroy objects in space as force application.[16]

Nuclear Detonation Detection

Space-based systems, ground-based systems, correlation center C2 systems, etc, provide the requisite timely warning and characterisation of nuclear detonations to support and follow-on decision making. In countering weapons of mass destruction (WMD), detection of nuclear detonations can be used to help identify proliferators.

Spacelift

Spacelift is the ability to deliver payloads like satellites or other materials into space. Spacelift operations deploy, sustain, augment or reconstitute satellite constellations supporting military operations, national security objectives and commercial customers. Space launches are usually planned several years in advance. Spacelift operations provide assured, responsive access to space with an emphasis on public safety.

Deterrence

Deterrence, as described by classical deterrence theorists like Herman Kahn and Thomas Schelling, is typically achieved by punishment or denial. Deterrence is persuading a potential enemy that it is in his own interests to avoid certain courses of activity. The purpose of deterrence is to influence someone's behaviour.[17] To deter, "the adversary must perceive that it will not be able to escape responsibility for an attack in space due to the own forces' ability to confidently attribute the attack." This threat of attribution must be communicated through a declaratory policy that the adversary can understand. In the concept of deterrence by attribution, a "deterrence by punishment strategy has more stringent attribution requirements."

If the deterrence by punishment is to be effective, the attribution information must be credible and available to share with a broad range of stakeholders. Deterrence is essentially a cognitive issue. The mind of a potential aggressor must be understood to achieve deterrent credibility. Attribution, though important, is not the "capability" most needed to achieve a deterrent threat.

By contrast, "deterrence by denial emphasises the ability to absorb an attack" and to communicate the resilience of own space capabilities through disaggregation, diversification, deception, protection, proliferation and distribution of space assets that will convince the adversary that it will be unable to achieve its objective.

When any country declares a deterrent threat to an adversary state, in any domain, that threat must be reinforced by a credible resolve to use force, not merely the capability to attribute and absorb attacks. The risk of deterrence failure increases when the threat to respond is not taken seriously. To be credible, deterrence must be based on armed capability and the perceived willingness to use it.

A framework for assessing and developing a credible deterrence posture should be based on a realistic assessment of what an adversary believes, not a mirror-image of our own views based on what we think they should believe. This requires innovative thinking and development of a tailored framework for implementing reliable space deterrence.

To provide effective deterrence in space, a nation must actively protect its space systems through a credible offensive, counterforce capability. The damage limitation measures such as active defence of critical space and terrestrial infrastructures are crucial to ensure credible deterrence.

Keith B. Payne, an expert on deterrence, argues that to exercise force projection, damage limitation measures such as "offensive capabilities for counterforce strikes, active defenses such as air and ballistic missile defenses and passive defenses such as physical protection and hardening against space-borne electromagnetic pulse (EMP) attacks are essential."[18]

James Finch and Shawn Steene have argued that we need to think about space deterrence as deterring attacks against space systems while bolstering an overarching deterrence posture.[19] They suggest an approach utilising the familiar means of enforcing cost, denying benefit and encouraging restraint. Through such an approach, it is thought that should deterrence fail in space, national leaders have options and capabilities that allow them to prevail in the broader terrestrial conflict.

Michael Krepon has defined space deterrence as "deterring harmful actions by whatever means against national assets in space and assets that support space operations."[20] He writes: "The key elements of space deterrence, as with nuclear deterrence, are secure retaliatory capabilities sufficient to deny advantages to an attacker, effective command and control mechanisms, and redundant safety and security mechanisms to prevent accidental as well as unauthorized use of military capabilities. In addition, successful deterrence requires situational awareness, attribution capabilities, as well as resilient space assets so that the United States is able to identify the perpetrator of harmful actions and continue to utilize space for national and economic security despite these acts."

Dissuasion

The term dissuasion is used when describing actions "that should be taken against those identified as posing a threat to a nation's interests prior to such potential adversaries having the actual capability to pose a danger." Paul Davis defines the concept as "deterring an action by having the adversary see a credible capability to prevent him from achieving potential gains adequate to motivate the action." A strategy incorporating dissuasion seeks to convey the futility of conducting a hostile act, causing a potential adversary's leadership to not pursue a military confrontation in the first place.

To be effective, dissuasion activities must occur before a threat manifests itself. Dissuasion includes "shaping activities," which are typically non military in scope and are conducted during peacetime.

A potential adversary may be dissuaded if it concludes that an attack in space will be ineffectual in achieving the desired effect. This is the domain of space mission assurance. Space mission assurance efforts consist of: defensive operations, reconstitution which includes launching replacement satellites or activating new ground stations and resilience which includes on-board protection elements.

Viable dissuasion measures include actions resulting in a potential adversary not seeking a military confrontation. Actions including distribution, redundancy, maneuverability and protection are all suitable for promoting dissuasion in space.

To dissuade aggression in space attacks, would-be aggressors must perceive that their attacks will be futile. Any space mission assurance efforts should be widely publicised to be effective in dissuading others.

A reliable and responsive space forensics capacity is required to assist in the attribution process following a hostile act. Space forensics includes catalog information, along with data and signal analysis from satellites or ground systems, to help identify details of a hostile act. Space forensics and information from law enforcement and intelligence community support the attribution process. A robust and effective communication capability to rapidly identify and attribute the source of attack help dissuade potential adversaries who would only attack if their identity remain unknown.

Rules of Engagement

Although the Rules of Engagement are not considered strictly law or a legal basis, the rules are shaped by the Laws of Armed Conflict (LOAC). These rules help shape the understanding of what is considered an appropriate use of force during either peace or conflict by a state's or coalition's fighting forces. It is expected that war in space will observe many of the same restrictions as warfare in the other domains of war. General John Hyten, U.S. Strategic Command Commander, support the view that the right of self-defence applies in space.[21]

It means, to achieve military objectives, creating orbital debris in space operations is permissible. However, during war, action should be taken to protect and preserve the natural environment in space. Debris generation not necessitated by mission accomplishment is prohibited. Any anticipated orbital debris resulting from an attack on a legitimate military objective should be considered during targeting analysis and selection.

In future conflicts, there may be the need to not only target a specific satellite but a specific subsystem on that satellite. Today's commercial satellites have multiple paying customers with different hosted payloads on each satellite. The military may use commercial satellites for some communications. Only that subsystem being the military object should be considered during the targeting process. Specific targeting will be required when considering jamming and interference of signal bandwidth used for military purposes. Targeting distinction between multiple hosted payloads or subsystems on a single satellite is needed. However, current technology and capabilities make targeting and engaging only a single sub-system on a satellite difficult.

Attachment to the principle of military necessity does not preclude responding to an armed attack in space in a different domain. If a system is attacked in space, a response can include actions on land, sea or in air. Needing to protect national interests in space through military action means potentially risking human life to defend and protect critical space assets. Responding to a hostile action through a different domain could be perceived as escalatory by an adversary. Suitable messaging regarding intent, objectives and capabilities should be organised well before the onset of hostilities.

Preemption or anticipatory self-defence. Preemption in space will need to fulfill the three preconditions: necessity, proportionality and immediacy. Space as a domain of warfare presents special challenges for preemptive action. Preemption in space necessitates capabilities and processes for observing what is occurring, categorising potential threats and communicating understandings with the international community.[22]

Depending on the magnitude and manner in which space assets are being threatened the decision to act preemptively is a political decision, There are a broad range of possible actions. It includes activities ranging from reversible like jamming to non-reversible like destroying critical satellite electronics and kinetic or non-kinetic actions such as an anti-satellite missile or a laser. This range of potential offensive actions to critical space systems pose the question what types of imminent hostile attack will warrant preemption. Some experts may question whether non-kinetic and reversible actions necessitate a military response. Due to these reasons, clarity is needed in military doctrine and Rules of Engagement, regarding the conditions justifying self-defence and preemptive action in space.

Strategies incorporating deterrence, preemption and dissuasion require excellent SSA, space forensics and resilience capabilities and a timely space attribution process. These concepts require more involvement of the legal community in advancing what constitutes hostile intent, hostile act and armed attack in the space domain. It should include definitions of Rules of Engagement. These efforts require communicating with the international community regarding these definitions and under what conditions self-defence and anticipatory self-defense are warranted. Space powers should be able to respond at any location and at any point within a space conflict timeline.[23]

Chinese Concept of Deterrence

Chinese concept of deterrence is fundamentally different than American and Western thinking. The Chinese concept of deterrence (weishe) includes a significant element of compellence and coercion. Dean Cheng has observed when describing the difference between Chinese and American views of deterrence, "The Chinese focus is on compellence, including coercion, rather than solely, or even primarily, on dissuasion. Thus, the idea of 'deterrence' is seen in both coercive and dissuasive terms." The Chinese see deterrence as a means to achieving political ends. Chinese deterrence goals include actions pursuing to intimidate the opponent through economic, diplomatic or military coercion in a way that directly affects an opponent's interests to compel him to submit to China's will.

In the 2001 edition of the Science of Military Strategy, the dual nature of this idea was highlighted in defining strategic deterrence as "a military strategy in which one displays or threatens to use force in order to compel the adversary to yield."[24] The 2013 Science of Military Strategy says that it is important to "not be afraid to (ganyu) use military deterrence methods, particularly in space, network and other new domains of struggle, to smash the enemy's warfighting command systems."[25]

China does not appear to be interested in "deterrence in space", or deterring an adversary from acting in the space domain or acting against space assets. Deterrence is thought of holistically and not isolated to each domain of potential conflict. China's strategists are focused on "deterrence through space", thereby integrating space activities with conventional, cyber and even nuclear to influence an adversary. Dean Cheng has observed, "This reinforces the point that, from the Chinese perspective, 'space deterrence' is not about deterring adversaries from acting in space, but exploiting space-related systems to achieve certain political and military aims (largely on Earth)."[26]

Affecting Strategic Positions

Emerging space powers will consider affecting strategic positions for the use of the military instrument of national power. Strategic positions may include high-value space assets or those considered of special importance.

There are several ways that an emerging space power may use to exploit strategic positions. Some of them are:

- Irreversible actions affecting a satellite providing specialised services. Can be done through kinetic or non-kinetic means.
- Conducting operations against a ground station through which a high-volume of satellite communication passes.
- Adversely affecting the manufacturer's facilities used in producing high-value satellites.
- Conducting land, sea, air, space or cyber operations against an adversary's land-based launch site. Limit an adversary's ability to reconstitute space systems damaged during a conflict.
- Damaging a space station which is a hub for scientific, commercial, logistical or military enterprise to curtail specialised activities and causing serious political repercussions.
- Adversely affecting permanent stations on the Moon or on other celestial bodies, as they will likely provide unique services or capabilities.

Protracted War

The purpose of protracting a conflict is to protect one's interests and prevent the enemy from accomplishing its aim until the situation changes in one's favour. Buying time through protracted warfare includes elements of defensive strategy. Minor actions can delay defeat, until allies or other forces can join the fight against the superior force. When seeking to protract a war until the situation changes in one's favour, the concept includes using either non-military or military actions against the adversary.

Examples of actions that may facilitate protracting a war include:

- Military actions consistent with a cumulative strategy and the indirect approach.

- Collective action with other states and space powers to enforce an economic embargo against an adversary to adversely affect its space-reliant commerce.
- Introducing legal actions into domestic or international courts to potentially delay an adversary's ability to pursue its immediate objectives.
- Releasing scathing media reports about an adversary's space activities to force an adversary to respond before resuming a contentious action.

Terrorists Actions

The terrorists may want anarchy, chaos or the disestablishment of a state. Terrorist may prefer to attack easily accessible locations that cause the most sensational reactions from the general population. Some potential space-related targets that terrorists may consider acting against include:

- Corporate headquarters involved in the development or use of space systems.
- Ground-based relay stations that support space-based commerce and trade because they are numerous and may not be well protected.
- Manned spacecraft readying for launch because the destruction will cause sensational reactions and result in media attention.
- High-value commercial space systems, such as those providing one-of- a-kind services or with high brand recognition.
- Manned space stations to cause catastrophic damage.

Space Treaties

There is no legally binding Treaties or Norms on the use of space, especially for weapons. Therefore, defining rules and norms for the responsible use of space has been a complicated and contentious issue. However, several attempts have been made but proved elusive for several reasons.

Defining what constitutes a space weapon is difficult. Terrestrial-based missile defence interceptors can also be used to destroy satellites.

Lasers, directed energy weapons, electronic jamming and offensive cyber tools can threaten satellites also. Defining an anti-satellite weapon (ASAT) is going to be more complicated. Even if an agreement is reached on the definition of an ASAT system, verifying compliance would prove challenging. It is debatable that the U.S. or Russia and China would agree to ban capabilities that are essential to protect their military operations.[27]

Arms Control and Norm Dynamics in Space. During the Cold War era, the placement of weapons of mass destruction (WMD) in space became an increasing concern for the international community. This led to the signing of the Outer Space Treaty (OST) in January 1967. This treaty banned states from placing WMDs in the Earth's orbit, on the Moon or any other celestial body. The treaty also promotes the use of space for peaceful purposes and explicitly mentions that the exploration of space and celestial bodies shall be carried out "for the benefit and in the interest of all countries, irrespective of their degree of economic and scientific development and shall be the province of all mankind."

The OST was ratified under the UN General Assembly in October 1967. The OST remains the starting point for all future discussions and agreements regarding international cooperation in outer space. As on 2020, 110 countries are parties to the treaty. The OST provides the basic structure on international space law, including the following principles:

- The exploration and use of outer space shall be carried out for the benefit and interests of all countries and shall be the province of all humankind.
- Outer space shall be free for exploration and use by all States.
- Outer space is not subject to national appropriation by claim of sovereignty, employing use or occupation or by any other means.
- States shall not place nuclear weapons or other weapons of mass destruction in orbit or on celestial bodies or station them in outer space in any different manner.

- The Moon and other celestial bodies shall be used exclusively for peaceful purposes.
- Astronauts shall be regarded as the envoys of mankind.
- States shall be responsible for national space activities, whether carried out by governmental or non-governmental entities.
- States shall be liable for damage caused by their space objects.
- States shall avoid harmful contamination of space and celestial bodies.[28]

The Outer Space Treaty (OST) was followed by other treaties such as the Rescue and Return Agreement (1968), the Liability Convention (1972) and the Registration Convention (1975). Nevertheless, the efforts to negotiate an International Code of Conduct in Outer Space have been unsuccessful and no consensus exists among the key players today.

Treaty (short name)	Date	Total Parties	Total Signatories
OST	1967	110	23
Rescue Agreement	1968	96	23
Liability Convention	1972	95	19
Registration Convention	1975	67	3
Moon Agreement	1979	18	4

The OST or any of the other treaties regulating the use of space never banned the militarisation of space or the placement of conventional weapons in the earth's orbit. On the contrary, it allowed the states to place offensive military assets in space without legal consequences. Moreover, it permits states to place passive military assets such as spy satellites, early-warning assets and military command and control assets. It blurs the distinction between defensive and offensive weapons that could be placed in space.

Recent trends in the development of space weapons have once again ignited the debate on the peaceful and military use of space. However, initial efforts by Russia and China to introduce a space weapons ban failed to gather support.

Major United Nations Space Treaties. There has been a number of attempts to prevent an arms race in space. The Conference on Disarmament has considered various proposals under the agenda item Prevention of an Arms Race in Outer Space (PAROS) since the 1980s. Another effort was the Chinese-Russian treaty proposal to ban weapons in space, formally known as the Treaty on Prevention of the Placement of Weapons in Outer Space and the Threat or Use of Force Against Outer Space Objects, commonly referred to as PPWT.

Initially, this was introduced by Russia and China in 2008. In revised form, it was introduced again in 2014. The treaty proposal was rejected by the U.S. due to the lack of a verification mechanism and restrictions on the development and stockpiling of ASAT weapons on the ground. The PPWT proposal also does not address the threat of space debris as a result of weapon testing.

Some Key Problem Areas to Address

Rand Corporation, in a report, identified five key problem areas that responsible space powers should address.[29] The problem areas are:

- Space Situational Awareness (SSA) and Space Traffic Management (STM).
- Debris mitigation.
- ASAT testing.
- Rendezvous and proximity operations (RPOs).
- Conflation of safety and security.

Presently there is no international body that provides global SSA and STM oversight. As a result, space debris threaten the safe and long-term use of space. The U.S. government sent out 655 emergency alerts to satellite operators in 2017, including 579 in LEO and watched 310,000 close calls. SSA becomes more complex, the more objects there are in space to track. According to NASA's Orbital Debris Program Office, "More than 21,000 orbital debris larger than 10 cm are known to exist. The estimated population of particles between 1 and 10 cm in diameter is approximately 500,000. The number of particles smaller than 1 cm exceeds 100 million." The collision of objects in space, in turn, creates more debris and is already a current reality.

Monthly Number of Objects in Earth Orbit, by Object Type

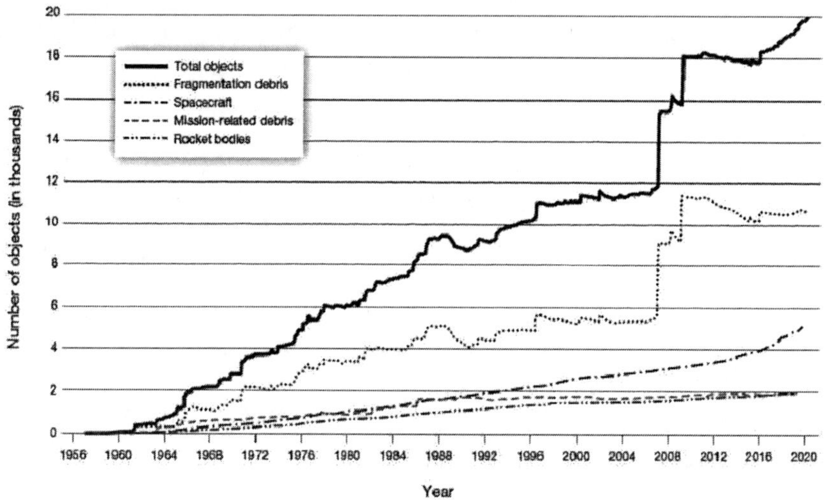

Source: Bruce Mcclintock et al., Responsible Space Behavior for the New Space Era, RAND Corporation available at: https://www.rand.org/content/dam/rand/pubs/perspectives/PEA800/PEA887-2/RAND_PEA887-2.pdf

NASA, in December 2020, released a handbook that details best practices for on-orbit conjunction assessment and collision avoidance. The handbook discusses the manoeuvrability, reliability, tracking and disposal of space hardware. Other topics include space vehicle and constellation design, prelaunch preparation and early launch activities, spacecraft trackability, automated trajectory guidance, manoeuvring, and in-orbit collision avoidance. Although it is a positive step, the approaches outlined in NASA's Best Practices Handbook are voluntary.

Today the framework of space activities is vastly different from that of 1967 when the OST was signed. Now, the world has more than 70 countries and multinational organisations that own or operate satellites. The global economy is intricately linked to space. However, several problems merit attention as space becomes more congested and contested. For example, SpaceX plans to launch thousands of small Starlink satellites to provide global internet service.

The U.S. Space Force shares information on the location of objects in space with more than 100 governmental, academic and commercial partner organisations from 25 nations through formal data-sharing agreements. It is progressively adding more parties to the list of users.

Such multilateral cooperative efforts could help the adoption of additional transparency and confidence measures. They may offer genuine hope of reducing risks and protecting freedom of access to space for all nations.[30]

GEOINT

"The term 'geospatial intelligence' means the exploitation and analysis of imagery and geospatial information to describe, assess, and visually depict physical features and geographically referenced activities on the earth. Geospatial intelligence consists of imagery, imagery intelligence and geospatial information."[31]

Geospatial intelligence refers to the collection of imagery or measurements from satellites and aircraft. Overhead observation often reveals information not readily apparent from other vantage points. During the Cold War, such information was primarily the domain of the intelligence community. However, there has been a civil component to demand such observations always. When used in a civil context, the term usually used is "remote sensing".

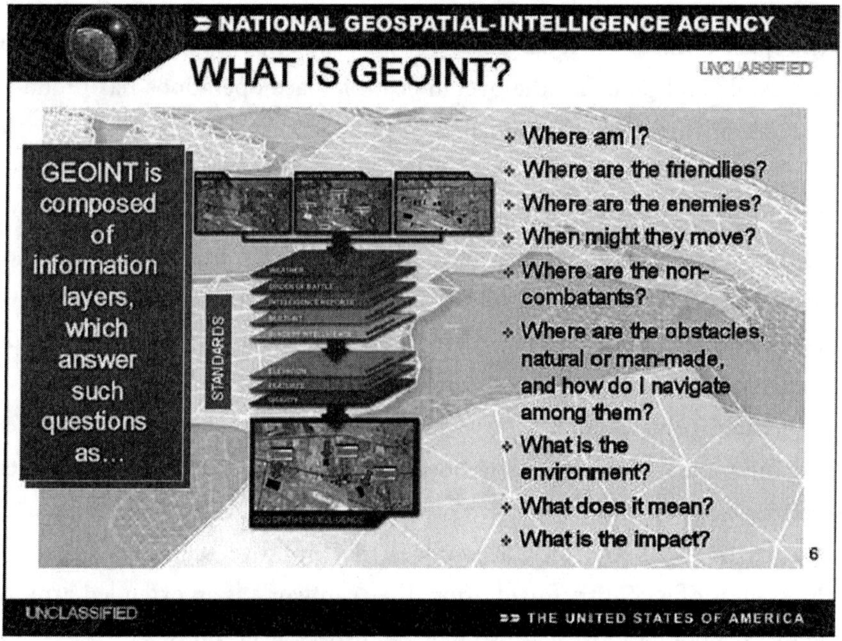

Source: Loren Thompson, 'Geospatial Intelligence Becomes A Focus Of Military And Economic Competition', *Forbes*, December 11, 2020, at https://www.forbes.com/sites/lorenthompson/2020/12/11/geospatial-intelligence-geoint-becomes-a-focus-of-military--economic-competition/?sh=5ba6519a3c5d

In the national security context, earth-observing satellites that collect imagery are a source of geospatial intelligence for a long time. National Reconnaissance Office of the Pentagon operates spy satellites using electro-optical and radio-frequency (radar) technology to generate detailed information about other states and non-state actors. This information is then analysed by the National Geospatial-Intelligence Agency and other consumers using powerful software tools to reveal valuable insights.[32]

Role of Private Players

The emergence of private players in the space domain has given a new dimension to the use of space and space security. Big companies like Boeing, Northrop Grumman and Lockheed Martin have been there in the space domain for some time. But the requirement to make space more accessible and reducing the overall cost of space operations has produced several private launch companies like Space Exploration Technologies (SpaceX), Blue Origin and Rocket Lab. Termed as New Space companies, they have brought about innovations in the space industry. Services such as high-resolution imaging, geo-location and remote sensing are now available through cube and microsatellites. These can be purchased on the commercial market. Earlier, these capabilities were accessible only with large satellites requiring significant investments.

These private players serve both government and non-government organisations. However, their business is largely driven by government contracts. Indigenously-grown private space industries help reduce the launch of assets and provide services that improve the space situational awareness of a country. In addition, they can work as an extended arm in a state's overall national space strategy and space operations.

The rise of commercial rocket and space services companies is not restricted to U.S. and Europe. Many private companies have come up in China and India, which can offer affordable and reliable launch services for small, micro and nanosatellites. Both China and India can lead the micro and small satellite market in the world and become a hub for affordable and reliable launches and space services.

The government of India is taking appropriate measures. On June 24 2020, the Indian Government created a new organisation known as IN-SPACe (Indian National Space Promotion and Authorisation Centre). IN-SPACe is a "single window nodal agency" that will boost the commercialisation of Indian space activities. In addition, the agency will promote the entry of Non-Governmental Private Entities in the Indian space sector.

The private players in space bring particular challenges on security. To conduct espionage operations against adversary states or conduct counter-space operations, a country can operate through private players. This will not be easily attributable directly to any state. Access to space becomes easy. This could open doors to non-state actors whose intentions may sabotage a country's satellites and communication networks and create havoc. States will have to deal with the potential threat posed by non-state actors.

Private space companies extend the capabilities of a country to operate in space. But it also raises the potential non-attributable threats from states and non-state actors.

Availability of the Commercial Sector in Crisis Situation. Many countries use satellite communication, remote sensing and global positioning services during normal military operations. As a result, they rely more on these technologies.

Due to the dual-use nature of many of the products and services provided by commercial space activities, it is difficult to differentiate between purely military and commercial endeavours and associated systems. There may be shared architectures where military-related communications are enabled by commercial satellites. There are implications of mixing military and commercial activities.

It is understood that commercial companies, especially homegrown, will support states in times of conflict if the applicable agreements are in place before the war starts. Militaries and commercial partners must create trust during peacetime.

Commercial space companies come under cyberattacks from individuals, foreign militaries or their surrogates. However, many commercial space capabilities are more robust and resilient than generally understood by policymakers and the military. Commercial satellite operators deal with various threats like jamming of satellite communications or cyberattack of networks every day. They have become more resilient. Several medium-to-large commercial space companies do their own research and development to improve operating under jamming or cyberattack conditions. The governments can benefit by applying the lessons learned from commercial partners.

Private operators and government organisations must understand certain important issues before any conflict to incorporate innovative commercial space capabilities. These areas of understanding are:

- The implications when commercial assets are employed to support military activities.
- Governments considering the ways and means needed to protect commercial space assets when employed to support military operations.
- Companies and their shareholders to consider the implications of commercial space assets becoming targets for kinetic or non-kinetic attack because of the services provided to governments during hostilities.
- For commercial remote sensing companies understanding the potential level of control that licensing nations may exert during hostilities.
- Establishing the most effective and efficient communication structure or architecture between governments and commercial partners enables the unimpeded flow of information during peace and conflict.
- Ensuring commercial partners have access to all necessary data and information to ensure they can provide the agreed-upon products and services during times of war.

Examples of Commercial Space Enterprises.

From the mid-2000s, start-up space companies started coming up. These start-ups entrepreneurs, some with impressive records of success, developed business plans and sought venture capital from investment firms and angel investors. These NewSpace companies are currently taking a leading role in space technological development by building the components, materials and rockets deploying a new generation of cell-phone-size satellites into space. Many of these companies, including SpaceX, Blue Origin and Virgin Orbit, are attracting the best and brightest young minds.

The technology of choice for many of these space start-up companies is the CubeSat, which is ten cubic centimetres, weighs about two pounds and generally costs less than $100,000 to build. About 60 companies now sell them. This allows governments and companies with relatively little financial resources to put a satellite into orbit for agriculture, oil spill or border monitoring like tasks. Some entrepreneurs envision potentially thousands of satellites being part of a mega-constellation in the decade ahead. A launch market has emerged that caters to the CubeSat market.[33]

SpaceX has become the operator of the world's largest active satellite constellation. As of now, the company has 242 satellites orbiting the planet. It has plans to launch 42,000 over the next decade, part of its ambitious project to provide internet access across the globe. These new satellites can revolutionise many aspects of everyday life, from bringing internet access to remote corners of the world to monitoring the environment and improving global navigation systems.[34]

Starship is different from any rocket that has come before it. After it gets operational, its payload capacity, size, ability to land and fly again and the number of vehicles that will be built, will eclipse anything built over the past 70 years of spaceflight. The dimensions of Starship are mind-boggling. When fully stacked, the 164-foot-tall vehicle is only the second stage of a much larger two-stage rocket. Combined, Starship and the Superheavy booster will stand some 400 feet.[35]

Unmanned orbital flights may commence in 2021 and private manned flights around the Moon as early as 2022. Recently SpaceX won the National Aeronautics and Space Administration contract to provide lunar landing services with a lunar variant of Starship. The company also plans unmanned flight tests to Mars in 2024. When it arrives, a single Starship/Superheavy will be able to place more mass in orbit during a single launch than the entire world managed in total in 2020.

There are several technical challenges. First, starship has to demonstrate that it can be reused after surviving landing. Second, it has not yet achieved orbit. Superheavy is still under construction and even when it flies, it will have only three of its planned complement of 37 engines. Finally, core capabilities such as orbital refuelling, crucial to advanced manoeuvre above the atmosphere and central to unlocking commercial and military space, still need to be tested. SpaceX is working to overcome these remaining technical obstacles.

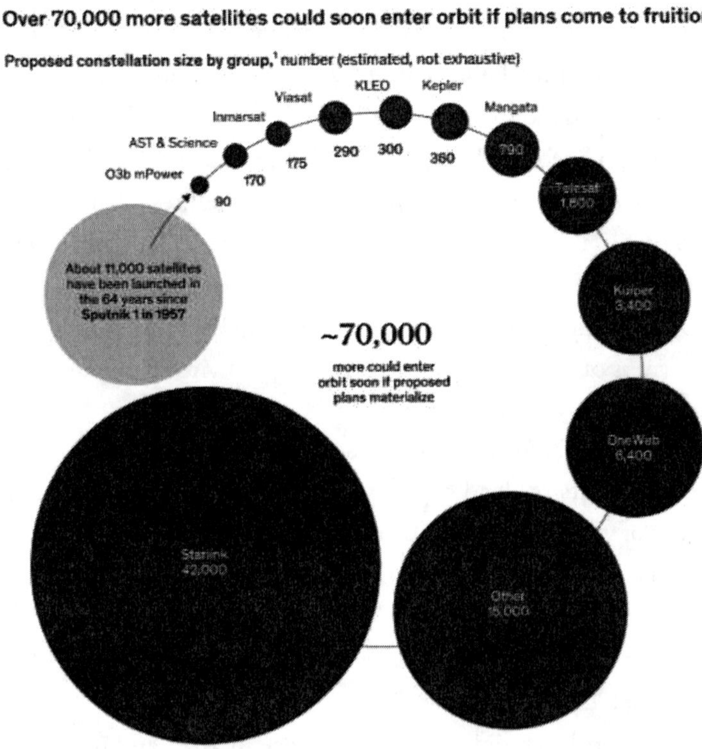

Source: Chris Daehnick and Jess Harrington, 'Look out below: What will happen to the space debris in orbit?', McKinsey and Company, October 1, 2021, available at: https://www.mckinsey.com/industries/aerospace-and-defense/our-insights/look-out-below-what-will-happen-to-the-space-debris-in-orbit

Emerging Capabilities and Future Trends

New Launch Vehicles. The commercial sector is now developing multiple new launch vehicles across small to heavy lift payload classes. In addition, many commercial launch providers are investing in innovative technologies and processes to lower launch costs and increase competitiveness. Some of the creative processes include rocket stages and booster reusabilities, like SpaceX's Falcon Heavy and the use of lower-cost propellants, like the liquefied natural gas used in Blue Origin's New Glenn vehicles. While technological innovations and new processes are expected to transform the launch market, the market still has persistent challenges including a highly competitive commercial launch market, historically low profit margins, missile technology proliferation concerns and technology and intellectual property export control risks.

Affordable Launch. Two key trends have enabled reductions in the cost of space launch. First, companies like SpaceX and Blue Origin have pioneered techniques to re-use launch vehicles, potentially saving significant savings. Second, many companies like Rocket Lab have begun introducing small launch vehicles empowered by new technologies such as additive manufacturing. These small vehicles provide lower total cost making them attractive to some users.

Smallsats. With reduced launch costs and the miniaturisation of computer components, small satellites have shown the way for more diverse uses of space. Countries like Mongolia and Ghana have been able to field satellites, as have universities, high schools and middle schools through programs like NASA's Educational Launch of Nanosatellites (ELaNa). Small satellites like CubeSats have also supported many commercial ventures, including Earth-imaging and communications services. However, small satellites and large constellations pose the risk of significantly increasing the quantity of debris in orbit.

Large Constellations. Large constellations have become cheaper as it is easier to launch large numbers of small satellites. As a result, large constellations can be predominantly helpful for lower-latency satellite communications and expand Internet of Things (IoT) applications.

New Space Applications. Commercial companies have offered recently serious proposals to undertake novel activities in space. With plans for private customers on suborbital flights by at least two well-financed companies, space tourism has arrived. Other activities include satellite servicing with specialised spacecraft, which repair or refuel existing satellites to extend their mission lifetimes, and commercial lunar and asteroid missions, which could provide data to space agencies and universities or even prospect for valuable resources.

Examples of Past and Current Commercial Space Activities

Activity Type	Example Companies
Satellite manufacturing	Northrop Grumman, Lockheed Martin, Boeing, Maxar
Launch vehicle subsystem manufacturing	Aerojet Rocketdyne
Launch services	Arianespace, Spacex, ULA, Northrop Grumman, Blue Origin
Telecommunication	Indium, Intelsat, Eutelsat, Direct TV, Sirius XM
Earth observation	Planet, Maxar
Space tourism	Virgin Galactic, Blue Origin
Satellite servicing	MDA, Northrop Grumman
Space station logistics	SpaceX, Sierra Nevada, Boeing, Northrop Gruman
Space stations	Axiom, NanoRacks, Bigelow Aerospace
Smallest manifesting	Spaceflight Industries, NanoRacks
Lunar delivery and space resources	Astrobotic, Moon Express, ConsenSys

Source: https://aerospace.org/sites/default/files/2021-01/Gleason-Dickey_SpacePrimer2_20210118_2.pdf, p. 21.

However, these emerging Commercial Space Enterprises raise a number of ethical, business and security hazards. Starlink, the mega-constellation launched by billionaire Elon Musk's company SpaceX would have 42,000 spacecraft. It seems that they represent a takeover of a shared public resource—the outer space. In the absence of any enforceable space laws, the takeover of LEO is likely to be a fait accompli.

The 21st century, will see a race between private companies to exploit space assets, mine space resources and ferry tourists. How do you deal with this irresponsible conduct, environmental apathy and unethical business practices? Today to ensure the safety, security and sustainability of space operations in the face of the growing number of space actors, space objects, space debris and adverse space weather phenomena; space governance needs enforceable and farsighted laws, planetary ethics, traditional wisdom and real-time and reliable data about orbital traffic.[36]

Cyber Security

Amid all the pomp, a critical danger has evaded notice. The deficiency of cybersecurity standards and regulations for commercial satellites, along with satellites' complex supply chains management and layers of stakeholders, leaves them highly vulnerable to cyberattacks.

If state-sponsored hackers or non-state actors can take control of these satellites, the consequences could be catastrophic. Hackers can shut down satellites or turn them into weapons, jam or spoof the signals from satellites creating a disaster for critical infrastructures like electric grids, water networks and transportation systems. In addition, some of these new satellites have thrusters that allow them to speed up or slow down and change direction in space. Hackers could change the satellites' orbits and crash them into other satellites or even the International Space Stations.

Makers of these satellites, like tiny CubeSats, use commercial off-the-shelf technology to keep costs low. The easy availability of these components means hackers can analyse and find vulnerabilities in them. Most of the elements depend on open-source technology. The hackers can insert back doors and other vulnerabilities into satellites' software.[37]

The highly technical nature of these satellites means multiple manufacturers are involved in making the different components. The process of getting these satellites into space is complicated, involving various companies. Once they are in space, the satellites' owners regularly outsource their day-to-day management to other companies. Additional vendor means, increase in the vulnerabilities as hackers have multiple opportunities to infiltrate the system.

Satellites are normally controlled from ground stations. These stations use computers with software vulnerabilities that hackers can exploit. If hackers infiltrate these computers, they could send malicious commands to the satellites.

While the U.S. Department of Defense and National Security Agency have made some efforts to address space cyber security, the pace has been sluggish. Presently there are no cyber security standards for satellites and no governing body to regulate and ensure their cyber security. Even if common standards are developed, there are no mechanisms in place to enforce them. Responsibility for satellite cyber security is with the individual companies that build and operate them.

Market forces work against space cyber security. As they compete to be the dominant satellite operator, rival companies are under constant pressure to reduce costs. There is pressure to speed up development and production. This makes it attractive for the companies to cut corners in areas like cyber security that are secondary to getting these satellites in space.

Even for companies that consider cyber security as of high priority, the costs associated with guaranteeing the security of each component could be prohibitive. This problem is more acute for low-cost space missions, where the cost of ensuring cyber security could exceed the cost of the satellite itself.

The complex supply chain of these satellites and the several parties involved in their management means it's often unclear who bears responsibility and liability for cyber breaches. Unfortunately, this lack of clarity has bred complacency and hindered efforts to secure these critical systems.

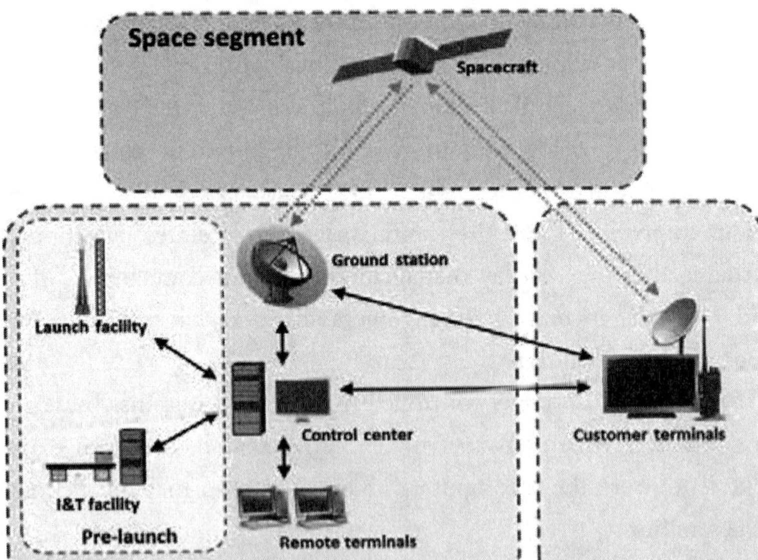

Source: M. Manulis, C. P. Bridges, R. Harrison, V. Sekar & A. Davis, 'Cyber security in New Space available at https://link.springer.com/article/10.1007/s10207-020-00503-w

Regulation is required. Certain experts favour strong government involvement in the development and regulation of cyber security standards for satellites and other space assets. There is a need to adopt a comprehensive regulatory framework for the commercial space sector. Satellite manufacturers may be told to develop a common cyber security architecture. Reporting of all cyber breaches involving satellites should be made compulsory. To prioritise cyber security efforts, there is a need to clarify which space-based assets are critical. Clear legal guidance on who bears responsibility for cyberattacks on satellites will ensure that the parties concerned take the necessary measures to secure these systems.

A multi-stakeholder approach involving public-private cooperation may be necessary to ensure cyber security standards. Whatsoever steps government and industry take, it is imperative to act now.[38]

Recent Developments

Secure Communications. Military space leaders are worried about fighting through jamming during the conflict. They are trying to develop a new, hard-to-jam Satcom system for troops in battle. U.S. is developing a tactical alternative to the Advanced Extremely High Frequency (AEHF) satellite network known as the Protected Satellite Communications (PTS) program. It is budgeted at a massive $2.4 billion through 2025. PTS would connect the battlefield operators and back to headquarters. Per se, PTS is not a satellite. Instead, a payload that uses a highly jam-resistant signal called the Protected Tactical Waveform (PTW). The payload could be fitted onto U.S. military or commercial satellites in Geosynchronous Orbit.

PTS includes a ground control element and a gateway to interface with the global DoD Information Network. User terminals will be developed and provided by the individual services using the system. The budget justification documents explain, "PTS provides worldwide and polar, beyond-line-of-sight, Anti-Jam (AJ), low probability of intercept communications in benign and highly contested environments. With its on-board payload processing and antenna design, PTS enables reliable tactical satellite communications within close proximities to adversarial jammers."

NTS-3. It is being built as one of the leap-ahead technology programs. It is designed to fill the gap in present Global Positioning System satellites (GPS III) capability by rapidly bringing online the long-delayed, anti-jam M-Code for military users. It is expected to be launched in 2023.

The new constellation will comprise a minimum of four, perhaps up to eight, satellites in Geosynchronous Orbit. The flying saucer-shaped satellites are small and can be launched rapidly and cheaply.

Unlike current GPS satellites, the navigational payload is fully digital. The software can be upgraded as new capabilities are developed. This will allow the satellites to keep pace with the threat. Digitising the Mission Data Unit (MDU) at the heart of the NTS-3 navigation payload provides the ability to change the satellite's frequency to avoid jamming and to increase power to blast the navigation signal through the white noise a jamming system creates.[39]

According to an Air Force Research Laboratory (AFRL) fact sheet, "NTS-3 will experiment with a new digital signal generator that can be reprogrammed on-orbit, enabling it to broadcast new signals, improve performance by avoiding and defeating interference, and adding signatures for detecting spoofing attacks."

Fully Networked C3 (FNC3). The Fully Networked C3 (FNC3) is designed to enable the DoD to communicate with all its tactical and strategic assets reliably. DoD is now looking for "Beyond-Line-Of-Site (BLOS) communications systems for airborne, surface, and subsurface systems that is compatible with both FNC3 enabled systems and legacy systems."

Beyond-Line-Of-Sight communications relayed through satellites usually require equipping platforms like aircraft, ships and ground vehicles with high-throughput voice and data links. BLOS communications can also be accomplished without using satellites. The alternative method include tropospheric scatter using microwave radiation, high frequency (HF) wireless, unmanned aerial vehicle (UAV) relays and passive reflector systems.

Laser Technology. It is on the edge of enhancing satellite communications through higher data-transfer rates and enhanced security. Data transmitted using radio waves grow weaker due to noise, disruption or the sheer volume of space. As activities move farther into space, latency issues create unacceptable delays for some applications.

By contrast, Lasers maintain signal strength over longer distances and employ shorter wavelengths, allowing exponentially faster data transfer. There is more regulatory freedom to experiment with communication lasers. Laser technology can advance LEO satellite connectivity as well as deep-space communications. Lasers are much more difficult to intercept. The development of laser communication will allow for satellite constellation growth, increased data throughput and greater security.

Radar. Defence and commercial satellites have been using electro-optical and infrared (EO/IR) cameras, aiming to image targets by creating a contrast between the desired target and its background. Such systems have limitations in tracking objects at a distance, especially under adverse conditions. Modern EO/IR sensors are degraded by cloud cover, heavy moisture and low light. Regardless of conditions, Synthetic Aperture Radar (SAR) is always available. SAR can produce two-dimensional (2D) or elevation maps useful for defence and civilian applications. In addition, SAR imagery improves orbital detection.

Reusable space launch. This has transformed the space industry by reducing the cost to orbit. Although earlier capsules or other components would be used only a single time, innovations have allowed rocketry firms to retrieve and reuse launch components, reducing cost substantially. SpaceX is leading in reusable rocketry. Other "new space" firms and aerospace incumbents are not far behind.

Rideshares and hosted payloads. Rideshares use the service of launch consolidators, allowing multiple satellites to deploy from the same launch vehicle. The launch consolidator company Spaceflight Industries wants to acquire capacity and provide rideshare services on all commercially competitive launch vehicles. The company tries to use various vehicles to launch the spectrum of satellites—CubeSats to large telecommunications satellites. The company assists in payload integration with the launch vehicle.[40]

Some of the benefits to the hosted payload customer include:[41]

- Shorter time to space because the development of an entire satellite system is not required.
- Lower cost because placing a hosted payload on a commercial satellite costs a fraction of building, launching and operating a dedicated satellite.
- A more resilient architecture by distributing assets over multiple platforms and locations.
- Increased access to space because the number of commercial launches each year provides multiple access to various orbital locations.

Earth imaging and remote sensing. There is a growing market for Earth imagery and associated information coming from satellite-derived data. One of the newer commercial entrants to the sector is Planet. On February 14, 2017, the company launched 88 Dove satellites into orbit, the largest satellite constellation ever placed in orbit. This Dove constellation enabled the company to reach its first milestone of imaging Earth's landmass every day. Currently, the company is operating over 200 Earth observation satellites, which is the largest satellite constellation.

Data analytics. Based on earth observation and geospatial location information, data analytics and other computationally derived products demand increases. Government agencies, commercial industries and financial markets can focus primarily on the resulting information and meaning ascribed to data and imagery. These groups need not develop, build and launch their own satellites. Governmental or non-governmental organisations are willing to pay for the analysis of the data collected by satellites.

The company Planet uses analytical methods and machine learning fed by global, daily earth imagery to detect and classify objects, identify geographic features and monitor change over time. The idea is to give governmental, non-governmental and commercial customers insights and actionable intelligence based upon the most recent imagery available. The company sees its analytical products being used in the following areas:

- Identifying new buildings and roads to update maps and charts, cataloguing urban development and determining change before and after natural disasters.
- Identifying aircraft and monitoring their movement over broad areas to understand the economic activity.
- Observing maritime vessels to determine "pattern of life" activity, as well as to track specific vessels for law enforcement.
- Detecting deforestation and monitoring land use.

Additive manufacturing. Additive manufacturing techniques enable commercial aerospace firms to develop new components for launch systems, satellites and other payloads at lower development and production costs, lower component weight and faster production schedules. It uses typically computer aided design (CAD) software or 3D object scanners to direct hardware to deposit material, layer upon layer, in precise shapes. While the terms 3D printing and rapid prototyping are often used to discuss additive manufacturing, each process is considered a subset of additive manufacturing.

Made In Space uses a 3D printer aboard the International Space Station (ISS) as a proof of concept and prototyping system. In addition, this additive manufacturing device is providing hardware manufacturing services to both NASA and the U.S. National Laboratory onboard. Much of additive manufacturing technology in the aerospace sector is still in a nascent stage and uncertainties remain.

Debris removal and mitigation. Due to growing concerns for space operations safety and preservation of the orbital environment, many companies are looking into options for active debris removal, particularly in low Earth orbit.

Space situational awareness. In recent times, there has been an increase in commercial space situational awareness (SSA) capability. SSA is foundational to all other activities that ensure access to and use of space. Commercial SSA capabilities are enabled by earth-based systems, including ground-based telescopes and radars.

ExoAnalytic Solutions seeks to preserve space as a safe, natural resource through persistent, automated and real-time SSA solutions. The company defines SSA as the ability to monitor, understand and predict natural and man-made objects in orbit around the earth. The company employs a global commercial SSA telescope network with more than 25 observatories and 200 telescopes to track man-made space objects within multiple orbital regimes, including geosynchronous earth orbits, highly elliptical orbits and medium earth orbits.

Using the globally collected SSA information, the company AGI uses software to model, analyse and visualise objects in space. Its products are used for space catalogue maintenance and observation processing, manoeuvre processing, sensor tasking, conjunction assessment and web-based visualisation. In addition, the Space Data Association uses the company's generated SSA information to provide satellite owner/operator information to facilitate safe space operations.

On-orbit servicing and proximity operations. An important activity enabling satellite servicing is rendezvous and proximity operations (RPO). These operations are relatively complex, with only a few companies or agencies being able to perform them. Some RPO activities include docking and undocking manoeuvres. Multiple companies are planning to offer on-orbit servicing, including seasoned space companies such as Northrop Grumman, MacDonald, Dettwiler & Associates and Airbus.

Stuart Eves has proposed several potential commercial areas for on-orbit satellite servicing. These proposed missions include: service life-extension or technology upgrades of operational satellites; relocation of satellites, satellite inclination lowering, satellite right ascension change, on-orbit refueling, robotic maintenance or repair, monitoring deployment of launch partners, testing space situation awareness capabilities, moving malfunctioning, "embarrassing" or defunct payloads into a "graveyard" orbit, disposing of any inconvenient or hazardous orbital debris, orbital slot occupation, security monitoring of existing satellites and apogee motor failure compensation.

Resource Extraction. Commercial companies and international organisations have discussed plans to mine the Moon and asteroids for precious metals and other vital resources. Some of the precious metals mined would be brought back to Earth for use, while other material would be used for fabricating large structures and components in space. However, challenges for extracting or mining resources in space include the lack of clear government oversight and a shared understanding of whether the activity is truly compliant with the Outer Space Treaty or not.

Space-based solar power. Space-based solar power is a concept that seeks to use large arrays of solar cells in orbit and then transmit the energy via microwave or laser to a terrestrial receiving station. Despite the theoretical potential, a design is yet to come out that would be affordable and profitable. In addition, energy transmission losses of both microwave and laser energy from orbit to the terrestrial receiving stations are high.

China

> "To explore the vast cosmos, develop the space industry, and build China into a space power is a dream we pursue unremittingly."
>
> —China's Space White Paper, December 26, 2016

Introduction

China's July 2019 defence white paper highlights the relevance of space in its national competitiveness. It states:

> "Outer space is a critical domain in international strategic competition. Outer space security provides strategic assurance for national and social development. In the interest of the peaceful use of outer space, China actively participates in international space cooperation, develops relevant technologies and capabilities, advances holistic management of space-

based information resources, strengthens space situation awareness, safeguards space assets, and enhances the capacity to safely enter, exit and openly use outer space."

China's President Xi Jinping stated that China's space program is "a powerful force for the realization of the rejuvenation of the great Chinese nation." According to Xi, building China into a strong space power is the "unremitting pursuit of the China dream." China believes that space contributes significantly to China's national power. Its space program is serving its political, economic and military interests. Thus, space is contributing to China's overall influence and helping to maintain China's national security.

China has released four space white papers, each entitled "China's Space Activities." It discusses China's space policy. For example, according to China's 2016 space white paper, China's space program must be able to:

- Independently innovate.
- Conduct cutting edge scientific discovery and research.
- Promote economic and social development.
- Guarantee national security.
- Exercise sound and efficient governance.
- Carry out mutually helpful international exchanges and cooperation.

Since 2000, China has made tremendous progress to become a strong space power. Today, China has more than 300 satellites, the second largest number of satellites in orbit. The reliability of its space launch vehicles is at international standards. In 2019, China exceeded all space powers with 32 successful launches whereas the U.S. had 27 launches. The majority of satellites launched annually have been remote sensing satellites, followed by communications, navigation and technology development satellites. China is fast narrowing the gap in quantity and quality of space technologies with global space powers.

Chinese Orbital Space Launches (1957-2019). China had more successful orbital space launches in 2019 than any other nation

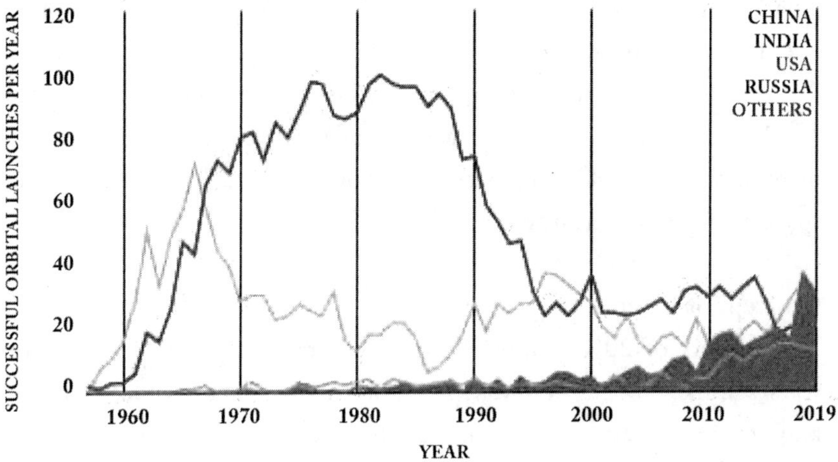

Source: http://www.milsatmagazine.com/story.php?number=1021469330

China is building a robust suite of counter-space capabilities that include direct ascent kinetic kill vehicles (KKVs), directed energy, electronic warfare, cyber and co-orbital satellite systems. The development of China's space capabilities is consistent with its progressively outward-looking and active military policy. Chinese missions to the moon have focused on analysing its composition, looking for potential rare minerals, water, and other resources like helium-3 that could be a revolutionary energy source. China's plan to build a base on the Moon in the 2030s is a "means to accomplish its goals of asteroid mining, deep space exploration and exploitation."[42]

Ye Peijian, Head of China's Lunar Mission stated, "The universe is an ocean, the moon is the Diaoyu Islands [Senkaku Islands], Mars is Huangyan Island [Spratly Islands]. If we don't go there now, even though we're capable of doing so, then we will be blamed by our descendants. If others go there, then they will take over, and you won't be able to go even if you want to. This is reason enough."

There is a probability that China will use "first presence rights" to justify lunar territorial claims, which cannot be prevented by the unverifiable and unenforceable outer space treaty and the current ambiguity in space law. The International Institute of Space Law Position Paper on Space Resource Mining says that "in view of the absence of a clear prohibition of the taking of resources in the Outer Space Treaty one can conclude that the use of space resources is permitted.[43]"

Concept of Operations

The authors of 2013 Study of Space Operations predicted that future wars will likely begin in outer space and that "achieving space superiority and cyber superiority is critical for achieving overall superiority and being victorious over an enemy." They argue that China must prepare for an enemy to attack from all domains, including space. The study identified outer space as one of five major military threats facing the PLA, along with nuclear, conventional, cyber and nuclear-conventional threats. It included space operations as one of nine "main operational activities" along with information operations, joint strike operations, air and missile defence, air and sea blockades, island seizure operations, area denial operations, border defence operations and cyber operations.

The authors conclude, "Whoever is the strongman of military space will be the ruler of the battlefield; whoever has the advantage of space has the power of the initiative; having 'space' support enables victory, lacking 'space' ensures defeat." The Study of Space Operations asserts that space warfare is inherently offensive in nature and that active offence is the only method for achieving victory in war.

In 2015, the PLA raised the Strategic Support Force to centralise and oversee its cyber, space and EW operations. China has taken a whole of force approach to future battle, wherein outer space and cyberspace capabilities are integral force multipliers. China has improved its counter space cyber arsenal to gain the upper hand during military confrontations.

The U.S. DIA, in their 2019 report, stated that "China emphasises offensive cyberspace capabilities as key assets for integrated warfare and could use its cyber warfare capabilities to support military operations against space-based assets." China's latest national defence white paper, released in July 2019, states, "outer space, electromagnetic space, and cyberspace" as a single, collective defence aim.

Given China's perceptions of the seriousness of space-enabled operations to enable beyond-line-of-sight operations for deployed Chinese forces, space and counter space operations will form integral components of PLA campaigns. The PLA also sees counter space operations to deter and counter a possible U.S. intervention during a regional military conflict. PLA analysts feel that "destroying or capturing satellites and other sensors" would make it challenging to use precision-guided weapons. Also, PLA writings recommend that reconnaissance, communications, navigation and early warning satellites may be amidst the targets of attacks arranged to blind and deafen the enemy.

Space Situational Awareness (SSA). SSA serves as the foundation for the safe operation of satellites and achievement of space dominance. SSA provides information needed for China to conduct targeting when interfering with the space use of an adversary and is essential for detecting interference with China's own space use. China has a vigorous network of space surveillance sensors capable of searching, tracking and characterising satellites in all Earth orbits. This network includes various telescopes, radars and other sensors that allow China to support missions, including intelligence collection, counter space targeting, ballistic missile early warning, spaceflight safety, satellite anomaly resolution and space debris monitoring.

The China National Space Administration supervises civil use of space and international cooperation. It established the Space Debris Observation and Data Application Center in 2015. According to the 2016 Space White Paper, China will continue to develop the space debris basic database and advance the development of space debris monitoring facilities, the early warning and emergency response platform, and the online service system.

Organisation

PLA plays a core role in China's space activities, making space and military activities inseparable. In 2018, when President Xi Jinping visited the Xichang Satellite Launch Center, he ordered the centre to focus on military training and research, enhance satellite launch and combat capabilities and integrate itself with the PLA's joint operation system.

Chinese military experts describe space assets as critical for carrying out joint firepower strike operations against an adversary. ISR satellites will be particularly important. These satellites would be tasked for collecting intelligence used by the PLA to build and update opponent targets, monitor and target enemy combat platforms and provide battle damage assessments after the initial wave of strikes.

To prepare for any operation, China's military space units are expected to continuously collect and analyse intelligence on enemy. For example against Taiwan, beaches, currents, tides, roads, bridges, waterways, electric power grid, reservoirs, oil and gas stocks, airports, seaports, command posts, ground force units and air defense networks would have to be under continuous surveillance.

Chinese satellites and near-space drones would provide wideband, high-capacity, jam-resistant, encrypted communications to all the units involved in the operation. Future Chinese space architecture will allow the PLA to amalgamate and connect all joint forces together into an organic system that allows operational commanders to find targets, decide how to strike them, send strike orders to forward units, neutralise targets, assess battle damage and consider whether or not re-strikes are required. The office overseeing China's manned space missions remained with the CMC Equipment Development Department, probably to avoid the appearance of militarising China's manned space mission.

To further integrate space into military operations, the PLA created the Strategic Support Force (SSF), an organisation that is, in part, responsible for elements of the PLA's space program. The SSF is a functional command that conducts strategic level space, cyber and electronic warfare operations. The SSF has two subordinate operational departments: a Network Systems Department responsible for executing strategic cyber and EW operations and a Space Systems Department responsible for space operations. The Space Systems Department is responsible for China's military space operations, including space launch and support, space surveillance, space information support, space telemetry, tracking and control and space warfare.

The raising of the PLA Strategic Support Force (PLASSF) Space Systems Department (SSD) is an organisational innovation that places all major components of China's space program under a unified command structure. The SSF Space Systems Department is responsible for nearly all PLA space operations, including space launch and support; space surveillance; space information support; space telemetry, tracking, and control; and space warfare. The SSD integrates space-related Research, Development and Acquisition, operations and training under a single authority.

The PLASSF Space Systems Department is central to China's ambitions in space. The PLA has already fielded electro-optical (EO), radar and other space-based sensor platforms that can transmit images of the Earth's surface to ground stations in near-real-time. China is investing heavily in EO, synthetic aperture radar (SAR) and electronic reconnaissance surveillance capabilities. The SSD has taken over almost every aspect of PLA space operations including space launch and support; space telemetry, tracking, and control, space information support, space attack and space defence.

The PLASSF Space Systems Department is responsible for space launch operations, space tracking and control and applied space operations.

The organisation of the PLASSF Space Systems Department is given below:

Table 2. SSF Space Corps Units		
Space Launch and Support		
Name	**Assessed Grade**	**Function and Description**
Jiuquan Satellite Launch Center [中国酒泉卫星发射中心] **20th Testing and Training Base [第20试验训练基地]**	Corps Leader grade	Oldest and largest launch site and the only one that conducts human space-flight launches.
Taiyuan Satellite Launch Center [中国太原卫星发射中心] **25th Testing and Training Base [第25试验训练基地]**	Corps Leader grade	The center launches satellites into sun-synchronous and low-earth orbits.
Xichang Satellite Launch Center [中国西昌卫星发射中心] **27th Testing and Training Base [第27试验训练基地]**	Corps Leader grade	The center launches satellites into geo-synchronous orbit. Maintains mobile tracking stations that supply data to other facilities.
Wenchang Aerospace Launch Site [文昌航天发射场]	Corps Leader grade	Completed in 2014. The center was built to use the new heavy-lift Long March 5 and to launch heavier payloads into orbit.

Source: Phillip C. Saunders, et al. (eds), *Chairman Xi Remakes the PLA: Assessing Chinese Military Reforms*, National Defense University Press, Washington, D.C., 2019.

PLASSF space launch operations are carried out from four launch complexes. The Jiuquan Satellite Launch Center (PLASSF Base 20) supports LM-2C, LM-2D, and LM-4 launches into LEO, as well as crewed space missions on the LM-2F. Base 20 is also a key facility for short-range ballistic missile, land attack cruise missile and space intercept testing. Subordinate units are responsible for space launch operations, launch tracking, missile testing, impact area management, transportation, propellant loading, and communications.

The Space Systems Department oversees at least six corps or corps deputy leader-grade operational commands responsible for space launch, tracking, and control. The PLASSF tracks and controls space assets through the Xian Satellite Control Center (Base 26) and the Beijing Space Command and Control Center in the northern suburbs of Beijing, which integrates space tracking data from ground and sea-based units. Three corps leader-grade space launch base commands are in Jiuquan (Base 20, aka Shuangchengzi), Taiyuan (Base 25, aka Wuzhai), and Xichang (Base 27). Base 27 probably oversees the launch complex on Hainan Island. These space launch centers also support ballistic missile and kinetic space interceptor testing. Newly raised PLASSF corps-level units suggest possible direct operational support to Theatre Command leaders in a contingency.

Space Launch Operations. PLASSF space launch operations are carried out from four launch complexes. Each is led by a corps or corps deputy leader-grade officer. The Jiuquan Satellite Launch Center (PLASSF Base 20) supports LM-2C, LM-2D, and LM-4 launches into LEO, as well as crewed space missions on the LM-2F. Base 20 is also a key facility for short-range ballistic missile, land attack cruise missile, and space intercept testing. Subordinate units are responsible for space launch operations, launch tracking, missile testing, impact area management, transportation, propellant loading and communications.

The Taiyuan Satellite Launch Center (PLASSF Base 25), headquartered in Shanxi's Kelan County, functions as China's primary platform for satellite launches into sun-synchronous orbit (SSO) as well as testing of medium and intermediate range ballistic missiles. In June 2019, Taiyuan established a maritime team and was responsible for the launch of the LM-11.

The Xichang Satellite Launch Center (PLASSF Base 27) is China's primary platform for launch of communication and weather satellites into GEO. Xichang reportedly had capacity to launch between eight and ten satellites a year. Base 27 was the launch point of the PLA's January 2007 test against an aging Chinese weather satellite.

Table 2. SSF Space Corps Units

Telemetry, Tracking, and Control (TT&C)		
Name	**Assessed Grade**	**Function and Description**
Beijing Aerospace Flight Control Center [北京航天飞行控制中心]	Corps Leader grade	Responsible for command and control of China's manned spaceflight program.
Xi'an Satellite Control Center [中国西安卫星测控中心] **26th Testing and Training Base [第26试验训练基地]**	Corps Leader grade	Core hub for China's telemetry, tracking, and control network. Maintains a nation-wide retinue of fixed and mobile TT&C stations.
China Satellite Maritime Tracking and Control Department [中国卫星海上测控部] **23rd Test and Training Base [第23试验训练基地]**	Corps Leader grade	Provides maritime TT&C for China's space launches and intercontinental ballistic missile tests. Maintains a small fleet of Yuanwang (远望) tracking ships.

Source: Phillip C. Saunders, et al. (eds), *Chairman Xi Remakes the PLA : Assessing Chinese Military Reforms*, National Defense University Press, Washington, D.C., 2019.

Base 26 has a role in monitoring and identifying debris and other objects in space. Base 26 is likely to oversee the Beijing Space Flight Control Center and its subordinate entities. The Base 26 space surveillance system may fuse data from other sources, including the China Academy of Science's Space Target and Debris Observation and Research Center in Nanjing. It supervises deep space tracking facilities in northeast China and oversee a tracking and control station on Duncan Island in the South China Sea.

The China Satellite Maritime Tracking and Control Department (Base 23, Jiangyin) is a corps leader-grade organization. Base 23 is responsible for sea-based satellite tracking, control, and launch vehicle transportation to Hainan. Seven Yuanwang ships are in operation as of 2019.

Table 2. SSF Space Corps Units		
Space-based C4ISR		
Name	**Assessed Grade**	**Function and Description**
Aerospace Reconnaissance Bureau [航天侦察局]	Deputy Corps Leader grade	Responsible for space-based intelligence, surveillance, and reconnaissance.
Satellite Communications Main Station [卫星通信总站]	Deputy Corps Leader grade	Responsible for space-based communications and data relay.
Satellite Positioning Main Station [卫星定位总站]	Deputy Corps Leader grade	Responsible for military use of the Beidou navigation system

Source: Phillip C. Saunders, et al. (eds), *Chairman Xi Remakes the PLA: Assessing Chinese Military Reforms*, National Defense University Press, Washington, D.C., 2019.

Initially, the SSF was not assessed to have complete control over China's ASAT capabilities. Experts believed that the responsibility for direct-ascent ASATs might be with either the PLA's Rocket Force, which manages China's nuclear arsenal or the PLA's Air Force. However, recent records show that the SSF has begun training specialised units with direct-ascent ASAT weapons capable of targeting satellites in LEO.

The following table shows the role military-civil space assets will play in future joint operations.

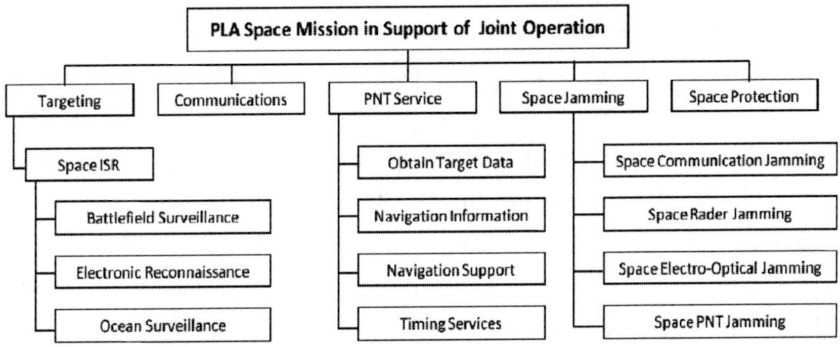

Source: Wang Yongping, (ed.), *Space Information Support Operations*, National Defense University Press, 2014, p. 126.

Employment of Chinese space assets in future joint military operations. Underscoring the military nature of China's space program, the informationisation plan says that CCP and state authorities at all levels will "accelerate the construction of military-civil and dual use global mobile communications satellite systems." It affirms that China will "advance military-civil fusion in the space domain and construct an integrated space-to-earth cyberspace infrastructure." Notably, the Beidou GNSS informationisation programs are primarily run by the Office of the Central Cyberspace Affairs Commission, the Central Military Commission (CMC) Equipment Development Department (EDD) and the CMC Joint Staff Department.

China's Demonstrated Space Capabilities

China's civil, military and commercial space capabilities are rapidly growing. China's civil space program is concentrated on its network of BeiDou positioning, navigation, and timing (PNT) satellites, comparable to the U.S. Global Positioning System (GPS). Since early 2019, Chang'e-4, the Chinese lunar lander mission that brought about a successful lunar rover called Yutu-2, has been operating an exploration mission on the far side of the Moon. China plans to follow up this mission with Chang'e-5, which aims to return samples from the Moon to Earth for further study. To sustain its growing space capabilities, China has built an expansive ground support infrastructure to support its increasing on-orbit fleet and related functions, including spacecraft and space launch vehicle (SLV) manufacture, launch, command and control (C2) and data downlink.[44]

China is improving its space launch capabilities so that it has an independent, reliable means to access space and compete in the international space market. Recent improvements decrease launch timelines, increase manufacturing efficiencies and also support human spaceflight and deep-space exploration missions. These improvements include new, modular SLVs that permit China to tailor an SLV to the specific configuration required for each customer.

Using modular SLVs can increase manufacturing efficiency, launch vehicle reliability, and cost savings for launch campaigns. China is in the early stages of expanding a super heavy-lift SLV similar to the U.S. Saturn-V.

China has made a "quick response" SLV to enhance its attractiveness as a commercial small satellite launch provider and to quickly reconstitute LEO space capabilities, which could support Chinese Space Launch Sites and Key Satellite Control Centers.[45]

In 2019, China's busiest launch site, the Xichang Satellite Launch Center, held 19 of China's 32 launches. Xichang, located in the south of China, is currently expanding by adding another launch pad to get along with China's growing national and commercial launch demands. After a 2014 declaration to allow private companies to develop SLVs, many new private, but typically state-backed Chinese companies started to develop and test new launch vehicles. The growth of China's commercial space companies has led to introducing new commercial policies in 2019 to regulate the growing commercial space launch sector better.

Chinese TT&C stations and international partners

The following ground stations have been identified as having been leased by cooperating with or directly constructed and operated by China's space programs. Chinese officials identify these as part of "China's network".

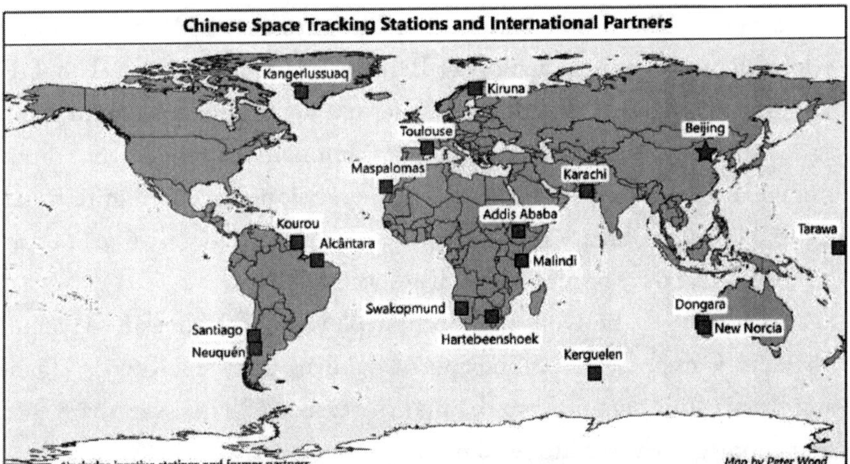

Source: Peter Wood, et al., 'China's ground segment: building the pillars of a great space power', China Aerospace Studies Institute.

Provision of Satellite Infrastructure, Launch Services. China has provided launch services to several countries. These satellites are launched from either the Xichang Satellite Launch Center in Sichuan Province, the Jiuquan Satellite Launch Center or the Taiyuan Satellite Launch Center in Shanxi Province. All these Satellite Launch Centers are operated by various PLA units. Terms and conditions of contracts and agreements between China and other countries regarding ground stations and other space infrastructure benefit Chinese interests vastly.

Sri Lanka's SupremeSat is owned in partnership with China Satellite Communications Co. This ownership structure suggests that China maintains access to the satellite's data and bandwidth. China and Sri Lanka also signed a Memorandum of Understanding to cooperate on BeiDou expansion in the Indian Ocean region including applications in fisheries and transportation.

In April 2019, China and Pakistan strengthened their cooperation in space, signing a cooperation agreement on crewed space missions. Space and Upper Atmosphere Research Commission (SUPARCO) of Pakistan is expected to establish a China-Pakistan space committee chaired by top officials from both countries to address future collaborations and issues.

BeiDou Global Navigation Satellite System (GNSS) **Achieving Global Reach.** China is deploying BeiDou as an alternative to U.S. GPS. The BeiDou system has a range of dual-use applications, including smart agriculture, land surveying and mapping, autonomous vehicles and drones, storage logistics, airport management, precision-guided munitions and combat drones. China and Russia have a strong collaborative relationship on the mutual development of their respective GNSSs.

As of 2019, BeiDou has been deployed in Indonesia, Myanmar, Thailand, Cambodia, Laos, Singapore, Maldives, Pakistan, Kuwait, Uganda and Russia. This demonstrates China's increased willingness to share access to its homegrown satellite system.

List of Countries That Have Had Satellites Launched in China

Country	Satellite Project Name	Launch Year	Launch Location	Status
Venezuela	Venesat-1*	2008	Xichang	Plan to launch fourth satellite (Guaicaipuro) in 2022.
	Venezuelan Remote Sensing Satellite-1 (VRSS-1)*	2012	Jiuquan	
	Venezuelan Remote Sensing Satellite-2 (VRSS-2)*	2017	Jiuquan	
Nigeria	Nigcomsat-1	2007	Xichang	Two new satellites under development by CGWIC as of Feb 2019.
	Nigcomsat-1R	2011	Xichang	
Bolivia	Tupac Katari (TKSat-1)*	2013	Xichang	Plan to launch second satellite in 2020–2021.
Ecuador	NEE-01 Pegaso	2013	Jiuquan	Last satellite launched by Russia in 2013.
Algeria	Alcomsat-1*	2017	Xichang	Considering launching second satellite under framework of 2020–2040 space program.
Sri Lanka	SupremeSAT-1*	2012	Xichang	Second satellite (SupremeSAT-2) delayed but expected to be launched imminently.
Pakistan	Badr-1	1990	Xichang	Last satellite launched in 2018.
	PakSat-1R*	2011	Xichang	
	Pakistan Remote Sensing Satellite-1 (PRSS-1)	2018	Jiuquan	
	PakTES-1A	2018	Jiuquan	
Indonesia	Palapa-D	2009	Xichang	Last satellite launched in 2017.
	Palapa-N1*	2017	Xichang	
Belarus	Belintersat-1*	2016	Xichang	Last satellite launched in 2016.
Laos	LaoSat-1*	2015	Xichang	Last satellite launched in 2015.
Brazil	CBERS-1*	1999	Taiyuan	Plan to launch CBER-4A during second half of 2019.
	CBERS-2*	2003	Taiyuan	
	CBERS-2B*	2007	Taiyuan	
	CBERS-3*	2013	Taiyuan	
	CBERS-4*	2014	Taiyuan	

* Satellite was developed either partially or fully by PRC entities.

Source: Mark Stokes, et al., 'China's Space and Counterspace Capabilities and Activities', Project 2049 Institution, March 30, 2020.

Pakistan was the first nation to deploy BeiDou. As of 2018, the system was undergoing trial operations in Karachi. During a May 2014 visit to China, a representative from the Pakistan Space and Upper Atmosphere Research Commission stated that BeiDou had successfully been applied to Pakistani urban management programs to assist with the urbanization process and allocation of resources.

Pakistan

Karachi Station

China has been helping Pakistan's missile and space industries for a long time. The Badr-I, Pakistan's first domestically produced satellite was launched by China in 1990. This program also extended to ground operations.

China's second overseas TT&C station was unveiled on October 1, 1999 at Karachi. It is housed inside the headquarters of Space & Upper Atmosphere Research Commission (SUPARCO), Pakistan's space agency. China signed a joint research agreement with Pakistan for space technology in 2006 which was extended in May 2007.

China Great Wall Industry Corporation, in November 2009, was contracted to support the construction of a ground TT&C system for Pakistan's 1R communication satellite (PAKSAT-1R). The included the Karachi main station and a secondary standby station in Lahore.

Overseas Tracking Stations. China is expanding its space R&D capabilities globally through the establishment of foreign space tracking and downlink stations overseas. As of 2019, the PRC had established four of these stations in various strategic regions around the world, sometimes in collaboration with host nations, to improve its capacity.

The data collected at Chinese overseas ground stations is subject to China's National Cyber Security Law. The law stipulates that "critical information infrastructure operators that gather or produce personal information or important data during operations" outside of mainland China may be required to store that information within China where the PRC deems it "truly necessary for business requirements."

Chinese Overseas Tracking/Ground Stations

Location	Date Established	Chinese Operator	Local Partner
Dongara, Australia	2011	China Satellite Launch and Tracking Control General (CLTC)	Swedish Space Corporation
Swakopmund, Namibia	2000	China Manned Space Engineering Office (overseen by CMSP)	Ministry of Education of Namibia
Neuquén, Argentina	2014	China Satellite Launch and Tracking Control General (CLTC)	Comision Nacional de Actividades Espaciales (CONAE)
Kiruna, Sweden	2016	CAS	Swedish Space Corporation

Source: Mark Stokes, et al., 'China's Space and Counterspace Capabilities and Activities', Project 2049 Institution, March 30, 2020.

Synthetic Aperture Radar Satellites. SAR satellites are a core component of the militarily relevant surveillance architecture supporting over-the-horizon (OTH) targeting of surface assets. SAR satellites use a microwave transmission to create an image of maritime and ground-based targets. They can operate at night or day and in all weather conditions. They are well suited for the detection of ships in a wide area. The PLA's first dedicated military SAR satellite was deployed in 2006. Since then, remote sensing satellites with a SAR package include the Gaofen-3, Yaogan-1, Yaogan-6, Yaogan-10, Yaogan-13, Yaogan-18, and Yaogan-23, and possibly the Yaogan-29. The China Aerospace Science and Technology Corporation (CASC) is the main contractor for the Chinese space program. CASC

Shanghai Academy of Space Technology (SAST) is the lead systems integrator for SAR satellites.

Satellite Communications and Data Relay. SATCOM will be important as the PLA operates farther from China's borders. The PLASSF Space Systems Department develops operational and technical requirements for dedicated military communications satellites, such as the Fenghuo and Shentong systems. The PLASSF Space Systems Department manages the PLA's SATCOM network. Since 2017, China has carried out verification testing of a wideband (Ka band) communications satellite. The SJ-20 satellite was launched from Wenchang on an LM-5 in December 2019 and validated a new-generation communications satellite bus, the DFH-5. The DFH-5 is China's heaviest satellite to date. The same platforms have been used for testing of laser communications and electronic propulsion. A new base command, notionally designated Base 37, was established in 2017 in the Beijing suburb of Mentougou. To expand the scope of its communications satellite architecture, China has fielded a data relay capability.

Two types of the Zhongxing satellite are used for military communications. One is a satellite series known as Fenhuo which provided SHF (C-band) and UHF communications and is said to be a satellite for the Qudian, China's first integrated command, control, communications, computers and intelligence (C4I) system. The other is a satellite series called Shentong, which is said to provide communications in SHF (Ku-band) to users on the ground.[46]

For the first time in the world, in 2017, China announced that it pulled off intercontinental quantum key distribution using the Quantum Science Satellite Mozi.

The main goals of the program are quantum key distribution from a satellite to ground station, a global-scale quantum communication network that uses satellites and optical fibre cables (OFC), long-range entanglement testing involving two ground stations over 1,000 km apart and a satellite, and ground-to satellite teleportation (sending quantum information from one location to another). In June 2017, China successfully entangled photons at two ground stations 1203 km apart, relayed through Micius.

Through this satellite China transmitted encrypted data and conducted a video communication. By 2030, China plans to start operating satellite-based, global quantum-encrypted communications. The PLA's use of such capability will make its communications far more secure.

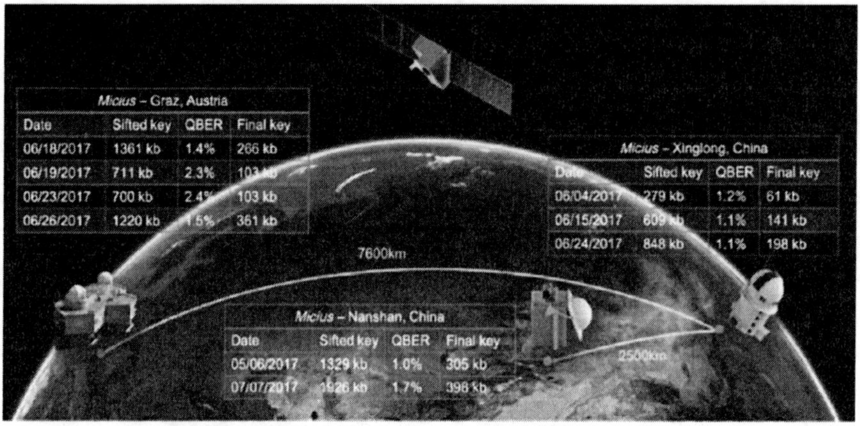

Source: Peter Wood, et al., 'China's ground segment : building the pillars of a great space power', China Aerospace Studies Institute.

It has been reported that, since the 2010s, China has conducted Rendezvous and Proximity Operation (RPO) tests frequently. RPO constitutes the technical foundation of space-based anti-satellite (ASAT) weapons.

Meteorology, Oceanography and Space Weather. The PLASSF manages military meteorological satellite data and supervises a specialised unit responsible for space weather analysis and forecasting. The FY-4, equipped with space weather sensors, is China's most advanced space asset providing meteorological support to PLA and other users. As a dual-use asset, FY satellite requirements have been developed by both the PLASSF and China Meteorological Administration (CMA), although their respective responsibilities remain unknown. The system also could provide measurement and signature intelligence (MASINT) data for PLA targeting. The PLASSF has launched at least 16 FY satellites.

An accurate assessment of current and future weather conditions, such as cloud cover, atmospheric moisture, winds, temperature, and ocean currents, is critical for various military operations. Weather satellites can measure electromagnetic conditions in the ionosphere that could affect OTH radar and communication systems. Meteorological and hydrographic satellites would facilitate PLA operations at sea at increasingly long ranges. Fengyun and Haiyang satellites collect and provide strategic weather and oceanographic data for civilian and military purposes.

Chinese National Spaceports

China currently has four active spaceports, which have collectively launched hundred of satellites and several astronauts or Chinese astronauts.

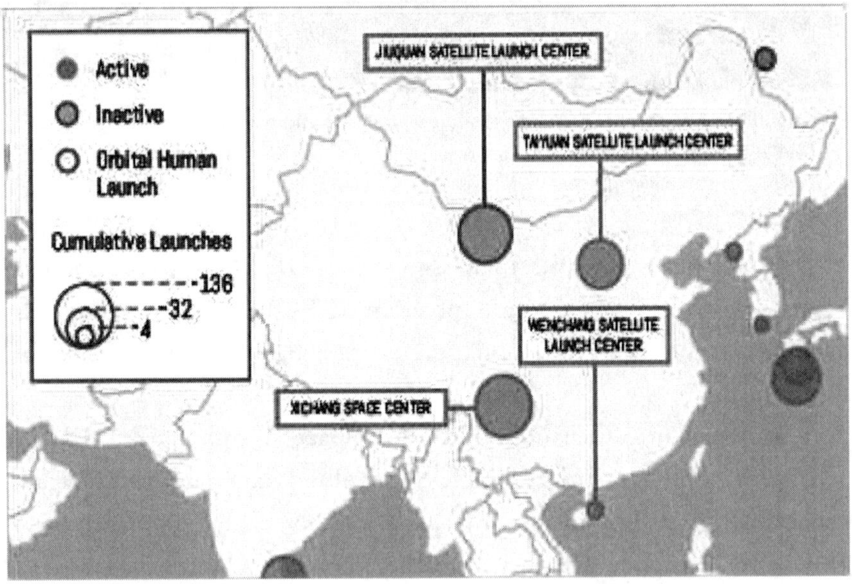

China became the third country to accomplish independent human spaceflight, in 2003, when it successfully orbited the crewed Shenzhou-5 spacecraft, followed by space laboratory Tiangong-1 and -2 launches in 2011 and 2016, respectively. China wants to assemble and operate a permanently inhabited, modular space station to host Chinese and foreign payloads and astronauts.

China is the third country to land a rover on the Moon and performed the first-ever landing on the lunar far side in January 2019. Since it is not feasible to communicate directly with objects on the far side of the Moon, a lunar relay satellite in May 2018 was launched to enable communication between the Chang'e-4 and the Earth.

China announced plans to assemble a robotic research station on the Moon by 2025. In addition, it has started establishing the foundation for a human lunar exploration program to put astronauts on the Moon in the mid-2030s.

With the successful landing of Zhurong rover on Mars on May 15, 2021, China became only the second nation to soft-land on Mars successfully, after the U.S.

Source: Image credit: China National Space Administration.

This photo is the first colour view of Mars from China's Zhurong rover, looking toward its rear, from its landing spot on a plain in Utopia Planitia following a May 14, 2021 landing. This image was released on May 19, 2021.

The Tianzhou-2 cargo spacecraft was launched from Wenchang Satellite Launch Center on China's Hainan Island on May 29, 2021, rising off the pad atop a Long March 7 rocket. The uncrewed Tianzhou-2 is carrying 4.69 tonnes of pressurised cargo and 1.95 tonnes of propellant. As per plan, the freighter will lift these goods to Tianhe, the 22.5-ton core module of China's prepared space station, which was launched to low Earth orbit on April 28, 2021.

China, of late, had some setbacks also. The 23-tonne core stage of a Long March 5B booster crashed back to Earth on May 8, 2021 ending ten controversial days aloft, that captured the world's attention. The Long March 5B launched the core module for China's new space station on April 28, 2021.

China has a number of methods at its disposal to carry out frequent satellite launches.

By global standards, in response to changes in the situation, the country has one of the highest abilities to launch additional satellites. If a satellite breaks down for any reason, China can launch an alternative satellite to reconstitute the satellite constellation relatively quickly.

Satellite Internet. Internet services in remote regions can be provided by satellites in high-altitude geostationary and medium Earth orbits. There is a growing need for connectivity in sparsely populated parts of China and in countries along China's Belt and Road Initiative (BRI). However, the services are costly and their latency i.e. the time required for a signal to travel between a satellite and Earth is high. The introduction of broadband internet from satellites in low Earth orbit can fill the gap in terrestrial communications and overcome weaknesses in existing satellite internet services.

China has showed its intention to deploy LEO satellite internet at scale. It has established China Satellite Network Group Co. Ltd., a state-owned enterprise (SOE) that will oversee the construction of a satellite internet mega constellation. This new SOE will manage the planning and operations of "Guowang" network of sub-constellations that may ultimately comprise about 12,992 satellites in LEO.

In April 2020, satellite internet was elevated to a top development priority when the National Development and Reform Commission

(NDRC) designated it as a type of "new infrastructure". Chinese experts are aware of the dual-use nature of the satellite internet mega constellations and their potential to augment C4ISR capabilities. The professionals feel that the future integration of satellite internet with technologies like 5G and IoT is inevitable. This would transform battlefield network information systems toward a "space-ground integrated three-dimensional structure." They recommend development of internet with technologies that incorporate "software-defined satellites" that can be quickly adjusted and updated according to variable user requirements.

Obstacles to Development of Satellite Internet. There are several difficulties for the rollout of a home-grown LEO mega constellation. Some of them are:

- Ability to compete with Western commercial space companies in terms of technological capabilities and access to necessary space resources is suspect.
- Lack of critical satellite construction and launch technologies that would enable constellations to be deployed quickly, at low costs and in large numbers.
- Frequency bands and orbital slots are scarce. Other countries are quickly acquiring these.
- Multinational deconfliction of in-orbit satellites and potential environmental consequences as the U.S., China and other countries deploy mega constellations in LEO.

Development of LEO satellite internet services by China is likely to be extremely costly unless several technological breakthroughs are achieved in the near term. A LEO satellite internet capability could improve the speed and coverage of Chinese military communications in distant or sparsely populated theaters. However, if China wants to sell satellite internet services outside mainland China, it would try to downplay the military affiliation, in light of the Huawei experience.[47]

ISR, Navigation and Communications Capabilities. The PLA continues to invest in improving its capabilities in space-based intelligence, surveillance, and reconnaissance (ISR), satellite communication, satellite navigation, and meteorology, human spaceflight and robotic space exploration. China employs a vigorous space-based ISR capability to boost its worldwide situational awareness. Though used for military and civil remote sensing and mapping, terrestrial and maritime surveillance and military intelligence collection, China's ISR satellites can provide electro-optical and synthetic aperture radar (SAR) imagery and electronic intelligence and signals intelligence data. As per data available till May 2018, the Chinese ISR and remote sensing satellite fleet contain more than 120 systems, a quantity second only to the U.S.

The PLASSF manages the application of data from space-based systems. It is responsible for managing the ground segments of the PLA's space-based ISR architecture, satellite communications network, China's BeiDou GNSS, and space-based meteorological and oceanographic system.

Chinese Satellites on Orbit, as of 1 May 2018

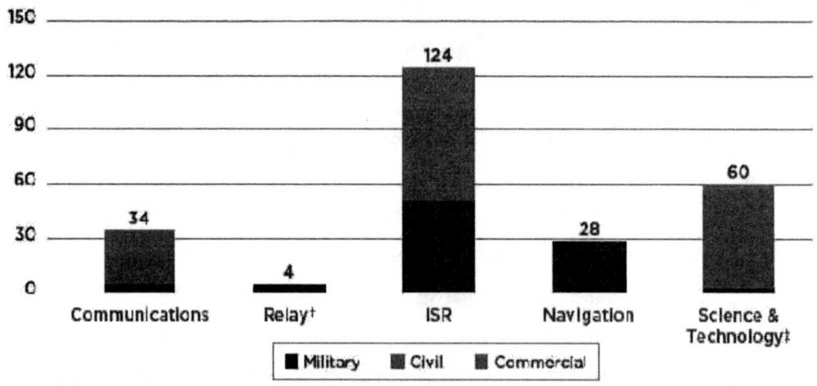

† Relay satellites enable communication between satellites outside the reception area of a ground station.
‡ Science and technology satellites are used for scientific research or testing new space technologies.

Source: 'Challenges to Security in Space', Washington, DC: Defense Intelligence Agency, January 2019, p. 19.

The PLA owns and operates almost half of these ISR systems. Maximum of these could support monitoring, tracking and targeting of U.S. and allied forces worldwide, including the Indo-Pacific region. They allow the PLA to maintain situational awareness of potential regional flashpoints. China owns and operates over 30 communications satellites, with four dedicated to military use. China makes its military-dedicated satellites domestically and its civil communications satellites incorporate off-the-shelf commercially manufactured components.[48]

China has embarked on many ambitious plans to propel itself to the forefront of the global satellite communications (SATCOM) industry. China is testing multiple next-generation capabilities, like quantum-enabled communications, which could supply the means to field highly secure communications systems.

China is improving its indigenous satellite navigation constellation. China offers regional PNT services and achieved its worldwide operating capability, next-generation BeiDou constellation in 2018. Along with providing PNT, the BeiDou constellation provides unique capabilities, including text messaging and user tracking, to facilitate mass communications between BeiDou users and provide additional C2 capabilities for the PLA.

China exports its satellite technology globally, including its indigenously-developed communications satellites. China intends to provide SATCOM support to users worldwide and develop at least three new communications constellations. China offered its BeiDou constellation with additional services and incentives to countries taking part in the BRI.

China's New Spaceplane. In September 4, 2020, the Chinese space plane was launched by a LongMarch 2F after orbiting Earth in LEO for two days. It successfully landed in northwest China on a five-kilometer runway. It is similar to the United States' X-37B spaceplane program. Experts are uncertain of the motivations behind or mission of this new space plane. It is unlikely to be used as a counter space weapon.

Counter Space Capabilities

The PLA continues to acquire and develop a range of counter space capabilities and related technologies, including ground-based lasers, kinetic-kill missiles, orbiting space robots and expanding space surveillance capabilities, which can monitor objects in space and enable counter space actions. China's reconnaissance and remote sensing fleet, as of December 2020, consisted of more than 200 satellites designed to collect data for civil, commercial or military owners and operators.[49] The PLA owns and operates about half of these systems, most of which could support situational awareness of regional rivals and potential flashpoints, while monitoring, tracking and targeting an adversary's forces.

The PLA has developed jamming and cyberspace capabilities, directed energy weapons, on-orbit capabilities, and ground-based ASAT missiles that can deny an adversary unimpeded use of its own satellite systems. The specific PLA service responsible for direct ascent ASAT operations remains unknown. Testing of kinetic kill vehicles (KKVs), high-powered lasers, co-orbital satellites, electronic jamming and cyberattacks have been reported. The opacity surrounding China's space programs suggests other clandestine counter space weapons programs may also exist.

Kinetic Physical Weapons. China has competent kinetic physical counter space capabilities and has proven this several times with a range of direct-ascent ASAT weapons tests. For example, in January 2007, it destroyed one of its defunct weather satellites in a successful test of a direct-ascent, anti-satellite (ASAT) missile, the SC-19 missile system, launched from a ground-based, mobile transporter erector launcher.

China has taken up an ambitious program to develop offensive space control capabilities. The SC-19 is an operational weapon system, able to engage targets in low earth orbit. China is now developing direct-ascent ASAT capabilities to reach targets in medium earth orbit and geostationary earth orbit. Moreover, China has developed a wide assortment of directed-energy weapons, including radio frequency jammers to block satellite communications and low and high power lasers to dazzle or damage optical sensors.[50]

The PLA is considering attacks against satellite TT&C facilities and launch sites. Such attacks do not require dedicated weapons and can be carried out with ballistic missiles, cruise missiles or special forces.

Use of Artificial Intelligence (AI). The South China Morning Post reported in 2019, quoting recently declassified government documents, how decade-old Chinese satellite technology has provided a base for "the development of new weapon systems powered by artificial intelligence." It is not clear how AI is utilised. The article reports that the new small satellites can be equipped with robotic arms for active debris removal missions. This technology is dual-use and could be used on a range of objects in orbit. It states that China has been developing and testing this technology since 2008. The document claims that the robotic arm technology has also been incorporated into "drones, smart weapons and robots. These satellites could remain attached to the debris it collects to avoid being tracked from the ground."

Non-Kinetic Weapons. China has highly sophisticated non-kinetic, electronic and cyber weapons, which have proven effective against space assets. According to the U.S. Director of National Intelligence, the technologies include directed-energy technology that can blind or damage sensitive space based optical sensors, such as those used for remote sensing or missile defence. In 2019, General John Raymond, Commander of U.S. Space Command and Air Force Space Command, stated, "we're pretty comfortable [in asserting] that they are developing directed energy weapons—probably building lasers to blind our satellites." It was reported in early 2020 that China had developed a prototype for an airborne laser weapon, capable of taking down incoming missiles or aircraft. In early 2019, the U.S. Defense Intelligence Agency stated, "China likely is pursuing laser weapons to disrupt, degrade, or damage satellites and their sensors and possibly already has a limited capability to employ laser systems against satellite sensors."

The PLA has an operational ground-based satellite electronic countermeasures (ECM) capability designed to disrupt adversary use of SATCOM, navigation, SAR, missile early warning and other satellites through use of jamming. The PLA acquired ground-based satellite jammers from Ukraine in the late 1990s. Since then China has indigenously developed satellite ECM. The PLA and defence industry are developing jammers capable of targeting satellite communications over a large range of frequencies, including dedicated military communication bands. The

PLASSF Network Systems Department probably carries out satellite jamming operations. As of now this cannot be confirmed.

Laser. China had been developing significant satellite lasing facilities. It announced an airborne laser in early 2020. China is pursuing these efforts in at least five different locations across the country. Reportedly in an uncorroborated assessment, one image depicts a suspected electro-magnetic pulse (EMP) simulator suspended between two structures. China is expected to deploy a laser weapon targeting sensors on LEO satellites by 2020.[51] U.S. DIA estimates that, from the mid-to-late 2020s, China may deploy higher power laser weapons that can attack non-optical satellites.

High-Power Microwave (HPM). China has displayed interest in developing HPM weapons for air and missile defence. However, adding a mobile HPM system to a satellite would depend upon further reductions in weight, size and power in addition to many other integration challenges unique to the space environment. China can launch a nuclear weapon into LEO. The resulting EMP from the detonation would cause indiscriminate damage to satellites. In addition, it would create a high level of radiation in LEO that could last for years. While China has the technology to field a nuclear-armed ASAT weapon, it appears to be focusing its efforts in other areas.

Electronic Warfare (EW). China possesses advanced satellite jamming capabilities. In military exercises the PLA routinely incorporates jamming and anti-jamming techniques against multiple communication, radar systems and GPS satellite systems.

China is developing jammers dedicated to targeting SAR aboard military reconnaissance platforms, including LEO satellites. China is improving jammers to target SATCOM over a range of frequency bands, including military protected extremely high frequency communications. On Mischief Reef of the Spratly Islands, China has reportedly deployed mobile jammers targeted at GPS and other global navigation satellite systems. Presently China can jam common satellite communication bands and GPS signals. In addition, China is developing jamming systems that will be able to target a large range of frequencies of commercial SATCOM.

A paper from the China Electronics Technology Group Corporation proposed solutions for "overcoming the high-power requirements for jamming U.S. millimeter wave (MMW) satellite communications by using space-based jammers hosted on small satellites, in a typical 'David versus Goliath' attack." The authors identified U.S. satellites that would be susceptible to such an attack, like "the Advanced Extremely High Frequency (AEHF), Wideband Global SATCOM (WGS) and Global Broadcast Service (GBS) satellite constellations." Another Chinese technical paper provides further insight into how China plans to jam GPS signals used by U.S. drones, e.g. the RQ-4 Global Hawk, over the Spratly Islands and the South China Sea.

A Chinese military analyst stated that China would detect an incoming drone strike through its early-warning radars and anti-access/area denial (A2/AD) systems. He added that China would shoot down the drone with its air defences and conduct a "soft kill" by jamming the drone's communications and GPS.

China has deployed military-grade truck-mounted jamming equipment in its buildup of military installations in the artificial islands in the South China Sea. U.S. officials endorsed that there are two islands in the Spratly Island chain that have been equipped with jamming systems for targeting communications and radar.

As per the National Interest, China has developed a J-16D aircraft equipped with jamming systems. This aircraft, which suspiciously looks like the U.S. Navy's EA-18G Growler electronic attack fighter, is equipped with several new antennas and conformal electronic- warfare arrays along the fuselage. The "D" in J-16D comes from "diànzǐ," the Chinese word for electronic.

In 2018, the SSF even carried out advanced military exercises simulating a complex electronic warfare environment with the "SSF base pitted against five PLA Army, Air Force, and Rocket Force units."

Cyber Warfare. China has displayed its ability to infiltrate satellite systems and take command, hack into organisations responsible for specific satellite operations and penetrate the networks of companies involved with geospatial imaging technology, big data and other advanced innovations crucial to space dominance. Through the reorganised Strategic Support Force (SSF) China has been integrating its advanced cyber capabilities with its counter space and electronic warfare operations.

China has been implicated or suspected in several cyberattacks against U.S. satellites. For example, in October 2007 and July 2008, cyberattacks supposed to originate in China targeted a remote sensing satellite operated by the U.S. Geological Survey called Landsat-7. These attacks have occurred through a ground station in Norway. Each attack caused 12 or more minutes of interference with ground station communications. However, the attackers could not gain control of the satellite.

In June and October of 2008, hackers from China attacked the National Aeronautics and Space Administration's (NASA) Terra Earth observation satellite. In these operations, the hackers "achieved all steps required to command the satellite but did not issue commands." A 2019 NASA Inspector General report references several Chinese cyber intrusions into NASA, including a 2009 Chinese cyberattack on the Joint Propulsion Laboratory (JPL), resulting in 22 gigabytes of data getting transferred to a Chinese IP address. Another transfer of data to Chinese IP addresses occurred in 2011 when "intruders gained full access to 18 servers supporting key JPL missions, including the Deep Space Network (DSN) and Advanced Space borne Thermal Emission and Reflection Radiometer mission and sensitive user accounts."

China could use its cyber warfare capabilities to support military operations against space-based assets. The PLA can carry out cyber espionage targeting foreign space entities. For example, the PLA unit responsible for conducting signals intelligence has supported cyber espionage against U.S. and European satellite and aerospace industries since 2007.

China is significantly increasing its development, testing and fielding of non-kinetic physical and electronic counter-space weapons. The operational deployment of lasers, competent of dazzling or blinding satellites, is in the offing. China is getting bolder with its electronic jamming and spoofing capabilities. It is probable that satellite jamming and spoofing capabilities will be deployed and used in areas of grey zone conflict, such as the South China Sea, and even to deter protests in Hong Kong.[52]

Shortcomings

Chinese military writings have identified its perceived shortcomings in China's space program. Some of them are:

- There is a possibility that essential Chinese satellites could be affected by hostile counterspace operations. Enemy forces could jam Chinese satellites in orbit and sabotage their ground support infrastructure.
- BeiDou satellites could be accidentally jammed by friendly air defence units.
- In the event of conflict, it is not clear what types of space assets are likely to be assigned to PLA commanders and how would they be used?
- It is not clear what responsibilities the SSF's space force has for anti satellite research, development, testing and operations.
- Whether the SSF has a role in ballistic missile defense (BMD) is unknown.
- Whether the SSF's authority in space and space-based C4ISR will rule out other services from developing, operating or maintaining their respectively space infrastructure for operations independently.
- Role of PLA Rocket Force and the PLA Air Force (PLAAF) which earlier had demonstrated some capability.

Experts from PLA recommend hardening satellites, camouflaging and concealing their operations centers, maneuvering when under attack, and augmenting the protection of ground stations. They also recommend using civilian satellites for military missions and stockpiling military satellites as a reserve that can be launched to fill coverage gaps and meet wartime needs. To reduce the risk of "red-on-red" jamming, they recommend that commanders coordinate operations and carefully control when and where electronic jamming is used.

Armed forces all over the world are known for vigorously defending their turfs. China is no exception. It is quite likely that the SSF's space mission may represent a bureaucratic solution to the previous fight for space primacy between the PLAAF and Rocket Force.

In August 2017, the DN-3 anti-satellite missile was launched from the SSF's Jiuquan Satellite Launch Center, which may signal that the SSF has responsibility for testing or fielding these systems. The current locations of many of China's offensive space capabilities, including its more experimental co-orbital attack capabilities such as the Shiyan-7 "robotic arm" satellite, remain unknown.[53]

Key Space and Counterspace Organisations. China's space program has a complex structure and consists of organisations in the military, political, defence-industrial and commercial sectors. The PLA has managed China's space program historically. It continues its efforts to improve China's capabilities in space-based ISR, satellite communication, satellite navigation and human spaceflight and robotic space exploration. State-owned enterprises are China's main civilian and military space contractors. China is placing greater importance on decentralising and diversifying its space industry to increase competition.

The Chinese government operates separate civil and military space organisations. The China National Space Administration (CNSA) falls within the State Council's State Administration for Science and Technology and Industry for National Defense (SASTIND) which is the primary organisation for China's civil space activities. A state-owned aerospace corporation, China Aerospace Science and Technology Corporation (CASC) is the primary developer of national civil space technologies. Military space activities are run through the People's Liberation Army (PLA). However, each of these entities collaborates with one another on developing space technologies.

Currently, the State Council's SASTIND is the primary civil organisation that manages and coordinates China's space activities which includes allocating space research and development funds. It also maintains a relationship with the PLA organisation that administers China's military acquisitions. SASTIND establishes policies and guides state-owned entities conducting China's space activities, whereas the State-owned Assets Supervision and Administration Commission provides day-to-day management.

SASTIND and the CMC Equipment Development Department, in June 2019, jointly created and released rules on manufacturing, test flights and launches of commercial rockets. The specific rules include the need for commercial rocket companies to obtain SASTIND's prior permission for research and manufacturing and to give prior notice to relevant departments when actually beginning research and manufacturing. The rules encourage companies to make maximum use of national resources for technology research, manufacturing equipment and facilities and launch sites.

In December 2019, the China Commercial Space Alliance was launched by entities including the China Space Foundation, China Volant Industry (CASIC subsidiary), China Great Wall Industry Corporation (CASC subsidiary) and Chinese Academy of Sciences Holdings. The Alliance plans to support member organisations through such activities as providing information under the guidance of the China National Space Administration.

China has expanded its Electro-Optical (EO) satellite network. EO satellites are assigned Yaogan and Gaofen designations. SASTIND manages the Gaofen satellite engineering program, suggesting its dual-use nature. At least eight Gaofen satellites, many equipped with an EO sensor, have been launched since 2013, with the latest (Gaofen-11) launched in 2018. Other Gaofen satellites are equipped with SAR and hyperspectral sensors. The Yaogan-28 was launched in November 2015. At least two of the Yaogan-30 series satellites where launched in 2016/2017 and are believed to carry EO payloads. The China Aerospace Science and Technology Corporation (CASC) Fifth Academy (China Academy of Space Technology [CAST]) is the lead systems integrator for EO satellites.

Currently, China's private space firms are in their early stages. It is premature for the military to use technologies or services that the companies developed. However, the Chinese version of New Space is growing at a rapid pace, supported by the government and the military under the military-civil fusion strategy. In the future the military is expected to adopt the technologies developed by the private sector and use them.

The CNSA serves as the public face of China's civil space efforts. China is using these efforts to augment relationships with countries worldwide. CNSA, in April 2018, stated that China had signed 21 civil space cooperation agreements with 37 countries and four international organisations.[54]

Key Organizations Involved in China's Space Activities

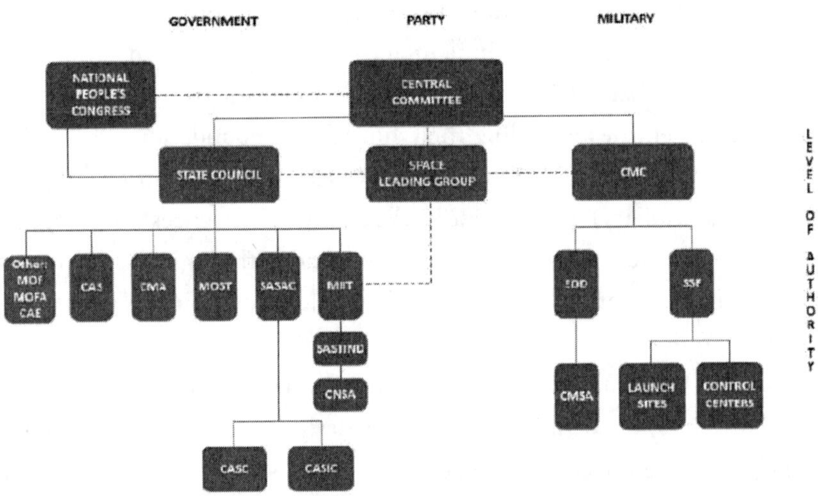

Source: Adapted for Marco Aliberti, *When China Goes to the Moon...* Springer International Publishing, 2015, p. 10.

Recent Developments in China

Since the 2010s enterprises known as "New Space" pioneered by SpaceX, founded by Elon Musk and Blue Origin established by Jeff Bezos have taken centre stage. SpaceX has been driving down prices of satellite launch services and planning the provision of an internet service enabled by a constellation of thousands to tens of thousands of satellites.

China has entered into this band wagon. As of 2018, 141 aerospace enterprises have been registered in China, consisting of 36 satellite manufacturing enterprises, 22 launch vehicle manufacturing enterprises, 39 satellite operation enterprises and 44 satellite applications enterprises. Some examples are:

- Established in 2015, Beijing Commsat Technology Development aims to launch
- 72 IoT satellites into LEO by 2022.
- Founded in 2016, Galaxy Space, has a scheme to provide high-speed global communications by launching up to 1,000 5G satellites into LEO.

Founded in 2016, Beijing Interstellar Glory Space Technology (iSpace)

- became the first Chinese private rocket company to successfully launch satellites with an independently developed rocket in July 2019. The solid propellant rocket Hyperbola-1 developed by iSpace was launched from Jiuquan Satellite Launch Center administered by the SSF.

India in Space Domain

Introduction

India is now a major space faring nation. Initially, the Indian space programme was focused primarily on societal and developmental utilities. Today, like many other countries, India is compelled to use space for several military requirements like intelligence, surveillance and reconnaissance. Hence, India is looking to space to gain operational and informational advantages.

India has had its fair share of achievements in the space domain. It includes the launch of the country's heaviest satellite, the GSAT-11, which will boost India's broadband services by enabling 16 Gbps data links across the country, GSAT-7A, the military communication satellite and the launch of the GSLV Mk III-D2, the GSAT 29. The Anti-Satellite (ASAT) test is an intrinsic part of today's geopolitics and the national security context.

India's space programme is self-reliant. India has achieved self-reliance in launch vehicles and satellite technology. India has been providing launch services to foreign countries. Space-related assets are extremely useful for military purposes. For example, ballistic missile defence cannot function without space assets providing communications and navigation.

Space applications like satellite communications, satellite imagery and surveillance and satellite navigation perform numerous functions. Satellite imagery helps damage assessment following an airstrike and satellite navigation guides precision missiles to their targets. India is facing a number of national security threats, including two-front war, proxy wars perpetrated by inimical neighbours, insurgencies, left-wing extremism, natural disasters and dangers along the Sea Lines of Communication (SLOCs). Space will play a crucial role in addressing these threats. Space is essential to the Indian Armed Forces for sustaining communications, logistics, missiles launch and guidance, weapons systems and Unmanned Aerial Vehicles (UAVs). Space for military applications is gaining momentum. INSAT and GSAT satellites for communications, Synthetic Aperture Radar (SAR) satellites, high-resolution panchromatic satellites, Indian Regional Navigation Satellite System (IRNSS) met a large part of space requirements of the armed forces. However, gaps continue to exist in India's space capabilities.

Space assets are of immense use in disaster management and humanitarian assistance. India is in the process of finalising its space policy. India's space policy should energise private industries to take part in domestic and global markets in launch vehicles and satellite manufacturing segments with increased entrepreneurship. Space assets should be protected for supporting civil space functions and national security objectives.

India is moving towards integrated application of different space technologies by use of satellite communication, navigation and imaging. These technologies are being used for social welfare purposes such as advancements in tele-medicine, tele-education, disaster management and search and rescue operations. Schemes like village resource centers and e-governance are significant for large populations, providing connection to the most remote places while ensuring transparency.

The commercial uses of space technology are popular. Around 900 television channels are available to viewers through Direct-to-Home (DTH) services. However, in commercial use of space technology, India is lagging behind. For example, Indian transponders are fulfilling only 40 percent of India's DTH requirements. The ISRO is trying to reduce this gap through the launch of new satellites to make Digital India a success. GSAT series of satellites will raise the capacity to 75 Gbps of data augmenting the existing bandwidth on ISRO's satellites.

Internationally, India is helping other countries boost their space technology and resultant services. In addition to hosting payloads and launching foreign satellites, India is also operating South Asian Satellite for the neighbourhood.

Characteristics of Indian Space

The government drives Indian space activities to meet national needs with a focus on self-reliance and security. ISRO drove commercial activities through its commercial arm, Antrix Corporation. It depended on the availability of spare capacity. All commercial space activities were closely regulated and controlled by the Department of Space (DoS). As a result, space commerce has not grown in India compared to other major space-faring countries. While India has achieved significant feats in space missions and allied activities, Indian space commerce accounts for less than 1% of the global market.

The current global space economy is around US$ 360 billion. It is split between upstream, midstream and downstream activities. Therefore, there is excellent scope for the commercialisation of the ground operations like mission support, satellite broadband gateways and 5G backhauling.

The Indian space program is totally state-driven. ISRO is around 70-80 per cent reliant on private-sector contractors for components and services. A huge number of Indian companies provide ISRO with launch and satellite components, the leaders being well known engineering and technology firms like Larsen & Toubro, Godrej, Walchandnagar Industries, and Tata Aerospace. There is a number of emerging new space actors , mostly start-up companies based in Bangalore. Majority of them are in the small satellite segment.[55]

India has a large base of SMEs for supplying parts and components for satellite and launch vehicle manufacturing. ISRO contracts these suppliers for meeting its demands. There have been initiatives to help private industry build capacity in system-level integration. However, they lack end-to-end manufacturing capabilities ranging from design to testing and launch. Currently, ISRO has adopted public-private partnership (PPP) policies to encourage companies to take up more production activities rather than part/component manufacturers. ISRO has formed a consortium of private industry players for Assembly, Integration and Testing (AIT) of 30-35 satellites.

ISRO has built a facility spread over 25 acres in Bengaluru where the amenities have been set up for use by the industry to encourage more private participation.

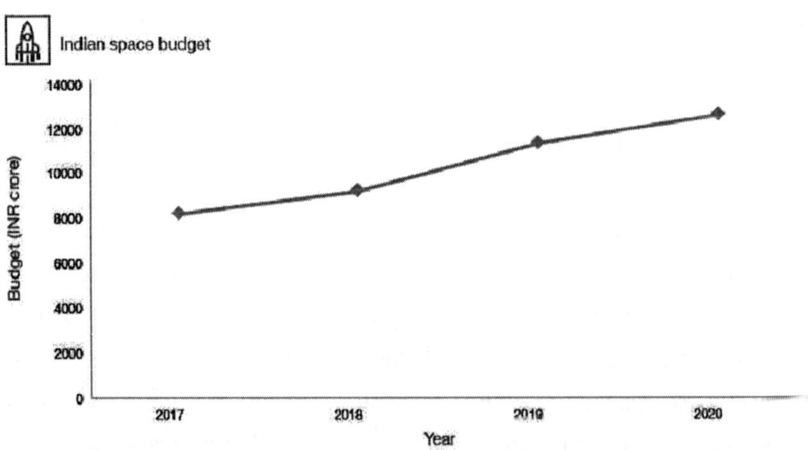

Source: *https://www.isro.gov.in/budget-glance, https://www.business-standard.com/budget/article/budget-2019-fm-hikes-dept-of-space-outlay-pushes-for-commercialisation-119070500973_1.html*

Size of India's space economy. The value of the Indian space economy is around US$ 7 billion. Of this, upstream activities contribute US$ 2.3 billion and downstream activities contribute US$ 4.7 billion.

With the current success of exploratory missions to Moon and Mars and the government's impetus on promoting space technology-based tools and applications, different avenues are opening up to tap the economic and commercial potential of space technology products and services. With significant advantages like a strong domestic manufacturing base, high demand for services, cost advantage, a large human resource pool and ability to use IT skills, the private space industry should take a more significant role in the space economy.

ISRO's existing space value chain mapping

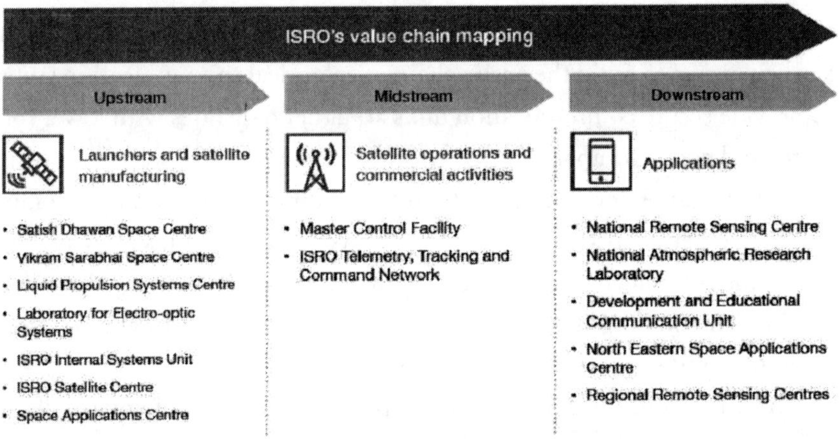

Source: Preparing to scale new heights: Enhancing private participation in India's commercial space sector, January 2020, available at: https://www.pwc.in/assets/pdfs/research-insights/2020/preparing-to-scale-new-heights.pdf?utm_source=dlvr.it&utm_medium=facebook

With the rising space-based needs of security agencies, ISRO will have to continue the normal development of remote sensing and telecommunications missions and deliver for national security requirements. If the government facilitates the development of spacecraft by the private industry, ISRO will be able to focus on the development of the next generation of technologies. Antrix initiated the project of small satellites to boost the new space ecosystem in India.

Launchers. ISRO has announced the building of an SSLV that can lift satellites up to 500 kg in LEO. For the production process, ISRO has been practising a subcontracting model for all its launch vehicles successfully. However, this model is not adequate to achieve cost optimisation and production efficiency. These objectives can be achieved by executing an end-to-end production set-up, with optimum numbers planned and transparently communicated to the industry. India's ability to stay at the forefront in an increasingly competitive space market depends on integrating private players into the ecosystem. There is a scope to commercialise the development of medium and heavy-lift launchers.

Communication. Satellite communication is the largest services market. There is increased interest in optical communication to overcome the constraint of the limited availability of radio frequencies. An Indian start-up wants to build the entire chain of an optical communication system to provide secure communication links at higher data rates with lower form factor and power compared to RF systems. Start-ups also develop ultra-high capacity transponders that operate in the millimetre wave frequency range to provide better spectral efficiency and a considerable unused bandwidth. These provide much higher uplink/downlink capacity per satellite. With the implementation of 5G, Internet of Things (IoT) and BharatNet, these satellite-based services will be in great demand.[56]

In India only a few industries possess the technology to design, manufacture, qualify and supply space subsystems like various sensors, inertial systems, control mechanisms, propellant storage and delivery systems thrusters, power systems and payloads. This can be addressed by a well-defined Transfer of Technology (ToT) policy.

International Partnership. India's most important international partner in space is France. It launched most of India's heavy-payload satellites. India and Israel have cooperated in developing advanced imaging and reconnaissance satellites, most prominently the RISAT-2. Using synthetic aperture radar, it is a day-night and all-weather radar-imaging satellite capable of monitoring India's border areas on a 24/7 basis. Another important partner is NASA, with which India has a long history of cooperation. However, cooperation was restricted because of the export control regimes and sanctions placed on ISRO following the 1974 and 1998 nuclear tests. After the 2005 U.S.-India civil nuclear agreement, things have improved.[57]

Indian Space Research Organisation (ISRO)

ISRO is now one of the largest space agencies in the world. It maintains a large fleet of communication, (INSAT)/Geostationary Satellites (GSAT) remote sensing, navigation and scientific satellites. It provides multiple application-specific products and tools for broadcasting, communication, disaster management, weather forecasting, GIS, cartography, navigation, telemedicine, among many other functions. ISRO has completed 118 spacecraft missions and 78 launch missions till 2019. Presently, there are 18 communication satellites, 21 conservation satellites and eight navigation satellites in orbit. These achievements display the rapid advancements made by the Indian space programme in manufacturing indigenous equipment to fuel its ambitions. ISRO's launch systems proved to be among the most reliable and cost-effective solutions globally and have attracted international customers.

In more recent achievements, ISRO has placed an orbiter around Mars and assisted in confirming the presence of water on the moon. In 2019, the agency tried to land a rover on the moon, but the mission partially failed when the lander could not achieve a "soft landing" and crashed.

India has joined the quest to explore other celestial bodies through missions such as:

- **Gaganyaan**. Sending humans in space and bringing them safely back to earth.
- **Chandrayaan 3**. To land safely on the moon, Chandrayaan-3 is likely to be launched in 2022.
- **Mangalyaan2**. Second Mars mission, this mission is likely to be an orbiter. Will be undertaken after the launch of Chandrayaan-3.
- **Aditya.** To study the outermost region of the sun, called corona. It would be placed into a point in space known as the L1 Lagrange point.
- **Heavy lift launcher**. Super heavy-lift launch vehicle, which is planned to have a lifting capacity of over 50-60 tonnes.

- **Geosynchronous Transfer Orbit (GTO).** Heavy-lift launch vehicle that can carry up to 16-tonne payloads to Geostationary Transfer Orbit.

Other emerging nations have benefitted from the progress made by the Indian Space Research Organisation (ISRO) in outer space technologies. India has signed 200 cooperation agreements with five international organisations and 51 countries for providing effective collaboration for peaceful use of outer space, data sharing, capacity building and policy coordination.

Antrix

Antrix Corporation Limited was raised in September, 1992 as a company under the administrative control of the Department of Space, Government of India. Antrix is the commercial arm of ISRO. It promotes and markets the products and services generated by the Indian space programme.

Commercially, a total of 328 foreign satellites from 33 countries have been successfully launched on board the Polar Satellite Launch Vehicle (PSLV). Revenue earned through these launches is $25 million. These launches were done through contracts that were signed with Antrix Corporation Ltd.

Major areas of work of Antrix Corporation are:

- Obtain licence from DoS/ISRO for SSLV technology and transfer it to the industry through sub-licencing.
- Provide launch services for customer satellites.
- Manufacture SSLVs in collaboration with the private sector.
- Production of Polar Satellite Launch Vehicle (PSLV) through industry.
- Production and marketing of space-based services.
- Transfer of Technology to the industry through sub-licensing.
- Market by-product technologies and products or services.

In 2019, the Government of India established the NewSpace India Ltd. (NSIL), whose purposes are almost identical to Antrix.

Space Policy

ISRO has always punched well above its weight. However, today, the Government space agency, by itself, does not have the capacity in terms of capital, skilled labour, equipment to develop and exploit all benefit single-handedly. This makes a strong case for unlocking the potential of private capital and skills. For example, DTH operators in India use 42 transponders from indigenous satellites and leasing about 67 transponders from foreign satellites. The policy needs to focus on creating a competitive and level playing field where new players can enter, receive mentorship and support from ISRO and flourish.

India's space ecosystem has seen significant government involvement, with ISRO spearheading research, manufacturing, launching, operating and maintaining objects in space. However, private sector involvement in space activities was limited to supplying parts and assembling blocks for ISRO.

All these are about to change. In a major policy change, the union government has permitted for the reforms in the space sector by allowing private players' participation. On November 20, 2020, the Department of Space unveiled its Draft Space RS Policy-2020 and Space RS NGP-2020 documents and sought comments from the public. ISRO has released the draft of a new Spacecom Policy 2020. This is the most significant development in the space sector since the formation of ISRO half a century ago.

Indian National Space Promotion and Authorization Center (IN-SPACe). IN-SPACe is an independent nodal agency under the Department of Space to allow space activities and usage of Department of Space owned facilities by non-government private entities (NGPEs) and prioritise the launch manifest. IN-SPACe will have a chairman, technical, strategic and legal experts in space activities, safety and from other departments, academia and industries and members of the PMO and Ministry of External Affairs. The decisions of IN-SPACe, shall be final and binding on all stakeholders. The NGPEs will not require to seek separate permission from ISRO for using its facilities.[58]

This has invited sharp reactions. Former ISRO chairman G Madhavan Nair said that this is an unwanted disturbance in the functioning of the Indian space programme. Trying to implement an unproven novel concept would result in killing the goose that lays the golden eggs.

Roles and Responsibilities. IN-SPACe will be established as a single-window nodal agency, with its own cadre, which will permit and oversee the following activities of NGPEs:

- Space activities include building launch vehicles and satellites and providing space-based services as per the definition of space activities.
- Sharing of space infrastructure and premises under the control of ISRO with due considerations to ongoing activities.
- Establishment of temporary facilities within premises under ISRO control based on safety norms and feasibility assessment.
- Establishment of new space infrastructure and facilities, by NGPEs, in pursuance of space activities based on safety norms and other statutory guidelines and necessary clearances.
- Initiation of launch campaign and launch, based on readiness of launch vehicle and spacecraft systems, ground and user segment.
- Building, operation and control of spacecraft for registration as Indian Satellite by NGPEs and all the associated infrastructure for the same.
- Usage of spacecraft data and rolling out of space based services and all the associated infrastructure for the same.

The Chairman of ISRO is also the Secretary of the Department of Space (DoS) and the Chairman of the Space Commission. The New Space Policy 2020 aims to decouple the policy, regulatory and service delivery roles of the ISRO. The incumbent ISRO will be restructured. Its commercial activities hived-off into a government-owned NewSpace India Ltd, leaving the organisation to focus on research and development, scientific missions and exploration.

K. Sivan, ISRO's chairman, categorically stated that "IN-SPACe will be a autonomous body, which won't be influenced by ISRO and it won't influence ISRO's work". However, he is also concurrently the secretary of the DoS and chairman of the space commission. Even if IN-SPACe is independent of ISRO, it cannot be truly autonomous to the extent that it is under the DoS. Among the first tasks would be the painful one of severing the roles of chairman of ISRO and secretary of DoS.

In the last two years, IN-SPACe is the second space organisation made by the government, The government, in the 2019 Budget had announced the setting up of a New Space India Limited (NSIL), a public sector company that would serve as a marketing arm of ISRO. Its primary purpose is to market the technologies developed by ISRO and bring more clients that need space-based services. That role was already being performed by Antrix Corporation, another PSU working under the Department of Space, and which still exists.

The government stated that it was redefining the role of NSIL so that it would have a demand-driven approach rather than the current supply-driven strategy. Rather than just marketing what ISRO has to offer, NSIL would listen to the clients' needs and ask ISRO to fulfil those.

In a lecture, Chairman of ISRO Dr K Sivan recently stated that ISRO intends to offload most of its space-related activities to industry and increase focus on advanced research. He said, "Future of space activities is now changing. Earlier all the space activities were done by only ISRO. Now, we are giving equal opportunity to private players also to do it. We want to hand-hold them to our [ISRO's] level so that most activities that ISRO is doing can be offloaded to industry, and we can spend more time on advanced research to take India to the next level (in the space sector)."

He was firm in saying that ISRO is not looking at collaboration with NGPEs at this stage. ISRO can only collaborate with partners with equal strength, like international space agencies, since NGPEs in the space sector are still in the growth stage. He added, "That is a process. We are hoping that once they grow to our level, then definitely we will be able to have collaboration."

Spacecom Policy 2020

Key Points of the Spacecom Policy 2020 are:

- The space policy has been drafted for reforming the Indian space sector.
- The policy will regulate the commercial use of satellites, orbital slots and ground stations for communication needs.
- The private players in the space communication sector will help India to keep pace with the increasing demand for satellite-based broadcasting, network connectivity and global mobile personal communication.
- The government wants private players to participate in the space sector as a vendor and partner.

The Spacecom Policy—2020 enables the activities of space-based communications under five major statements. Spacecom Policy-2020 states that the Government of India shall:[59]

- Adopt measures to monitor and authorise the use of space assets for communication to or from Indian territory.
- Ensure protection of space assets already put in place and adopt measures to bring in more space assets under the administrative control for enhancing the ability to utilise space-based communication for national needs.
- Promote increased participation of commercial Indian industry to provide space-based communications both within outside and the country.
- Concentrate on realising space-based communication systems to address the requirements that cannot be effectively, affordably and reliably satisfied by the private Indian industry either due to national security concerns or economic factors.
- Provide a timely and responsive regulatory environment for the commercial Indian industry to establish and operate space-based communication systems.

The Salient Features. The new policy will enable India to meet the growing demand for satellite-based broadcasting, network connectivity and global mobile personal communication. It will help India attain a significant position in the worldwide space communication sector. The salient features are:

- Only Indian entities will be allowed to seek authorisation for orbital slots for new satellites, services based on existing satellites and new ground stations.
- There are no restrictions regarding satellite owning, ground session setup and providing services to ordinary people.
- Private industries are allowed to use the ISRO satellites and they can have their own satellites.
- Any company sending a communication satellite in space will also be responsible for any damages to other objects in space and the environment.

There are issues. For example, take the satellite industry. Each one satellite company requires a frequency allocation license from a national agency that coordinates the frequency allocation with the International Telecommunication Union (ITU).[60] There was no clarity on how a private satellite operator would do that. Agencies involved are the Department of Telecommunications which allocate the frequencies, the Department of Space and some other departments. With the creation of INSPACe and the new draft SATCOM policy, the procedure will become much simpler, with IN-SPACe being the nodal agency for this. Regarding the remote sensing policy, it only covered the usage of satellite imagery and not the operations of earth imaging satellites until now. All purchases had to go through the National Remote Sensing Centre (NRSC). The process adds a time delay. With the setting up of INSPACe and the new draft of the remote sensing policy, the process has become simpler. Anything above 50 cm resolution is free to procure and sell, which would be a massive boost to the sector.[61]

Indian Space Association (ISpA)

Prime Minister Narendra Modi, on October 11, 2021, launched the Indian Space Association (ISpA). It is an industry body of various stakeholders of the Indian space domain.

The Prime Minister said, "ISpA is a premier industry association of space and satellite companies, which aspires to be the collective voice of the Indian space industry. It will undertake policy advocacy and engage with all stakeholders in the Indian space domain, including the government and its agencies. These reforms will provide opportunities for both industry and academia."

The members of ISpA include government bodies Organisation (ISRO) and private telecom companies. The founding members include leading domestic and global corporations that have advanced capabilities in space and satellite technologies such as Bharti Airtel, engineering firm Larson & Toubro, and other companies such as Nelco of Tata Group, Sunil Bharti Mittal's OneWeb, Mapmyindia, Walchandnagar Industries and Alpha Design Technologies and Ananth Technology Limited . Other core members include BEL, Centum Electronics, Godrej, Hughes India, Azista-BST Aerospace Private Limited and Maxar India. The first few start-ups to be members include Pixxel, Astrome Technologies, Agnikul Cosmos, Digantra and Skyroot Aerospace.[62]

Lt Gen A.K. Bhatt (retd) from 11 Gorkha Rifles who commanded the Chinar Corps at Srinagar and had been Indian Army's Director General of Military Operation will be the first Director General of ISpA while Jayant Patil, senior executive vice president, defence, L&T-NxT, will serve as chairperson.

Till recently, the ISRO's private engagement model has been the one of sharing technological know-how or intellectual property with companies. ISRO has a monopoly over purchase of their products and services. Private players have been demanding for greater involvement in India's space sector to make ISRO more competitive with leading global players. The present government's decision aim at long-term technological, economic and industrial gains.

The space-based communications network in India, has taken off with number of global and Indian and companies showing interest in providing high-speed and affordable internet connectivity to inaccessible areas also. This includes Sunil Bharti Mittal's OneWeb, SpaceX's StarLink, Amazon's Project Kuiper, U.S. satellite maker Hughes Communications, etc. By late 2022, OneWeb is expected to offer its high-speed, low latency connectivity services in India. StarLink and Amazon have shown interest for a licence to offer satellite-based Internet services. SpaceX is also willing to invest in Indian space segment.[63]

The expansion of the internet in India is vital to the present government's project of a digital India where a bulk of government services would be delivered directly to the people. Though the government aims to connect all villages and gram panchayats with high-speed internet through BharatNet, internet connectivity in hilly and far-flung remote areas are still a challenge. To overcome this problem, satellite internet will be crucial where terrestrial networks have not reached.[64]

ISpA will drive space reforms based on "four pillars" of space technology. They are:

- The freedom of innovation in the private sector.
- Preparing the next generation for the tomorrow of the space industry. Making the government act as an enabler.
- Ensuring the space sector is used as a standard resource for the human progress.
- Development projects are being overseen by satellite imaging, space technology is being used in settlement of Fasal Bima Yojna claims and disaster management planning and the NAVIC system is helping fishermen.

ISpA will focus on capacity building and creation of space hubs and incubators in the country for private space start-ups. It will work in conjunction with NSIL, a central public sector enterprise under the Department of Space (DOS). NSIL works as the commercial arm for ISRO. ISpA will also work with IN-SPACe, which acts as a regulator facilitating the use of government facilities to private companies. IN-SPACe will make sure a level playing field for private companies to use Indian space infrastructure and a friendly regulatory environment.

ISRO will continue to function as the core space organisation in India with decision-making authority related to activities, missions and projects. It will focus more on Research and Development (R&D), exploring new technologies, and planning new space missions.

This reforms will enable and promote private players to carry out independent space activities, facilitate services and technology created by the ISRO for utilisation by the private sector, arrange regulatory and policy inputs and promote an conducive ecosystem for start-ups, MSMEs and academia.[65]

ISpA is expected to do the following:

- Engage with all collaborators in the Indian space sector. Be the collective voice of the Indian space industry, undertake policy advocacy including the government and its other agencies, NSIL IN-SPACe, among others.
- Make India technologically advanced, self-reliant and a leading player in the space arena.
- Support space start-ups and work towards facilitating and enabling private companies to work in coordination with IN-SPACe and ISRO.
- Formulate an enabling policy framework that achieves the government's vision of leading commercial space exploration and space-based communication.
- Work towards building world wide linkages for the Indian space sector to get more investments and develop critical technology to create more high-skilled employment.
- Concentrate on the creation of space hubs and incubators and capacity building in the country for private space start-ups.

Why ISpA? The reasons are:

- Lack of policy revision in the past. Inadequate funding to ISRO.

- Shortage of private industries specialised in space technology. They lack in developing world-class software, and advanced material science industries in India.
- Currently, most of the materials and software are imported. A huge gap exists between Indian and other advanced countries in the space field. Advanced countries develop most of their requirements in-house.
- To fill this huge gap between demand and supply more industries are needed.
- Has the potential to generate 10 to 15 times of the current revenue. This will generate a lot of employment and develop much-advanced technology.
- Through the help of private agencies invest heavily in material science, material industries, electronics industry, software industry, start-ups, and many more.

What hasn't Changed

Though the new policy has significant clarity compared to the earlier SATCOM Policy and norms, there are areas of concern. The availability and allotment of orbital resources, such as orbital slot, frequency and coverage, have not been deliberated in the new policy. Currently, the wireless planning and coordination wing of the Ministry of Communications is the official body to coordinate with the ITU on behalf of India for securing these resources. The allocation of spectrum is undertaken through the National Frequency Allocation Plan, 2018 and under the Indian Telegraph Act. This process is complicated and time-consuming. The new policy needs the operational licenses to be secured from the ministry of communications or broadcasting.

The new policy falls short of achieving a single-window clearance system for potential applications seeking authorisations for launching and operating SATCOM assets. The new policy and norms do not define the composition of IN-SPACe, the regulatory body for commercial space activities and the extent of the powers of regulation. The Department of Space and IN-SPACe have been given authority to formulate policy guidelines for submitting applications, processing and grant of authorisations without laying down the limits of the powers of each body.[66]

The intent of the new norms and policies is laudable. However, the potential for achieving ease of doing business metrics for the satellite communications industry remains unrealised. Excluding foreign entities altogether from the new policy and norms scheme raises concerns about whether or not the new policy and norms comply with international obligations under the provisions of relevant Bilateral Investment Treaties. They are corollary to India's membership in the World Trade Organisation. Furthermore, the requirement of bringing Non-Geostationary non-Indian orbital resources (NIOR) under Indian administrative control curbs the ability of Indian entities to cooperate with foreign satellite service providers to act as aggregators and distributors of their capabilities in India. It is a subject of debate whether the objective of self-reliance should be realised at the expense of facilitating international partnerships.

Suppose the new policies and norms are to achieve the stated objective of promoting commercial space. In that case, it must first involve the joint and consolidated efforts of the Ministry of Communications, Ministry of Information and Broadcasting, Ministry of Home Affairs, Ministry of Defence, along with the Department of Space to work out a new and revised policy that consolidates the mandates of the provisions of the Indian Telegraph Act along with security considerations into a single window system for receiving and processing applications for space activities. Authorisation for launching satellites and operational clearances cannot be two independent regulatory streams. This will only lead to uncertainties on timelines and outcomes.[67]

Armed Forces

In June 2018, the U.S. raised a separate branch of the armed forces known as the Space Force to protect U.S. space interests. In 2015, China created the Strategic Support Force to carry out space and cyber operations and information and electronic warfare. Russia has military space command

and operational capabilities. Recently, France has announced that it will establish a space command to protect its space assets and interests. The need to save space assets is an inescapable requirement now.

India realises this reality and the need to re-organise and re-structure the entire National Security Complex. It is the most important task ahead of the Indian Nation-State, especially if India wants to become a global power. The role of space-based communications and C4ISR assets complemented by other ground-based SSA components will be crucial for waging war to preserve peace through the deterrence of war.

Indian armed forces had been aware of the importance of space in today's warfare. Therefore, the first integrated space cell within the Headquarters of the Integrated Defence Staff was created in 2008. This cell was formed to create synergy between the Department of Space, ISRO, civilian space agency and the Ministry of Defence and the military. These different institutions interact with each other about requirements, capabilities, and relevant policies.[68]

In 2019, the Union Government announced the creation of a new agency called the Defence Space Agency (DSA), comprising members from the Army, Navy and Air Force, and supported by a new research organisation, the Defence Space Research Organisation (DSRO). Defence Space Agency (DSA) comprises members from the Army, Navy and Air Force. The DSRO is a research organisation to facilitate the development of space technology for military purposes. DSA may be a precursor to something like that of a space command in the U.S., integrating space assets from the army, navy and air force and formulating strategy. The DSA, commanded by an air force two-star rank officer, began with a staff of about 200 officers taken from the three services and took over the duties of some existing military organs, including the Defense Imagery Processing and Analysis Center(DIPAC) and the Defense Satellite Control Center (DSSC). The DSRO and DSA will form the pillars of India's military space operations.

On March 27, 2019, Prime Minister Narendra Modi addressed the nation, announcing that India had successfully tested an ASAT weapon, becoming the fourth nation to acquire this capability after China, the United States and Russia.

India had about 25 satellites, of which four were dual-use. The armed forces were relying on those four satellites. However, they did not have a dedicated military satellite till August 2013, when the first satellite was launched for the Indian Navy for maritime communications. Before that, India was relying on Inmarsat, a British commercial satellite communication provider. This had obvious security implications. The next military satellite will serve the Indian Air Force. Indian Army and will likely have a delayed launch.

To translate the above needs into an operational capability, India may have to launch 17 satellites into various orbits every year. Moreover, 28 smaller satellites may also have to be launched as part of constellations that cater to diverse C4ISR needs. The Small Satellite Initiative needed to build small satellite capacity in the country may also require the launching of 100 small satellites in the five to 100 kg class.

India needs 16 PSLV, 7 GSLV and 7 Agni 5 based launchers in every year to meet this requirement.

Apart from the requirements for satellites and launchers, many technology areas require urgent action for development to meet operational needs. Some of these critical areas are:[69]

- Antenna Technology used for meeting SSA, SAR and C4.
- Infrared Technologies and Imaging Sensors.
- ELINT Technology Development.
- SAR weight reduction initiatives.
- Improved Integrated Optics for Imaging sensors.
- Data Processing especially SAR data processing.
- Small satellites related developments.
- Tracking Data Relay Satellite System (TDRSS) Compatibility related developments.
- Use of open source data for strategic work.

India should have a space doctrine for armed forces. The Takshashila Institution, a Think Tank from Bangalore, has published a Discussion Document on Space Doctrine for India- 2021.

India is taking baby steps to develop space warfare capabilities. There is a need for a fast, aggressive approach as we are already considerably behind the space powers. Some feel India should take a leapfrog approach to catch up with lost time. The creation of Space Forces by the U.S. is an example. This would facilitate the defence of India's growing satellite networks and lay the foundation for coercive action against adversary networks. It would require substantial financial support.[70]

India needs to augment and reorganise its space organisational structure so that the armed forces can take full advantage of the country's space assets. Integrating the various SSA and C4ISR capabilities into a seamless network to facilitate real-time action will be the key. In addition, training personnel for the military application of space technology will need major emphasis. Space plays a significant role in meeting national security needs. It is also used extensively in India's social and development sector, with at least 60 departments using space services to pursue its developmental agenda. However, there has to be a balance between national security challenges and societal needs.

India has been committed to the peaceful use of outer space. She believes that space technology can provide innovative solutions to developing countries for meeting their Sustainable Development Goals (SDGs). India has concluded space cooperation programmes with 51 countries and five multilateral organisations. India has helped improve capacity building by training nearly 3,000 officials from about 109 countries.

With the present state of global politics, a new arms race in the form of military-oriented applications for space is becoming dominant.[71] India should secure its territory, address threats and have unhindered use of the outer space. The capability to use space for commercial, scientific and military purposes has become a critical factor of national power. India's growing use of space could make its space assets attractive targets for adversaries. Some critical technological developments make this threat a reality. This threat is aggravated as many space-denial capabilities can be employed covertly or with deniability in peacetime or situations short of war.[72]

Recommendations

Today India is a major space power. The ability to use space for military, commercial and scientific purposes has become a critical determinant of national power. Space plays a significant role in meeting national security needs. India's growing use of space could make its space assets attractive targets for adversaries. India's space programme has grown hugely over the past decade but without an overall strategic plan. As India's power and influence rise, there must be greater clarity on what it wants to attain as a nation in its overall security architecture. While there are significant opportunities to integrate satellite-based technologies into the defence realm, there is a need to plan this technology integration carefully. India has lacked an overall National Security Strategy that lays out its long term goals and objectives and within each of the essential security components.

Some critical technological developments that make the space threat a reality are:

- Kinetic systems such as direct ascent and co-orbital anti-satellite weapons,
- Non-kinetic systems such as cyberattack and electronic warfare capabilities, as well as directed energy weapons,
- Supporting capabilities such as sensors and computation.

This threat is also aggravated because many space-denial capabilities can be employed covertly or with deniability and in peacetime or situations short of war.

India has many external security challenges in the form of two-front war and internal security challenges. The internal security challenges include cross border terrorism, attacks on cities like Mumbai and sensitive military installations like Pathankot and Uri and Surveillance on Left Wing Extremism infested areas. Our space capabilities require surveillance of our cross border areas, vast coastline and water spaces and LWE affected areas. The importance of this capability for offensive operations like raids need no elaboration.

Space Strategy

India does not have a National Security Strategy document. That does not mean that India does not have an overall security strategy. But the strategy document helps to provide a broad direction on various security-related issues. Non availability of National Security Strategy document has not stopped the Indian Navy to articulate India's Maritime Strategy. Indian government must publish its space strategy, preferably signed by the Prime Minister. It should factor in the growing requirement of space assets in social, economic and security areas. India's Space Doctrine should be published by the Defence Space Agency signed by the CDS. Reasonable assumptions can be made. Path taken by India Navy can be followed. At least a draft space doctrine can be made and circulated within academia, industry, think tanks and subject matter experts to get inputs from all the stakeholders before arriving at a final Space Doctrine.

Increasing deliberation, interaction and debate among the stakeholders are important as defence strategists and planners today face highly complex challenges. However, the answers are not clear. Capabilities designed to advance one objective may, in turn, undermine others. Integrated strategy requires balancing capability development for effect in a crisis or conflict.

The following may be considered for inclusion in National Space Strategy:[73]

- How will India use space, both commercially and militarily, in her grand strategy?
- Command and control structures for offensive and defensive use of space and maintenance of space deterrence. Which agency or agencies would control which activity should be clearly spelt out.
- Our stands on anti-satellite weapon, space situational awareness and International code of conduct.
- How do we integrate SSA and C4ISR?
- Under what circumstances offensive use of space will be undertaken? This would bring clarity to both the minds of adversaries as to what might provoke a military response in terms of jamming, blinding, destruction and interference.

- How space assets will be used to deal with Internal Security challenges of India?
- Cyber challenges to outer space.
- The role of private and non-state actors in space. How will private actors get involved in space strategy?
- What are the different postures that we will adopt as a warfighting strategy with respect to the available capabilities?[74]
- How space and cyber tools be integrated with other capabilities to support strategic and tactical deterrence objectives?
- How do we measure victory in a future conflict? Which types of space and cyber tools will be helpful and necessary for prosecuting the war and then for securing the peace?[75]
- How do we ensure that missile-warning infrastructure of radars and satellites can determine whether there is a ballistic or a hypersonic missile attack on us?

There are sensitive issues. India's approach for utilisation of space for strategic and security purposes has been kept at low key. India has used some of the space assets within legally accepted limits of the Outer Space Treaty (OST). ISRO has stringent firewall rules to keep away civilian space assets for fear of restriction imposed by world powers.

Without waiting for publication of India's Space Doctrine, Army can simultaneously work in Indian Army's doctrine on Space Warfare. Being such a large force, it has a maximum stake in space domain. Resources in space in terms of funds, personnel, capabilities are limited. Therefore, Indian Army must put its best foot forward to get its legitimate and well-deserved share of space capabilities.

Organisation

India needs to augment and reorganise its space organisational structure so that the armed forces can take full advantage of the country's space assets. Integrating the various SSA and C4ISR capabilities into a seamless network to facilitate real-time action will be the key. In addition, training personnel for the military application of space technology will need significant emphasis.

There are major issues of command and control. At the apex level, India's space forces shall operate under the Cabinet Committee on Security (CCS). The decision to employ space forces offensively will also reside with it. Clear and distinct command and control channels have to be well established with due care as political leadership, bureaucracy, ISRO, DRDO and armed forces at the highest level are involved.

At the level of the armed forces, present collaborative working arrangements may not the best way to fight a war. There are space segments in every service. The current DSA or the future Space Command do not have executive authority over them. They remain under the command of respective services. For training, policymaking, interaction with industry/academia/subject matter experts, fund allocation, etc., the role of DSA is well understood. However, on operational matters, the respective space segments follow their operational branches directions. If there is any difference of opinion, the services space segments follow the orders of their respective services. This is unlike the model of U.S. where the space segments come under space command. With the proposed theatre command, this issue must be resolved beforehand. The author recommends that for the theatre command, at least, the space segments should be part of DSA or Space Command.

As explained earlier, space and cyber are intimately interlinked now. Both the cyber and space domains are global commons. There is a close integration and dependency between these domains. The Armed Forces are getting increasingly dependent on both cyber and space domains for fighting an integrated battle. There is a need to evolve a synergistic approach to fight a war in these domains. We must analyse the issues involved deliberately and take appropriate actions at strategic, operational and tactical levels. These organisations in the armed forces remain stove-piped. Efforts to integrate strategic planning should be pursued in parallel with efforts to integrate space and cyber policy planning to ensure that capabilities and organisation at the policy level proceed at a similar pace as operational capabilities.

Placing space and cyber under the same policy management construct as other areas that are key for long-term competition and deterrence may be a promising near-term option.[76] Today there is hardly any horizontal integration. The process of horizontal integration at every level must be started now with well thought out organisations in place.

Both for offensive and defensive ballistic missile systems, space plays a vital role. The role of Strategic Forces Command and DRDO should be clear and there should be no organisational ambiguity. Is the SFC now under the command of CDS? What is the staff support with the CDS for handling SFC? Similarly, for BMD the role of DRDO should be clear. The role of DRDO and the newly raised Defence Space Research Organisation (DSRO) should be distinctly demarcated.

DEFENSE INTELLIGENCE AGENCY

WASHINGTON, D.C. 20340-5100

U-08-0780/CE

To: Distribution List APR 2 8 2008

Subject: Establishment of National MASINT Management Office

1. In his 22 December 2007 memorandum, the Director of National Intelligence (DNI) assigned the MASINT Services of Common Concern (SoCC) to DIA on behalf of the Intelligence Community (IC). In response, on 6 March 2008, I established the National MASINT Management Office (NMMO) to manage and execute the MASINT SoCC and other related activities. The NMMO reports directly to me, and I have appointed Colonel Aldon Purdham, USAF, as its Acting Chief.

2. To ensure these SoCC responsibilities are executed in the best interest of the IC and its customers, I have directed a mission analysis be accomplished for each of the DNI-assigned SoCC and other significant MASINT-related activities. Colonel Purdham will lead this effort and will provide me with a report detailing its conclusions and recommendations. I will rely on this report to finalize the NMMO's responsibilities, organizational structure, and composition.

3. The unique perspectives of each organization involved in MASINT activities are paramount to the success of this mission analysis. For this reason, I request that each of your organizations provide a senior representative at the GG-15 or O-6 level to participate in this effort. NMMO will convene the first Working Group meeting on 30 April 2008, 0900-1500, in Room 1320 of the Clarendon Building, 3100 Clarendon Blvd, Arlington, Virginia. Subsequent meetings are planned for the same time and location on 7 and 14 May 2008. Please provide the name of your representative by 23 April 2008 to [ ] (b)(3) 10 U.S.C. 424; (b)(6)

4. I look forward to your assistance in implementing the NMMO. That assistance is indicative of the very cooperation I intend for the office to embody as it strives to foster enhanced success across the MASINT Community and to its customers.

There is minimal ELINT capability with Indian DIA. The MASINT capability of India is in an absolute minimum category. India has to take urgent steps to develop MASINT capability at all levels.[77]

Conclusion

Offensive space capabilities such as small co-orbital satellites, satellite jammers and spoofing technologies can produce significant benefits. Offensive capabilities will give a clear advantage against defensive abilities, as defending and hardening satellites is expensive and infeasible. The weaponisation of space adds complexity to the existing dynamics of deterrence and warfighting.

However, space warfare and advanced space-based weapons will not change the nature of warfare. It will affect the character of how war is conducted. The application of space-based technologies is unlikely to win wars by itself. Although space-related technology may provide a tactical advantage in combat, it is doubtful that a single technology will decide the outcome of a conflict.

Space warfare's character will be different from conflict in other domains. Space strategy deserves a separate context and vocabulary to facilitate a practical understanding and its implementation. When considering the span of space activities, they are frequently divided into four major areas: civil, commercial, intelligence and military. These four sectors are useful when describing the means available to achieve political and national ends in space.[78]

Technology and innovation will be the primary drivers of competition in space. The proliferation of private space companies will play a prominent role in shaping the dynamics of cooperation, competition and deterrence in space.

Notes

1. Joint Chiefs of Staff, Space Operations, Joint Publication 3-14 (April 10, 2018), p. ix, at www.jcs.mil/Portals/36/Documents/Doctrine/pubs/jp3_14.pdf.

2. JP 3-14, Space Operations, CH 1, October 26, 2020, at https://www.jcs.mil/Portals/36/Documents/Doctrine/pubs/jp3_14ch1.pdf?ver=qmkgYPyKBvsIZyrnswSMCg%3d%3d
3. U.S. Joint Doctrine Publication, JP 3-13.1.
4. Dr. Rebecca Reesman and James R. Wilson, 'The Physics of Space War', The Center for Space Policy and Strategy, October 2020.
5. Bob Preston, et al., 'Space Weapons Earth Wars', Santa Monica, CA: RAND, 2002, at https://www.rand.org/pubs/monograph_reports/MR1209.html.
6. Todd Harrison, 'International Perspectives on Space Weapons', The Center for Strategic and International Studies (CSIS), May 27, 2020, at https://www.csis.org/analysis/international-perspectives-space-weapons
7. Joshua Carlson, 'Full Spectrum Space Deterrence: From Laws to Technology', Honors Theses, University of Nebraska-Lincoln, (2021), 304, at https://digitalcommons.unl.edu/honorstheses/304
8. Michael P. Gleason and Peter L. Hays, 'A Roadmap for Assessing Space Weapons', Center for Space Policy and Strategy, Space Agenda 2021, at https://aerospace.org/sites/default/files/2020-10/Gleason-Hays_SpaceWeapons_20201006_0.pdf
9. USSTRATCOM, Space Control CONOPS, 2004.
10. Air Force Doctrine Publication (AFDP) 3-14 Counterspace Operations, Space Situational Awareness, January 25, 2021, at https://www.doctrine.af.mil/Portals/61/documents/AFDP_3-14/3-14-D04-SPACE-SSA.pdf
11. Space Situational Awareness Efforts, GAO Report, GAO-16-6R, at https://www.gao.gov/assets/gao-16-6r.pdf
12. Recommendations on Trust and Interoperability in Space Situational Awareness Data National Space Council Users' Advisory Group Technology and Innovation Subcommittee, September 2, 2020, at https://www.nasa.gov/sites/default/files/atoms/files/white_paper_on_saa_data_findings_and_recommendations_rev2020-10-22b.pdf
13. Lt. Col. Kelly J. Hand, Maj. Richard Benz, Maj. Thomas Holts and Capt. Travis Longmire, 'Environmental Space Situation Awareness and Joint Space Effects'.
14. Major Giuseppe Valentino, 'IT AF, JAPCC, Using the Space Domain An Intelligence', Surveillance and Reconnaissance Perspective available at: https://www.japcc.org/using-the-space-domain/
15. Brian W. Everstine, 'Raymond: Expect the Space Force to Provide Tactical ISR', May 12, 2021, at https://www.airforcemag.com/raymond-expect-the-space-force-to-provide-tactical-isr/
16. FM 3-14, Army Space Operations, October 2019.
17. James P. Finch and Shawn Steene, 'Finding Space in Deterrence: Toward a General Framework for Space Deterrence', *Strategic Studies Quarterly,* vol. 5 no. 4 (Winter 2011), 1www.dtic.mil/dtic/tr/fulltext/u2/a569581.pdf

18. Michael P. Gleason and Peter L. Hays, 'Getting the Most Deterrent Value from U.S. Space Forces', Space Agenda 2021, Center or Space Policy and Strategy, Aerospace Corporation, October 27, 2020, p. 1, at https://aerospace.org/sites/default/files/2020-10/Gleason-Hays_SpaceDeterrence_20201027_0.pdf.
19. James P. Finch and Shawn Steene, n. 17.
20. Michael Krepon, 'Space and Nuclear Deterrence', in Anti-satellite Weapons, *Deterrence and Sino-American Space Relations*, Michael Krepon and Julia Thompson (eds.), The Stimson Center, September 2013, p. 15.
21. Chairman of the Joint Chiefs of Staff Instruction, 'Standing Rules of Engagement', in Operational Law Handbook, 16th edition, eds. Rachel Mangas and Matthew Festa, Charlottesville, VA: The Judge Advocate General's Legal Center and School, U.S. Army, 2016, pp. 95-110, at www.loc.gov/rr/frd/Military_Law/pdf/OLH_2015_Ch5.pdf
22. The White House, 'The National Security Strategy of the United States of America', December 2017, p. 31.
23. General John Hyten in 60 Minutes, 'The Battle Above', David Martin, original air date, August 2, 2015, at www.cbsnews.com/news/rare-look- at-space- command-satellite- defense-60- minutes-2/
24. Peng Guangqian and Yao Youzhi, (eds.), *The Science of Military Strategy,* Beijing: Military Science Publishing House, 2001, p. 230. Referenced in Kaufman and Hartnett, 'Managing Conflict: Examining Recent PLA Writings on Escalation Control', p. 54.
25. Shou Xiaosong, (ed.), *The Science of Military Strategy,* Beijing: Military Science Press, 2013, p. 129. Referenced in Kaufman and Hartnett, 'Managing Conflict: Examining Recent PLA Writings on Escalation Control', p. 56.
26. Dean Cheng, 'Evolving Chinese Thinking about Deterrence: What the United States Must Understand About China and Space', Backgrounder No. 3298, The Heritage Foundation, March 29, 2018, p. 2, at http://report.heritage.org/bg3298
27. John Lauder, Frank G. Klotz, and William Courtney, 'How to Avoid a Space Arms Race', RAND Corporation, October 26, 2020, at https://www.rand.org/blog/2020/10/how-to-avoid-a-space-arms-race.html
28. UN, Treaty on Principles Governing the Activities of States in the Exploration and Use of Outer Space, Including the Moon and Other Celestial Bodies, New York, 610 U.N.T.S. 205, January 27, 1967.
29. Bruce Mcclintock, Katie Feistel, Douglas C. Ligor and Kathryn O'connor, 'Responsible Space Behavior for the New Space Era', RAND Corporation, 2021.
30. John Lauder, Frank G. Klotz and William Courtney, 'How to Avoid a Space Arms Race', October 26, 2020, at https://www.rand.org/blog/2020/10/how-to-avoid-a-space-arms-race.html
31. National System for Geospatial Intelligence, Geospatial Intelligence (Geoint) Basic Doctrine, April 2018.

32. Loren B. Thompson, 'Geospatial Intelligence: A Test Case For Washington's Emerging Industrial Policy,' Lexington Institute, February 2021.
33. Jennifer Alsever, 'Space Startups are Booming in the Mojave Desert', Fortune, February 20, 2017, at http://fortune.com/2017/02/20/space-startups- travel-satellites/
34. William Akoto, 'Hackers could shut down satellites–or turn them into weapons', Phys Org, February 12, 2020, at https://phys.org/pdf500726447.pdf
35. Jeff Becker, 'A Starcruiser for Space Force: Thinking Through The Imminent Transformation of Spacepower', War on the Rocks, May 19, 2021, at https://warontherocks.com/2021/05/a-starcruiser-for-space-force-thinking-through-the-imminent-transformation-of-spacepower/
36. Susmita Mohanty, 'Outer Space, the next Wild West', November 2, 2021, at https://www.eurozine.com/outer-space-the-next-wild-west/
37. William Akoto, n. 34.
38. William Akoto, University of Denver, Hackers could shut down satellites – or turn them into weapons, The Conversation, February 13, 2020, at https://theconversation.com/hackers-could-shut-down-satellites-or-turn-them-into-weapons-130932
39. Theresa Hitchens, 'New GPS Sats Can Maneuver & Resist, Jamming, Breaking Defense', February 26, 2020, at https://breakingdefense.com/2020/02/new-gps-sats-can-maneuver-and-resist-jamming/
40. 'Services', Spaceflight, at http://spaceflight.com/services/
41. 'Benefits of Hosted Payloads', Hosted Payload Alliance, at www.hostedpayloadalliance.org/Hosted-Payloads/Benefits.aspx, accessed on August 8, 2018.
42. Namrata Goswami, 'China's Get-Rich Space Program', *The Diplomat*, February 28, 2019 available at: https://thediplomat.com/2019/02/chinas-get-rich-space-program/
43. Tyler Farley, 'China's Space Program & Its Growing Threat to U.S. Interests, Patterson', Journal of International Affairs, September 5, 2019, at http://pattersonjournal.com/2019/09/05/chinas-space-program-its-growingthreat- to-u-s-interests.
44 Milsat Magazine, at http://www.milsatmagazine.com/cgi-bin/display_article.cgi?number=1021469330
45. New DIA Report, 'Challenges to Security in Space', Offers Copious China-Related Information, at https://www.andrewerickson.com/2019/02/new-dia-report-challenges-to-security-in-space-offers-copious-china-related-information/
46. Rui C. Barbosa, 'China Launches Shen Tong-1 Military Satellite via Long March-3A', NASASpaceFlight.com, November 24, 2010.
47. Brian Waidelich, 'A Chinese Starlink? PRC Views on Building a Satellite Internet Megaconstellation', China Brief, Volume 21, Issue 20, October 22, 2021.
48. New DIA Report, n. 45.
49. Military and Security Developments Involving the People's Republic of China, Annual Report to Congress, Fiscal Year 2000, Office of The Secretary of Defense, at https://media.defense.gov/2021/Nov/03/2002885874/-1/-1/0/2021-CMPR-FINAL.PDF

50. Todd Harrison, Kaitlyn Johnson and Thomas G. Roberts, 'Space Threat Assessment 2018', Washington, D.C.: Center for Strategic and International Studies, April 2018, p. 8, at https://www.csis.org/analysis/space-threat-assessment-2018
51. Bill Gertz, 'Satellite Photos Show Chinese Anti-Satellite Laser Base', The Washington Free Beacon, April 1, 2019.
52. Todd Harrison, Kaitlyn Johnson and Thomas G. Roberts, n. 50.
53. Mark Stokes, et al., 'China's Space and Counterspace Capabilities and Activities', Project 2049 Institution, March 30, 2020.
54. Maj Gen PK Mallick, VSM (Retd), 'India in Space Domain—Pathbreaking Developments', Vivekananda International Foundation, October 2021, at https://www.vifindia.org/brief/2021/october/29/India-in-Space-Domain-Pathbreaking-Developments
55. 'India's Space Program: Challenges, Opportunities, and Strategic Concerns', The National Bureau of Asian Research, February 10, 2016, at https://www.nbr.org/publication/indias-space-program-challenges-opportunities-and-strategic-concerns/
56. Preparing to scale new heights: Enhancing private participation in India's commercial space sector, PwC India, January 2020, at https://www.pwc.in/assets/pdfs/research-insights/2020/preparing-to-scale-new-heights.pdf?utm_source=dlvr.it&utm_medium=facebook
57. India's Space Program: Challenges, Opportunities, and Strategic Concerns, n. 55.
58. Dhinesh Kallungal, 'IN-SPACe mandate creates flutter in scientific community', newindianexpress, August 3, 2020 at https://www.newindianexpress.com/states/kerala/2020/aug/03/in-space-mandate-creates-flutter-in-scientific-community-2178292.html
59 No.C.19013/48/2012-Sec.3 (Vol.III) October 15, 2020 available at: https://www.isro.gov.in/sites/default/files/draft_spacecom_policy_2020.pdf
60. Abhinav Singh, 'India's space policy benefits from greater clarity, feel experts,' *The Week*, December 7, 2020, at https://www.theweek.in/news/biz-tech/2020/12/07/indias-space-policy-benefits-from-greater-clarity-feel-experts.html
61. Maj Gen PK Mallick, VSM (Retd), n. 54.
62. Pranav Mukul and Aashish Aryan, 'Explained: Public-private partnership breaches space frontier', Indian Express, October 13, 2021 at https://indianexpress.com/article/explained/indian-space-association-narendra-modi-7565248/
63. Sandhya Ramesh, 'Modi launches Indian Space Association, plan is to open up sector to start-ups & private firms', The Print, October 11, 2021 at https://theprint.in/science/modi-launches-indian-space-association-plan-is-to-open-up-sector-to-start-ups-private-firms/749018/
64. 'What are Indian Space Association?', *Business Standard*, at https://www.business-standard.com/about/what-is-indian-space-association#collapse

65. Vishal Kumar Singh, 'Why the Indian Space Agency needs privatization?', Part-1, July 29, 2020, at https://medium.com/@vishal.ks.iitg/why-the-indian-space-agency-needs-privatization-part-1-dc3b3a3bb9ca
66. 'Spacecom Policy 2020: What Is New And What Remains Normal?', at https://www.marketscreener.com/quote/stock/SATCOM-SYSTEMS-LTD-56537250/news/Spacecom-Policy-2020-What-Is-New-And-What-Remains-Normal-31685245/
67. Ashok G.V. and Maithry Kini, 'India: Spacecom Policy 2020: What Is New And What Remains Normal?', Mondaq, November 4, 2020, at https://www.mondaq.com/india/broadcasting-film-tv-radio/1001238/spacecom-policy-2020-what-is-new-and-what-remains-normal
68. India's Space Program: Challenges, Opportunities, and Strategic Concerns, n. 55.
69. Ibid.
70. Robert Farley, 'Managing the Military Problem of Space: The Case of India', The Diplomat, April 19, 2021, at https://thediplomat.com/2021/04/managing-the-military-problem-of-space-the-case-of-india/
71. Rajeswari Pillai Rajagopalan, Pulkit Mohan and Rahul Krishna, 'India in the Final Frontier: Strategy, Policy and Industry', ORF Special Report No. 100, January 2020, Observer Research Foundation, at https://www.orfonline.org/wp-content/uploads/2020/01/ORF_SpecialReport_100_Space.pdf
72. 'A Space Doctrine for India', Takshashila Discussion Document 2021, V 1.0, March 16, 2021 at https://takshashila.org.in/wp-content/uploads/2021/03/A-Space-Doctrine-for-India.pdf
73. Maj Gen PK Malick, VSM (Retd), 'Cyber and Space Strategy For India', at https://indianstrategicknowledgeonline.com/web/1%20Cyber%20and%20Space%20Strategy%20for%20India.pdf
74. Pranav R Satyanath, 'Takshashila Review Paper', Space Power and Space Warfare: A Review Paper, December 11, 2019.
75. Benjamin Bahney, 'Space Strategy at a Crossroads Opportunities and Challenges for 21st Century', Competition Center for Global Security Research Lawrence Livermore National Laboratory, May 2020 at https://cgsr.llnl.gov/content/assets/docs/space-strategy-at-a-crossroads.pdf
76. Ibid.
77. Rajeswari Pillai Rajagopalan and Narayan Prasad Nagendra, 'Creation of a defence space agency: A new chapter in exploring India's space security', Observer Research Foundation, February 23, 2017, at https://www.orfonline.org/expert-speak/creation-of-a-defence-space-agency-a-new-chapter-in-exploring-indias-space-security/
78. John J. Klein, Space Warfare: Strategy, Principles and Policy, Abingdon: Routledge, 2006.

6 Summary of Recommendations

Information Domain

National Level

Responsibility. Responsibility of carrying out psychological/information operations should be clearly given. It should be MHA or a specific organisation under NSA working within National Security Council Secretariat (NSCS). The NSCS is the appropriate agency to be made responsible for information operations, The organisation should have experts from psychology, sociology, media, area specialists, language experts, legal, armed forces, political science specialists, foreign affairs, country experts, communication and social media.

Right Terminology. Terms like information operations, psychological operations, strategic communications, influence operations, perception management, public information operations, public field diplomacy etc are being used. For influencing the minds of people across the border and within the country in counter insurgency/counter terrorism operations, psychological operations and perception management may be used respectively.

Strategy and Doctrine. Indian government must enunciate a formal integrated strategy for Psychological Operations encompassing all facets of Psychological Operations at international, national, concerned ministries and armed forces level.

Organisation. A formal organisation to carry out this task should be put in place. It should have close ties with government, industry, academia, think tanks, and public interest groups.

Coordination. The organisation at the apex level should link executive leadership and implementation officers across departments and agencies and reduce the emphasis on differences and credit for successes.

Factors to be Considered. The various factors to be considered are:

- Current objectives, outcomes under present conditions, target groups or actors.
- Most likely strategies to influence the targeted groups and yield desired outcomes.
- Authority/influence of targeted group leaders over their supporters/followers.
- Sources and information channels target audiences use.
- Target audiences attitudes.
- The messages they receive.
- Likely message sources, content and formats to be accepted by them.
- Type and number of messages to be sent to them to achieve influence objectives.

Legal Measures. To control use of social media by our external and internal adversaries, legal course has to be taken. Present action against Twitter is a case in point.

MoD Level

Organisation

No inter service organisation exists for carrying out psychological operations. It is not recommended that MoD be the lead agency for psychological operations at the national level. However, the responsibility for perception management within the country specially in J&K and North East States may be undertaken. For Left Wing Extremism affected states, the same should be done by MHA.

MoD should immediately:

- Define information warfare.

- Develop an information warfare operational concept/doctrine.
- Subordinate select organisations under a designated leader for information warfare.

Information warfare in armed conflict is a threat to morale of service personnel, command and control of forces and relations with local people in the area of operations. MoD must acknowledge that service members are being targeted in unconventional and subtle ways by our foes. MoD should:[1]

- Initiate action to defend its service members and their families.
- Initiate an anti-disinformation training program to educate and minimise the reach and impact of foreign agents online.
- Coordinate with intelligence agencies.
- Put in place the necessary people, policies, programs and partnerships to defend against these new threats in the information environment.

Indian Army

Perception Management. Indian Army should take the lead and become the lead agency for carrying out perception management in J&K and North East States. Formal organisations and mechanism should be put in place at strategic, operational and tactical levels.

Intelligence Organisation. Indian Army's intelligence organisations and staff at every level must be a part of the information warfare battlefield.

Talent Management. There is a general shortage of talent in this critical field. Talent management is not a key result area of MS branch. Present system is incapable of maturing talents in critical capabilities and maintaining the talent not just to be competitive but also to win. Innovative solutions must be found to attract talent, nurture them and look after their carrier progression.

The following is recommended in no particular order:

- Generously resource information power.
- Give greater emphasis and priority to information effects in operational planning and execution.

- Increase the prestige of personnel carrying out this task.
- Integrate physical and information power.
- Use information power extensively in operations below the threshold of conflict.
- Carefully record and document own operations.
- Produce high-quality video, digital and other information products.
- Focus on maintaining the support of domestic audiences.
- Standardise the processes associated with the Information Environment to be consistent with and part of other routine staff processes.
- In coordination with the MoD seek expanded authorities to operate in the Information Environment short of declared hostilities and in CI/CT Ops.
- Increase education and training to reflect the increasing importance of these capabilities and their role in future conflicts.
- Take steps to close capacity gaps in key capability areas, including cyber, influence, operations security and military deception.

Some factors to be considered for planning purposes.[2]

- IO is not well understood in the armed forces.
- Success in IO requires prioritising intelligence support for IO.
- IO objectives must be clear and precise.
- Consider the information environment from the population's perspective.
- Things do not always happen for the reasons you think; causation can be complicated when behaviours, perceptions, cognition and culture are involved.
- Every operation is an information operation.
- IO can deliver effects on enemy forces and commanders and on civilian populations.
- Adversaries can do things that you cannot. Be prepared for them.
- Information-related capabilities that are not well integrated with operations are vulnerable to being overwhelmed.

- It can take years to build credibility but only minutes to destroy it.
- Effective information operations cannot be an afterthought. If IO is part of planning, it is more likely to be part of the plan.
- If effects in and through the information environment are important to the commander, they should feature prominently in the commander's intent.
- Manoeuvre and fires generate effects in the information environment, too.
- Plan for friendly-force mistakes and adversary propaganda.
- All communications are potentially global. What you do and say here can have effects elsewhere, and vice versa.
- IO is like fire-support coordination; it is an integrating function.
- Information-related capabilities can have lengthy timelines for both execution and results.
- Events do not always unfold according to plan, so prepare IO branches and sequels.
- Warfare, including information warfare, involves trade-offs.
- The efforts planned and coordinated by IO need to be monitored and assessed; otherwise, you are shooting in the dark.[3]

Cyber Domain

National Level

India should make a small Group of Ministers for giving leadership and strategic direction. Priority and allocation of resources for offensive and defensive actions should be clear. Plans should be for long, medium and short term. A Deputy National Security Adviser for Cyber at the secretary-level should be appointed directly under NSA to oversee issues like cyber security, cyber diplomacy, capacity building, espionage and offensive cyber operations. A comprehensive national cyber strategy and national cyber security strategy should be published separately.

Cross-government audit across defence, security and intelligence agencies under the arrangement of the Cabinet Secretary should be conducted regularly. India should develop an operations approval framework incorporating a small standing cadre of National Security Council personnel and interagency "approvers" to streamline decision making for both offensive and defensive cyber operations.

The exchange of technologies with countries like Israel, Taiwan, Japan, Australia, Ukraine, Belarus, South Africa, Sweden and France should be explored. India should support bilateral and multilateral activities in international bodies of like-minded nations to protect cross-border critical infrastructure and create common standards. Through cyber diplomacy our adherence to international law should be demonstrated to the international community.

We must give clear signals to adversaries, both state and non-state actors and cybercriminals, about punitive actions to be taken by the government if they transgress boundaries. We should continuously review and assess the effectiveness of ongoing operations within a clear legal and ethical framework.

The vulnerabilities equities process must be coordinated at the government level. This process helps the security agencies decide when to remain quiet about a vulnerability so that own intelligence agencies can exploit it and divulge it so that it can be patched, enhancing everyone's cyber defences.

The government should lead in developing and implementing standards and best practice in emerging niche technology areas. Public key cryptography, quantum computing, and artificial intelligence are some fields the government should lead in research and development.

India is increasingly becoming a space power. There are a lot of vulnerabilities in the space sector. Our space assets and support infrastructure must be protected from cyberattacks.

Cyber activities of criminals, state and non-state actors, need to be curbed. Offenders have to be apprehended and prosecuted. Cyber laws and procedures have to be suitably strengthened/amended to combat transnational cybercriminal activities. This should be done in consultation with the private industry.

The incident of the recent compromise of widely used enterprise IT systems (SolarWinds), reportedly by Russian intelligence and Russian cyberattacks against Ukraine's critical infrastructure are well known. In case of such happening in India, what should be our action? What offensive cyber capabilities should we develop? Should war game all these likely eventualities and take action accordingly.

The responsibilities should be made clear. For example, who should take action against ransomware crime group, terrorist operation online or state actors like China or Pakistan?

Critical Infrastructure. Though a lot of work has been done to identify critical information infrastructure and responsibilities for cybersecurity of respective sectors, a lot remains to be done. In all such sectors, regulators have to be appointed, and clear-cut responsibilities have to be given. Space sector should be included in the category of critical information infrastructure.

The NTPC and other public sector undertakings may be well off in cyber security. The same cannot be said about the arrangement, say, in a state-owned hydroelectric plant that is also connected to the national power grid. A hacker could easily get into the national power grid through this poorly protected power plant and create mayhem at a time of their choosing. What can India do to prevent this type of incident?

Exchange of Information. Exchange of information about any breach of security and mitigation measures must be strengthened between the private and the public sectors. Institutional mechanisms have to be put in place. Trust has to be developed between them. The industry does not trust intelligence agencies easily.

Research and Development. Funds for research and development have to be spent judiciously and prioritised. The private sector must contribute to cyber-related research and development.

The Private Sector. A vast majority of our cyber infrastructure is owned and operated by the private sector like the internet service providers. The government should closely work with the private sector in three areas:

- Setting the conditions for a truly secure cyber infrastructure.
- Significantly empowering private sector defensive capabilities.

Providing for interoperable capabilities and joint exercises in the event that a national crisis requires the government to assist the private sector more directly or to respond directly against a threat to the nation.

Consider creating an India version of the Information Sharing and Analysis Centers (ISACs) and Information Sharing and Analysis Organisations (ISAOs) of the U.S. The Government of India should assist the private sector in their cyber security efforts and help facilitate critical cyber security information sharing, both among private sector actors and between the government and the private sector.

The government should have programs that provide the private sector with threat information data and other forms of assistance designed to help private organisations improve their cyber security postures.

Threat information sharing is significantly more efficient when automated, relying on standardised feeds and formats to communicate key pieces of data. The NCIIPC and the CERT-IN should encourage automated sharing of threat information and push for greater interoperability between such initiatives, including the incorporation of confidence levels in the sharing of cyber threat indicators (such as IP addresses and MD5 hashes).[4]

Ministry of Defence (MoD)

The role of armed forces for the protection of critical information infrastructure, including the private sectors, should be clearly defined. What happens when the armed forces are called in an aid to civil authority in case of some cyber calamity?

- Should extensively use cyber training ranges. Preferably Indian Army should take the lead.
- Should develop and implement professional development courses to build leaders and elite forces in the Cyber branches of all services.
- The MoD and the Army should leverage appropriate expertise outside the military from academia, industry and individuals to augment their cyberspace planning, operation and capability development.

- Should establish a Centre of Excellence (CoE) for cyber. The Indian Army can be the lead agency as it has already a CoE at MCTE, Mhow.
- Coordinate with the services and integrate cyber operations and related activities.
- Should develop theories of cyber operations at strategic, operational and tactical levels.
- Should encourage open discussion regarding the future evolution of military cyberspace in terms of tasks, authorities and organisational structures.
- Should consider raising an organisation like U.S. Department of Defense, Defense Information Systems Agency (DISA) which provides, operates and assures command and control and information sharing capabilities in direct support to war fighters, and national level leaders across the full spectrum of military operations.
- Should create a mechanism to ensure that bugs are not present in the procurement of equipment and supply chain management system.
- Should define Rules of Engagement for armed conflicts.
- Should lay down human resource development policies for the Armed Forces in the cyber domain. It will require drastic changes to attract and keep talents in such niche technology areas. The RM should direct the Chiefs of the Army, Navy and the Air Force to direct their military secretary branch and its equivalents to treat the cyber career field as a national security priority, where promotion boards must understand the cyber mission as a priority and facilitate recruitment, retention and career-long professional development in cyber expertise.
- Create a red team for performing operations on MoD critical systems and critical infrastructure.
- RM should get regular updates on identified challenges, plans and progress.

- Direct DCA to develop cyber capabilities/effects, focused on adversary military targets, which should include:
  - o Development of infrastructure and tools to support own forces.
  - o Ensure operational experience and an appropriately skilled workforce.
  - o Create agility to respond to dynamic situations/opportunities.
  - o Develop a deliberate plan and acquisition strategy that leverages existing infrastructure and identify where new infrastructure and tools are required.
  - o Develop a plan for joint space strategy, exercises and ultimately operations with and alongside other nationals cyber organisations operating as joint teams.
- Ask DCA to establish and enlarge professional military education opportunities at all levels, allowing military personnel to work in cyber-related private sector positions. Should encourage greater commercial exchange opportunities to improve skills and operational understanding.
- Create a mechanism to coordinate national cyber priorities and private-public collaboration across the spectrum of peace, no war no peace and war. DCA should play a key and unique role in this.
- The Office of Net Assessment in HQ IDS should institute a continuous strategic net assessment process to support our own operations. This process should leverage the Intelligence Community, industry, academia and integrate red team assessment activity for measuring our effectiveness in cyberspace.
- Should coordinate with MHA, Ministry of Law and Intelligence Agencies to review existing laws governing action in cyberspace. Should update or draft replacement language to protect own people and promote national interests in cyberspace.

Cyber Security Audit of MoD Organisations and Defence Industrial Base. Currently, NTRO does not carry out a cyber security audit of MoD organisations. The networks of the armed forces must be audited. Similarly,

Defence Research and Development Organisation (DRDO) networks and organisations, Defence Public Sector Undertakings (DPSUs) and Ordinance Factory Board (OFB) organisations must be audited. Under the 'Make in India' campaign, several private sector organisations have become a part of the defence industrial base eco-system handling sensitive equipments and accessories. Cyber security standards for these defence industrial base organizations must be spelt out clearly. Some responsible agency like the NTRO should carry out their cyber security audit.

War Gaming of Probable Events. Probable scenarios in a realistic environment should be war-gamed to determine the vulnerabilities in our systems and take appropriate remedial measures. For instance, just before a conflict in India's North East, the power grid and railways communications network fails, adversely impacting the large-scale movement of men and material of the armed forces. How do we overcome such situations? War-gaming scenarios like these will help identify and plug weaknesses.

Development of Crypt Analysis Capability. India does not have any high-grade decrypting capability. The introduction of 128 or 256 bits key has made code-breaking extremely difficult. However, the U.S.'s National Security Agency (NSA) and the UK's Government Communications Headquarters (GCHQ) already possess this capability, as do perhaps Russia and China. India must start the process of developing this capability. Cryptographers, mathematician and analysts with the power of super computers must get together to develop this capability. Collaboration with countries like Ukraine, Belarus, South Africa, Iran and Russia can be explored.

Forensic Labs for Embedded Hardware and Software. India is the world's biggest importer of military equipment, with plenty of electronic hardware and software components. No country shares its codes. There is always a chance of embedded hardware and software in these weapons platforms. What is the mechanism to check whether there is any malware in the increasingly sophisticated technology areas? What is the mechanism in the procurement of equipment procedure and supply chain management system to ensure that bugs are not present? While procuring, some legal and business clauses can be incorporated. But there is no getting away from India having its testing facilities. This is extremely niche technology and costly, but it needs to be developed.

Command and Control Set-up. There should be no ambiguity in the responsibility of organisations for cyber operations. For offensive cyber operations, the interplay between the Ministry of Defence, the armed forces, Ministry of Home Affairs and intelligence agencies (internal and external) and NTRO needs to be clearly demarcated. Who will carry out offensive cyber operations in a conflict scenario? Can an intelligence agency do it, bearing in mind the rules of engagement or the laws of armed conflict?

Collaboration with Friendly Countries. India should actively collaborate and exchange information with friendly countries like Japan, Taiwan, Vietnam and Australia. For developing niche technology, counties like Israel, Ukraine, Belarus, Romania and South Africa can be approached.

Indian Army

Offensive cyber operations at strategic, operational and tactical levels are not recommended. The following capabilities should be built into tactical levels:

- Collect intelligence by rapidly exploiting captured digital media.
- Counter and exploit adversaries' unmanned aerial systems.
- Protect friendly unmanned aerial systems operating in the area of operations.
- Gaining access to closed networks in or near the area of operations, including extracting and injecting data.
- Using electronic warfare systems as "delivery platforms for precision cyber effects."
- Exploiting new devices emerging from new trends and opportunities.
- Conducting cyberspace intelligence, surveillance, and reconnaissance (ISR) operations.
- Engaging in offensive social media operations.

The Army may look into similar organizations like U.S. ARCYBER and can take up certain actions which are applicable to us.

- Its Cyber Protection Brigade (CPB) trains and deploys specialised Cyber Protection Teams (CPTs) to defend key cyberspace territory. CPB augments network defence against sophisticated and persistent cyber threats. The CPB has two battalions with 20 CPTs to support the Army.
- 915th Cyber Warfare Battalion (CWB) trains and deploys 12 Expeditionary Cyber Teams (ECTs) to augment corps and below formations. ECTs would provide offensive Cyber, IO and EW capability to tactical units. Each of 12 ECTs will have organic cyber development capability, network support and capability to operate independently or as integrated into a supported unit headquarters.
- 1st IO Command (1st IOC) is U.S. Army's only active duty IO brigade. This is under a Force Design Update (FDU) that reorganises the Brigade to increase the number of IO Field Support Teams (FSTs) available and add capacity.
- Offensive Cyber Operations (OCO) Signal Battalion is being raised by late 2021, which will provide critical, dedicated support to Army cyber forces and Joint operational missions.
- 780th Military Intelligence Brigade (Cyber) is the U.S. Army's offensive cyberspace operations element to USCYBERCOM. It provides 21 teams in support of National and Combatant Command requirements.

Army Cyber Group of Indian Army should create teams with requisite human resources, technology and equipments to send them to a threatened or affected area. They should fall back after doing the needful.

In U.S. teams from the most elite and niche technology cyber warfare experts of Tailored Access Operations (TAO) of NSA get embedded with appropriate levels in the battlefield for carrying out sophisticated cyber operations. Indian Army should have similar arrangements with NTRO. The procedures should be rehearsed well in advance and glitches sorted out.

Bug Bounty Program. U.S. Army conducts bug bounty program to incentivise security research and reporting of real-world security vulnerabilities in exchange for monetary rewards. This helps in resolving the vulnerabilities before they are exploited by adversaries. The last bug bounty program was held from January 6, 2021 to February 17, 2021.

Bug bounty programs are an effective force multiplier for securing critical Army networks, systems and data. By crowdsourcing solutions with the help of the military and civilian ethical hackers, the existing security measures are complemented.

The participants had identified 238 vulnerabilities, including 102 rated high or critical and designated for immediate remediation. More than $150,000 was awarded to eligible civilian hackers in bounties during Hack the Army 3.0.[5]

Indian Army should also organise such bug bounty programs to identify vulnerabilities in their network and take remedial measures.

Space Domain

National Level

National Space Strategy. India must publish its national space strategy.

The following may be considered for inclusion in National Space Strategy:[6]

- How will India use space, both commercially and militarily, in her grand strategy?
- Command and control structures for offensive and defensive use of space and maintenance of space deterrence. Which agency or agencies would control which activity should be clearly spelt out.
- Our stands on anti-satellite weapon, space situational awareness and International code of conduct.
- How do we integrate SSA and C4ISR.
- Under what circumstances offensive use of space will be undertaken. This would bring clarity to both the minds of adversaries as to what

might provoke a military response in terms of jamming, blinding, destruction and interference.

- How space assets will be used to deal with Internal Security challenges of India.
- Cyber challenges to outer space.
- The role of private and non-state actors in space. How will private actors get involved in space strategy?
- What are the different postures that we will adopt as a warfighting strategy with respect to the available capabilities?[7]
- How space and cyber tools be integrated with other capabilities to support strategic and tactical deterrence objectives?
- Which types of space and cyber tools will be helpful and necessary for prosecuting the war and then for securing the peace?[8]
- How do we ensure that missile-warning infrastructure of radars and satellites can determine whether there is a ballistic or a hypersonic missile attack on us?

Organisation. India needs to augment and reorganise its space organisational structure so that the armed forces can take full advantage of the country's space assets. Integrating the various SSA and C4ISR capabilities into a seamless network to facilitate real-time action will be the key.

Command and Control. At the apex level, India's space forces shall operate under the Cabinet Committee on Security (CCS). The decision to employ space forces offensively will also reside with it. Clear and distinct command and control channels have to be well established with due care as political leadership, bureaucracy, ISRO, DRDO and armed forces at the highest level are involved.

Linkage between Cyber and Space. There is a close integration and dependency between cyber and space domains. Today there is hardly any horizontal integration. Efforts to integrate strategic planning should be pursued in parallel with efforts to integrate space and cyber policy planning to ensure that capabilities and organisation at the policy level advance at a similar pace as operational capabilities.

Navigational Capabilities. Indian Regional Navigation Satellite System (IRNSS) constellation provides accurate position information to users in India and the region extending up to 1500 km from its boundary. This capability has to be augmented for Agni and BrahMos missile systems. India needs to step up its PNT capabilities and measures against jamming and spoofing of India's satellites.

Counter Space Operations and ASAT Capabilities. Though India has displayed its ASAT capability, the target was own satellite whose orbit and every other details were known. To target an adversary satellite will be a different ball game. Therefore, India has to constantly improve this capability and carry out simulation tests like war game scenario.

Counter space operations will not necessarily be anti-satellite systems shooting down satellites. Indian capacity to use non-kinetic means should be improved in a big way.

Capability Development in Niche Space Technology Areas. Some of the major space-based components required for India's fledgling space capabilities are:[9]

- A robust SSA capability comprising radar, optical and laser tracking facilities complemented by an organisational and human resource base that is able to operationally monitor the space environment.
- A four-satellite constellation of advanced communications satellites in GSO that use ion propulsion for carrying out vital C4 functions.
- A constellation of 40 satellites in LEO that provide Internet services for the military.
- Three clusters of 3 satellites each for performing the ELINT function.
- A constellation of 12 EO and SAR satellites in appropriate Sun Synchronous Orbits (SSO) for meeting ISR needs.

- A constellation of 24 small satellites in LEO for meeting ISR needs during times of crises.
- Three Tracking Data Relay Satellite System (TDRSS) satellites in GSO for performing the tracking and data relay functions needed for a C4ISR capability.
- Two operational satellites in GSO along with 3 orbiting satellites in an 800 km SSO for meeting operational weather requirements.
- Seven satellites in Geostationary and Geosynchronous Orbits for meeting core navigation functions.
- A 24 satellite constellation in MEO, established over ten years, for providing an indigenous navigation solution.

To translate the above needs into an operational capability, India may need to do the following:

- Launch 17 satellites into various GSO, SSO and other orbits every year.
- 28 smaller satellites to be launched as part of constellations that cater to various C4ISR needs.
- The Small Satellite Initiative needed to build small satellite capacity in the country. May also require the launching of 100 small satellites in the 5 to 100 kg class.

India requires 16 PSLV, 7 GSLV and 7 Agni 5 based launchers every year to meet this requirement. This is a tall order.

Apart from the requirements for satellites and launchers, many technology areas require urgent action for development to meet operational needs. Some of these critical areas are:[10]

- Antenna Technology used for meeting SSA, SAR and C4.
- ELINT Technology Development.
- Infrared Technologies and Imaging Sensors.
- Improved Integrated Optics for Imaging sensors.
- SAR weight reduction initiatives.
- Small satellites related developments.
- Data Processing especially SAR data processing.

- Use of commercial open-source data for strategic work.
- Tracking Data Relay Satellite System (TDRSS) Compatibility related developments.

There are also many technology areas where Indian capabilities have to be significantly enhanced to meet medium, and longer-term anticipated needs. These include:

- Ion Propulsion.
- Satellite to satellite and satellite to ground Laser Communications.
- Secure Communications specially Quantum Communications where China has taken the lead.
- C4 Network Operations integration of space and other networks.
- Networked LEO Communications Satellite systems architecture and design.
- Operational use of GSLV Mark 3.

Important Issues

Commercial satellite imagery suppliers currently provide high-quality data that could cater to many military needs. However, the current model of using onboard storage and a network of suitably located ground stations may be inadequate for collecting ISR data. India's storage and data handling capability need augmentation.

The IRNSS that India is developing for providing navigation services for civilian and military use is based on geostationary and geosynchronous satellites. It is very different from the architectures of the systems being established by the other major space powers. India will need to add a complement of orbiting satellites in a phased way to improve accuracies. Following is required:

- National capabilities to build small satellites need to be enhanced through a small satellite initiative.
- Capacities for building and launching more PSLVs should be created to cater to the increasing demand.

- The slight modifications needed to convert the Agni 5 into a space launcher for smaller satellites need to be carried out on a crash basis.[11]

Priority should be given to investments in improved space domain awareness capabilities, including more space-based sensors, better integration with commercial and friendly foreign government systems and the use of artificial intelligence to analyse data and form a better understanding of capabilities and intentions.

Decision-makers should ensure that programs designed to increase survivability, redundancy, reusability, resilience, rapid replacement and disaggregation of critical space assets receive continued support, specially financial allotments.

It is important that policymakers and strategists must view space systems as a critical infrastructure of the nation and not just a support structure for force enhancement and terrestrial operations.

MoD

Command and Control. For offensive and defensive ballistic missile systems, space plays a vital role. The role of Strategic Forces Command and DRDO should be clear and there should be no organisational ambiguity. The role of DRDO and newly raised the Defence Space Research Organisation (DSRO) should be distinctly demarcated.

Role of Intelligence Organisations. Intelligence Organisations are the biggest consumers of space capabilities. National Technical Research Organisation (NTRO) is a big player in the space and ISR domain.[12] It comes under the National Security Advisor in the Prime Minister's Office. NTRO reportedly operates Technology Experiment Satellite(TES), Cartosat-2A, EMISAT and Cartosat-2B, besides two Radar Imaging Satellites, namely RISAT-1 & RISAT-2. Very Long Range Tracking Radar (VLRTR) systems are functioning under MoU between NTRO and IAF for realising Missile Monitoring System for detection of spaceborne threats in aid of Ballistic Missile Defence.[13] Other intelligence agencies like R and AW, Aviation Research Centre(ARC) etc.

also operates space assets. Is there a need to put these assets under DSA or future space command when they create the necessary capabilities to handle these assets? There is a need for a formal coordination mechanism between all the agencies. Since it is the armed forces who have to take the final action at the end of the day, it will be prudent that the armed forces be given the lead role. The Balakot strike has given an idea of how space based ISR assets can be coordinated. However, it is an isolated, one-off incidence. During the war, will this system work, or there is a need for an institutional mechanism? Turf war is a universal phenomenon. The political leadership must take a call, keeping in view the overall strategic security issues.

Training

We should establish a CoE on Space Warfare to develop expertise for space. Staffed by military personnel, civilian government employees and academics, a centre of this nature would serve as a pathway for increased bilateral cooperation and collaboration on addressing space-based threats, including counter space cyber capabilities.

We require highly trained and capable human resources. Development of human resources requires time. Somehow it has not got due attention. Armed Forces have to take action on mission mode.

The Armed Forces are getting increasingly dependent on both cyber and space domains for fighting an integrated battle. There is a need to evolve a synergistic approach to fight a war in these domains. We must analyse the issues involved deliberately and take appropriate actions at strategic, operational and tactical levels

Capacity Building

Space Situational Awareness (SSA) and C4ISR capability. We cannot afford to ignore Space Situational Awareness (SSA) and a C4ISR capability. Integrating the various SSA and C4ISR capabilities into a seamless network that facilitates real-time action should be the space strategy's key organisational and institutional component.

Signal Intelligence. COMINT and ELINT together are named as signals intelligence (SIGINT). Satellites can monitor many types of activities in the electromagnetic spectrum. SIGINT also includes capturing of telemetry signals with emphasis on missiles. The ground-based SIGINT equipment has inherent limitations due to radio line of sight and threat of equipments getting compromised. SIGINT payloads on an elevated platform like satellites would boost the capability tremendously. Presently Indian armed forces have minimal space-based SIGINT capability. India will need more space-based SIGINT capabilities. India should establish ISR capability to monitor Indian Ocean Region (IOR) and Tibet Autonomous Region (TAR). India has not launched and operated an ELINT cluster yet. India has to develop a more significant number of ELINT and Imagery Intelligence (IMINT) satellites to increase revisit times and improve resolution. This is a crucial requirement even for a limited regional ISR. Reducing this gap must be taken up on a priority basis.

Measurement and Signature Intelligence (MASINT). MASINT is technically derived intelligence data other than imagery and SIGINT. MASINT is scientific and technical intelligence information obtained by quantitative and qualitative analysis of data (metric, angle, spatial, wavelength, time dependence, modulation, plasma, and hydromagnetic) derived from specific technical sensors to identify any distinctive features associated with the source, emitter or sender and to facilitate subsequent identification and measurement of the same.

MASINT includes:[14]

- Radar Intelligence (RADINT)
- Radio Frequency/Electromagnetic Pulse Intelligence (RF/EMPINT)
- Acoustic Intelligence (ACOUSTINT)
- Laser Intelligence (LASINT)
- Nuclear Intelligence (NUCINT)
- Unintentional Radiation Intelligence (RINT)
- Electro-optical Intelligence (ELECTRO-OPTINT)
- Materials Intelligence

- Chemical and Biological Intelligence (CBINT)
- Directed Energy Weapons Intelligence (DEWINT)
- Infrared Intelligence (IRINT)
- Effluent/Debris Collection
- Spectroscopic Intelligence

MASINT provides the capability to:

- Use automatic and aided target recognition.
- Penetrate man-made and natural camouflage.
- Detect recently placed mines.
- Counter stealth technology.
- Detect natural and artificial disturbances on earth surface not detected by other means.
- Provide target identification through munitions and sensors.
- Enhance passive identification of friend or foe.
- Detect the presence of CBRN agents, including before, during and after employment.
- Detect signature anomalies that can affect target sensing systems.

In the U.S. Department of Defense (DoD), the Defense Intelligence Agency (DIA) provides central coordination for MASINT collection efforts. Each service, in turn, has a primary command or staff activity to develop requirements and coordinate MASINT effort. In 2008 DIA raised the organisation for MASINT. DIA of HQ IDS should perform the same duties.

MoD should improve integration with commercial space operators and leverage existing space systems for national security purposes. Should incentivise investments in better passive defences for commercial space systems.

Further analysis and gaming are needed to explore grey zone competition in space to find out whether it is advantageous or not to do nothing in response to an attack or threat of attack.[15]

Use of commercial Space data. Commercial Space data can improve the resilience of Space-based ISR asset in limited satellite availability or in cases of limited national contributions. Some key factors are:

- What is the role of commercial imagery in the national security space community? Can the commercial satellite providers be intertwined into the architecture of ISR to be provided to, say, command HQ of services or theatre command when it comes up?
- High-resolution, persistent, global commercial imaging of the Earth will reveal the location and activities of its own forces in a near real-time. How will the Indian Armed Forces deal with this?

Some of the issues which should be discussed threadbare are:

Information about the adversary. How much do we know about the capabilities of adversaries in the space domain? Some relevant queries are:

- **Reconnaissance and surveillance**
  - o What are the near-space and space reconnaissance and surveillance systems (organic, commercial, third-party) available to support military operations?
  - o Does the enemy use space reconnaissance and surveillance for strategic or tactical operations?
  - o What are enemy tasking, collection, processing, exploitation, and dissemination capabilities for space reconnaissance and surveillance?
  - o Does the enemy have the ability to receive and disseminate information promptly to support the targeting process?
- **Missile Warning.** What threat ballistic and cruise missile assets are available to friendly space-based warning systems can collect and accurately identify potential threat missile systems.
- **Environmental Monitoring.** What space weather and remote sensing assets are available to support the enemy? What is the doctrinal employment of these systems?

- PNT
    - o To what degree does the enemy rely on PNT?
    - o What are the critical adversarial capabilities that rely on PNT?
    - o How is it incorporated into critical operations? What are other PNT alternate capabilities?
- SATCOM
    - o What key military and commercial SATCOM systems does the enemy employ?
    - o What is the reliance of the enemy on SATCOM to perform effective mission control?

Answer of the above questions will give us our capability gaps which should be plugged.

Indian Army

Most of issues covered under MoD are equally applicable to the Indian Army. As a component of MoD, Indian Army should implement the recommendations given above at Army HQ level.

Without waiting for publication of National Space Strategy or Defence Space Strategy Indian Army can simultaneously work in Indian Army's doctrine on Space Warfare. Being such a large force, it has a maximum stake in space domain. Resources in space in terms of funds, personnel, capabilities are limited. Indian Army must put its best foot forward to get its legitimate and well-deserved share of space capabilities.

Notes

1. Herb Lin , 'On the Integration of Psychological Operations with Cyber Operations', January 9, 2020, at https://www.lawfareblog.com/integration-psychological-operations-cyber-operations
2. Christopher Paul, et al., 'Lessons from Others for Future U.S. Army Operations in and Through the Information Environment', RAND Corporation, 2018, at https://www.rand.org/pubs/research_reports/RR1925z1.html
3. Christopher Paul and William Marcellino, 'Dominating Duffer's Domain', RAND Corporation, at https://www.rand.org/content/dam/rand/pubs/research_reports/RR1100/RR1166z1/RAND_RR1166z1.pdf

4. Maj Gen PK Mallick, VSM(Retd), 'U.S. National Cyber Strategy and Department of Defence (DoD) Cyber Strategy: An Analysis,' VIF.
5. Bill Roche, 'Latest Hack the Army bug bounty wraps up, increasing network security', June 10, 2021, at https://www.army.mil/article/247381/latest_hack_the_army_bug_bounty_wraps_up_increasing_network_security
6. Maj Gen PK Malick, VSM (Retd), 'Cyber and Space Strategy for India', at https://indianstrategicknowledgeonline.com/web/1%20Cyber%20and%20Space%20Strategy%20for%20India.pdf
7. Pranav R Satyanath, Takshashila Review Paper, 'Space Power and Space Warfare: A Review Review Paper', December 11, 2019.
8. Benjamin Bahney, 'Space Strategy at a Crossroads Opportunities and Challenges for 21st Century,' Competition Center for Global Security Research Lawrence Livermore National Laboratory, May 2020, at https://cgsr.llnl.gov/content/assets/docs/space-strategy-at-a-crossroads.pdf
9. S. Chandrasheka, 'Space, War & Security–A Strategy for India', National Institute of Advanced Studies, December 2015, at http://isssp.in/wp-content/uploads/2016/03/Space-War-and-Security-_A-Strategy-for-India.pdf
10. Ibid.
11. Ibid.
12. RS Bedi VrC, 'NTRO: India's Technical Intelligence Agency', *Indian Defence Review*, Issue Vol. 23.1 Jan-Mar 2008, at http://www.indiandefencereview.com/spotlights/ntro-indias-technical-intelligence-agency/
13. Major Achievements of Ministry Of Defence from May 2014 to Present Ministry of Defence, at https://archive.pib.gov.in/4YearsOfNDA/Comprehensive-Materials/defence.pdf
14. Measurement and Signature Intelligence (MASINT), at https://fas.org/irp/program/masint.htm
15. Todd Harrison, Kaitlyn Johnson and Makena Young, 'Defense Against the Dark Arts in Space: Protecting Space Systems from Counterspace Weapons', Center for Strategic and International Studies, February 25, 2021, at https://www.csis.org/analysis/defense-against-dark-arts-space-protecting-space-systems-counterspace-weapons

7 Conclusion

Information Domain

The instruments of national power refer to the tools a country uses to influence other countries or international organisations or even non-state actors. There are four recognised instruments of national power; diplomatic, informational, military and economic. Information continues to remain silent, under-resourced and under-used as an element of national power.

The information environment comprises social, cultural, technical, cognitive and physical attributes that act upon and affect knowledge, understanding, beliefs, world views and ultimately, actions of an individual, group, system, community, or organisation.[1] Operations in the information environment are the sequence of actions with the universal purpose of affecting the perceptions, attitudes and decision-making of relevant actors.

Currently, in almost all countries there is no recognised defence ministry to resource, develop policy, guide and coordinate information operations. Information operations do not have geographic or even functional boundaries.

A whole-of-nation approach should be specified with a related structure, authorities and resources. The primary actors in Information Operations framework should include intelligence agencies specially counterintelligence specialists, social media, the public, the private sector together with other government agencies and international partners. MHA, MoD and Ministry of Law and Justice should make an Information Operations-Counterintelligence Plan. Though the external and internal intelligence agencies are known to have taken part in information operations, they cannot be the lead agency for the national information operations.

The private sector has some of the most cutting edge, innovative capabilities to detect and repel information operations' threats. But, the private sector does not have the authority to reach beyond the defence of their own networks. Strength of a democracy is in its innovativeness. We must get our top talents from private sector. We must collaborate with innovative commercial business partners.

The experts believed that there is a necessity of an Information Operations-Offence Fusion Center capability, where artificial intelligence can be used for offensive purposes. Artificial intelligence is used to produce realistic fabricated audio and video , automated, personalised disinformation and influence campaigns; bot-driven denial-of-information attacks. and manipulation of information availability.[2]

A digital framework that consolidates, analyses and contributes to the decision-making of huge data sets can achieve remarkable effects with today's AI capabilities, such as refuting disinformation, network attack solutions etc. Presently, big data analytics and artificial intelligence are being used. The data collected include adversarial behavioural modelling, detection of disinformation, inference learning, pattern recognition, etc.

Artificial intelligence remains a core technology with game changing capabilities. As per the journal Small Wars and Insurgencies on the impact, artificial intelligence has on Sub conventional Warfare, "fake news reports with realistic fabricated video and audio can be generated with the help of artificial intelligence. Artificial intelligence can be leveraged in various ways to achieve instantaneous and short-term effects, like creating shock and awe, causing panic, and disorder."

However, problem is that 99 per cent-plus of the data that U.S. Department of Defense collects remains dark and never exploited. They remain in stovepipes, idle.[3]

We should develop a legal framework closely reflecting rules of engagement consistent with the CI/CT ops and conventional warfare we are or likely to be engaged. The rules of engagement must ensure response actions can both keep pace with the threat and be unambiguous.

The role of the Ministry of Defence during any form of influence operation must be carefully vetted. The capabilities of cyber weapons must be studied to ensure no inherently indiscriminate act occurs.

Information warfare capabilities must be integrated with conventional warfare for success on the modern battlefield. Information warfare's ability to drive offensive operations while denying or manipulating enemy perceptions of the battlefield will not get us victories in isolation. Information warfare capabilities defined as combat capabilities will only be effective in the context of consequences. Ultimately war is won in the land, which involves violence, killing people and destroying things.

A growing population of strategic thinkers in the western world are exploring the concept of cognitive war. They think that irregular and unconventional methods and means, including non-lethal and non-kinetic delivery and effects leveraging digital connectivity, have changed the centre of gravity of political conflict from a clash of arms on the traditional battlefield to a narrative contest among the population. In this process, traditional concepts of violent political conflict linked with boundaries, levels, thresholds and phases are acutely disrupted.

Cognitive warfare is an attack on our way of thinking. It is not only about the conduct of warfare but about whole-of-nation security and prosperity. One of its exclusive properties is the extent to which we do it to ourselves. We take part. In the age of hyper-connectivity, the adversary need only show up, inject, nudge, exploit and disappear. The concept of below the threshold conflict becomes meaningless when we prove ourselves capable of losing without fighting.

Cyber Domain

The cyber realm is unique in terms of warfare, primarily because it is an entirely manmade domain of conflict. Cyberspace engagements can happen almost simultaneously, instantaneously, continuously and globally. Success requires a whole-of-government approach that aligns to the interconnected battlespace—a domain that does not recognise territorial borders, sovereign territory or areas of conflict.

The demands for security, privacy, intellectual property protection, open access, innovation, and free information flow involve difficult trade-offs. There is a real problem in balancing the principle of freedom of expression on the Internet and cyber security where people with malafide intentions can be identified and stopped. Both the concerns are genuine. There will always be tension between securing cyberspace and promoting internet freedom. However, they are not fundamentally opposite. The government, academia, industry, NGOs, and activists all have to work together to make the difficult choice between security and freedom and combine both aims. After the recent Solar Winds hack during a Senate Armed Services Committee Hearing, in March 2021, lawmakers, private companies, intelligence officials and the White House have all called for greater information sharing between the private and public sectors.

Now the armed forces think that cyberspace can be exploited with appropriate tools and techniques to achieve tactical, operational and strategic effect. Much of this activity would support conventional military operations like command and control, reconnaissance and situational awareness, operational and tactical planning, logistics, and supply.

To provide information advantage for commanders and decision dominance, it will require a range of capabilities to include cyber, intelligence, psychological operations, public affairs and space. Today's strategic leaders should be fully conversant of what is taking place in cyberspace. The threats, risks and vulnerabilities lie and are evident in their deliberations on how effectively military operations could meet these challenges.

However, there are challenges in integrating cyberspace and information operations (IO). Today synchronising and coordinating information-related capabilities together in a coherent strategy is piecemeal and limited. We have to be imaginative, within the constrains of law, policy and capabilities, in integrating cyberspace and IO capabilities to counter and contest our adversaries.

This challenge is not new. Cyber is a subset of information operations. Nation states are employing IO continuously short of armed conflict. They do not see any difference between cyber and IO. They understand the importance of connectivity, content and cognition. The relationship between cyber operations and influence operations has to be understood and find ways to integrate these capabilities.

The following need deliberate consideration:

- The intelligence requirements for successful information operations generally are not accounted for in the kinetic targeting model.
- Increased intelligence support for IO targeting and do it at scale.
- What activities in cyberspace come under traditional military activity? Can armed forces use this to legitimise its cyber activities?
- Management of data to ensure rapid and timely support to commanders' decision-making.
- Role of the private sector in seizing and maintaining the cyber initiative.
- Measures to minimise or eliminate redundancies, overlap, and waste when each service has developed cyber capabilities.
- Can and should military defend the civilian critical infrastructure upon which it relies to execute its missions?
- Rules of Engagement (ROE) for operational commanders to respond with latitude to enable action like in other domains.
- What is (and should be) the role of DOD in defending our nation from cyberspace threats?

In most of the armed forces of the world there is no separate specific organisation for carrying out Information Operations. Except possibly China, Cyber, EW, Space, PsyOps—all operate in distinct silos and there is little horizontal integration. Cyber war is glamorous, gats maximum attention and funding. Information Warfare does not have that gravitas and the organisation, funding and personnel support are mostly poor.

Though Cyber Warfare is a subset of Information Warfare, there is a growing tending to subsume Information Warfare activities under Cyber Warfare. The recent statements of Lt Gen Stephen G. Fogarty, the U.S. Army Cyber (ARCYBER) Commander, are testimony to this thinking.

In 2018, Lt Gen Stephen Fogarty committed to a strategy for transforming ARCYBER into an IW command by 2028 by converging the Army's IO, cyber operations, and electronic warfare (EW) capabilities within ARCYBER. He stated at TechNet Augusta on August 20, 2019, "The intent is to provide a proposal that will change us from Army Cyber Command to Army Information Warfare Command because we believe that is a more accurate descriptor of what I'm being asked to do on a daily basis."[4] He stated that the cyber and electromagnetic activities sections the Army is creating at each echelon from brigade to corps, will become information warfare sections next. Army Cyber Command will change its name to reflect its mission in the information environment. However, specifics have not been finalised. Service-centric capabilities does not generate the jointness and unity of effort, particularly in the ubiquitous, transitory information operations environment.

Lt Gen Stephen Fogarty said, most of its personnel, time, and bandwidth remained devoted to defending U.S. networks around the world. ARCYBER is increasingly delegating network security to Network Enterprise Technology Command (NETCOM), freeing up Fogarty's Fort Gordon, Ga. headquarters to do more cyber offense and online information & influence operations.

May be, other armed forces of the world can take a cue from U.S. ARCYBER.

Space Domain

The scale of economic activity that space adds to the global economy is worth about $500 billion per year. Space is set to grow into a trillion-dollar industry encompassing communications, technology, tourism, mineral wealth and cheap environmentally friendly renewable energy sources for the benefit of everyone on planet Earth. Strategic rivalry, competition and war in and about space are inevitable. History tells us that conflict and war will follow us into space.

Much of the world's critical infrastructure such as communications, transport, energy, agriculture, financial transactions, environmental and weather monitoring, food and other resources management and defence depend on the space infrastructure which includes ground stations, satellites, and data links at national, regional and international levels.

Commanders of the armed forces at all echelons must understand the fundamental principles and advantages space operations bring to armed forces operations, the disadvantages associated with not understanding space capabilities and the impact to mission operations when friendly forces are denied the use of space capabilities. Space operations bring essential capabilities with unique tools to influence, enable and enhance all mission areas in unified land operations. Unit commanders must have a clear understanding of the space capabilities available that contribute to mission operations and how best to utilise those assets.

Space and Cyber Space Interplay. Outer space and cyberspace are the two commons upon which today's information society depend. Space and cyberspace are increasingly interdependent. Space operations depend on the Electro-Magnetic Spectrum (EMS) for the transport of information and the control of space assets. Many cyber space operations occur in, and through, the space domain via the EMS, resulting in an interdependent relationship between space and cyber space. There is a close integration and dependence between these two domains.

Satellites and other space assets, are vulnerable to cyberattacks. New vulnerabilities and threats to space assets are created by the increased link between space and cyberspace. The sheer scale of data gathered, processed and transmitted by satellites on a daily basis offers great vulnerabilities to be exploited by a cyberattack. Space and cyber capabilities ride on common infrastructure. That bit of data may ride on fibre for a while before going up through a satellite and back down through another terrestrial network. The space and cyberspace capabilities are distributed, networked and global. Both cyber and space capabilities face common threats. Both depend on the IT infrastructure and electromagnetic spectrum that affords great capabilities but create cross-domain vulnerabilities and challenges. An attack on space capabilities may start in cyberspace and attempts to hack our cyber capabilities get routed through space.[5]

Risks associated with cyberattacks are: taking physical control of satellites like manoeuvring a satellite to collide with another satellite, 'decaying' or lowering its orbit so that it re-enters the Earth's atmosphere and burns up or deliberately overexposing a satellite's solar panels to highly energetic ionising solar radiation, causing irreparable damage.

Cyberattacks on satellites include jamming, hacking and spoofing attacks on communication networks, attacks on the ground infrastructure such as satellite control centres and targeting control systems or mission packages. Possible cyber threats against space-based systems include state vs state military actions, well-resourced organised criminal elements seeking financial gain, terrorist groups wishing to promote their causes, even up to the catastrophic level of cascading satellite collisions and individual hackers who want to exhibit their skills.

The armed forces are getting increasingly dependent on both cyber and space domains for fighting an integrated battle. There is a need to evolve a synergistic approach to fight a war in these domains. We must analyse the issues involved deliberately and take appropriate actions at the strategic, operational and tactical levels.

Information, Cyber and Space Domain

Commanders at all echelons must understand the fundamental principles and advantages information, cyber and space operations bring to all Army operations, the disadvantages associated with not understanding their capabilities and the impact to mission operations when friendly forces are denied the use of these capabilities. These operations bring essential capabilities with unique tools to influence, enable and enhance all mission areas in unified land operations. Unit commanders must have a clear understanding of these capabilities available that contribute to mission operations and how best to utilise those assets.

We must remember that information, cyber or space can enable a military operation. They cannot win the war on their own. "In our effort to capture the leading edge of the info age, it is important to remember that at night, in the rain, attacking uphill in the mud, it is the quality of the leadership, not the speed of the processor, that will carry the battle."

WHO IS WINNING ?

Notes

1. 'Joint Operations', Joint Publication 3-0, October 22, 2018, at https://www.jcs.mil/Portals/36/Documents/Doctrine/pubs/jp3_0ch1.pdf?ver=2018-11-27-160457-910#page=105
2. Malicious Use of AI, January 11, 2021 at https://img1.wsimg.com/blobby/go/3d82daa4-97fe-4096-9c6b-376b92c619de/downloads/MaliciousUseofAI.pdf?ver=1553030594217
3. Michael Brett, et al., 'Artificial Intelligence for Cybersecurity: Technological and Ethical Implications', Center for Cyber and Homeland Security at Auburn University, 2017 at http://www.jstor.org/stable/ resrep21461
4. Mark Pomerleau, 'A new name—and focus—for Army Cyber Command?', C4ISRNET, August 22, 2019 at https://www.c4isrnet.com/show-reporter/technet-augusta/2019/08/21/a-new-name-and-focus-for-army-cyber-command/
5. Maj Gen P K Mallick, VSM (Retd), 'Cyber and Space Strategy for India, Military Strategy for India in the 21st Century', CLAWS, at https://drive.google.com/file/d/1tzcDdEENIiC9AX2nep7i1NOxaSOzKtCQ/view